India and Jambu Island

India and Jambu Island

SHOWING CHANGES IN BOUNDARIES AND RIVER-COURSES OF INDIA AND BURMA FROM PAURANIC, GREEK, BUDDHIST, CHINESE AND WESTERN TRAVELLERS' ACCOUNTS

AMARNATH DAS

Gian Publishing House

GIAN PUBLISHING HOUSE
PUBLISHERS OF BOOKS ON HUMAN CIVILIZATION
29/6 SHAKTI NAGAR, DELHI-110007

First Reprint in India, 1986

Printed at Goyal Offset Printers, Delhi-110035
and published by Smt. Gayatri Garg
for Gian Publishing House, Delhi-110007

PREFACE

The informations contained in this book were originally intended as an appendix to a book on Rivers and Irrigation that I was writing. I realised however that mere dogmatic assertions of the conclusions as regards the very great changes that India has undergone will not be accepted by many; there will be others who would refuse to accept identifications of ancient places, quite different from what they hitherto have been, without sufficient proof. An attempt to amplify the account of the changes, giving very short reasons in support of the identifications, was found to be too long a note to go as an appendix; the idea also struck me, that these proofs will not be of interest to the readers of River engineering. I have therefore thought it best to release these notes as a separate volume.

As will be seen, the outcome of the investigations, has been to show from Ptolemy's account, and confirmed by other Greek writers that in the 2nd Century A.D.,—

(*a*) Southern India was an island, known as Taprobane island and separated from the mainland by a shallow sea;

(*b*) the Ganges river flowed through the Vindhyas, passing by Palamau, and entered the sea through the Mayurbhanj States, at some distance to the west of the present outlets;

(*c*) the Indus river flowed by a channel, at some distance east of the present channel and emptied into the sea, at the north-eastern corner of the Rann of Cutch;

(*d*) the Guzerat peninsula did not exist;

(*e*) the Narmada river, crossed the Tapti river and fell into the sea which at that time intervened between the mainland of India and Taprobane island;

(*f*) the southern end of Malay Peninsula was an island, named by subsequent European travellers as Java, the Less, separated from the mainland of Burmah;

(*g*) Central Siam was an inland sea, the Great Gulf (Magnus Sinus) of Greeks, and the "Red South" of the Chinese.

(*h*) the Irrawadi flowed into this Great Gulf.

Going back to an earlier stage, to the accounts given in the Pûrânas, the nine-island stage of Bhâratvarsha (India) has been speculated upon, and it has been shown that Jambû-ḍvîpa island was Burmah, at one time an island separated from India and China. The subsequent changes involving the changes of courses of the Brahmaputra to India, and of Irrawaddy to its present course into the Gulf of Martaban have also been described.

Further, from the accounts in the Mahâbhârata, and Râmâyana, supported by those given in the Pûrânas, it has been shown that the theatre of Mahâbhârata episode was in Burmah, whereas that of Râmâyana was in Lower Burmah and Western Siam, Lanka being represented by the Thaton and Amherst districts and an area to their west which have subsequently gone under the sea.

The discussion of Buddhist accounts of the neighbourhood of Palamau, which was necessary in tracing the course of the Ganges in the beginning of the Christian era, brings out the fact that Gautama Buddha's birth place and travels lay within a comparatively small area; Palamau being Palibothra, Kapilavastu being Rajakheta lying 60 miles west of Palamau, Kusinagara being Kerwa near Paharbula (Pava) lying 100 miles south-west of Palamau, Mahabodhi site being about 40 miles south-southwest of Palamau or 20 miles west of Netarhat, Varanasi-nagara of Buddhists being Barwenagara lying 20 miles south of Netarhat, and Bimbisar's capital Rajgriha lying close to Daltonganj.

20, Bethune Row,
Calcutta, July, 1931.

AMARNATH DAS.

CONTENTS

LIST OF MAPS, ETC.

INTRODUCTION

The object in view in the following notes is to trace as far as possible the remarkable changes that have taken place in the configuration of India during the course of the last twenty centuries, and in particular to the changes in the course of the river Ganges during that period. The minor changes in the course of rivers in the delta of Bengal during recent years of which we have greater details, will not be discussed here.

The information regarding the geography of India, and casual references to location of places, rivers etc., are contained in

(1) Greek accounts,

(2) Early Buddhist literature, which found its way outside India, to Tibet, China, etc., at an early period.

(3) Chinese travellers' accounts.

(4) Accounts by travellers from Arabia, Italy, etc.,

(5) Hindu literature, *e.g.*, Vêdas, Pûrânas, Mahâbhârata, Râmâyana, etc.

(6) Local literature, and accounts by European travellers from about the fifteenth century A.D.

Ordinarily one would expect that the Hindu religious books would furnish the most ancient accounts and should thus appear first in the list, but I have put them fifth in the list because of the fact, that, except the Vêdas which contain meagre geographical information, the other books, *viz.*, the Pûrânas, Mahâbhârata, Râmâyana, etc., were revised and rewritten at a fairly recent period, probably 11th to 13th century A.D., with so great changes and additions that they have depreciated their value as reliable ancient accounts. Though it is certain that some of the Pûrânas at any rate, were extant, long before the Christian era, the later additions and changes introduced as the colonization of Aryans in India extended, and added to this the purpose of assimilating the identity of places in their new colony, named after places of hallowed memory in their previous colony, have made the accounts so obscure that it has rendered it very difficult, and in some cases impossible to sift the old accounts from the new.

The Greek accounts have their value in the fact that, they have not been tampered with to any extent. Then again the outstanding work of Ptolemy, who has given not only the account but a regular map, has given us material for a complete geography of India in his day; the verification of this map and account, by that given in the Periplus of the Erythrean Sea, puts its value and accuracy beyond any doubt. The failure of proper appreciation of the changes which the configuration of the country has undergone, and their possibilities, has led the antiquarians to depreciate the value of Ptolemy's work, and to identifications in directions very wide of the mark, as they have all started on the assumption that India was always, what it is today.

With the reascendency of Brahmanism in India after Buddhism, the Buddhist literature seems to have been gradually destroyed in the country of its origin, but some of the books found their way to other countries, notably to Tibet and China, at an early date. Some of these books were extant in the country to which they were exported, even before the 1st Cent. A.D. and have escaped chances of interpolation and have thus their great value as unchanged authentic records of the time they were written. It is for this reason that I have placed them second on the list.

The Chinese and Arabian travellers made their appearance in the field later, and it is after them that the European travellers came in.

The more recent local literature also furnish us indications of recent changes, particularly of rivers in the deltaic region of Bengal. As in this book only major changes have been dealt with the materials available from this source have not been utilised except so far as they relate to such major changes.

From what I have said above, it is clear that the first complete and reliable account of India, is that of Ptolemy (140 A.D.), and it is accompanied with his map; his account is also in agreement with the account of the coast as given in Periplus of the Erythrean Sea (80 to 89 A.D.). It is on this ground that I have thought fit to start with Ptolemy's map and account as the basis of my investigations.

After the outline of India as given by Ptolemy is demonstrated, the work of finding out the previous conditions as given in the Pûrânas, and of development subsequently to his time is rendered easy, and this arrangement has been followed.

The changes which the geography of India has undergone, are very rapid indeed. The proper realisation of the influences which have brought them about, will only be possible when the reader is acquainted with the work of construction carried out by the sea, and rivers, in particular circumstances, and these are being dealt with, in the book on rivers which I am now writing. My indifferent health, is delaying its progress, and as an interest may be awakened in some readers of this book, to know the reasons underlying such far-reaching changes, I would mention here some of the very important operations involved :—

(1) The littoral drift of materials by the sea into convenient recesses on the coast; this has played an important part in joining Taprobane with the mainland, along the general line of the coast.

(2) The sea tides meeting in a comparatively narrow belt of the sea intervening between the mainland and an island, or between two big islands bring the drift materials from both ends and deposit them in the tidal meeting ground; when such tides do not meet in the belt, the result is, that the materials which enter into it, pass out again, but directly this stage is altered to one of meeting of tides inside the

belt, the filling up of the deep sea to a shallow one is a rapid process. This process must have operated on the sea between India and Taprobane island, as also in the sea between Burmah and Lankâ island (Thaton-Amherst districts as island).

(3) The sea tide of great intensity impinging on the coast-land exerts a pressure, the accummulated effect of which is to squeeze the soil along the coast and raise it up, forming the coastal dunes; this action of the sea tides in forming hills would be accentuated when there is moist soil, or better still impounded water behind such coastal hills; the pressure on the coastal land will be greater, the steeper and deeper the coast, and wider the tidal range. This action has operated, in frequently dislocating the courses of rivers formerly flowing through the Vindhyas by raising the heights of this range, mention of which fact is insistently repeated in the Pûrânas; in raising the western coast of India from Bombay to Kanara and forming the continuous Western Ghats directly ridge was thrown up along this coast after Ptolemy's time; in raising the ridge and forming the range of hills between the Isthmus of Kra and Isthmus of Ligor soon after the land was formed along this line joining the Malay Peninsula to the mainland.

(4) The filling up of inland shallow seas and recesses by rivers will be rapid, when this silt is not moved by littoral drifts to the deep sea in the neighbourhood. This action has operated on the final reclamation of the land between Taprobane island and the mainland from the silt of the rivers; this is also responsible for the reclamation of Central Siam.

(5) A river, when it flows through a narrow gorge of a mountain range, and its flow is intermittent, will open out another channel if other weak points in the range are offered to it; the channels through such gorges are open to greater danger of filling up, if the rainfall in such hills continues in the up-stream end

of the gorges inducing side slips and bringing in materials for blocking up the channel, when the river is not receiving any large rainfall in its upper catchment area to maintain a supply for scouring out such materials as soon as they are dropped in. This condition was responsible for the several changes of the outlets of the Ganges through the Vindhya Range.

If these points are remembered, the lay reader will very easily appreciate the forces of nature which have operated to bring about the far-reaching changes which India and its rivers have undergone during the last twenty centuries, as also the sequence of the changes in the courses of the rivers described in this book particularly those described in Chapters V, IX, and XII.

CHAPTER I

TAPRCBANE ISLAND OF PTOLEMY IS THE PENINSULAR PORTION OF INDIA, SUBSEQUENTLY JOINED TO MAINLAND

The first and most remarkable point brought forth from Ptolemy's map is that Taprobane Island shown in his map, is portion of the present peninsular portions of India, which has later on been joined with the mainland of India which latter then extended to some distance to the south of the Vindhya range, the southern boundary of the mainland then extending east to west, almost parallel to the Vindhya range. It would be convenient in this connection to trace the coastline of the mainland starting from west near Bombay proceeding eastwards in the first instance, and then to trace out the coastline of the Taprobane Island as it was in Ptolemy's line.

(A) Coastline Bombay to Vizagapatam.

The point on the west coast from which the coastline turns sharply towards east is Simyllar, a Cape, which has been identified with Chaul by Yule while Pandit Bhagvanlal Chiranji suggests Chimala in Trombay I, east of Bombay. The point in any case is somewhere in the neighbourhood of Bombay and then turning sharply towards east, the next point on the coast is Baltipatna; Periplus mentions that after Semulla, the local marts are Mandagora, Palaipatmai, etc., and this Palaipatmai is evidently Baltipatna of Ptolemy. Yule identified Baltipatna or Palaipatmai doubtfully into Daibul whereas Fra Paolino identifies it with Balaorpatam a point placed too far south to make it possible to accept, and both these cases the identifications suggested are along the coast as it is now.

If we however turn towards east, the town of Pala to southwest of Lanauli seems to offer a satisfactory identification, the town being an emporium, was named Pala-patan which is rendered by Ptolemy into Baltipatna. It is further reasonable to assume that the small river flowing from Lonavla northwards by Kalyan must have flowed southward when it had a much nearer outlet to the sea in that direction and that Pala-patan was the port on the mouth of this river. It is also on this assumption, that it is possible that the village Patan, much nearer to Lanauli and one mile southeast from Karle station may have been the position of the mart at an earlier date than Pala itself and that as the land extended further to the sea southwards the port was shifted to Pala. These are ancient places as the ancient Buddhist caves and other ruins in the neighbourhood testify.

The next point east of Baltipatna, and near to it Hippokoura. Pandit Bhagwanlal Chiranji identifies it with Ghoda-bandar, quite in a different direction, while Yule suggests Kuda near Rajapur. As the sea was shallow at this locality, the marts were mostly situated on the mouths of the rivers, and those situated at the mouths of the small rivers naturally were named after the name of the river itself, and I have therefore no hesitation in identifying Hippokoura with a town on the Ghod river where it had its outlet to the sea in Ptolemy's time, that is, at the mouth of the Ghod river at that time. This indicates its location at Poona, a portion of the upper courses of R. Bhima was very likely the lower reaches of the Ghod river with its outlet at Poona.

Next we find the coast abuts on the Pirate country, Ariake of the Pirates, and in this country are the towns of Mandagora, Byzantion, Khersonesos, Armagara, and a mart Nitra. In the map Ptolemy shows the inland country of Viri pirates. Periplus also mentions the pirates between Khersonesos and the island of Leukê. This area of the sea must have been shallowest and full of islands referred to both by the Greek writers and the Arabian travellers; this afforded the people of the locality ample chances of their piratical expeditions. Pliny also refers to the pirates of Nitrias infesting the coast near Muziris, and the sea very shallow at the place, so that navigation in the sea at the locality was by vessels without rudders. It is therefore certain that Ptolemy referred to pirates, and that Mr. Campbell's suggestion that by Ariake Andros Piraton, he meant not the pirates but Andrabrityon is not to be taken seriously. The pirates referred to are therefore the "Viri" pirates, and the present district Bhir is just where the Viri country is shown. There is therefore the obvious identity of the district.

Mandagora is identified with Madangarh by Burgess, Yule etc. Even on their assumption of the coast line of the sea, the position indicated scarcely corresponds. The village Mandavagaon Bharata a little to west of Dhond however clearly indicates the situation as it corresponds exactly to what is indicated by Ptolemy.

The next point on the coast is Byzantine; Mc-Crindle, sticking to the present east coast, suggests the identity with Vijaydurg on Vaghotan River in Ratnagiri. The position as indicated points out the identification with Visapur, or Vijaypura in Ahmednagar District or its neighbourhood. The position of the old town of Belvandi or Belvandi Kothar a little to the south of Visapur appears to me to answer more to the possible location, and I am inclined to prefer to this identification, considering the position, the similarity of the name, and the antiquity of the place.

The next point is Khersonesus for which no exact identification has been suggested, except that Mc-Crindle would place it near Goa. The location however leads to its identification clearly with Sonari on R. Sina a little to the north-west of Parenda. Periplus mentions Kaineitai island near what is called the Khersonesos, places in which are pirates and after this the island of Leukê. This island Kaineitai would appear to be Srigonda or Shrigonda or Chamargonda, which Taluk of Ahmedabad must then have been an isolated area in the shallow sea, the pearl fisheries of which were famous as mentioned in Kautilyas' Arthashastra (Ch. IX, in Shamashastry's Translation).

We come next to Armagura near the mouth of the Nanaguna river. As regards the Nanaguna river, the position will be discussed later on (Chapter IV), but the identity of Armagura with the present town of Amirguda south-east of Parenda and southwest of Barsi, appears to be obvious.

The next point is Nitra, an emporium; it is thus to be presumed it is on the mouth of a river, and a river from which it had its name. I have no hesitation therefore in adopting a location at the mouth of river Trina at the time, and this location would put its situation on river Trina a little to the west of Tadwalla.

The coast of Ariake, is now passed, and then comes the coast of Limyrike, with the following points on the coast in order :—Tyndis City, Bramagura, Kalaikarias, Mouziris emporium, mouth of river Pseudostomos, Podoperoura, Semne, Koreoura, Bakerei, mouth of river Baris.

Tyndis is identified by Yule with Tanur or perhaps Kadal-tundi near Bepur, both doubtfully. The position shown in the map would lead us to fix its identity with Tadwalla.

For Bramagura and Kalaikareas I have no suggestions to make, except that they have to be looked for on or near the road from Tadwalla to Latur, or that the position of Bramagura is put by Ptolemy a little to the west of where it should be and that Amba of Amba-garh represents Bramagura.

Next we come to Mouziris an emporium; here again as on the case of many of the other emporia, the name of the emporium is taken from the river at the mouth of which it stands, which is made clear in the accounts in Periplus (*vide* Chapter II) where it distinctly states that the port lay on its own river. The point of debouchure of river Manjira would therefore offer a key to its location and that point would be where the road from Amba to Owsa crosses the river Manjira.

Pseudostomos must have been the mouth of a silted up river which was of large dimensions at the previous time. Its course will be discussed later.

Podoperoura is obviously Burdapur.

Semne and Koreoura would be near, or at, Varval Rajura; I am however unable to suggest identification of the names.

Bakerei is undoubtedly Bhokar about 25 miles east of Nander. This is one of the cities founded by Barkarîkâ the daughter of Satasrînga, the grandson of Rîshabha deva of *Jains*.

After Bakeroi comes the mouth of River Baris, this mouth lying between Bakeroi and Melkynda. As Melkynda is undoubtedly Balkonda, both from its name and situation, the mouth of the Baris must have been at Bhaisa. The course of the river will be discussed later on.

Next comes the coast along the country of the Aioi, and the places on the coast are:—Melkynda, Elangkon or Elangkor, a mart; Kottiara the metropolis; Bammala; Komaria a cape and town.

Elangkon, corresponds to a point in Kona-Samudram.

Kottiara the metropolis is perhaps Nizambad or the old city Indur.

Bammala is without doubt Vemalwada; it was situated inland at the head of a V-shaped gulf as indicated in Ptolemy's map.

Komaria is Kamareddipet. This locality has lost its importance as after the sea receded from the place, the course of the river Godavari which subsequently formed the drainage artery of the country, was at a distance from the place. This locality seems to have been of importance as a place of pilgrimage and north of it is Ramareddipet, the place of Râmêsvar Sîva and west of it is Siddhipet, the place referred to in Periplus where men and women wishing to consecrate their closing years came to bathe and engage in celebacy. This Kûmâri is mentioned as a sacred place in the Pândya kingdom in Mahâbhârata (Vana, sec. 88), next to Sûrpâraka and also next to Vaidûrya mountain, making it clear that the Pândya kingdom of Nagpur is indicated. Brahma Pûrâna (Ch. 28) mentions that near southern sea is Odra or Utkala where exists Konâdîtya (Konaraka, of Puri) and on that sea coast is the sacred Râmêswar Sîva and visiting that Kâmâri gives merit equivalent of a Râjsûya sacrifice. This Kamaraddipet, sacred to Kâmâri Sîva is the southernmost point of the Indian sea coast as it was in Ptolemy's time. After this the coast turns northwards into the Kolkhic Gulf.

Now comes the Kolkhic Gulf abutting on the land of the Kareoi, with the following places on the coast :— Sosikouri, Kolkhoi, an emporium, mouth of river Solen. the Kolkhic Gulf afforded the pearl fisheries as noted by Ptolemy, and this is to be expected as the sea tides meeting from the Bay of Bengal to the east and the Arabian sea to the west were rapidly filling up the central portion of the rift between the mainland and Taprobane island in this neighbourhood affording facilities for pearl fishing in shoaled up sea. Kaûtîlya in his Arthashâstra, in his statement of pearls, seems to have indicated this locality as the pearl producing area, as he says (Ch. XI) that "the Superintendent of Treasury shall examine pearls of Tâmraparnî, Pândyakâvata, Pâsa, Kûla, Chûrna, Mahêndra, Kardam, Srotasî, Hrada, Haîmavata." Tâmraparnî no doubt refers to Taprobane I.; Pandyakâvata is a river in Pândya country, and this Pândya country can only refer to the Pândya country of Nagpur, which is shown abutting on the coast lying next to the Kolkhic Gulf to its east; Küla is given by the commentator as Kaûlêya, *i.e.*, belonging to the coast, and this is presumably the Kolkhic Gulf of Ptolemy; Pâsa is represented by R. Pus meeting the Penganga at a point near Waronda from where sea was near to this coast; Kardama is a river, of which the locality given by Mr. Shamasastry as in Persia, but it is obvious that Kaûtîlya refers to Kardama river, now a tributary of the Godavari meeting the latter about 30 miles to the east of Nirmal and Balkonda, which from its location indicates that it debouched on the Kolkhic

Gulf; Hrada is also given by the commentator as a pool known as Srîghanta, but its location is fixed by M. Shamashastry near the sea of Barbara beyond India, though it is clear that the coast near Shrigonda in Ahmednagar Dt. of Bombay which was then on the sea coast, must have been meant by Kaûtîlya. The subsequent entire withdrawal of the sea from this area may have afforded the bringing to surface of rich find of pearls, and I am not sure whether the lower area of the Gulf derived its name subsequently as Manthani, that is, where the sea was dewatered.

Of the coastal towns, I am not able to fix the positions, but Kolkhoi, emporium, as in the other cases, must have been on the mouth of a river, and that river the Kardama river, the position thus deduced would bring it to near Lakhsetipet. Sosikouri would then be near Jagtial. R. Solen is shown as falling into the Kolkhic gulf a little to the east of Kolkhoi and Lakshsetipet must be taken as a point near to this mouth.

Following next, comes the Orgalic gulf, abutting on the land of the Pandion, with the following places on the coast :—Kory or Kalligikon, a cape; Argeirou, a town; Salour, a mart. The Orgalic gulf, as it was situated at that time near the strait between the mainland of India and Taprobane Island, was the first to silt up and so must have been very shallow at that time and the water white with the admixture of the vast quantity of silt-laden water brought by the River Solen and this perhaps led to the name of the gulf itself as Orgalic or the town on it as Argeirou, the name of the river, Kardama or "mud" river, also indicates the sea to be a muddy one. As regards the country abutting on it being the Pandya country there is no doubt about it. In pre-Buddhist times, Ceylon and Dekkan are ignored and in Buddhist times the most southern town given is Patethâna, and beyond Kalinga forest, Bherûkachchha and Suppâraka there is no mention of southern India or Ceylon (Rhys David's, Buddhist India II, P. 23, 31); as a matter of fact the Pandya kingdom of southern India was founded in the 5th Century A.D. (Mont Martin, British Colonies III, 41), or in any case did not come to be of any importance till then. Kâlîdâsa in describing Raghû's march has the following sequence:—after crossing river Kapîsâ reaches Utkal, *i.e.*, Orissa; then Mahêndra mountain which is unmistakably the Eastern Ghats of Orissa; then the Dakhîn Country on the sea coast; then R. Kâvêrî which is Kheberus of Ptolemy or Wain-Ganga river as I will show later on; then Malaya Mt., *i.e.*, the outcrop of hills from centre of Vindhyas; then southern Pândya kingdom after which again is Malaya Mt., and then Dardûra Mt., both being part of the Vindhya range. This shows that this southern Pândya kingdom, named southern to distinguish it from the northern Pândya kingdom of Indraprastha, was south of the Vindhyas and east of Kheberus. Kâlîdâsa also mentions here, that the Pândya Kings presented Raghû with pearls where Tâmraparnî and the sea met, indicating the existence of pearl fisheries in the sea between Pândya kingdom and Tâmraparnî or Taprobane Island. In introducing the different princes present in Vîdarbha at the Syambara of princess Indûmatî, next to the Kalînga King is introduced the King of the Pândya country, who is the King at Nagpur. This enables us to fix with certainty the Pandion country, extending from the Vindhyas to the sea coast at that period, with headquarters at Nagpur, and this could not therefore apply to the later Pândya kingdom in southern India.

Cape Kory must be a point near Manthani, and it is to be looked for near if not the same as Pratap-giri.

Salour is Sirpur, the headquarters of the taluk.

For the town Argeirou, I am unable to suggest a definite indentification, but it was at the mouth of the Kardam river.

Then follows the country of the Batoi with the following coastal points:—Nikama, the Metropolis; Thelkheir; Koroula, a town.

Nikama, the metropolis is without doubt Rajura or old Manikgama.

Koroula is Churul or Juna Churul on river Wainganga.

Thelkheir must therefore be looked for between the two towns above, *i.e.*, near Keljhar Railway Station.

After the Batoi country, follows the Paralia country of the Toringoi and the points on the coast are :—Mouth of river Khaberos; Khaberis an emporium, Sabouras, an emporium. Paralia as used here may not be after all the Greek term for coast as suggested by Yule, and it refers to the coast of Parla, with its capital at Parla-kot on the Kotri river.

Khaberos river is Kâvêrî or Ardhagangâ of old, and with the outlet to the sea near to it from near Jubbulpore, it is to be expected that the Narmadâ had previously the southern outlet to the sea and the course of the river Wainganga clearly, indicates that it was so. In Ptolemy's time this outlet had closed, and the Narmadâ river, or rather the Nanaguna river of Ptolemy had formed an outlet westward towards Bombay. In Brahma Pûrâna (78) it is stated that "Gangâ, issuing from the Hîmâlaya, flowed through the centre of Bhâratavarsa, towards the eastern sea, and in her passage was cleft into two branches in Mahêswara's belly, one branch proceeded by the south of Vîndhya mountain and is known as Gaûtamî Gangâ, while the other branch proceeded by north of Vîndhya mountain and is known as Bhâgîrathî Gangâ". This indicates that at one stage the overflow of the Ganges carried it through the rift in the hills north of Jubbulpore and east of the Bhanrer range and that the point of bifurcation was in Mahadeo Hills. The Brahma Pûrâna then (Chap. 79-115) gives the places of pilgrimage on the Gaûtamî Gangâ from which it is possible to trace the course of the river as it then existed. The river after bifurcation, met the Nîla-Gangâ, *i.e.*, the Sîprâ, after which it met the Süvarnâ river and the Kâdravâ river and then met the Pravarâ river and passed by Nîvâsapûra, *i.e.*, Nevasa in Ahmednagar district of Bombay. This course indicates that the river flowed along Narmadâ up to Hoshangabad, and then flowed southward by the course of Tapti river up to near Malkapur from where it left the line of the Tapti, and proceeded southwards to its outlet by several branches to the sea towards the south, and this course is exactly what is shown as the Nanaguna river by Ptolemy. In Padma Pûrâna (Svarga, 6) it is stated that "Narmadâ starts from Amarkantaka hills behind the Kalînga country; west of Amarkantaka, the Narmadâ meets with rivers Kapîlâ, Bîshalyakaranî and Udvâsa; after this is the Narmadâ-Kâvêrî sangam, the famous place of Kûvêra's religious meditations. In Agnî Pûrâna (113) it is given that "from the Amarkantaka hills to the junction with the river Kâvêrî, the bank of the Narmadâ is a sacred place." These statements enable us to fix without doubt the place of bifurcation of the river Narmadâ and Kâvêri to the west of Amarkantaka as is to be naturally expected if the contour map of the locality is studied. The exact spot is suggested by the name Chhindwara or 'Chhînna-dvâra' which means literally "the closed gates" of the river. This Chhindwara is the ancient Chhindwara town a few miles to the west of Jubbulpore and it will thus be realised that when this "gate" was open and the combined river received in turn the spill of the Ganges from the Himalayas, the Kâvêrî formed the main river with the southern sea very much closer to the point of bifurcation *via* Kheberus, and the Narmadâ its effluent which flowed by a circuitous route to the sea near Bombay. Khaberos river is therefore no doubt the Kâvêrî of old, a branch of the Gangâ and that after the spill of the Ganges was cut off from the north and the river bed also was raised where it penetrated the hills near Nainpur, the stream was diverted to the Narmadâ system finally, and lost its importance but the remnant of its course no doubt is left in the river Wain-Ganga and its northern length from Amarkantak to Chhindwara had its flow reversed and thus included as a portion of the Narmadâ river. The mouth of the river Kheberus must therefore be looked for a little to the south of Garh-Chiroli, and Chichbori, on the road from Mul to Garh-Chiroli represents the Khaberos emporium of Ptolemy, the mouth of the river itself being very near to, and east of it.

Sabouras emporium, is perhaps Surya-garh, situated on a tributory of the Indravati river. This is perhaps the same as Sopatma of Periplus, Surya-pattana being contracted to Sopatma.

The Arouarnoi coast follows next with the following points on the coast :—Podoukê, an emporium; Melangê, an emporium; mouth of the river Tyna; Kottis; Manarpha or Manaliarpha, a mart. Podoukê is an emporium and is therefore to be looked for at the mouth of the next river to the sea that was, and this would lead us to fix the position on the point where the Indravati river, which as a river of anterior drainage retains the alignment of the old sea coast here, received its next tributary, *i.e.*, Bhamragarh. Above Bhamragarh on the river is Pothungoli which is Podoukê.

Similar consederations lead us to fix the position of Melangê emporium at the junction of Indravati river with its tributary that comes next higher up the river, and that gives us the village Lanka for Melangê.

The next point is the mouth of river Tyna. This is evidently the river Indravati, which had its direct outlet to the sea to the east of Lanka, as a matter of fact skirting eastward even of Pindikonda, the outlet being near Pothikal. This river was one of importance and indications point out to the conclusion that this was the eastern Tâmraparnî river flowing from eastern Malaya mountains. It would perhaps be convenient here to state the reasons for such a conclusion as the identification of other places particularly of R. Manda depend on them. The following list shows the names of rivers as flowing from the mountains shown opposite to them as given in some of the Pûrânas.

Purana	From mountain	Rivers.
Vâyû (45)	... Sûktîmâna	Rîshîkâ, Sûkûmârî, Mandagâ, Mandabâhînî, Kûpâ, Palâshînî.

Purana	From mountain	Rivers.
Brahma (19 & 27)	Sûktîmâna	Rîshîkûlyâ (Sûbîkâlâ), Kumâra (Kûmârî), Manûgâ, Mandagâmînî, Kshayâ, Palâshînî.
Matsya (114) ...	Do.	Kâshikâ, Sûkûmârî, Mandagâ, Mandabâhînî, Krîpâ, Palâshînî.
Vîshnû ...	Do.	Trîshâmâ, Aryakûlâ.
Kûrma (46) ...	Do.	Rîshîkûlyâ, Trîshâmâ, Gandhamâdanagâmînî, Kshîprâ, Palâsînî, Rîshîkâ, Vansakârînî.
Skanda (Mahêsvara Kûmârîkâ 39) ...	Do.	Rîshîkûlyâ, Kûmârî.
Vâyû (45) ...	Mahêndra	Trîshâmâ, Krûtûkûlyâ, Ikshûlâ, Trîdîbâ, Lângûlînî, Vansadhârâ.
Brahma (19 & 27)	Do.	Trîsandhyâ, Rîshîkûlyâ, Lângûlînî, Vansakarî.
Skanda (Mahêsvara Kûmârîkâ 39)	Do.	Trîsâmâ, Rîshîkûlyâ.

Of these rivers the Rîshîkûlyâ falls on the Bay of Bengal, just below Chilka Lake, Vansadhârâ at Colingapatam, Lângûlînî past Chicacole, retaining their names unaltered and this enables us to deduce that Mahêndra Gîrî is part of the Eastern Ghats lying in Orissa. Further, as these sets of rivers are shown as flowing from Mahêndra, as also Sûktîmâna, these names are interchangeable or that Sûktîmânâ is a section of the Mahêndra mountain, and that, the western one. The following list obviously brings in the rivers of the contiguous hills, as they include the names of some of the rivers in the foregoing list, or that the name of the hills are mixed up.

Purana	From mountain	Rivers.
Vâyû (45) ...	Malaya	Krîtamâlâ, Tâmraparnî, Pûspajâtî, Utpalâvatî.
Brahma (27) ...	Do.	Krîtamâlâ, Tâmraparnî, Pûshyajâ, Pratyalâvatî.
Matsya (114) ...	Mahendra	Krîtamâlâ, Tâmraparnî, Mûlî, Sabarâ, Vîmalâ.
Vîshnû ...	Malaya	Krîtamâlâ, Tâmraparnî.

Purana	From mountain	Rivers.
Kûrma (46) ...	Malaya	Krîtamâlâ, Tâmraparnî, Pûspavatî, Utpalâvatî.
Skanda (Mahêsvara Kûmârîkâ 39) ...	Do.	Krîtamâlâ, Tâmraparnî.
Agnî (118) ...	Do.	Krîtamâlâ.
Vâmana (13) ...	Sûktîmâna	Krîtamâlâ, Tâmraparnî, Vanjûlâ, Utpalâvatî, Sûnî, Sudâmâ.

This also indicates that Malaya hills, are also contiguous to, or part of, the Mahêndra-Sûktîmâna system and it is the eastern section in Bastar District. The Krîtamâlâ river, also called shortly Krîtâ (Skanda, Avantya-Rêvâ, 3) is evidently the Kotri flowing north to south along the east of Bastar district and had its outlet to the sea near Suryagarh. The Utpalâvatî or Pratyalâvâtî is the Tel river flowing from Malaya hills in Bastar district northwards, and it is now a tributary of the Mahanadi river and had lent its name to that river as the Chîtrotpalâ river. Sabarâ is the Sabari river. Having now fixed the disposition of some of the rivers, the Tâmraparnî, referred to in the list can only apply to the important river left in this area, and that is the upper reaches of the Indrâvati river flowing past old Bastar and this important river is therefore the Tyna of Ptolemy, and it had its oulet to the sea below Pindikonda, very likely near Dantewara. There was an obvious attempt to transplant the Râmâyana places in this direction as accretion proceeded southwards, for which Orissa derived its reputation as Kîskîndhyâ, and we find Chitrakut on the Indravati, near Bastar and Lanka on the sea, representing Melangê of Ptolemy as shown before. Arising out of this, it will be convenient to identify Manda river of Ptolemy here, as this river is shown as flowing from the Mahêndra Mt. eastwards to the Bay and from its name evidently is the same as Mandagâ of Vâyû and Matsya Pûrânas, Manda-gâmînî of Brahma Pûrâna, or Gandhamâdana-gâmînî of Kûrma Pûrâna. It is accordingly a river flowing from Mahendra mountain and near the Rîshîkulyâ river, and the location indicated shows it to be the same as the Vansadhârâ river flowing from Mandagar, east of Bhowani Patna.

Kottis is the point on the southern sea coast coming next to the Tyna mouth. This is Konda, situated as it was on the mouth of river Sabari.

Manarpha or Manaliarpha mart comes next on the coast, and this is Maniamkonda on the then mouth of the next small river flowing to east of Malkangiri, which river became a tributary of the Sabiri river, on the sea coast receding at this point.

The coast of Maisolia follows next, with the following points on the coast :—

Mouth of river Maisolus; Kantakasylo, a mart; Koddoura; Allosygne, a mart; point of departure for ships for Khryse. Maisolia is perhaps Mâhîsîka-janapada. In Vâyû Pûrâna (45) repeated in Mârkandêya Pûrâna (57) Mâhîsaka is placed next to Kalînga. In Matsya Pûrâna, the sequence is also Navarâshtra, Mâhîsîka, Kalînga. Brahma Pûrâna also gives the sequence as Mahârâshtra, Mâhîsaka Kalînga, Abhîra etc. This is also confirmed in the lists given in some of the other Pûrânas. From the list of rivers flowing from Mahêndra, Sûktîmâna and eastern Malaya mountains, it appears that Manjûlâ or Vanjûlâ would claim its place between Tâmraparnî and Vansadhârâ, and that this is perhaps the same as Mûlî river of Vâmana Pûrâna which would be where Maisolus is shown. This Mûlî or Manjûlâ or Vanjûlâ therefore appears to be Maisolus and that Maisolus country is Mâhîsîka. This area would appear to be south of the Matsya country, which is placed in the following sequence in the Mahâbhârata (Bhîsma 9) :—Sûrasêna, Kalînga, Bodha, Malaya, Matsya, Mûkûta etc. In Râmâyana (Kishkindhya 41) Matsya is placed next to Kalînga. The Eastern Matsya-dêsa must have been to the north of this area of Maisolia, and possibly extended at a time southwards and that the Machkund river is the central river from that area to the southern sea as it existed at an early stage and this would indicate that the Machkund river is the same as Mûli of Pûrânas and the Maisolus river of Ptolemy and it corresponds exactly to the location indicated by him.

The mouth of the river Maisolus is therefore the mouth of the river Machkund, and with the sea coast as it was in Ptolemy's time, the mouth was on the sea itself near Kondakamberu.

Kantakasylo mart or rather an emporium as noted on the map is the port at the mouth of the above river, that is Kondakamberu itself.

Koddoura is not doubt Chodavaram.

Allosygne mart is Simhachalam.

The Point of departure for ships bound for Khryse is the next and final point in this west and east coast as it should be. It is without doubt Vizagapatam, which literally indicates it is the port from which ships branch off and that is evidently the case as this port standing out at the angle of the mainland would command the routes to Khryse, *i.e.*, Sûvarnadvîpa or south Burmah, as also the northern route towards the delta of the Ganges at that period.

The sea coast of India was therefore generally in a west to east direction from Bombay to Vizagapatam.

(B) CIRCUIT OF COAST OF TAPROBANE ISLAND AND ITS INTERIOR TOWNS AND RIVERS

Having now traced the southern coast-line of the mainland of India, I now proceed to trace out the coast-line of Taprobane island as described by Ptolemy, in the order given in his descriptive outline of the Island.

Boreion Akron, or the North Cape, the nearest point of the Taprobane Island from the mainland of India is evidently within the area of Medak, and Sangareddipet would seem to be the point indicated. In fixing the the northern head of the island I think Ptolemy has placed it a little to the west of what its relative position should be with the mainland and has thus mentioned that this North point is near to C. Kory of mainland instead of its being nearest to C. Kommaria. This is very likely due to the fact that navigation along the direct route from Kommaria to North point must have been very difficult owing to the tides strengthening in the narrow neck of the sea as it was, and that the usual route for vessels from mainland to Taprobane was from C. Kory, and so it was considered to be the nearest point.

The next point is Galiba, which is undoubtedly Gulbarga or ancient Kulbergha.

Margana comes next on the coast and this is Mudgal. This ancient city was evidently the headquarters of the powerful Mûdgal tribes which were supposed to have sprung from the Rîshî Vîsvâmîtra (Harîvamsa 28), and described as sons of the Rîshî, where Mûdgal is placed next to Gâlava on the list, and later on are mentioned to Sâlankâyanas of southern India, which confirms the location as it is expected to be.

Iogana, is to be looked for near Gadag, ancient Kratûka, the name Iogana, is perhaps of the port near Annigeri a little to the west of Gadag.

Anarismoudon cape is Honawar, ancient Honnavura, the name Anarismoudon is evidently from Honnavura Samudram, as it is this point in which the coast line emerged or projected into the Samûdra or Ocean, the other portion of the coast being mostly behind the multitude of islands which then existed on the coast and later joined with the main island.

Sindokanda town comes next on the coast. It is shown some distance south of Anarismoudon and the identification presents some difficulty. The town Siddapur a little to the north east of the Gersoppa falls however would from its name location on the coast as it was then, and its antiquity appear to offer an identity as Siddapur is in the area of Sîddhakhanda. The river Sharavati probably had its outfall into the sea between Honawar and Siddapur and is therefore part of the river Soana of Ptolemy.

The haven of Priapis comes next, and the town of Bhatkal or Sasagudi or southern Manipur of old is evidently the haven indicated. The Lingsagur area clearly indicated the position of a vast inland lake of Taprobane Island, which must have drained into the Arabian Sea by the rivers Varada and Sharavati and the coast here offered maritime facilities and was the haven of Lingsagur from which the name was adopted by Ptolemy.

Then comes Anoubinagara which is no doubt the present town of Nagar, or ancient Badnur. The name Badnurnagar is distorted to Anoubinagara.

Prasodês bay comes next. This is no doubt the low ledge on the sea face lying between Mangalore and Kesargarh, which ledge extends inland to a width of more than 30 miles. This bay is no doubt the same as that to which the tax collector of Red Sea, Annus Proclamus, was drifted, when he landed at Taprobane, and the port in which he landed which he calls Hippouri is no doubt Kudre-mukh which in Tamil means horse-mouth. Before the sea receded this town must have been on the coast. The contour map further shows that the appearance of the bay as it must have been suggestive of the mouth of a horse. A further confirmation of this identification is forthcoming from the fact that this bay was the point of debouchure of one of the main rivers draining the Megisba lake in the interior, and that this river is Palaesamundus and the Capital city Palaesamundus was on the banks of that river, and near to Hippoura. This line of river is easily traceable on the line of the lakes that still exist along the Vedavati and Hagari rivers, and the old city Brahmasamundra indicates the position of Palaesamundus city of Proclamus. Just above the gulf itself and near Halebid are the ruins of ancient Dwarasumudram, or the gateway of the huge inland lake of Megisba which was of the nature of an inland sea. Why the name of the gulf is Prasodês I am unable to suggest definitely but it may possibly be Pârsva-dês, that is, the country on the side (of the island of Taprobane); or that it is Brahmasamudra corrupted to Palaesamundus bay Proclamus, and Prasodês by Ptolemy.

The next point is Dionysos extrema or Headland of

Zeus. This cape is the jutting out point that was opposite Hippoura, and that is Brahma-giri which agrees both in name and location.

Noubertha town comes next on the coast. The situation corresponds with Manantoddy or ancient Manantawadi, the name evidently is derived from the name of the taluk of which Manantawadi is the chief city, the town itself being on an eminence or hill is called "betta", *i.e.*, Weinad-betta, which distorted to Noubertha.

Odoka comes next, a town of importance and this is unmistakably Ootaca hill or Ootacamund. The extensive ruins of the old port is down the hill and when the sea receded and the port ceased to be a port there was nothing left to induce a population to exist in the old place which must have as usual in these cases become unhealthy, and the inhabitants must have gradually gathered round the more agreeable and salubrious location at a higher altitude.

The river Azanos, flowed into the sea, on the coast between Noubertha and Odoka. The upper courses of the Cauvery river evidently had an outlet towards the west coast when the sea was nearer, and the course would be expected to be *via* Kollegal, Ramasamudram, and Chamrajnagar, falling into the sea in the gulf above Odoka. The broad bed of the Cauvery river between Kollegal and Hagenakallu falls, indicates this conclusion. On the sea receding from Ootacamund coast, the river bed levels retrograded and as it became higher, it cut open the present course by Hagenakallu falls, the present course of the Cauvery below the falls having been worked out in two stages, *i.e.*, a direct southern outlet by Karur when the sea coast existed there, and on the sea receding from Karur, the sharp turn towards the east from above Karur and exit towards the east coast.

The coast now turns sharply towards the east and the next point is Orneon headland and the location points to its identity with Coimbatur or Koyamathura, the ancient place Perur 3 miles south of the city is perhaps the cape indicated. It is remarkable that evidence of intercourse with the Romans is forthcoming along this line of the country, which was the former coast-line in the beginning of the Christian era from the fact that finds of old Roman coins in this area of the Coimbatur District is common as noticed by Mr. Sewell (Sewell's Madras, P. 214). This is another proof of the sea coast and ports of communication with the western countries having been in this line which only can account for these finds.

Next on the coast is Dagona, a city sacred to the Moon. This is to be looked for in the neighbourhood of Tiruppur. In the Coimbatore District the prevalent worship seems to have been of Somêsvara Swâmî, ancient temples dedicated to whom, exist in this area. The other alternative identification which suggests itself is that Dagona may be Sendamangalam, or Chandra-mangalam, literally meaning the place sacred to the Moon, and a comparison of the two names will make it apparent that it is possible that the Greek name is one corrupted from the Sanskrit name; this ancient town is situated near Salem, and the central section of river Cauvery on an affluent of which this town is situated, must have had an outlet to the sea near Perur when the coast was nearer to the river there as in Ptolemy's time; it is likely that Ptolemy placed the city on the coast, though it lay on the river in the interior, simply because the river was then navigable and the city on it was an emporium, and its distance from the coast was under-estimated.

Korkobera town, is obviously the very ancient city of Karur which was for sometime the capital of the Keralas.

Next comes the cape of Dionysos, shown on the map as Bacchi town. This from its position is unmistakably Srirangam, and the fact that it has been the headquarters of the Vaishnavites of old, explains the name of Bacchi given to the town.

Ketaion Cape is no doubt Pattukottai from which point the coast now sharply turns towards the north.

After the coast turns northwards and a little beyond the bend the R. Barakes falls into the sea. The drainage of the basin at the head of the Cauvery as already indicated previously was effected by the river Azamos flowing to Arabian sea.

The drainage of the Cauvery basin lower down was effected eastward and the resulting stream was the Barakes and its alignment as indicated by Ptolemy was along the upper course of the southern Penner and then the Vasisthi river. The name of the river is possibly derived from Adîkêsa, which form of Sîva was worshipped in this part of southern India, the river having its source in the Chhina-kesava hills, where the worship of Adîkêsa was most prevalent.

Bokana town comes next on the coast and this is possibly Mukkan, 15 miles northwest of Tindivanam Railway station. At the foot of the hills are remains of the old town (Sewell's Madras, P. 208). The coast here has accreted considerably as a result of the silt brought in by the three big rivers Cauvery, Penner and Palar which are now draining the whole width of the peninsula east-wards, after the west coast has been raised and drainage towards that coast shut out since Ptolemy's time. This explains why Mukkan is so far inland now. This is the district in which the chiefs who flourished in the fourteenth century and called themselves Udaiyar, and the name which first powerful chief assumed was Bukkana, have left inscriptions, showing that they traced their descent from ancient kings of names hallowed in the locality.

The haven of Mardos or Mardoulamne is unmistakably the Madras or Mândrâj coast. This coast here has under-gone subsidence, as along the coast there is evidence of remains of structures under water. Madras city as we see now is more or less a recent one, but there is no doubt that the flourishing old city existed in the neighbourhood, but now submerged under water, and the new city is partly part of the higher level portion of the old city on the coast.

Aberatha town, I am inclined to think, is misplaced by Ptolemy on the coast, and that it is the famous Kânchîpûra of old, or present Conjeeveram, which is to the south west of Madras instead of north of it as shown by him. The name is from Ekâmranâtha, the form in which Sîva is worshipped here with his wife Kâmâkshî Dêvî.

Solis port, or Heliou limen, or haven of the Sun is the next port on the coast. This is Shriharikota which is now an island between the Pulicat lake and the sea; Capt. Neubould (J.A.S.B. X, 105) refers to traditions that the old city here was founded by Trîsankû of the Solar race and that the ruins of the city are still to be seen under water. The establishment here of the king claiming descent from the Solar race also explains the name of the port as given.

Aigialos Megas, or the great coast comes next. This is Anantasâgaram, which literally means "great sea" or "great sea coast". This place is now several miles inland to the west of Nellore but it is easy to see that this coast set back from the general coast line as it is shown by Ptolemy, was possibly shallow and has been reclaimed rapidly by the silt brought in by the northern Penner river. As repeated by Mr. Sewell in his List of Archeological remains in the Presidency of Madras, this tract of the Nellore district was uninhabited till a comparatively recent period, and like the Cuddapah, Bellary, Anantpur and Kurnool Districts formed part of the great wilderness of Dandaka, which indicates the reclamation of the inland lake Megisba as referred to already, and after the lake was reclaimed the whole of the silt of the rivers were available for forming deltas on the sea coast, which led to the rapid reclamation of the Ananta-sagaram.

The next point is Prokouri, a town and this is without doubt Kandukur.

In the map we find a town Enanera shown between Prokouri and Rizala, but omitted in the accounts. This town Enanera is evidently Ongole-nagara on the coast.

The haven of Rizala is next on the coast, and this is evidently the ancient city of Chezarla, 14 miles east-north-east of Narasaravupeta in Guntur District. The coast here has also been reclaimed to a good width since Ptolemy's time for the reasons already given for similar reclamation of the Anantasagaram coast to its south. Chezarla contains the ancient temple of Kopotêsvara, connected with the episode of King Sîvî's sacrifice.

Oxeia, a headland comes to the north of Rizala, and this is as we should expect to find as the north end of the Nallamalai range ran into the sea at the point in a sharp tongue, at the base of which the river Kistna flowed into the sea; the ancient prosperous city of Amarâvatî marks this spot which is no doubt the headland referred to by Ptolemy, since whose time, the Kistna has accreted its delta several miles beyond this point.

The river Ganges falls into the sea above this headland and this Ganges is no doubt the Kistna river, which is the Dakshîn or southern Gangâ. This river was perhaps also called Nîlgangâ, the name preserved in the name of the town on the river where it skirts the famous Sri-sailam.

In Brahma-Pûrâṇa, where the accounts of sacred spots on the Gaûtamî Gangâ are concluded, the last portion of the list (Ch. 169-173) is evidently a later interpolation, where instead of Gaûtamî Gangâ of the Vîndhyas, the Ganges of Taprobane has been referred to, where it says "on the south bank of the Gangâ and north of Srî-gîrî is Bhîlla Tîrtha, with Adîkêsa Mahâdêva installed there." This also confirms that the river was once named Gangâ.

Spatana haven comes next on the coast. This haven I am unable to identify definitely but it is quite possible that it was situated on a blind inlet of the sea and that Satttampalle, the old headquarters of the taluk of that name may possibly be the haven referred to.

Nagadiva or Nagadina is Nandigama. This town was evidently situated in an area which was an island, with the sea to its north, east and south, and separated from the mainland by the Kistna river, and an effluant of the same which is now the lower end of the Paler river. This island was one of the Nagadivas, or Nâga islands, as is evidenced by the numerous Nagakals and Serpent stones found all over this district.

After this comes an inlet of the sea, the Pati Bay. This must be the low area to the east of the Muneru river stretching from Jaggeyampeta to Khammamett.

Anoubinagara would accordingly be identified with Khammamett.

The next point is Modottou, a mart. This is the famous place Warangal, the name Modoutti is from Mathwada, the village in suburbs of Warangal, which place was the headquarters of the Moudouttoi people. This is evidently the clan Madhûchchhanda, claiming their descent from Visvâmîtra as given in the Harîvamsa.

After this is the mouth of the river Phasis. It will be seen that the river Kistna received a very large number of tributaries, such as Bhima, Dindi, Peddavagu, Halin, Musi etc., to its left which now flow southwards. All these rivers would have flowed to a nearer outlet to the sea to their north if the sea was there. As this was the case, it is to be expected that the whole of the Mahbubnagar district would drain northwards and the result would be the river as indicated by river Phasis. The line of the river was very likely from Gadwal *via* Mahabubnagar and then falling into the sea to the east of Hyderabad city.

The point beyond the mouth of the river is Talakory or Aakote, which I would unhesitatingly locate at Golconda north of Hyderabad.

The circuit of the coast then is completed by return to the North Cape, and the coast of Taprobane island was therefore as shown in the map annexed.

As regards the people living in the Taprobane island, as already referred to, the Harîvamsa mentions the progeny of Vîsvâmîtra, representing some of the different of clans who occupied southern India. In Chap. 27 the names of these clans as given are :—Kâtyâyana, Rênûmâna, Sânkrîtî, Gâlava, Mûdgala, Madhûchhanda, Dêvala, Astaka, Kachchhapa, Pûrîta; Pânî, Babhrû, Kârajapa, Dêvarâta, Sâlankâyana, Vâskala, Lohîtya, Yamaduta, Karîsî, Sausrûta, Sandhavâyana; Yâgnavalka, Amagharsana, Udûmbara, Abhîglâna, Târakâyana, Chûnchûla, Bâdarâyana. I have already mentioned that the Galava of Gulburgha are the Galiboi of Ptolemy, and Mûdgala are people living in modern Mûdgal which corresponds to Margana of Ptolemy. Sânkriti were people living next to Galiboi, and Sângaraddipet which is the country near the North Cape of Ptolemy shows their location. Next to them the Moudouttoi which is evidently Madhûchchhanda of Harîvamsa, living near Warangal or Mathwadi which is Modoutton of Ptolemy. The Sennoi, I am inclined to think, are the Sâlankâyanas, who must have been in this locality at an earlier stage but gradually spread themselves to the Vengi-desa in Godavari District as reclamation of land in that area proceeded and we find them established there in the 5th Century A.D. as a branch of the Pallavas. The Sandokandoi are the Sândhavâyanas, and the Bumasanoi sounds like that of the Amagharsanas. The Tarkhoi are the Tarakâyanas of Harîvamsa, or Târakshara of Mârkhandêya Pûrâna which correspond to Târakshatî of Brîhat-Samhîtâ, which also mentions Bhakkanas in the neighbourhood who are no doubt Bokanoi of Ptolemy. The Markandêya Pûrâna has Konkana in place of Bhakkana of Brîhat-Samhîtâ, and this southern Konkana is placed by Cunnigham at Anagundi on the Tungabhadra, long way to the northwest of the locality indicated by Ptolemy. Tarakhoi, as Târakshatî of Brîhat Samhîta, is then the locality indicated in North Arcot, and it is possible that Arcot is shortened Târakshatî, I am therefore inclined to think that Cunnigham's Konkana is not Bhakkana or Bokanoi. The Anouragrammoi appears to correspond to Renûmâna of Harîvamsa their headquarters is clearly Hampi or Vijayanagara. The country of the Bumasanoi is round Brahmasamûdra, and the name of the country has possibly been put in place of the name of the people inhabiting it. The Nageiroi are no doubt the Nâgas of Nakadouba (*Vide* next para), as this is the area in which the Manîâkkhî nâga had his Kingdom of old. The names corresponding to the Rhogandanoi and Diorduloi are not traceable in the localities indicated in the map; this is the area to which the Harî-worshippers of Burmah and Lankâ gradually migrated when driven out after the Mahâbhârata war.

As regards the interior cities, Anourogrammon the royal residence, is Hampi as already pointed out in the preceding paragraph. Maagrammon the metropolis, as shown, would be Nagar Karnul or Nagad Karnul. Podoukê is no doubt Hosdurga, and Oulispada is Solapaddi, 28 miles west of Salem, situated on the left bank of the Cauvery river. Nakadouba or Nakaduma is very likely Konganapuram south of Solapaddi and west of Salem which was perhaps the headquarters of the Kongu-desa which included Salem and Coimbatore districts.

The courses of the rivers of Taprobane have already been dealt with in some cases in discussing the identification of the coastal towns. The course of the river Soana is from Podoukê to the sea between Anarasimoundon and Sindokadê. The source at Podoukê is clearly distinguishable, as the inland lake Vanivilas sagar near Hosdurga still indicates, and it is from here that a connection with the upper Tungabhadra river existed as the broad bed of that river from Shimoga to its junction with the Varada river indicates. From this junction point to the sea near Honawar was presumably by the Varada river. After the inland lake Megisba was reclaimed in part, the reclamation of the Prasodês gulf must have been rapid and with it the retrogression of bed of the river Palaesamundus which was the bigger outlet of the lake towards the Arabian sea. This process must have closed this outlet and the Soana river outlet then must have come into being as the predominating drainage line towards the west of the island. Why the name of the river is Soana, I am unable to suggest at present but it is at this locality that we should look for the Samanga country mentioned in Padmapûrâna (Svarga 3) and Mahâbhârata (Bhîsma, 9), where it is placed near southern Konkana and Manî-Malaya, and that this is the Shimoga district and that the name Soana is a corruption of Samanga.

River Azanos is clearly the upper Cauvery of which the flow has since being reversed, from Sivasamudram, and that the river Shimsha was the connection from this point Sivasamudram above the Cauvery falls, to the central Megisba lake. The name Azamos is presumably a corruption of Shimsha. The course of river Barakes has already been traced when dealing with the location of its mouth on the coast line. It is the river, made up partly of the upper portion of the southern Penner river, and the Vasisthi river and the name is derived from the country of its origin in Chhinna-kêsava hills, a country where Shiva in his form of Adikêsa was worshipped. The northern Penner flowing by Nellore and the southern Penner, which falls into the sea south of Pondicherry and north of Cuddalore, were at an earlier stage than Ptolemy's, one river, and thus the portion of the Madras Presidency bounded by this system of rivers to the north, west, and south and on the east by the sea coast of Madras and Anantasagar, was an island. This was at one stage, one of the Nâga Dvîpas, where worshippers of Ananta Nâga were predominant settlers.

River Ganges of Taprobane island is the lower courses of the Kistna river, with a part of its tributary the Tungabhadra. It is the Nîlgangâ of southern India as would appear from the name of the town on it. The flow in the upper part of the Tungabhadra which was towards the western coast must have been reversed with the reclamation of sea coast on that side, and similarly the upper portion of the Cauvery must have had an outlet northwards by the river Phasis as shown by Ptolemy, from where the flow has already been diverted when Godavari basin filled up.

Of the River Phasis, the probable course has already been indicated while dealing with the portion of coast line at the north end of the Taprobane island. The course of the river was from Gadwal, *via* Mahbubnagar and falling into the sea east of the city of Hyderabad.

(C) SMALLER ISLANDS ROUND TAPROBANE

A short reference of the islands in front of Taprobane will perhaps be desirable. The number of islands given is 1378. After the circuit of the coast that has been given above, it will be realised that the whole of the west coast has been reclaimed to a good width, as also the sea lying between Taprobane and the mainland of India. In the west coast, the Western Ghats now afford a continuous high ridge, and as this area was the sea, the only conclusion is, that in this area the sea was dotted over with innumerable islands and rocky eminences, and the intermediate vallies were gradually filled up by materials from the denudation of the hills of these islands, which valleys have also been raised higher and higher since then, from denudation of materials of still higher hills. Combined with this there is no doubt that the sea waves and tides striking on the coast have also contributed to the upheaval of land level along the coast. The islands of moderate size, to call for notice, are however small, and the names of only 19 islands are given, and their position indicated in the map from which it is not difficult to locate them as below :—

(1) Ouangalia or Ouangana—This is Yenagar, about 36 miles east of Sholapur and 50 miles north-west of Gulbergha. This locality includes Nalgir, and also high hill (2,164 ft.) near Jaoli in the neighbourhood, which indicates the site of the island.

(2) Kanathra—This is the area round the hills near Ladwanti (2,057 ft.) about 24 miles north of Gulbergha. The name is preserved in the Benithora river which skirts these hills.

(3) Aigidion—is the Belgaum area.

(4) Orneon—is to the east of Belgaum and the locality would be Gokak hill and the area round it.

(5) Amminê—is the country round high hills of Anmad near Castle-rock, to the east of Marmagao.

(6) Monakhê—is evidently Mangalore and the country round which was an island off the Prasodês gulf.

(7) Karkos—is Kesargad and the hilly country round it as also Chandragiri, which was also an island off the Prasodês gulf.

(8) Philekos—This island is Pollachi and the country round it.

(9) Eirene—is Ernakulam area.

(10) Abrana—Trivankura or Travancore.

(11) Kalandadroua—is possibly slightly misplaced, and it is the southern portion of Travancore, the area round Agastyamal̆ai hills, the name of the island was derived from the port of importance near Ambasamudram, the port being Kallidaikuruchi.

(12) Bassa—This island consisted of Varushanad range of hills.

(13) Balaka—The location of the island is unmistakably Madura and the country round. Why the name of the island is Balaka I am unable to suggest. It may either be from Villeyakundum north of Madura, or from Vêlâkûlam which means the sea coast proper, the Vellakul̆am indicated in the village about 10 miles east of Paramagudi on the Vaigai.

(14) Alaba—the north-western portion of the island of Ceylon; the name to be seen in its main river Aruvi-Aru or Aruvi river.

(15) Goumara—is Kûmrâra-dvîpa. This is the southern or main portion of the island of Ceylon.

(16) Zaba—is the northern portion of Ceylon island consisting of Jaffna and the small islets round it which is even now practically an island and not yet fully joined on to the Ceylon island.

(17) Zibala—was an island off the coast of Anantasagaram or the Great coast of Ptolemy, and it is therefore the island situated in the portion where the coast line was set back, and that is just to the north of the northern Penner river where it now falls into the sea, including the Kaval̆i taluk of Nellore district. The ancient port Zuvvaladinne from which the island derived its name, still exists as a port.

(18) Nagadiva—This island now forms the area on the southern bank of the Godavari river, stretching from its banks, south to Ellore. The area is full of

Nagakal relics strewn all over the place, and the village Nagavarama seems to indicate the headquarters when this part of Godavari district was originally occupied by the Nâgas, till they were superseded by the Sâlankâyanas of the Pallava dynasty.

(19) Sousoura—The position of this island is to the west of the second barriar of the Godavari river stretching as far as the Pakhal lake.

There are the following islands shown in the map of Intra-Gangam India (Tab. X of Ptolemy's map of Asia) which are not given in the accounts.

(1) Heptanesia—This is evidently an island formed out of a group of Seven divisions, from which the present district of Satara, the ancient Saptarshî or Seven Rîshîs' place of Vîshnû-Samhîtâ, is formed.

(2) Pepperina—The island situated to east of Heptanesia and includes in it Adarki.

(3) Trinesia—to the east of Pepperina is the Pandharpur area.

(4) Leukê island, situated between Trinesia and Vangana or Ouangana of the foregoing list is one of the two Leukê islands and is the Sholapur area.

(5) Trikadiva to south of Heptanesia is the Kolhapur area.

(6) Milizegyris island, from its position, is the Ratnagiri district area, including Ratnagiri, and Vijaydurg.

(7) Kory island—This island seems to be referred to also as the Leuke island situated between Taprobane island and the mainland of India, in the mid-passage of the mostly frequented route for crossing the sea here in the Greek period. This is therefore the second Leukê island also referred to as the island of the Sun and includes in it Udgir or Udaygiri, the hill of Sunrise from which it has probably received its name.

CHAPTER II

CONFIRMATION OF THE SOUTHERN COAST-LINE OF INDIA BY PERIPLUS OF THE ERYTHREAN SEA

At the outset it is desirable to remember that Ptolemy's Geography was written about 140 A.D., whereas the date on which Periplus of the Erythrean Sea was written is about 80 to 89 A.D. that is about 50 years earlier. The account in Periplus is from its unknown author's personal observations and accordingly the description of the coast as given by him refers to that date. Ptolemy's information is however from informations gathered by him from people who navigated to the east, and careful as he was in collecting and verifying such information, the fact remains that the accounts given to him were partly personal and partly hearsay and as such may have been of an earlier date in particular instances. The coast-line, and the sea lying between India and Taprobane was undergoing rapid changes and the accounts therefore are expected to be different in some localities, and the comparative dates of the two descriptions also cannot be always taken as a guide in judging the changed conditions of the coast.

In describing the western coast above Bombay, or rather near Broach, the description given in Periplus is that "from Barygaza (Broach) the coast turns southwards and the country from here is called Dakhinabades, which in the language of the country means southern country. Of this country that part which lies inland towards the east comprises a great space of desert country and large mountains abounding with all kinds of wild animals and is inhabited right across to the Ganges by many and extremely populous nations." This description makes it clear that the Dakshinabades or the southern India of his time stretched from this coast of Barygaza gulf eastwards up to the Ganges, and that the southern coast therfore was in a general direction west to east from the Bombay coast to the Ganges mouth, and so ignores the triangular protuberance of the southern or peninsular part of India.

This description further says that Paithana 20 days' journey southwards of Barygaza, and Tagara 10 days' east of Paithana are cities in this south country. Whatever may be the identifications of these cities, they are at no great distance, and the southern country, therefore did not stretch far out southwards than 20 days' journey from Broach, and so could not possibly have extended to southern Indian Peninsula as now. Further the identification of Paithana with present Paithan on the upper Godavari being obvious and accepted by all authorities, the assumption that southern boundary of India running at no great distance from this town is a natural corollary.

Periplus then says that, "After Kalliena other local marts occur, *viz* :—Semulla, Mandagora, Palai-Patmai, Meleizeigara, Buzantion, Toparon and Turrannosboas; you come next to islands of Sesekreienai, Aigidioi and Kaineitai near what is called Khersonesos, places in which pirates, and after this island of Leukê; then follow Naoura, and Tundis, the first marts of Limurike and after this Mouziris etc."

The paragraph preceding this description is concluded by saying that "their (Paithana and Tagara) commodities are carried down in wagons to Barugaza along roads of extreme difficulty. The length of the entire journey to Limurike is 700 stadia and to reach Aigialos you must sail very many stadia further." I have quoted this in detail as this description has an inportant bearing. It shows that the journey to Limurike, and carriage of commodities were preferred *viâ* road to Barygaza instead of the ports on the southern coast which were nearer; that the land distance from Barygaza to Limurike was short, only about 700 stadia, but by the sea was very much longer as it is indicated that sailing is by Aigialos island

and that to do this you have to sail very many stadia further. The reference to the pirates on this coast and impetuosity of tides, which evidently made navigation by sea-going crafts not merely difficult, but afforded facilities for piracy, makes it clear, why the ports on this coast were not resorted to by sailors ordinarily, and that the through navigation on the coast from Barygaza gulf to the Limurike coast was by a circuitous route, going very much farther out from the coast and skirting the islands mentioned, *viz.*, Sesikreienai, Aigidion, Kaineitai etc. This journey thus being by a circuitous and tortuous route and through the openings between the large number of islands which existed here, explains why the description omits the change of direction of the journey, on this coast, notably the change from north to south, to one of west to east at Semulla.

It is clear that the author of Periplus must have sailed by the circuitous route indicated and that the information regarding the marts in Dakhinabades coast between Barygaza gulf and Limyrike coast is from heresay information and this will be apparent from a critical reading of the description. The names of marts mentioned in this coast agree with those given by Ptolemy as shown below.

Periplus.		Ptolemy.	Remarks.
Semulla	...	Simylla	
Mandagora	...	Mandagara	
Palai-Patmai	...	Balti-Patna	
Meleizeigara	...		
Buzanteon	...	Byzanteion	
Toparon	...		No suggestion for identification.
Turranasboas	...	Nitra	On river Tirna, or Trînâ or Trînavahâ.

The order in which the marts occur in Ptolemy's map differ from that given in Periplus which no doubt is to be expected as the latter is heresay accounts of a cursory nature.

Meleizeigara is evidently Milizigyris island of Ptolemy, and Keineitai Island would appear to be Shrigonda, or

Chamargonda area, which was an island with the famous pearl fisheries mentioned by Kaûtîlya in Arthashâstra. Periplus then describes the coast to which its author evidently returns, namely, the coast of the mainland in Limurike Kingdom, and the first ports there, are, Naoura and Tundis. Naoura appears to the Nander now on the Godavari and Tundis must have been close to it, possibly at the mouth of the Ashna river.

Periplus here mentions Mouziris which is evidently not visited by him for reasons already explained, and it answers to the location given for it by Ptolemy, *i.e.*, on the Manjira river, which is also made clear in Periplus by saying that the port lies on its own river, an assumption already made by me in locating some of these ports. Another fact stated, is also interesting, namely that the journey from Mouziris to Nelkunda, which is Nelkynda of Ptolemy, could be done, either by sea or river, the distance being the same. A glance at the map would show that the Godavari river, portion from Sonapet to Nander and on to Balkonda by rivers Godavari and Siddha with a connecting channel would afford such a route, Ptolemy's Pseudostomos river intervening. This river Pseudostomos must have been at an earlier stage a navigable river of great importance which afforded passage of ports to the interior, and as it had two connections with the sea, one near Mouziris and the other near Nelkynda, it afforded these alternative routes to the interior, and this is what is stated by Pliny who says that, "by sea, nearest mart of India named Muziris is reached, a place infested by pirates of Nitrias, where goods have to be transferred to boats; another convenient harbour is Neakyndon, which is called Bakare".

Periplus then states that after Bakare, occurs the mountains called Pyrrhos (red) towards the south near another district called Paralia, where are pearl fisheries belonging to king Pandion and a city named Kolkhoi. Here again it appears that navigation along the shoaling coast is difficult and vessels have to go farther out into the sea, and thus leaving Bakarê coast, they proceed south towards the island which contained the hills of Nalgir, that is the "red hill" or Mt. Pyrrhos, and Udgir.

This island is also the same as Leukê or "white" island of Ptolemy, the name taken from Udgir, or Udayagîrî or the hill of Sunrise. Skirting along this island, the passage was back to the coast near the Pandian-cum-Paralia district.

Here Periplus gives the names of places on the coast in the following order :—Balita, Komar, Kolkhoi, where are King Pandion's pearl fisheries, Argelou where in the gulf is Epiodoros island where are also pearl fisheries. Balita is Bammala of Ptolemy; the next three places bear practically the same name as in Ptolemy, and in the same order. Epiodoros island is evidently the cluster of hills on the left bank of the Indravati river in its lower reaches, and it includes in it Bhopal-patnam, the patnam or port of Bhopal which is corrupted to Epiodoros; the village Mati-murka in this area indicates, as its name implies, where pearl fisheries existed.

The ports here mentioned in Periplus are :—Kumara, Podoukê, Sopatma. Kumara and Podoukê are Kommaria and Podoukê of Ptolemy. It is not a matter of surprise that Periplus omits to mention the ports between these distant points, as the sailing by its author was for a through journey and he avoided entering into the two gulfs, namely the Kolkhic and the Orgalic gulf, and in such a journey starting from Kommaria, the first port on the coast in the direct route to sight, would be Podoukê. The port Sopatma is obviously Suryagarh or Suryapattan or Sabouras of Ptolemy.

It is only after this that Periplus refers to Taprobane island. It describes that "Near the region which succeeds, where the course of the voyage now bends to the east, there lies, out in the open sea stretching towards the west, the island now called Palaisimoundon but by ancients Taprobane. To cross over to the northern side of it takes a day. In the south part it gradually stretches towards the west till it nearly reaches the opposite coast of Azania."

It has already been referred to once, that the author of Periplus must have navigated from Simylla onwards, leaving Taprobane hidden behind the series of islets between which and the mainland of India he travelled and he thus misses Taprobane, till he comes near Podoukê. Further it is evident, that the through traffic in vessels between the western countries with the Gangetic delta and Burmah was not much, as there is frequent mention that merchandise from China was carried either overland or carried to the east of the Taprobane island and thence it was carried either overland or by local flat boats of small draft to the west coast of the island, for export to western countries and *vice versa*. It is for this reason that the generally adopted local trade route from India to Taprobane was confined mostly to the eastern end of the intervening sea. Both these reasons explain why it is, after coming to this end of the intermediate sea, that Periplus mentions Taprobane Island, as his information about it must have been gathered from the ports he touched on the Indian coast. The sea between India and Taprobane had already shoaled to such an extent that "In these marts (Podoukê, Sopatma) are found coasting vessels which trade as far as Limurike and another called Sangara, made by fastening together large vessels formed each of a single timber and also others called Kolandiophonta which are of great bulk and employed for voyages to Khruse and the Ganges", as stated in Periplus. Now, a Sangara is not the Malayalam "Changadam" as suggested by McCrindle; the term Sângada is still used in Bengal to apply to crafts made up by tying usually two boats side by side; further the term is applied very largely to crafts made by tying two "Sâltees" side by side, and a "Saltee" is a dug-out made from a single timber usually of Sâl (Shorea Robusta) baulk. This is exactly the craft described in Periplus, and these crafts can only be used in very shallow water, as the freeboard left is little, the crafts from the nature of their construction cannot be large, as a matter of fact ordinarily a saltee does not exceed 30 ft. in length, 3 ft. in width and 2½ ft. total depth. It will thus be realised that the sea along its borders had by then dwindled to mere backwater swamps right through from Podoukê to Lymurikê, if not further. The fact that Sangara as a craft survives in the present Gangetic delta leads also to the assumption that these crafts were able to ply all over the delta even up to the Kalinga coast, and that this could only have been possible, if the system of inland channels as in the Sundarbans swampy area, extended along the Orissa coast. The huge size of the Taprobane island must have given the idea that at the end remote from the Masalia coast, the island protruded almost near to Azania or Africa. This is an idea which can only come if peninsular India was Taprobane, and not if Taprobane was Ceylon.

Passing Masalia, Periplus says that "the course turns eastwards across a neighbouring bay and to Desarene, the coast is northerly, after which it turns east again and sailing into the ocean far to the right and coast to the left you reach the Ganges." This shows that the course from Vizagapatam was north-east, and it is from here that the "Ocean" is met with to the right and the coast-line indented with the bay. This is another proof that from the time the Barygaza gulf is passed, and up to Sopatma near Vizagapatam on the Masolia or Kalinga coast, the journey is through an inland sea, and that the inland sea lay between Indian coast and Taprobane, and it is after emerging from the Masolia coast that the passage comes out to the Ocean again. The description of the course from Vizagapatam to the mouth of the Ganges, would be quite correct, if we remember two points of difference from present conditions namely (1) that the Orissa coast was then set back a little further in, than now, and (2) that the Ganges mouth was not at Saugor island but much towards the west, in the Keonjhar-Mayurbhanj zone.

The description given in Periplus of the Erythrean sea is limited eastwards to the Ganges mouth.

CHAPTER III

TAPROBANE ISLAND AND SOUTHERN COAST OF INDIA AS DESCRIBED BY OTHER GREEK WRITERS

HERODOTUS

Herodotus writing in 408 B.C. gives very meagre information. He has no reference to Taprobane, and both Carey, and Talboys Wheeler are agreed that Herodotus' India extended only to the valley of the Indus, and a little towards it southwest. The inhabitants were (1) Fishermen living in the marshes of the Indus (2) the nomad Padeans (3) the Vegetarians and (4) the Calatians. This gives an indication merely that Indus valley was still in the making, and that the inhabited or populous India barely extended beyond Guzrat.

KTESIAS

Ktesias, writing in about 398 B.C. has little more to say than Herodotus. He alludes to Pandore living in the valleys, presumably Indus valley; nothing beyond this area is mentioned.

MEGASTHENES

Megasthenes, who was in Palimbothra between 302 B.C. and 288 B.C., with the information gathered by him on the spot, gives much more information than his predecessors. He was however never down on to the coast-line and his information about southern India, and the coast is therefore meagre and from hearsay accounts. Further, these hearsay accounts were not reliable as the Mayurian supremacy had not then been established in southern India, *i.e.*, India south of Vindhyas, and the unsettled conditions of the country with petty states at feud with each other prevented the free intercourse of people between north and south. It is evident that for information about the distant countries he depended on the Brahminical sources as given in Pûrânas etc.

In Fragment LVI (Mc Crindle's translation) Megasthenes gives details of the tribes in India, and in doing so he has grouped them according to their positions. The tribes from the Indus to the Iomanes mostly consist of tribes living next to the Indus stretching towards its east and south, and have been identified with the Rajput clans, and then south up to Surat, and then towards the east to Charmae and next the Pandae, and then back to the area near Patala island at the mouth of the Indus. It will thus be seen that he does not mention any tribes southwards of the coast-line in Ptolemy's time as now depicted by me. As regards the Pandae, Magasthenes has defined the location clearly as he says in Fragment LVIII that "Herakles begat a daughter in India, called her Pandaia, assigned to her that portion of India lying southward extending to the sea." In the list of tribes previously referred to, he puts Salabastrae and the Horatoe with a fine city as also another Automela, an emporium on the coast on confluence of 5 rivers; next the Charmae, next the Pandae with women ruler descended from Herakles. This also appears to be the last tribe mentioned by him towards Iomanes. Now Horatae has been identified with Saurastra or Surat; I am inclined however to think that Salabastrae is Saurashtra, and Horatae is Maharashtra; whatever it is, the localities do not much differ and the fine city referred to is very likely Barygaza and the emporium Automela is Omenagar of Ptolemy which is Sangamner as I will show later on. In that case Charmae is the same as Limyrika of Ptolemy or Limurka of Periplus, and next Pandae must be the Pândya kingdom of Nagpur as discussed before in connection with the identification of Ptolemy's coast-line at Orgalic Gulf. River Iomanes is therefore R. Iobares of Arrian who says "Iobares river flows through Surasenoi country of Herakles," or Kheberos of Ptolemy. The Pandae referred to by Megasthenes cannot therefore be the Pândya kingdom of Madura in southern India.

In the portion to further east the southernmost point mentioned in Fragment LVI is Cape Kalingon and town of Dandagula, which shows that north of Godavari was the limit of India at that end. The southern coast-line was therefore east to west from south of Colinga to the south of Surat.

We are now in a position to follow the boundary given by Megasthenes in Fragment IV, where he says that "India is bounded on the north by extremities of Tauros, and from Ariana to Eastern sea by Parapomisos, Hemodes, and Himaos Mountains, on the west the Indus, but south and east sides which are both greater than others run into the Atlantic Ocean. The shape of the country is rhomboidal each of the greater side exceeding the opposite by 3,000 stadia which is the length of the promontory common to south and east coasts which project equally in these two directions. The length from west to east up to Palibothra measured along royal road is 10,000 stadia. Beyond Palibothra by the Ganges by guess is 6,000 stadia. Total 16,000 stadia."

Arrian, who gives the same boundaries, has given the following further details about the measurements "The western boundary from source of Indus along the river to the ocean is 13,000 stadia plus 3,000 stadia of jutting out country, a total of 16,000 stadia, which is the breadth of India. The length west to east up to Palibothra 10,000 stadia plus 10,000 stadia headland projecting to the sea, a total of 20,000 stadia". Reconciling these two accounts we have the shape of India as below in Fig. 1.

A look at this skeleton boundary of India, compared with the boundary as given by Ptolemy presents a striking similarity, and the coast-line of India to its south seems to have been much the same as depicted by both these authorities.

About Taprobane, Megasthenes says in Fragment XVIII, that "Taprobane is separated from the mainland by a river; the inhabitants are called Palaiogonoi", in Fragment LIX, he gives the size of the island as 7,000 stadia long and 5,000 stadia broad and that it is possessed

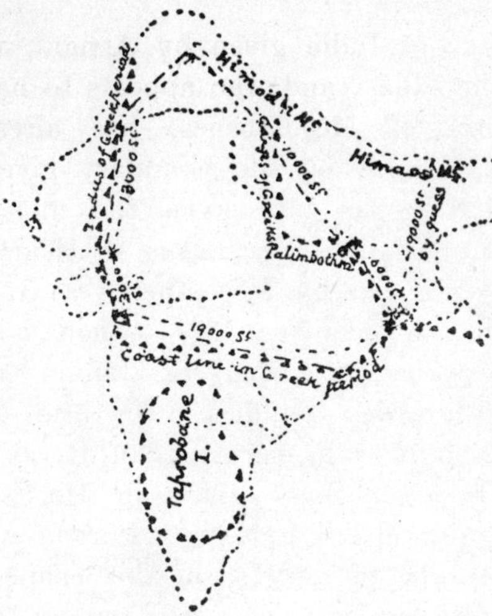

FIG. 1.—Skeleton Boundary of India as given in Greek Accounts.

of 750 villages; in Fragment XIX he says that trees grow in the Indian sea. All these accounts confirm the boundary of India and Taprobane as given by Ptolemy. The size of Taprobane makes it clear that it is the peninsular portion of India and not Ceylon. As distinguished from the Ocean mentioned by him, must be the sea intervening between India and Taprobane; it had already shoaled up as evidenced by the statement that trees grow in the Indian sea. When he says that Taprobane is separated from India by a river, it may be one of two things, (1) either seeing that in India, rivers of the dimensions of Ganges, which he says has an average width of 100 stadia (11 miles) and depth of 20 Orguiae (fathoms), he termed the shallow sea separating the island with a width of 30 miles or so at the narrow part, a river, (2) or, that used to dialect of Persia, then prevalent, he was led to this confusion as sea here may have been termed "Dariya" which was rather elastic, meaning anything between a big river and a sea.

ARRIAN

The boundary of India given by Arrian, who wrote in the 2nd century B.C., and who appears to have drawn on the materials of Megasthenes, has already been referred to when discussing the boundary given by the latter. Arrian, too, has not given the name of any tribes in southern India. He makes it clear that the name of the river given by Megasthenes as Iomanes, is river Iobares, in Surasenoi country, which is also the country of Herakles of Dionysos family and that Herakles' daughter was Pandaia. He also says that "Indians say Dionysos was earlier than Herakles by 15 generations." The geneology given in Harîvamsa Ch. 30-32, which is also given in Matsya Pûrâna with slight modifications, will be of interest in this connection and is therefore reproduced here.

Nahûsa (married Bîrajâ)

Yatî	Yayâtî	Samyâtî	Ayâtî	Yâtî	Sûyâtî

Yayâtî (married Devayani) (married Sharmistha)

Yadû (Established in North eastern India)	Tûrvasû (South east India)	Drûhyû (Eastern India)	Anû (Northern India)	Pûrû (Central India or Kûrû Pânchâla Kingdom)

Tûrvasû
Vanhî
Govânû
Traîsânû
Karandhama

Marûtta	Bharata (In Matsya Pûrâna)

Marûtta
Sammatâ (daughter, married Samvarta)
Dûshmanta
Karûtthama
Akridâ

Pândya	Kêrala	Kola	Chola

To these four children belonged thriving countries of Pândya, Chola and Kêrala.

The above geneology shows that Nahûsha or Dêva-Nahûsha is Dionysos of Arrian and that Akrîda is Herakles of Arrian and Megasthenes. Pândya is shown in the Harîvamsa as son of Akrîda instead of daughter. In Matsya Pûrâna, the name of the sons of Akrîda are given as Sandhâna, Pândya, Kêrala, Chola and Karna, which shows that interpolations are introduced here, as colonisation extended later on to the peninsular India after reclamation of the sea lying between Taprobane and India proper. The location of original kingdom of first southern India Pândyas is however indicated by Tûrvasu's kingdom which lay to the southeast of India in its older limits, that is the Nâgpur area in Central Provinces.

STRABO

Strabo writing in 21 A.D. defines limits of India as given by Megasthenes. In case of the Taprobane island however, he says "it is distant from Koniakoi in the southern extremities of India, 7 days' voyage southwards with bad vessels and wretched sails; other islands lie between it and India but Taprobane is farthest south." As this description is further detailed by Pliny no remarks are offered here.

PLINY

Pliny writing in 77 A.D., says that "formerly the journey from India to Taprobane was done in papyrus boats in 20 days, but with better boats now in 7 days from Prasii. The island begins at the Eastern sea and lies extended over against India east and west. The sea between India and the island full of shoals not more than 6 paces deep but in some places deep for which vessels are built with prows at each end to avoid turning round." This description is very clear showing that the southern coast of India was in an east to west line, that northern coast of Taprobane was lying parallel against this coast, that the intervening sea was shallow to an extent that vessels of very small draft even were liable to be grounded all along its expanse. This description cannot apply to Ceylon as Taprobane, and is a clear indication of Taprobane having been peninsular portion of India, and the sea lying between it and India already shoaled to an extent, to make it impossible for navigation for deep draft vessels of those days which were not much deep.

Pliny then gives an account of Taprobane as found by Annius Proclamus, a collector of Red sea revenue, who was accidentally wafted by wind, and landed at Hippouri, a port in Taprobane. This account is also given by Appollonius of Tyana in his account of the second embassy to Rome. Pliny's account gives greater details as follows.

"Proclamus landed at Hippouri, a port in Taprobane. They learnt that there is a harbour to south adjacent to city Palaesamundus, the most famous city in the island. In the interior is lake Megisba 375 miles in circuit from which flow river Palaesamundus towards south, having 3 branches, one past Palaesamundus and a third branch Cydara flow north towards India. The nearest point to India is Cape Koliacum, 4 days sail from the island and midway lies the island of Sun. The sea is of vivid green color with great number of trees growing at the bottom, which sticks in rudders of boats.

"By sea, nearest mart of India named Muziris is reached, a place infested by pirates of Nitrias, where goods have to be transferred to boats and Kaelobothras was sovereign of the place at the time: Another convenient harbour is Neakyndon, which is called Bakare; there Pandian was king in the interior at Modura; pepper is carried from district Kottonara to Bakare in canoes."

This description of Taprobane agrees with the Taprobane island of Ptolemy as I have sketched out. The port Hippouri, is without doubt Kudremukh port, situated on the north promontory of Prasodes gulf of Ptolemy as already referred to in connection with the identification of the latter. The city Palaesamundus is Brahmasamudra city on the Vedavati river. The interior lake Megisba is indicated by the extensive low area of districts Raichur,

Kurnool, Anantapur and Cuddapah. Why this was a lake in the early part of the Christian era will be realised from the following facts.

(1) The monsoon rainfall in the area must have been very heavy indeed with the broad belt of shallow sea lying between India and Taprobane to its north, the shallow seas in the Anantasagaram (Nellore district) to its west penetrating inland, the shallow sea to the south very much nearer to the tableland of Mysore. A look at the contour map of the Peninsula of India will show that the above conditions brought the seas in very close proximity to the hills which induced extensive precipitation of clouds.

(2) The rapid shoaling of the seas right round the island seriously blocked the drainage outlets or rivers of the island. To the north of the island the filling up of the sea along Godavari Valley, choked the outlets to a much larger extent than on the other sides. To the east the Anantasagar filling up choked up the Penner outlet. To the south the islands were accreting and threatening to join with the main island, that is, the area consisting of Cochin, Travancore, Tinnevelly, Ramnad and Madura, was forming one mass of land with the south of Taprobane island, thus blocking up the outlets in that direction. To the west the vast number of rocky islands on the coast were joining on to the mainland and thus closing the mouths of many rivers on that side.

These two conditions would for the time induce water logging in the central low part of the island and we are therefore not surprised to find the vast inland lake Megisba, which must have extended over the low line area of the four districts already mentioned. The name Megisba, having some connection with Mâhîsaka or Mahîsamandala of Southern India, which is part of Mysore, and a colony of the Mâhîsmatî Kingdom of the Narmadâ Valley.

The Palaesamundus river had, it is stated three branches. These three branches are not difficult to locate; one was the Vedavati-Hagari system flowing into the Prasodês bay of Ptolemy or Hippouri, *i.e.*, having its mouth near Dvarasamudram or present Halebid; the second branch is Ptolemy's Soanus; the third branch Cydara towards India is Ptolemy's Ganges, modern Kistna, the name is either Sîva-dhârâ or Srî-dhârâ as the river passes by Srî-sailam and through country where Adîkêsa Sîva was held in esteem.

As regards C. Koliacum, it is no doubt Cape Kory of Ptolemy, and the Sun Island or the eastern Leuke Island is the Kory Insula of Ptolemy. The sea between India and Taprobane, of green colour, shoaled to an extent that rudders of boats stick to the bottom, is exactly the same condition as given by other Greek authorities. District Kottonara is Kanathra island of Ptolemy.

The description given of Muziris (Muziris of Ptolemy), Nitrias (Nitra of Ptolemy), Neakyndon (Nelkynda of Ptolemy), Bakara (Bakare of Ptolemy), seem to agree fairly well with the accounts given by Ptolemy and other writers and does not require further comment.

KOSMAS INDIKOPLEUSTES

Monk Kosmas writing in the first half of the 6th Century A.D. says that "Taprobane is a large oceanic island, goes by the Indian name of Sielediba but by Greeks Taprobane. Around it is a great number of islands all of them having fresh water and cocoanut trees; they nearly all have fresh water close to their shores. The island 300 Gaudia (900 miles) long and equally broad. From remote countries China and other marts in that direction, the island receives silk etc., and these again pass on to the other ports to Male where pepper grows and to Kalliena where copper is produced."

"Sindu is the frontier country of India. The following are the most famous commercial marts in India—

Sindus, Orrhotha, Sibor, Male which has five marts which export pepper, Parti, Mangarouth, Salopatan, Nalopatan, Poudopatan. Then out in the ocean 5 days sail is Sielediba, which is Taprobane. Then again further away on the mainland is mart Marallo, then Kaber, then China.

"Sielediba being thus in a central position with reference to India receives wares from all marts and distribute again over the world, thus becomes a great emporium."

This shows that the Taprobane island still existed as an island, in the first half of the 6th Century A.D. but that the sea has silted up to such an extent that deep water channels were furrowed out against the coasts of the large number of smaller islands in the sea round Taprobane, a condition which we would expect when the sea bed itself is in its last stage, as an area with water surface. Further the islands shown as Heptanesia, Trikadiva, Pepperina, Trinesia, Leuke, Oungana, had joined on to the mainland as the names of the marts in the pepper country give names which are on the forward line on the islands, and the names of intermediate ports between Semylla to Podoperoura are omitted, as evidently they have ceased to be ports any longer and were now inland places. The ports mentioned by Kosmas in this length, *i.e.*, between Orrhotha which has been identified with Surat and Poudopatana, which is Ptolemy's Podoperoura, are Sibor Male, Parti, Mangarouth, Salopatan, Nalopatan. Sibor is evidently Srivardhana port at the mouth of the Savitri river, after which is Male the greatest port and city of the pepper growing country, and this is evidently Sangamesvar, at the confluence of Vena and Kistna rivers, in Satara district, the ancient name of the city is Mahuli and of which very extensive remains exist to show its prosperity of old. It is quite possible that at the stage referred to by Kosmas this port was accessible not only by the route south of Heptanesia island, *i.e.*, the Vasisthi river valley which was the sea-coast, but also by an opening along the valley of Savitri and Vena rivers. The next port in the pepper country is Parti, which is perhaps Pandharpur, and then Mangarouth which is Mangalvedha, and then Salopatan which is Sholapur, and then Nalopatan which is Naldurg, and then it joined on to the original coast-line of Ptolemy at Poudopatan or Burdapur.

Kâlîdâsa writing in about 4th to 6th Century A.D. in describing the peregrinations of Raghû (Raghûvamsa, IV, 53 to 58) refers to the reclamation of the sea in this corner of India already effected; that the sea was forced back by Parasûrâma's arrow, from the base of the Sahya hills, and that the powerful western Kings were established there, accepted defeat and Raghû retired from Trîkût hills (Junnar) where he was paid tributes from those princes, "as if the reclaimed corner of the ocean came to Raghû to pay tribute"; this indicates that Trikut was once the former sea coast, and the sea reclaimed beyond this point.

Kosmas' further emphasis of goods from Eastern countries being dumped on the east coast of the Taprobane island and transferred to the west coast for export to the western countries and *vice versa*, coupled with the fact that he mentions only the pepper-country marts referred to above and then jumps on to only two marts Marallo and Kaber on the eastern length of the old coast, shows that the through maritime traffic by the sea between India and Taprobane was a thing of the past, the sea having been reduced to swamps, and the seatide influence was felt so little inland that the small islands are now full of "fresh water" a statement to which he gives prominence to indicate the change has taken place from salt to sweet water.

It is superfluous to repeat here again that Kosmas' description, cannot apply to Ceylon as Taprobane, and that his Taprobane is peninsular portion of India, which was almost joined on to the mainland towards the west or Bombay coast, though towards the east, that is, the lower vallies of the Godavari and the Kistna were still unreclaimed but shoaled up sea.

CHAPTER IV.

COURSES OF RIVERS FALLING INTO THE SEA ON THE SOUTHERN COAST OF INDIA AS GIVEN BY PTOLEMY, AND IDENTIFICATION OF TOWNS LYING NEAR THEM, AFFORDING A FURTHER CONFIRMATION OF THE COAST LINE AS TRACED BEFORE

NANAGUNA RIVER

The course of this river from its source onwards was as follows :—Starting from near Amarkantak, it followed the course of the present Narmadâ river by Jubbalpore, Narsingpur, Nemawar, to Chandgarh where the Chhota Tawa joins the Narmadâ; from this point the river struck southwards, penetrating the Satpura range, following the course of the Chhota Tawa river, by the valley through which the G. I. P. Railway line is carried now, passing by Khandwa, and then joining the Tapti river course near Burhanpore; from this point it followed the course of the Tapti river for a short distance up to Jalgaon; from Jalgaon it left the Tapti and turned southward again by the Girna river valley in the neighbourhood of Chalisgaon; from Chalisgaon, the river flowed southward by the valley lying between the Satmala and Ajanta ranges, flowing past the old town of Patanen near Taloda, joining the Pravara river at Sangamner; it is from this point Sangamner, which is Omenagar, that the river branched into three streams, the western Goaris falling into the sea near Shahapur north of Kalyan, the central stream Binda river flowing a little to the south of the above flowing by the valley of the River Bhima at its source and falling into the sea at Bombay, and the third or eastern branch flowing by Nevasa and Paithan and then turing southwards made straight for its outlet through the centre of Bhir district and falling into the sea near Barsi. Though above Jubbalpore, the course of the river was towards Amarkantak as mentioned above, Ptolemy very likely took the remnant of the old connection with the Ganges, from Chhindwara towards Sihora as the main river course.

It would at first sight appear that the course of the river that I have sketched out is an arbitrary assumption and the assumption of subsequent changes to the present conditions of the rivers is equally arbitrary, and the only merit the sketch has, is that it agrees with the alignment of the river as has been given in Ptolemy's map. I propose therefore to show at first that the river course at one time was, as indicated above, and then identify the sites on or near the bank of the river as given in the map and then to show that the subsequent changes to course of the river that have taken place are just what are to be expected.

That the course of the river at one stage, was along the course indicated, is given in casual references in many of the Pûrânas, but here I refer only to the Brahma Pûrâna, as in it, a fairly complete account of the course of the river is given. In chapter 78 it is stated that "the sacred stream Gangâ descended from the Hîmâlaya, to Bhâratvarsa, flowing through the centre of which it proceeded towards the Eastern sea. She was however divided into two streams in the belly of Mahêsvara, one branch proceeding south of the Vîndhya mountain and is called the Gaûtamî Gangâ, the other branch flowing along the north of the Vîndhya mountain, and is called the Bhâgîrathî Gangâ." Then in Chapters 79 to 115, it gives details of the sacred spots on the Gautamî Gangâ. That the Narmadâ is the Gaûtamî Gangâ, will be clear from a reference to Skanda Pûrâna, (Avantya Khanda, Ch. 3), where it is stated that "River Narmadâ, rising from the Rîksha mountains, obtained a boon from Shankara by which she became famous as the southern Gangâ". The

Mahadeo range of hills, south of the Bhanrer range, shows the place where in the belly of Mahêsvara, the northern main river was originally divided into two branches. It is also clear that this Gaûtamî Gangâ, could not possibly have had its offtake at the Mahâkâla range near Ujjaînî, an attempt to fix to which point is made in later interpolations. This Gaûtamî Gangâ, therefore unmistakably takes off from Jubbalpore, and is the Narmadâ in this length. A comparison of the names of sacred spots on the Gaûtamî Gangâ as given in the Brahma Pûrâna, referred to above, with the names given on the Narmadâ river in Skanda Pûrâna, Avantya Khanda, Rêvâ 63 *Et. Seq.*), discloses some names in common, notably of Kûmâratîrtha, Manînâga tîrtha, Rînamochana tîrtha, Chakra tîrtha; this also shows that these two rivers are the same. It is then that we find that this Gaûtamî Gangâ lower down receives the Sûvarnâ, Kâdravâ, rivers, and that next it receives the Pravarâ river, at the confluence of which is Nîvâsapûra; next it meets the Vrîddhâ river. These rivers are maintaining their old names, the Kadwa now a tributory of the Godavari, joining the latter about 50 miles below Nasik, and the Pravarâ, another tributory meeting the Godavari at Pravarâ Sangama, and Nevasa or Nîvâsapûra is on the Pravarâ but now about 8 miles above the confluence or Sangama with the Godavari. These facts make it clear that the Narmadâ at one time flowed through the Nasik district towards the south and that Kadwa and Pravara were its tributories. That being so and with the sea close to this point to its south and west as in the beginning of the Christian era, this is the point at the head of its delta where its branching out into effluents is to be expected and Sangamner points out to the spot. The name Sangamner, ancient Sangamana-nagara, shows both its importance of old, and as the place of "confluence of rivers" Further the similarity of the name with Omenagar of Ptolemy leaves no doubt about its identity with the latter. Its relative situation with the points fixed along the coast line also agrees very well. Between

Salabestrae country, which must be Surat, and Charmae-Pandae country, which represents southern Central Provinces, Megasthenes (Fragment LVI) places the Horatae country with a town Automela an emporium on the coast on the confluence of 5 rivers. This Automela as described tallies very well with Omenagar or Sangamner; there were two more effluents at the time, and the Ghod river falling into the sea at Hippokoura, and the Muli river or Muralâ of Sanskrit literature, with its flow reversed, falling into the sea at Byzantui are the obvious probabilities.

In Skanda Pûrâna, (Avantyakhanda, Rêvâkhanda, ch. 5, 6) we find it stated that "Narmadâ has its source in the Rîkhsa mountains, flows by Trîkûta hills". Trîkûta hills have been identified with Junnar, lying near Sangamner to its southwest which also confirms the alignment of the river as adopted.

Of the three effluents shown in Ptolemy's map, the western branch Goaris possibly followed the course of the Pravara river from Sangamner to Akola which is reputed to be Agastya-Asrama of old and then struck south along the bed of the river Mula which is supposed to be the ancient and sacred stream Mûralâ, following up which valley, it fell into sea near Kinowli to the southwest of Shahpur which latter is Sippara of Ptolemy.

The second branch starting from Sangamner, southwards, following practically the route of the present road from Sangamner to Poona until it met the Indrayani river bed from which point it proceeded up that river bed, and then by the Patal Ganga river falling into the sea at the Bombay Harbour area; the name Benda as given to this river by Ptolemy is a corruption of Indrayani, and Dounga is very likely Bombay itself. The third and eastern branch, shown as the main river Nanaguna, flowed from Sangamner eastwards by what is now the Pravara river for a short length not up to but in the direction of Nevasa, or Nîvâsapûra of the Pûrânas, and Banausi of Ptolemy; and then made for, and followed, the bed of the Sina river, a tributory of the Bhima, till it debouched on the sea near Barsi, between Sonari and Amirguda, which correspond to Khersonesos and Armaguda of Ptolemy as already described before.

Having now fixed the position of the deltaic effluents of the Nanaguna river, I now proceed to identify the places along its course from its Delta to its source.

Olokhoira in the Piratic district of Bhir, lying between the Nanaguna and the Binda branches of the river, is Rahuri Khurd, an ancient town in Ahmadnagar district.

Omenagar is Sangamner or ancient Sangama-nagar as already referred to.

Gamaliba is very likely Gangapur, a little to the northeast of Nevasa.

Deopalli is Devagaon near Ellora.

Botana, or Baithana, the royal city of Polemaious, is Patanen, a village now deserted, lying 10 miles south-south-west of Chalisgaon, below the Satmala hills. The extensive ruins of Brahmanical and Jain temples in this village, attest to its former prosperity and being the headquarters of the local kingdom at an early period.

This is the point in which the river formerly started penetrating the Sahyadri range, and which must have suffered from flooding and severe physical changes which brought about its downfall from a prosperous city, when the outlet of the river southwards to the sea was closed.

Tagara from its position in the map must be close to Jalgaon if not Jalgaon itself. The city must have been an extensive one as described by the Greeks, and I am not quite sure whether Takerkheda, lying between Jalgaon and Amalner, perpetuates the name of old Tagara.

Sarisabis, is where the Biswa river, or rather the Biswa and Purna combined, joins the Tapti, and that is, the modern village Changdeo a little below Burhanpur.

Malippala is Pal to the west of Burhanpur. This is another place which must have suffered from severe flooding at the time the connection with the Narmada was being cut off as a result of retrogression of bed levels of the Tapti river. The name is from the "great" Pal or Mahâ-Pal; the towns in the neighbourhood have this eulogising prefix attached to their names, *e.g.*, Maharala, Mahamandli.

For Tabaso, I am unable to fix the exact position. It is suggested by Yule and others that Tabaso is from Tapasir or Brahman ascetics, a large colony of whom must have resided in the locality. The location indicated is south of Mândhâtrî Khêtra, the Kingdom of Kârtya-Vîrjya Arjjûna. The river Tawa or Tava seems to have existed as a loop of the Narmadâ river at this place, the main river hugging the northern edge of the valley at the base of the Vindhya range, while the Tava river ran along the southern edge of the valley along the base of the Mahadeo hills. This river is now seperated, the Chhota Tava and Tava being now at a considerable distance from each other, but this valley indicates the place of the Tabaso Kingdom, and I am inclined to think that Khandwa points to be the likely location of Tabaso itself.

Anara is represented by Nemawar in eastern Indore area.

Nygdosora is represented by Narasînghapûr or present Narsingpur.

Adeisathra, does not appear to have any connection with Ahîchchatra of old. Its position is to be looked for between Narsingpur and Jubbalpore, which brings us to the neighbourhood of Chhindwara. Chhindwara, is evidently the Chhînna-dvâra, or "closed gate" of river Gangâ, where it formerly fed the Narmadâ-Kâvêrî system of rivers with its spill water, and which was "Chinna" or cut off later on. I am unable to suggest how the name Adeisathra comes, but I hope a study of the locality will bring this out. This Chhindwara is the old city about 30 miles to the west of Jubbalpore and not the later headquarters of the district of the same name.

Agara, is no doubt Garha near Jubbalpore, the famous place where the Chandel Rajas had built later on one of their eight forts (Arch. Survey of India VII, 21).

The course of the Nanaguna river is now traced completely. The gradual changes that have taken place in its course will be dealt with later on, in connection with the changes of the courses of the main rivers south of the Vindhyas which are all co-ordinated and so cannot be conveniently considered separately.

Why the name of the river is Nanaguna has been a matter of speculation hitherto, and is likely to remain so yet. That the name is Nana-guna, because it offers many beneficial qualities is a suggestion scarcely admissible. It is more likely that it is a corruption of Dakshîna-Gangâ.

PSEUDOSTOMON RIVER

It is obvious from the contour map, that the basin of the Purna river, the largest tributory of the Tapti, which lies to the south of the Mahadeo Hill Range, must have drained formerly to its nearer outlet to the sea southwards; fortunately the name in different sections of the former river have still been maintained and there is therefore no difficulty in tracing the course of this former river, and this is the river which answers to the alignment of the Pseudostomon river as given in Ptolemy's map. Ptolemy terms the river mouth as Pseudostomos or "false mouth"; this obviously means that the mouth shown to the west of Burdapur (Podoperoura) near Amba had already silted up, which is to be expected, as at this point the sea coast must have shoaled earlier than at others, owing to the high lands of the Balaghat range running close by, and several big islands existing off the coast. A little raising of the bed of the river at its outlet was sufficient to divert the bulk of the river discharge to the channel passing by Nander; as the silting of the coast-line proceeded further, diversion of the river, first eastwards to the Penganga, then the Wardha river must have taken place, and finally to the Tapti as now.

The course of the former Purna river, is indicated by the portion of southern Purna river from its junction with the Godavari near Palam, then passing by Purna Railway station lying between Parbhani and Nander, up to the bend at Bamni, then striking north towards Kata-Purna river, joining the same near Basim, then following the course of the Kata-Purna till it joins the northern Purna river near Lakhpuri; from here the course ran along and up the northern Purna river to near Ellichpore from which point there seems to have been a connection with the Wardha river. The course of the lower reach of the river from the Purna Railway Station to the sea, consisted of the portion of the present Godavari river course up to its junction with the Wun river at Sonepet, then along the course of the Wun till it fell into sea near Amba. The remarkable trend of the courses of the three rivers, northern Purna, Kata-Purna, and southern Purna, in one general direction from the Mahadeo Range towards the southern sea of India that was in Ptolemy's time shows they were one river, and the silting of its mouth as also of interior sections due to piracy by other rivers which had already set in by Ptolemy's time, also shows why the mouth of the river is named Pseudostomos and the river itself Pseudostomon.

It remains now to identify the towns on or near its course, in further support of the alignment adopted. I proceed from the point of outfall upwards. The mouth of the river is between Muziris and Podoperoura, that is a point very near to and east of Burdapur. The silted up mouth did not afford facilities for a port and there is remnant of no town of importance here. The next town up the river is Paloura, which is no doubt Palam on the Godavari river. Next comes Kouba which is the point of meeting of the R. Kupra with the Purna, the name Kouba being corrupt Kupra.

Nurulla is at the junction of the Penganga and the Kata-Purna; the portion of Penganga intercepted by the Purna and lying to the west of it, was not part of the Penganga when Purna was the main river running north and south and the name of this river is perhaps preserved in the town Lawalla, which is the same as Nurulla of Ptolemy.

Karoura, the royal city of the Kerobothros comes next near the bank of the river. Kerobothros or Kêrala-pûtras, represents the kingdom of Kêrala, coming next to the Pândya Kingdom of the Surasênas, which I have shown (See Ch. III.) to be the Nagpur area. Kêrala Kingdom, occupied by the people who claimed their descent from Kêrala, one of the sons of Akrîda (Herakles), was therefore one of the Nâga kingdoms next to Pândya kingdom of Nagpur, and the area lying between Pseudostomon and Baris, must have included the kingdom of Kerobothros. I have no hesitation therefore in identifying Basim, ancient Vasukipura, with Karoura. The locality contains ruins to show its prosperity of old. The name Karoura, may be a contraction of Kêrala-pûra, that is the head-quarters of the Kêrala kingdom. A point for consideration also arises whether the Purna is "Varûna" of the Pûrânas (Brahma Pûrâna 81) and that it had a connection with the Arna river near Basim is obvious as the head of that river comes to within 15 miles of this point. Arna would obviously be "Arûnâ" mentioned in the Pûrânas, and near their Sangam or confluence and near the Kshîrâvdhî or "Yellow Sea" is Manînâga's royal residence and which is "Garûda" tirtha. The name "Garûda" tirtha, the situation at the confluence of Arûnâ and Varûnâ, and the headquarters of Manînâga, a worshipper of Vâsûkî, who had also his place Nagathan in the suburbs of the city, seems to point out its identity with Karoura, regia "Kerobothri", or "Garûdapûtras".

Kourellour is Kuran, or Kurankhed on the Katapurna where the Railway line from Akola crosses it.

Petirgala is Patur on the road from Akola to Basim.

Kalligiris is Akola itself.

For Modogoulla I have no suggestion to make.

Sirimalaga is Shirala-gaon, on the road from Amraoti, and at a distance of about 24 miles from it.

Soubouttou is Saur, 4 miles to the west of Shirala. This is evidently Sobhâ-râshtra, referred to by Kaûtîlya as a beryl producing place, which Bhattasâlî in his commentary places in Vîdarbha or Berar.

Hippokoura, the royal city of Baleokouros is Ellichpur, or as the local name properly spelt is Ilîchpûra, the city of the Ilich or Baleokors, which is very likely Rûlîka people living near the Vindhyas mentioned in Padma Pûrâna.

Tiripangalida is Ner Pinglai.

Indê is Benoda, about 5 miles west of Warud.

The course of the Pseudostomon is now completely described. For the sequence of changes on the reclamation of the Southern sea, the high level of the Ajanta range which the river penetrated played an important part, dividing the drainage basins, the southern portion of it draining into the Godavari, which came into being with the death of the southern sea, and northern area draining into the Tapti river. As the Godavari outlet was established towards the east, part of the bed of the southern Purna was appropriated by the Godavari, and the short bit intercepted between the former sea and the Godavari, had its flow reversed and is now the Wun river. The northern portion of the river found an outlet to the Tapti, and the connection with the Tapti being now the main northern Purna river, the name of the main river was applied now to the whole length up to its junction with the Tapti. The portion left to the south of the river, came then to be known as the Kata-Purna, or the "separated Purna" river.

BARIS RIVER

A look at the relief map will show that the alignment of courses of the Baris and the Kheberus at their upper reaches ran through low-lying areas, which were accordingly densly wooded two thousand years ago. This explains why the rivers were very much lacking in prosperous towns on or near their courses. To these areas the wild tribes and Naga worshippers must have penetrated, as occupation by civilised settlers spread from Surat on the west and Kalînga on the east along the southern sea coast of India at the time. This absence of towns on the banks makes it difficult to trace the courses of the rivers accurately, and the jungly nature of the country made it difficult for the Geographers of old to get information of the interior country correctly and would explain why Ptolemy has gone outside the mark to fix the comparative positions of the towns of which he has fixed the sites on the map. This fact should be borne in mind here. Further, the basins of the Baris, Solenus and Kheberus lie in this central level area of which the near outlet to the sea having since been closed, and the area being low, the balance of water levels of rivers which had small slopes, was affected seriously, with the result that, avulsions of river courses were numerous, and no trace of continuity of old beds are traceable. This additional difficulty in tracing the courses of the rivers in this area has also to be kept in view.

As explained, there is no distinct general line of bed of river indicated for the Baris, and the course of the river jumps from one river to another frequently, and it has been fixed only with reference to the towns whose sites can be identified. I now proceed to trace the course, starting from its outfall to the sea, upwards.

The mouth of the river lies between Bakarê and Melkynda, which would be near Bhaisa at the foot of the Nirmal range.

Morunda is the next town shown to the east of the river. This is without doubt Waronda in the Parbhani district of Hyderabad.

Next we have Koreour town on the west bank. This would be the junction of Kiadho river with the Baris, and the point is Hadgaon, or a little to the north of it. The name Koreour is from Kiadho.

It would be best here to identify the towns lying near Koreour and to its west. Adarina is Arni on River Arna. Bideris is Pusad or ancient Pusadi on River Pus.

Arembour comes next, on the Baris, on its west bank. This is no doubt Bori on the river Aran, the name evidently is from Aran-Bori.

To the east of the river, a little away from the bank now comes Tittoua, which is unmistakably Yeotmal or Yewatmal.

A little to the north comes Selour which is Sirpur on the Wardha river.

Further to the north of Selour comes Mendêla which corresponds to Deoli, an ancient town.

On the opposite or west bank in the interior here is Aloe which is Lohi on the north bank of the Aran and about 12 miles to the east of Karanja Bibi.

To the north of Aloe is Punnata town, where is beryl. In fixing the site of Soubottou with Saur about 20 miles to the north-west of Amraoti, it has been shown that Saur is Sobhâ-râshtra referred to by Kaûtîlya in his Artha-shâshtra, as a "Kâcha-manî" or beryl producing country, which his commentator Bhattasâlî makes it clear is in Vîdarbha or Berar, in which this area lies. This is therefore the beryl producing area of old and Amaraoti agrees with the site of Punnata as given in Ptolemy's map. Amraoti is therefore Punnata. The name evidently is from Pûrnâ-Tata, or bank of the Pûrnâ river; a look at the map will make it evident that the Pûrnâ very likely had its main stream by the river channel which passes from near Ner Pinglai and passes to the west of Amraoti within 5 miles, and joins the Purna river near the bend at Asra, in Kaûtîlya's time, that is, about four and a half centuries before Ptolemy.

Mastanour comes next, a little to the north of Punnata. This is no doubt Bisnur.

Further north comes Passagê, which is evidently Paradsingha to the east of Katol, in Katol taluka.

After leaving Pasagê to its west the source of the river Baris penetrates the valley which has been adopted by the Nagpur-Chhindwara railway line.

The course of the river Baris can now be traced completely and starting from the sea to the source it will be as below :—From its mouth west of Bhokar, it goes north till it meets the Penganga river to east of Waronda, then along Penganga for a short distance to near its junction with Kiadho, then striking north makes a short cut to the

Penganga again, the remnant of the channel still traceable; then along the Penganga northwards up to its confluence with the Aran; then follows the Aran up to Bhatgaon, from which point it goes north towards the Wardha river by the dead channels passing to the west of Yeotmal, joining the Wardha at Saongi; from here along Wardha river to Rohna, south of Arvi, then adopting the beds of the Dham, and the Jam, crossing the Kanhan, enter the Mahadeo Range, towards Chhindwara. The name Baris like that of the next river Solen is to be explained from the assumption that the Narmadâ or rather the Gaûtamî Gangâ, had several effluents southwards, penetrating the Mahadeo range, and the Baris river was connected with Bararewa river and the Solen with the Soner river, both of which are now small tributories of the Narmadâ, but these were at one time head channels of the Baris and the Solen. The same argument applies to the Kheberus as has already been shown that Kheberus was an effluent of the Narmadâ or Gaûtamî Gangâ (*vide* Ch. 1 A).

SOLEN RIVER

In tracing the course of this river, the same method as for the Baris will be adopted, that is, identifying the towns on or near the banks of the river, beginning from its mouth and proceeding to its source.

The mouth of the river was a little to the east of Kolkhi on the Orgalic gulf; this would therefore be a point little to the south of Asifabad.

The first town up the river, and to the east of it is Akour, which is represented by Wakri north of Asifabad.

Mantittour comes next to the west, at some distance from the river, and is Mandar, 4 miles south of Wun.

Modoura, the royal city of the Pandion, comes next on the bank. This city is near Nikama on the coast which I have already shown is Manikgam or Rajura.

The site to which Modoura obviously corresponds is that of the city Chanda and there appears to be no doubt that Chanda is Modoura of Ptolemy. This former capital of the Nâga kings is mentioned in most references, as Madhûrâ. As the name sounds much as Mathûra, the epithet "Dakshîna" or southern Mathûrâ was adopted to distinguish it from the Mathûrâ of Northern India. With the later growth of the Pândya kingdom in Madras Presidency, attempts were made to assimilate Madura with the southern Madhûrâ. Ptolemy puts Madhûrâ as Modoura of the Pandions, and to distinguish Mathûrâ from it, the latter is mentioned as Modoura of the gods. It is clear that wherever Madhûrâ is mentioned in Sanskrit or Pali literature, generally this is to be taken as the Madhûrâ of the Nâga kingdom of Pândyas in the Central Provinces. The position of Madhûrâ is indicated clearly in a curiously interpolated reference when dealing with the sacred places near the Sâbhramatî (Sabarmati R). Padma Pûrâna (Uttara Kh. 141) says that "Dharmâvatî and Gangâ sangama or confluence is a sacred place; after which is Madhûrâ-pûrî, the temporary refuge of Harî, who was in fear of Jarâsandha; Harî established Madhûrâ Daîtya in this place". Gangâ referred to here is Pengangâ and Dharmâvatî is the Dham river, which flows by Wardha and falls into the Wunna which again joins the Wardha river which latter meets the Penganga about 10 miles west of Chanda. It will readily be understood that at one stage the Dharmâvatî river was the main river of the system up to Chanda, and that it was only when the discharge of the Baris in its upper reaches was being gradually diverted eastwards owing to its mouth closing up on the sea receding, that the Wardha became the larger stream and thus appropriated to itself even the name of the Dharmâvatî river in its lower reaches. The Kathâ Sarît Sâgara, which though written at a later date but contains reiteration of older information, says that (II, XIII) Lankâ island to Madhûrâ the journey is by sea and (II, XIV) Madhûrâ to Vîndhya forest is 63 Yojanas. The position is thus fixed near the sea coast, and 200 miles from the Vîndhya forests, which is on the southern slope of the Vindhyas as indicated in that book elsewhere.

This also would fix the position of Madhûrâ near Chanda, at a time the sea ran close to it as shown in Ptolemy's map. The Vâyû Pûrâna (99) says that "Nâga kings will at first enjoy Champâvatî-pûrî and then Madhûrâ-pûrî"; the prosperity of the Champâvatî-pûrî as the capital may have been a short one as it is stated that the capital was shifted to Madhûrâ after only 6 kings had reigned there. Champâvatî is very likely Nâgpur itself, a point to which I will refer in connection with Korindiour. The Vîshnû Pûrâna however furnishes information which is important, as it shows that when the Nâga kings were reigning at Madhûrâ, accretion of land was proceeding along this sea coast at a rapid rate, and it indicates the locality also by mention of Kâmâra coast, as the limit of accretion at this stage. The Vîshnû-Pûrâna says that "Vîndhyasaktî was the most powerful king of the line of Vrîsa, of foreign origin." The Vâyû Pûrâna says that Bhogî, son of Nâga king Shêsa, was the first of the kings of foreign origin, of the Nâga line. The Vîshnû Pûrâna, then goes on to says that "Vîndhyasaktî was superlord, and 9 kings of his line reigned for 106 years after which kings of lower origin will prevail who will reign the country, joining on to the mainland, the sea coast land, Dâvvî, Kovvî, Chandrabhâgâ river side land, up to Kâmâra coast." This Kâmâra coast is no doubt Kommaria of Ptolemy, present Kamareddipet. All these go to show the Nâga kingdom, in this neighbourhood and Chanda is the site of Madhûrâ or Modoura, Regia Pandion, of Ptolemy.

Tangala is the next city in the interior to the west of the river; this is Talegaon, south of Wardha and west of Hingan ghat.

The next town, longway up the river, to west is Peringkarei. This is Gondkhairi on the main road, and 10 miles to the west of Nagpur.

On the opposite side in the interior here is Korindiour which is represented by Kamptee or Kamthi near Nagpur. This agrees as far as the site is concerned; the difficulty is regarding the origin of the name. This locality was unmistakably, the headquarters of the Nâga kings who raised themselves by claiming descent from the Pândû dynasty. Nagpur was the capital of these Pându kings as stated by Kâlîdâsa in Raghûvamsa (VI. 59, 60); the Nâga river runs close by. The city claims antiquity. All this point out to this city having been one of the capitals of the Nâga kings and if Chanda is Madhûrâ, then Nagpur is Champâvatî. Kamthi appears to be corrupt Champâvatî, or Champâvatî is Sanskritised Kamthi, Korindeour in that case is very likely Kamthinagar or corruption of Champâvatînagar.

There is no other town on or near the banks of the Solen river above this point. The course of the river starting from its outfall to the sea, proceeding up its course is now traced. The mouth of the river is a little to the south of Asifabad, the length of the river from the sea to Asifabad or Janakpur being along the small tributory of the Peddavagu river; from Janakpur, it followed the Peddavagu river up its course, from which it joined the Penganga lying within a short distance; from here it followed the course of the Penganga to its junction with the Wardha river near Chanda; it then turned north following the course of the Wardha up to its junction with the Wunna; then followed the Wunna, almost up to its source near Nagpur, from where it jumped to the course of Kanhar river, making a sharp turn towards the east, till it joined the Wain-ganga near Bhandara, from which point it followed the course of the Wain-ganga up its source up to the base of Mahadeo range.

The river Solen, was at an earlier date then Ptolemy's, an effluent of the Narmadâ, or rather the Dakshîna or Gaûtamî-Gangâ. The point in which this river penetrates the Mahadeo hills, brings it within easy range of the Soner, now a tributory of the Narmadâ.

This Soner appears to be river Sûrasâ one of the fifteen effluents of the Dakshîna Gangâ or Narmadâ as mentioned in Skanda Pûrâna (Avântya, Rêvâ, 3). This would explain the name Solen, corrupt Sûrasâ-nadî.

KHABEROS RIVER

In discussing the site of Khaberis port at the mouth of the Khaberos river I have already pointed out (*Vide* Ch. I. (A)) that this river is the Kâverî river, an effluent of the Dakshîna Gangâ or Narmadâ, bifurcating from the same from near Amarkantaka. Though this was one of the biggest rivers with a perrenial flow at one time, we find that by Ptolemy's time the river had lost its importance, as the lack of prosperous towns with the single exception of Orthoura, the royal city of the Sornagos indicates. It is not convenient to trace the course of the river, from a single point on its banks, and which also seems to be a township which was stuck to for a longer time, as it was the headquarters of the kingdom previously and must have been an extensive city, than others on the bank of this river, which must have been depopulated and deserted owing to serious unhealthy climatic conditions brought about by the spill of the Gaûtamî-Gangâ river being cut off, from its head. The river when it received the spill of the Gaûtamî-Gangâ had already done its work by building up the tableland to its west in the area lying between the Khaberos and the Solen, which we find full of townships and colonised by the Brahmans (Brakhme Magoi). The importance and populous character of this tableland have possibly misled Ptolemy in exaggerating its dimensions, and this also explains why the courses of these two rivers are actually very much nearer to each other than shown by Ptolemy. As there is only one town on the river, which has also lost its importance owing to unhealthy surroundings and is scarcely traceable now, it would be best now to proceed at first, by tracing the towns situated in the interior and lying between the rivers Solen and Khaberos.

Bata, is Bhatala lying to northeast of Warora, and about 10 miles from it.

Talara is Talodhi an ancient town on the road from Chanda to Nagpur, reached from Talodhi road station of the Nagpur-Chanda railway.

Abour is village Gabori, 20 miles to the south of Talodhi.

Kalindoia is Kalari about 25 miles north of Talodhi, near the road to Nagpur.

Eikour is not traceable.

Kaliour is Ekalpur on the Garhvi river, about 20 miles east-south-east from Brahmapuri.

Brakhmi, a large city, of the Brakhmanoi Magoi, who occupied the country from the Bettigo to the Batoi country, is unmistakably Brahmapuri, a town of great importance still and the ancient ruins in and near about the place speak of its prosperity of old.

Now that the interior towns have been dealt with, the two towns, Orthoura, the royal city of Sornagos, on the river itself near Bere, and Sangamarta, a town near its source remains to be fixed up, before tracing the course of the river.

Orthoura, the royal city, has evidently been deserted and ruined after the river spill was cut off. No big township stands on the site now, as the site is almost contiguous to Bere, which is without doubt Waria-garh. The extensive width of the Kobragarhi river which flows past Wariagarh, over its length from Wariagarh to its junction with the Wainganga, shows that when the Wainganga bed levels were raised in its lower reaches with the sea receding from its mouth, the river tried to break through the Kobragarhi river bed, which was widened out as a result, the spill escaping over the country to its south. The mischief owing to the flooding must have been done by wiping off Orthoura city, and Wariagarh escaped as it was situated on the fringe of the high land to the east of Orthoura. Local investigation will, I hope, enable us to fix the site of Orthoura and I can only now suggest that this city was at the confluence of the Kobragarhi and the Wainganga rivers, which is about eight miles to the west of Wariagarh, and Orthoura Regia will be in the proximity of Armori, if not Armori itself.

Sangamarta near the source of the river, is Mandla itself or a little to the east of it, that is, intermediate between Mandla and Amarkantaka. It is in this neighbourhood that the hallowed confluence of Narmadâ and Kâvêrî was at one time. Padma Pûrâna (Svarga, 6) fixes the spot thus "Behind Kalînga country is Amarkantaka mount, in which flows Narmadâ river; west of Amarkantaka is Kotîtîrtha, the place of Jalêsvara Rûdra, and burnt Trîpura; next and near is confluence of Narmadâ with Kapîlâ and Vîshalya-karanî rivers; next to this is Narmadâ-Kâvêrî Sangam, or confluence of these two rivers." Agnî Pûrâna in giving a list of sacred places, mentions (Ch. 113) *inter alia* "Narmadâ river portion from Amarkantaka to the confluence of Kâvêrî, Srî-mountain, the place of meditation of Hîranya Kasîpû" as one of these sacred spots. This fixes very nearly the spot at which the Kâvêrî as an effluent of the Narmadâ, separated from the latter river, a point to which I have already referred to (Ch. I (A)) where I have shown the Kheberos river is Kâvêrî, an effluent of the Narmadâ or Gautamî-Gangâ. Mandla city which claims antiquity from the extensive ruins in it as also its neighbourhood, appears therefore to be Sangamarta, lying to the coast of Kheberos. The name is very likely derived from Sangama-tîrtha, the sacred confluence of Kâvêrî and Narmadâ.

The course of the Kheberos river, from the sea to its source would therefore be as follows :—Mouth of the river near Chichbori; then up the Wainganga river to its junction with the Garhvi, west of Wariagarh; then up the Garhvi river, for a short length, and then striking westward till it joins the Sat river which is followed to its source, and then joins the course of the Bagh river, then the Son and Banjar up to Mandla where it penetrates the Mahadeo range.

TYNA OR TYNDIS RIVER

As in the case of the Kheberos, the best course would at first be to refer to the identification of the townships lying between the Kheberos and the Tyna, and then those lying on or near the banks of the river itself.

Bere as already noticed is Waira or Waira-garh.

Of Karmara, I have doubts for its identity but it will be in the neighbourhood of Dudhmala on the Katni river lying awout 25 miles south of Waira-garh.

Magour is Musrum-gond lying 20 miles north-north-west of Suryagarh (Sobara emporium).

Pikendaka is Pindi-Konda in Bastar district 16 miles east of Dantewara.

Poleour is Nalwara, 10 miles west of Kondegaon, across the river.

Phrourion, or the "fort" is Antagarh, the terminus of the metalled road, running south from Raj-Nandgaon.

Tennagora is Dangarh, about 50 miles south-west of Raj-Nandgaon lying on the road from it. The towns on the east side of the river will now be considered.

Keraugê is Khairagarh, 30 miles north of Raj-Nand-gaon.

Karigê is Koregaon, lying south of Dhamtari and north of Kondegaon, on the road between them.

Iatur is Bastar itself.

Ikarta is Bakti or Baktigura.

Malanga, the royal city of Basaronagos is Malkangiri.

The course of the river, from sea to the source would therefore be, with its mouth near Pothikal, passing by Dantewara joins the Indravati at Tumnar; then up the Indravati to Chitrakot; then following the tributory of the Indravati, passing by Kondegaon, joins on to Mahanadi for a short distance after which it appropriates the bed of the Tandula, till it reaches and joins the Sembarsa, following which it made for Khaira-garh, where it entered the foot of the Maikal Range.

The name of the river, I have already discussed in dealing with the coast-line [Ch. I, (B)].

MAISOLUS RIVER

The towns in the interior to the west of the river have already been dealt with. Those on the river itself are few, namely Skopoloura, Koroungkala, and Pharytra or Pharetra.

Skopoloura is Kottagama on the Bhaskel river. The name has probably some connection with the river on which it stands.

Koroungkala is Korenga, lying across the river.

Pharytra or Pharetra is Parvatipura or Parvati-puram in Vizagapatam district.

In the interior to the east of the river is Pityndra the metropolis which no doubt is Padwa, on the old main road from Chodavaram to Jeypur.

The course of the river Maisolus from sea to the source was therefore as follows :—

From its mouth at Kondakamberu northwards following the Machkund river to Jayantigiri; then joining the southern effluent of the Indravati river near Koraput, passing near Dandwara, Nowrangapur, then turning westwards to within 10 miles from Jagdalpur then turning north along the Bhaskel river to near the river Tel. As regards the name Maisolus, I have already dealt with this point in connection with the coast-line [Ch. L(A)] and have shown that it has reference to the southern Matsya country of which the name is still retained in the name of the Machkund river.

CHAPTER V

RECLAMATION OF SEA, BETWEEN TAPROBANE ISLAND AND SUB-VINDHYA MAINLAND OF INDIA, AND ROUND TAPROBANE, WITH CONSEQUENT CHANGES IN RIVER COURSES

Having now established that the southern Indian Peninsula was detached from the mainland of India in the beginning of the Christian era, and also defined exactly the boundary of the Peninsular island at that period, I propose now to offer short general remarks on Taprobane island, the progress of reclamation, and speculation into the past.

The name of the Taprobane island, and the frequent changes its name has undergone is explained from the fact, that the island was in the making. The nucleus of the island remained, but much of it was very near or below the sea level before the Christian era, and it is not difficult to conceive that the whole area of Taprobane, consisted of small islands, and in Ptolemy's time we see many of these islands joined to form one island of big dimensions, but a good portion of its interior still remained jungly as the dearth of townships in the central portion shows, though prosperous ports had sprung up on the coast, and the island already controlling the transference of merchandise between the seas lying to the west and east of India, as navigation between the island and mainland had become risky owing to shoals and facilities for piracy, and navigation by small coasting vessels not possible in the outer sea, except for a limited period outside the monsoons. Three hundred years previous to this we find Megasthenes stating (Frag. LIX) that the island has no cities but only 750 villages; the houses were made of wood and occasionally of reed; that (Frag. XVIII) half the island is occupied by wild beasts and elephants, and man claims the other part.

Proclamus' account also shows that about Megasthenes' time the island possessed an inland sea Megisba of huge dimensions, showing habitable land along the fringe of the island, and a few habitable lands in the interior. Dîpavamsa (I. 45) written in the 5th Cent. A.D. says that Bûddha joined Lankâ island with Gîrîdvîpa to let men go to Lankâ and to allow Yakkhas and Pisâchas to go to Gîrîdvîpa, and separated the islands again after interchange of inhabitants was effected, which proves, that the islands were then in a very critical stage of transition, their joining and separation again, taking place with slight fluctuation of the sea-level or equally slight subsidence of land. The Mahâvansa, (I, XI) records that "in Devanâmpiya Titta's reign (307 B.C. to 267 B.C.) a miracle happened; precious metals and gems buried in the earth rose to the surface, and treasures sunk in the ships wrecked in the neighbourhood of Lankâ, as also naturally engendered there, rose to the surface; pearls rose up from the Ocean stood on a ridge on the sea shore;" it also records (I, XXII) that "the Uttîya province near the sea was submerged by the ocean during Dûttha Gâmanî's reign (161 to 137 B.C.)". Portion to the north-east of Ptolemy's Taprobane island still retained its name Nâgadvîpa or island of Nâgas, the inhabitants being termed Nagadiboi, showing that this portion was an island shortly before that time, and the rivers Ganges and Phasis of Taprobane mark out the cleavage line between Nâgadvîpa and the rest of the island. The bed of the Northern and Southern Penner rivers, indicates, another such cleavage line, which must have separated the hilly region of Chittoor, North Arcot and South Arcot districts as an island. The existence of Nallamalais range as an island shortly before Ptolemy's time does not require much imagination.

The reasons for the rapid change of the name of the island having been found, it remains to find out what the origin of these names are. Palaisamundus the earlier name is no doubt Pâra-samûdra, which means "lying across the sea" by which name these islands, while in the making, were referred to. Kaûtîlya in his Arthsâstra (321, 300 B.C.) mentions "Pâra-Samûdra" as one of the Coral producing areas, and Bhattasâli in his commentary says that Sîmhala island is meant by "Pâra Samûdra". Padma Pûrâna in giving a list of Janapadas (Svarga Ch. 3) mentions this as "Samûdra", and in Mahâbhârata (Bhishmâ 9) we find this is mentioned as "Samûdra-Nîkûta", both indicating countries across or in the sea, which were used at that time to denote the islands near the then mainland, which were then coming to be of importance as Janapadas, or peopled areas. After this stage had passed, more definite names, than mere "sea islands" were adopted, and we find the name Tâmraparnî, in Sanskrit, or Tâmbapannî in Pâlî or Taprobane of the Greeks applied to it.

The division of Bhâratvarsa into 9 islands as given by some of the Hindu Books, is given below :—

Puranas.	Islands.
Vâyû ...	Indra-dvîpa, Kasêrû, Tâmraparnî, Gabhastîmâna, Nâgadvîpa, Saûmya, Gândharva, Vârûna, Seagirt-Bhârata-dvîpa.
Brahma ...	Indra-dvîpa, Kasêrûmân, Tâmraparna, Gabhastîmân, Nâgadvîpa, Saûmya, Gândharva, Vârûna, Sea-girt island.
Matsya ...	Indra-dvîpa, Kasêrû, Tâmraparnî, Gabhastîmân, Nâgadvîpa, Saûmya, Gândharva, Vârûna, Seagirt Bhârata island .
Vîshnû ...	Indra-dvîpa, Kasêrûmân, Tâmraparna, Gabhastîmân, Nâgadvîpa, Saûmya, Gândharva, Varûna, Seagirt Bhârata island.
Skanda ...	Indra-dvîpa, Kasêrû, Tâmradvîpa, Gabhastîmân, Nâgadvîpa, Saûmya, Gândharva, Vârûna, Kûmârîkâ.
Sîva ...	Indra-dvîpa, Kasêrû, Tâmraparna, Gabhastîmân, Nâgadvîpa, Gândharva, Chârana, Seagirt Bhârata island.
Agnî ...	Indra-dvîpa, Kasêrû, Tâmra-varna, Gabhastîmân, Nâgadvîpa, Saûmya, Gândharva, Vârûna, Bhârata-varsha.
Vâmana ...	Indra-dvîpa, Kasêrûna, Tâmraparna, Gabhastîmân, Nâgadvîpa, Katâha, Sîmhala, Vârûna, Kûmâra-dvīpa.

It will be seen from the above table that the name of the island, varied slightly, as "Tâmra" or Copper,

"Tâmra"-varna" copper-colour, "Tâmraparna" copper leaf, "Tâmraparnî" copper leaved. The latter may also indicate "huts of copper colour." The Mahâbhârata in Bhîsma Parva (Ch. 6) states that "Sasa-sthâna is the second island of Jambûdvîpa or Sûdarshandvîpa, and that this is included in Bhâratavarsha. In Sasa-sthâna is Tâmraparnî hills and Malaya mountain." This gives an indication of Tâmraparnî island deriving its name from the name of the hills in it, which is Tâmraparnî, and which is next to Malaya Mountain or Malaia Montes of Ptolemy, and that leaves the Galibi Montes, in the north of the island to be Tâmraparnî hills of Mahâbhârata. This may also be assumed to be the case, as the upper and eastern portion of the Kistna river must have had an outlet westward to the sea, and that Tâmraparnî river from Galiboi Mountain must have been in existence. As the sea was reclaimed and land raised, the flow was reversed, and its name was merged on to that of the bigger river Kistna, though we find a remnant still left as the Tamraparni-Ghataprabha tributory of the Kistna shows. The Skanda Pûrâna has given an inkling as to the period in which the division of Bhâratvarsa into the 9 islands as above existed, as it says (Kûmârîkâkhanda, 39) that "in Kalîyûga the institutor of alien religion is Rîshabha; his son Satasringa, who divided Bhârat-Khanda amongst his eight sons and one daughter, and named them Indradvîpa, Kasêrû, Tâmradvîpa, Gabhastîmân Nâga, Saûmya, Gândharva, Vârûna and Kûmârîkâ." The time of Rîshabha, the Jain hierarch, is about the 6th Century B.C. and it gives an indication that Nâgadvîpa was then not merged into Taprobane, and that Kûmâra-dvîpa, by which the Skanda Pûrâna refers to the area near Bombay was also then an island, the lower courses of the Nanaguna and Mais rivers indicating the line of separation.

This would indicate that certain portion of the island at any rate was named Tâmraparnî by the Jains at an earlier period, but that Hindus particularly the bigot section like Kaûtîlya, still persisted later on in ignoring this, and mentioning the island as merely Pâra-Samûdra, and that Buddhists in turn revived the name Tâmbapannî. Whatever it is, the name itself is perhaps from a copper colour view the island may have presented from the sea, or from the copper-colour cottages made of weeds and leaves by which they were made. Subsequently we find Sieldiba and Serendib, both corruptions of Sanskrit Sîmhala-dvîpa used indiscriminately to apply to Taprobane. This is due to the colonists from Thaton migrating in large numbers to the Eastern coast of the island and as the migration of the first large band of colonists started when there was a split in the Thaton Kingdom at the death of King Thiha Radza in 543 B.C., they and the subsequent colonists wanted to name their new home after Thiha Radza, which in Sanskrit is Sîmha Râjâ, and the new home they named was Sîmhala or Sîmhala-dvîpa which was corrupted to Sieldiva, Serendib etc. As these colonists were pressed on southwards by the stronger people migrating from southern India, they gradually made their way from Taprobane to Ceylon, naming the latter island subsequently as Sîmhala, and to obliterate the memory of their hard struggle with the people of southern India, the migration was recorded as one directly to Ceylon. The coincidence of the date of death of Thiha Radza of Thaton, with the date of advent of Vîjaya in Sîmhala proves the source of migration and I will show also later on that Lankâ of Râmâyana was Thaton and its neighbourhood, a good portion of the island lying to the west of Thaton having now been submerged under the sea (*vide* Ch. XI).

Subsequently as the island Taprobane joined with the mainland, it lost its name as an island altogether and merged into India.

A few words on the progress of the reclamation of the sea between Taprobane and India will be of interest.

We have seen Megasthenes (302 B.C.) saying that Taprobane was separated from India by a river, *i.e.*, at the nearest points, the distance could not have been great, and he says the sea shallow; subsequently Ptolemy shows the distance fairly great. Though Megasthenes' information was evidently not one gathered by him with sufficient caution or independent verification like that of Ptolemy, yet we cannot dispose of his statement as very inaccurate, merely on the assumption that the changes in the sea must have been gradual and that, it is not conceivable that the sea which subsequently filled up, was wider in Megasthenes' time than it was in Ptolemy's time 450 years later. The statement from Mahâvansa already quoted, shows that there was a depression of sea level in Devanâmpiya Tissa's reign (307 B.C. to 267 B.C.) while it records an accession of sea level in Dutthagâmanî's reign (161 to 131 B.C.). Here we have these statements where dates are available, which help us to explain that it was possible that the sea belt between Taprobane and India was narrow in Megasthenes' time owing to a temporary depression of sea level but widened again subsequently with an accession of sea level. Another contributory cause of the intermediate sea being narrow like a river in Megasthenes' time is perhaps the cutting off of Ganges' spill over the Vindhyas through the rivers south of Vindhyas for some time previous to Megasthenes' period, and its broadening again later on brought about by the main Ganges past Palibothra closing up for a time, thus re-establishing the spill south of Vindhyas again, previous to final diversion eastwards.

The Mahâbhârata (Vana 114) describing the wanderings of the Pândavas, mentions that "after Gangâsâgara sangama, the Pândavas made their way by sea coast, to Kalînga country, where the river Baîtaranî flows. North of the river Baîtaranî is hilly country occupied by Dvîjâtîs (Brahmans). Brahmâ made a gift of the hilly country here to Kasyapa, but falling into the hands of men, this country in rage, subsided to Rasâtala (Sea level), but through the power of Kasypa's austerities, was again raised above the sea, at a distance of 1,300 yojanas. From Kalînga, it appears like a raised ledge in the sea, and the chanting of Vaîkhânas Mûnîs could also be heard." It is not possible to fix the date of these events, but as the locality is at the end of the sea we are dealing with, this information is of importance showing that there was an accession of sea level at one stage and then again a depression. The comparative levels of sea and land did undergo fluctuation, before the final settled conditions prevailed, and sea was steadily reclaimed.

Regarding the final reclamation we find it referred to in many Indian literature that Parasûrâma by his arrow shifted the sea from the Bombay-Malabar coast, and the reclamation of this coast is supported by local tradition all along this coast. Thus Sewell mentions in his List of Antiquarian Remains in the Presidency of Madras (I, 240) that south Canara district traditions maintain that it has been reclaimed by Parasûrâma; similarly Malabar District traditions maintain that it was reclaimed by Parasûrâma and its history obscure till 14th Century A.D.; (I, 254) that little is known of Cochin District before 8th Century A.D., and (P. I, 271) hardly anything is known of Tanjore district till 11th Century A.D.; (P. II, 141) that there is no evidence of Kingdoms in Deccan anterior to 4th Century A.D.; (II, 195) that local tradition says of reclamation of Malayalam country by Parasûrâma and of emigration of 64 villages of Brahmans to it; (II, 237) that Travancore Râjâs claim descent from Chera King Bhanu Bikram whom Parasûrâma placed on the throne of south Kērala after it was recovered from the sea by him. Montogomary Martin (The British Colonies P. 41-43) says that Pândya Kingdom of Madras was formed as late as the 5th Century A.D.; that Kêrala of southern India which includes Malabar and Kanara, was colonised by Brahmins from Hindustan in 1st to 2nd Century A.D.; that Konkan in early times was a wild tract as it still now remains thinly inhabited by Marhattas; that the Mahârâshtra country is vaguely noticed in early records. In Harîvamsa Ch. 95, Srîkrishna addressing Bhârgava Râma (Parasûrâma) when he met him in Karavîrapura city on River Venâ at the foot of Sahya hills said that "By your arrow you made the sea recede here, and raised the site of Sûrpâraka City 1,000 cubits, and established the town there; you forced your way beyond the coast-line of the western sea, and established populous human habitation on the upheaved land there at the base of the Sahya hills. Skanda Pûrâna (Vîshnû Khanda, Pûrûshottâma Mâhâtmya, I) mentions that Pûrûshottama Khêtrâ (Puri district area) is upheaved land from sea, girt by sandy shores, with Nîlgîrî hills in its middle and lies south of Mahânadî river.

It would appear however that in the west coast, which was dotted with islands, the reclamation of the sea from the material from the Indus mouth spread by the littoral drift of material from north to south was progressing. We find therefore that Kâlîdâsa writing in the 5th Century A.D. describing Raghû's march for conquest (Raghû Vamsa IV, 32-53), proceeds from Eastern Sea coast or bend of the Bay of Bengal westward visiting the countries in the following order :—

Sûmha, Vanga, Mid-Ganges islands, Kalînga, Mahêndragîrî, South sea coast hallowed by Agastya, Kâvêrî river, base of Malaya hills, Southern Pândya Kingdom, Darddûrâ, Sahya-gîrî, Kêrala, Mûralâ river, Princes of western countries who came and paid him tribute which appeared as if the sea which gave up land to Parasûrâma came himself to pay him tribute at Trîkutâ hills, Pârasîkas and Yavanas. Further that the huge army of Raghû when encamped at the base of the Sahya hills, preparing for an attack on the Princes of the western countries appeared as if the sea which receded by force of Parasûrâma's arrow, had again advanced to the base of the hills. Here we find it clear, that the Malaya hills mentioned with Darddûra, is an outcrop of the Vindhyas and is not the Malaya-gîrî of southern India ; that southern Pândya Kingdom is the Nagpur Kingdom. Taprobane island was therefore still separated from the mainland, but we find considerable reclamation had already taken place in the Bombay coast, where, as indicated by Kalîdâsa, the sea coast was near Trîkûta hills (identified with Junnar, Bhagwanlal Indraji's early History of Guzrat, 57) that is, at the mouth of Goaris river of Ptolemy previous to his time but the sea along the coast had already been reclaimed to a good distance westward, where powerful western Kingdoms were established by the 5th Cent. A.D.

Monk Kosmas writing in 535-547 A.D., says that Taprobane was a large Oceanic island in Indian sea, called by Indians Sieldiva, by Greeks Taprobane, 900 miles long and equally broad, around which are numerous islands.

I refer now to a remarkable passage in Kâdamvarî of Bâna Bhatta who thrived in the beginning of the 6th Century A.D., where the poet says that (Stanzas 44-46) "The place (Agastya's âsrama in Vîndhya forest) is girt by River Godâvarî, which like a dutiful wife, followed the path of the Ocean when drunk by Agastya." Here we find a clear statement that the ocean is already dried up, and that the river Godâvarî has taken its place; the river had a small nucleus in the mainland of India, and as the sea receded, the Goâvarî river took up the function of draining the area thus reclaimed, and so "followed the ocean on its death" a very apt description indeed. It is thus to be presumed that the Taprobane island joined on to the mainland in the 5th Century A.D., in its central portion, though considerable portion of the gulf still remained, particularly to the east which now forms the lower Godâvarî basin. It is perhaps this eastern gulf in the form of a vast lake which Bâna Bhatta refers to as (Kâdambarî 47-48) "the Pampâ lake, near Agastya âsrama, standing like a second ocean made by the Creator in rivalry with Agastya, which is a peerless home of waters and of which the depth and extent none can tell". The subsequent filling up and reclamation of the eastern and western ends of this intermediate Indian sea must have been by a gradual process. Mention of Agastya drying up this ocean has been made in several Indian books but as this does not enable us to fix the time, the passages need not be quoted except one or two, where the information is of interest as giving a little further detail which will be useful in discussing the process by which the sea was filled up. Padma Pûrâna (Srîshtî, 19) says that "Agastya, after stopping the Vîndhya hills from increasing in height, proceeded south to the sea, and drank the whole of the sea-water; on the representation of the devas, Vîshnû assured them that river Gangâ will again replenish the dry sea with water; Dêva-nadi, flowing in a reverse direction, emerged at Pûshkar, near Agastya âsram." In Mahâbhârata it is mentioned that (Vana, 104-105) "Agastya mûnî stopped the Vîndhya from growing further, having drunk the ocean water, forced the Kâlakêya Dânavas to flee to Pâtâla as refuge, after which he refilled the sea with yellow water." In Harîvamsa, we find it stated that (Harîvamsa, 94) "in Sûrpâraka in the base of the Sahya hills and on the coast of the Western sea, Bhârgava (another name of Parasûrâma) is established after removing the sea from the coast"; and that (Harîvamsa 53) "Brahmâ with Kasypa, was sitting on the west coast of the Eastern sea, when the devas accompanied by the sea and Gangâ came there; the sea, with salt water waves was eroding the coast, on seeing which Brahmâ made the sea calm." All the above indicate the sea drying up and the locality indicated is the sea running East and West and lying between Taprobane and India of Ptolemy.

That the progress of filling of the eastern and western portion of the sea from Ptolemy's time was gradual and slow will appear from the fact even so late as 1030 A.D. Alberuni in his travels (Ch. XVIII) after Somnath, passes south to the coast in Laran country, then Vallabha, Kanji, and Darwad; next a great gulf in which lies Singaldib; round this bay lies city Panjayavar fallen into ruins, King Jaur having built city Padnur towards the west; next on the coast is Unamalnara, then Ramesher opposite Serandib. This shows that by 1030 A.D., the Bombay coast ridge had extended as far as Dharwad district, but that inlets and indentations still remained, or perhaps had opened up as a result of fast closing up and shutting out of the connections with the inland sea by a ridge which must have been forming proceeding from north to south thus scouring out the single opening which remained. Padnur referred to by Alberuni is not Nagar or ancient Badnur but possibly Savantavadi or Vadi or Vadinagara and the gulf indicated is very likely one which would occupy the gap between the Taprobane island coast to the east, and the islands Orneon, Aigidion and Ammine to the west, all these islands having been joined together with the mainland to the north. A point to note in Alberuni's account here, is, that he makes a distinction between Singaldib and Serindib, referring to what was formerly Taprobane island, and still maintained its appelation in some localities in peninsular India, by the term Singaldib, and referring to Ceylon as Serindib.

Marco Polo's journey in India was in about 1293 A.D. His journey seems to be both by land and water, so it is not, clear from his itinerary as to how much was then land and how much water in the area between India and Taprobane in his time. It would however be of use investigating his journey here, as he seems to have gone through the inland route and not by the outer sea as is suggested by Yule and others. Marco Polo (Bk. III, Ch. XVI) sails "from Seilan I., proceeds west 60 miles to Maabar Province, which is styled India the Greater, and is on the mainland; Sunder Bundi Deva is King of Maabar; the sea here forms a gulf between Seilan Island and the mainland; all round the gulf is shallow 10 to 12 fathoms and pearl fisheries; the pearl fishers first go to Bettelar and then 60 miles into the gulf". Here he mentions from heresay accounts that body of St. Thomas lies buried in a little town in Maabar province. Then "leaving Maabar 1000 miles north he comes to Mutfili Kingdom, ruled by a widow queen the country producing diamonds"; then from heresay account evidently he says "Lar is a province lying towards west of St. Thomas' resting place, and that Cail is another city in Maabar, and it is a port for sailing to Harmos and Arabia". Resuming the account of his journey he proceeds (Ch. XXI) "quitting Maabar 500 miles southwest come to Coilum, the pepper country; (Ch. XXIII) proceeding further Comari Country; (Ch. XXIV) west of it 300 miles is Eli Kingdom with no harbours and full of pirates; (Ch. XXV) west of this great Kingdom of Meliber and near it Guzerat, the sea full of pirate vessels; then Thana and Kambaet and Semenat, and then Kesmacoran the last Kingdom and boundary of greater India." Yule and others have taken his journey to be round the peninsula of India, suggesting Mutfili as Telingana, St. Thomas as Madras, Maabar proper as Tanjore, Comari as Cape Comorin, Coilum as Travancore, and then to Tana, Cambaet etc., on the Bombay coast. Marco Polo makes a distinction, then still existing, of India the greater or the mainland, which distinctly indicated the peninsula still considered partly detached, a tradition natural, when the island Taprobane was detached only 6 centuries before his time, and the intervening sea not filled up along its whole length. This shows his Maabar province is the east and west country south of the Vindhyas; the term Maabar is obviously Mahâbhârata, which is corrupted to Maabar, and of which the sense is carried in his description that it is a province of *India the Greater*. His first landing in India from Seilan I, is therefore in Orissa, and the King at the time was Kêsarî Narasîngha Dêva, who is no doubt the King Sundar Bandi Deva of Senor Polo. Seilan from where Polo comes, is Thaton coast or old Lanka Island as I will show later on, this locality was. The Seilan island he refers to later on in defining the gulf as lying between Maabar and Seilan, is however part of Taprobane or peninsular India. The colonists to Thaton to the Madras coast of Coringa, maintained a close contact with the country of their origin and the name of their new home and original home were much confused for a long time, until their exit from the latter was completed. We find therefore here a great gulf south of Orissa, shallow and with pearl fisheries in it, the pearl fishers having their headquarters at Bettelar which is no doubt Waltair, from which point southwards the gulf began. From this point the account is a little confused, but it appears that he goes from Maabar, that is from the first place landed by him at Maabar, that is Orissa south to Mutfili Kingdom, 1000 miles northward.

This journey seems to be by land, and indicates his

proceeding more west than north, and arriving at Warangal. From here 500 miles he comes to the pepper country, which is perhaps Golconda, then to the Comar country, and Eli Kingdom of pirates, which is no doubt the Kûmarîkâ Khanda area of Skanda Pûrâna, that is the country abutting on the Bombay coast. It will be seen in his accounts, that he does not mention the nature of journey from Warangal to the Comari country, and it is only after this he mentions Eli Kingdom on the sea with no harbours, which indicates shallow sea and backwater, and it is after this he mentions the sea at Melibar coast, full of pirate vessels. This shows that the interior of the Bombay coast silted up except for shallow backwater swamps, the central portion joined from there eastward, to the gulf below Orissa which was shallow, and ran inland almost up to Warangal.

Another three centuries, and we find Bombay coast completely reclaimed even to the interior areas as shown in Sanson de'Abbevils map of 1652 A.D., given in Charles Danvers' book, Portuguese in India. This map shows however that a considerable area at and above the mouth of the Kistna still unreclaimed, a good portion of the Kistna and Guntur districts being still under water. A point of great interest to note in this map is that the mouth of the Godavari had temporarily closed, and that the river had appropriated to itself the Indravati-Tel Channel, for its main outlet to the sea for the time being. That the Godavari had its mouth near about the present mouth before this time is clear, as the cape above its mouth is marked as C. de. Godavari, and it is very likely that a small channel still remained but it was so insignificant near the coast at its mouth at the time of de'Abbevil that he has omitted to show the channel altogether. With the progress of reclamation, the bed of the Godavari must have been raised sufficiently high at its junction with the Pranhita, so as to raise its water level to a height sufficient to reverse the direction of flow in the Indravati, and discharge a considerable quantity of its flow, into the Indravati-Tel-Mahanadi system, even in the 12th Cent.

when the Puri temple was constructed, and the river afforded sufficient water for safe navigation, as we find that stones for the temple were brought from the hills by the Chitrotpala river. The Brahma Pûrâna (Ch. 46-47) says that "King Indradyûmna arriving at Pûrûshottama (Pûrî), found the Mahânadî river, issuing from Vîndhya mountain and flowing into the sea, passed by this area, and this river, which is also known as the Chîtrotpalâ river falls here to the southern sea, the confluence was visible from that place; for construction of the temple, the Princes of Kalînga, Utkala, and Kosala, sent artisans to Vîndhya hills to quarry stones from the base of the hill and despatch them by cart and boat to Pûrûsottama." It has already been shown [Ch. I (A)] Tel is Chîtrotpalâ river and the passage quoted from the Brahma Pûrâna indicates that this river, at the time of construction of the Pûrî Temple, was the main feeder of the Mahânadî, since it had then become of such importance as to threaten for the time to assert its name to the whole of the lower reaches of the river. De'Abbevil names this river as Guenga, and the reason seems also to be obvious; the Penganga and Wainganga, which make up the Pranhita were then more important rivers than the Godavari, and this must have lent the name to the river; it is also very probable that the Penganga and Wainganga from the point of their junction at Seoni, or from a little below that point may have had a shorter direct connection Indravati, a good way from its junction with the Godavari, which explains the name Guango applied to this river and that the closing of Indravati-Tel connection and coalescing of Wainganga system with Godavari through the Pranhita, was subsequent, to 1652 A.D. DeAnville's map, given with Orme's History, shows the state of affairs as indicated, as it shows the Godavari a smaller, river running parallel to the larger river Gunga to its north, which is evidently the Pen-ganga and Wainganga system, joined on to the Mahandi river, through the Indravati and Tel rivers. Moll's map, attached to Dow's History of Hindoostan, indicates Godavari, joined on to the Wainganga-Tel-

Mahanadi system, which is the next stage; the final stage we find in the 18th Century, that is Godavari through its independent present outlet restored at old Godavari point, and its connection with the Tel-Mahanadi system completely cut off. It is at this stage, that the whole of the Godavari and Wainganga system discharge was concentrated again to the present outlet past Rajahmundry, and the little gulf completely filled up with the large quantity of silt brought down to this delta.

How or when the islands to the south of Taprobane were joined to the latter has not been fully investigated by me yet. This point, a minor one for my purposes here, will be taken up at a future date if my health permits of it.

We are now in a position to consider the changes in the rivers, south of the Vindhyas, consequent on the Taprobane island joining on to the mainland and thus their outles to the southern sea cut off.

We find in Ptolemy's map that all the rivers flowing from the Vindhya range, flow into the intermediate south sea, mostly in a north and south direction. The Paurânic lists also indicate this, and some of the Pûrânas have gone out of their way to distinctly mention this fact of their making for the south and the south sea. Thus the Brahma Pûrâna (Ch. 70) says that "In Bhâratvarsha, lying between Hîmavâna and Vîndhya mountains, are six rivers representing gods; between the Vîndhya and the southern sea are six rivers, born of devas. The six river flowing from the Vîndhyas, *in a southern direction,* are :—Godâvarî, Bhîmarathî, Tûngabhadrâ, Vênîkâ, Tâpî, Payoshnî; the six rivers from the Hîmâlaya are :—Bhâgîrathî, Narmadâ, Yamûnâ, Sarasvatî, Vîsokâ, Vîṭastâ." Vâyû Pûrâna Ch. 45, says that "from Sahya-pâda, flowing *in a southern direction,* the rivers are :—Godâvarî, Bhîmarathî, Krîshnâ, Vênî, Vanjûlâ, Tûngabhadrâ, Sûprayogâ, Kâvêrî." In the list of rivers from Vîndhya, which includes Tâpî, Payoshni, Nîrvîndhyâ, Bhadrâ, Nishadhâ, Vênvâ, Vaîtaranî, Sîtîvâhû, Kûmûdvatî, Toyâ, Mahâgaûrî, Dûrgâ, Antahsîlâ, there is no mention of the direction of flow. In Matsya Pûrâna (Ch. 114) practically the same list as in Vâyû Pûrâna is repeated, with similar remarks, that is, direction of rivers from Sahya given, as flowing towards the south, and no mention of direction for rivers from the Vîndhya. This indicates a condition similar to that gives in Ptolemy's, but it is clear that these lists where inserted in the texts are subsequent additions made at a much later period, as we find in the lists, the rivers from Sahya hills, had already advanced over newly formed land a considerable distance along the Bombay coast, the lists including, Godâvarî, Bhîmâ and Vênâ, which at the time had already formed their upper courses, but flowing into the gulf which penetrated inland from Bombay coast. I have mentioned this fact here to show one stage of the river channels of which we have an inkling from the recorded lists on which would be able to base our theories of the sequence of the changes that took place.

In order that the lay reader may realise the nature of the work of agencies which have brought about the changes in this particular area that we are considering, it would be necessary to mention in brief what these are.

First, the sea waves, ordinary and tidal, on striking the coast, exert a pressure. Ordinary surface waves exert comparatively small pressure, but as their frequency is great, about one for every 3 min. their action is not negligible, where the sea is subject to high winds and resultant waves comparatively high and the slope of the coast fairly steep. That their action is indicated in seismograph records at Kolaba (S. K. Banerjee, D.Sc., in *Pravâsî*, Srâvan, 1337 B.S.) and that storm waves in Madras coast, affect the sensitive Seismograph established in the Alipore Observatory, shows the intensity of action is not to be neglected, and with their action repeated, they crumple up and raise the level of the land along the coast. The pressure of tidal waves is very much greater, but their frequency is less, only twice a day. The pressure exerted by them is however, over the whole depth of the coast, and thus, is very great indeed where the coast is steep and deep; but as the pressure is brought to bear on the coast gradually, their effect is not noticeable in the Seismograph records. The combined action of these is to raise the land along coasts, forming dunes, which can scarcely be explained merely as the action of winds. A glance at the map of the world will show the highest mountains, occur, where the coast of the ocean is steep and deep, the Andes and Rocky mountains being notable examples. For mountains in the interior, we have in most cases, evidence of the sea existing at their base at some remote period. Then again when a tongue of land has the sea on both sides, the action in raising the land will be much more pronounced. A soil saturated by water logging behind the coast will accelerate the process of raising of the height of land. The sea we find was near the base of the Vindhyas, and the Gangetic trough kept saturated at a high level, when the river Ganges had no exit eastwards through the low Bengal delta as now; it is on this account that the Vindhya range was getting higher and higher, a process which was arrested only after the sea receded, a fact insistently repeated in the Pûrânas etc., and which we cannot dispose of by suggesting that it is mere fancy. The Padma Pûrâna (Srîshtî, 19) says, "When Vîndhya was increasing in height, Agastya, proceeded towards the south, telling Vîndhya to remain in that condition, until his return. Agastya then accompanied by devas proceeded to the sea shore, drank the sea water, and then defeated the Kalakêya Dânavas of whom the survivors retired to Pâtâla. The Dêvas then finding the sea dried up, appealed to Vishnû, who assured them that river Gangâ will again replenish the sea with water." Referring to Pâriyâtra hills, or the Aravalli Range portion attached to the Vîndhyas, the Harîvamsa (Ch. 191) says "To show obeisance to Krîshna, the Pariyatra hills became a mere "shâna" or grind stone; Nârâyana, pleased at this, offered this boon to this hill that it will become famous as the Shânapâda, and that it will grow in height vying with Sûmêrû peak." In Mahâbhârata it is mentioned (Vana, 104, 105) that "Agastya Mûni stopped the Vîndhya's growing further, drank the sea water, and forced the Kâlakêya Dânavas to take refuge in Pâtâla and then, filled up the sea again with *yellow* water." It will thus be seen that the Vîndhya hills were growing or increasing in height as long as the south sea was near its base to its south, and stopped growing only when the sea was dried up or receded. The fact that the sea was again filled up with water, does not mean that there was an encroachment of the sea again as it is made clear that the area was flooded subsequently with water of river Gangâ, the water being yellow or silt laden showing that the area was cut off absolutely from influence of sea tides.

Secondly, currents are produced in the sea, by tidal movements, such currents being affected also by ocean currents, and when approaching the coast, by the configuration of the ocean and sea troughs and the coastal line. Thus the tidal movement entering a gradually converging, bay will gain impetus and increase its force of current and height of wave. The Bay of Bengal presents one such example, whereas the Arabian sea does not present this facility in the sea itself, and it is only in the north-east angle of the sea, that is, near the Guzerat peninsula that we find this favourable condition over a small area of the Arabian sea. Where the currents strike the coast, and thus obstructed by firm land is forced to run along the coast, the mass of water in motion carries with it a vast amount of loose materials particularly un-consolidated silt brought to the sea by rivers, and distribute the same in recesses on the bank, or at points where the tidal current is forced to come to a halt from the nature of the coast, coming to an end or converging into shoals. Where the sea runs into rifts or openings, like that between India and Taprobane island of Ptolemy, the currents may at one stage pass from one end to the other, when materials with it will be transported from one end of the rift to the other if the velocity is sufficiently high. If the velocity however falls short, the materials will be deposited in the rift itself, thus closing up the rift in time. If the tides from both ends meet in the rift, the deposit of materials in it would be very rapid and the rift closed quickly. In both these cases, where there is a tendency of the current slackening in a rift, thus inducing deposition of materials and building up of land, this process will be maximum where the velocity of the prevailing littoral drift is first checked. Thus, if the direction of the prevailing littoral drift in the Guzerat coast is from north to south, and the sea rift open west to east as in Ptolemy's time, we would expect accretion of land at the northwest corner of the rift, *i.e.*, a tongue of land forming from the southwest corner of the mainland, and extending southwards like a ridge in continuation of the west coast.

Thirdly, the fine silt carried by rivers, and which gives a yellow colour to the water, is held in suspension even with very small movement of the water, but is precipitated when salts are mixed with it. Before the river comes to the sea, salts are mixed occasionally, either from disintegrated vegetable matter in swamps and beels, or rarely from inland salt deposits; the bulk of the silt is therefore carried to the sea and river mouth, where the salt of sea water finally acts as the agent for inducing the rapid precipitation of silt. The silt deposit is therefore concentrated ordinarily at the mouths of rivers forming deltas, and the bed of the river is raised at the mouth. If the river bed is raised at any such point, it will not remain as an abrupt bar in the bed, but the river will gradually work to ease off its bed slope above keeping to the normal bed slope as unaltered as possible. This means the bed level above will also be raised to a considerable distance above. This is known as retrogression of the bed level of a river. When the sea recedes away from the mouth of a river, as the sea level is fairly the same in a locality, retrogression of levels will take place, to a height, which would be represented by the normal fall of bed of the river over the additional length of channel. Similar retrogression of bed will be involved in the upper reaches of a river if its bed level is raised in gorges and narrow river valleys, by side slips of the hills, or upheaval from other causes. When the bed of a river is raised for any such causes, the river will, if facilities are available for a flow in other directions, owing to slopes of land in such direction now being steeper, change its course to that direction either over the land or over other existing river channels furrowing out the channel finally to adjust its requirements.

Fourthly, where small islands jut out along the sea coast, leaving opening between them, through which the sea tides penetrate inland, the travel of materials through such openings, inland, will take place, but the velocity being unrestricted and in some cases increased as a result of forced passage of the water through a restricted passage, the materials will not deposit between the islands, but will be carried inland, until the water spreading itself to a larger area, beyond, loses its velocity, and then the velocity is damped and materials come to a standstill. The result is a fanshaped deposit of materials in the interior, at a distance from the sea, spreading out the tide water over a long length of a bar in the form of an arc of a circle. This in turn prevents entry of the great tidal volume of water, by holding up the backwater above it and thus reducing the "head" of discharge at the point of entry for a considerable time in each cycle of tide. This induces further deposit of materials, and brings about the total closure of the gap between islands, leaving marshes and backwater and lakes behind them.

Fifthly, a consideration of second and third items, will make it clear that when a river discharges silt-laden water at its mouth in a sea coast where the action of littoral drift is strong, the materials are carried away in suspension to a long length of the coast, thus retarding the progress of building up of the land at the delta or river mouth. When a river discharges at a point where the littoral drift is weak, or where, as in the case of a shoaled up sea lying between the mainland of India and Taprobane island as they were in Ptolemy's time, the littoral drift is absent, the whole quantity of silt will deposit at the shoal at the mouth of the river, rapidly filling up the shoal, and extending its operation forward into further areas of the sea at a quick pace.

Sixthly, when a river, runs through gorges, or deep valleys with high hills abutting, the channel is liable to be raised or closed up by side slips of hills into the channel, or, from materials washed down the hill-side by local heavy rainfall on the hills, when there is a dry spell in the basin above. The latter condition is not infrequent in an extensive country like India, where storms penetrate inland to the upper basins of large rivers very occasionally, whereas nearer the sea coast where the rivers eventually penetrate into the hills and ghats near the sea, the storms are frequent and thus rainfall precipitations are frequent and heavy.

We will now proceed to consider the case at issue, and at the outset, we should know how the sea tides and littoral drifts proceed along the coast of India. The tides generated by the attraction of the Moon and the Sun, appear first as a primary ocean wave in the southern ocean, South of 60 lat. S., travelling in the direction of the transit of the Moon, that is from east to west. Sir George Airey has calculated this wave to be of about 2 ft. height in the spring tides and 0 ft. 9 in. in the neap tides. From this, the tides into the seas are propagated, and as expected, they proceed at an angle towards the north to the coasts of the continents. Thus the tidal wave proceeds past the west coast of Australia into the Indian ocean, deflected further to the right partly by the south equatorial current, and partly by the torsion of the earth under what is known as Ferrel's law. As the wave reaches near India, travelling at an angle, but in a general north westerly directions, it reaches the Bay of Bengal, first, striking the east or Coromandel coast near Madras, and then parting north and south; on the Arabian sea side, owing to this angle of travel, the wave strikes the African coast and deflected back along the Arabian and Persian coast to Indian coast near mouth of Indus, and the west or Malabar coast being on the lee side, the effect of the directly propagated wave is retarded and minimised. The littoral drifts are therefore mainly, in the east or Coromandel coast, from Madras northwards to the head of the Bay where it is retarded, and Madras southwards to Ceylon; on the west or Malabar coast, it is mostly from north to south. A comparison of the mean establishments (or the time after the transit of the Moon that the tide reaches a port) of the coastal ports, shows that the sea tide reaches Madras at 8h. 6m., Cocanada 8h. 51m., Vizagapatam 8h. 23m., Marmagao 11h. 8m., Bombay 12h. 14m., corrected to Indian Standard time on a day that the Moon's transit is at midnight, the Establishments of these ports being 7h. 87m., 8h. 50m., 8h. 28m., 10h. 33m. and 12h. 14m., respectively. There is no reason to assume that the condition of the sea tides have been altered materially, and it will be seen therefore that the sea-tide reached the eastern end of the intermdiate sea between India and Taprobane of Ptolemy, *i.e.*, between Cocanada and Vizagapatam, about 2½ hours earlier than the western end between Marmagao and Bombay. As long as this sea was broad and deep, the tide from east to west could therefore flow freely, as the distance was only 500 miles or even less over the narrow portion which would take about 3 hours, but would come to a halt at the Bombay coast as by the time it reached that coast the Arabian sea tide would be felt. Under these conditions, the whole mass of silt brought into this sea by the large rivers from the Vindhyas which flowed into it, moved on to the Bombay coast and was deposited along that coast where the tides met; for a similar reason, the detritus and silt that was brought by the Indus, Mais and Namadus on the west coast, travelled southward and was carried down by the littoral drift, and deposited at the same spot. These actions combined, led to the very rapid accretion of the land on the Bombay coast, which we have found to be fact borne out by tradition. After the ledge near the Bombay coast was built up along the sea face, the next step was the bulding up of the ridge in continuation of it, southwards, the progress of which was also accelerated by the existence of islands in that locality. It is thus that we find the land along coast below Bombay, reclaimed below up to Dharwad, though an opening to the sea still remained below this tongue of land, which was the opening at the western end of the intermediate sea, which must have been now a fairly narrow gulf lying between Taprobane and the accreted Bombay coast, extending southwards. The effect of shoaling, lengthening, and narrowing of the intermediate sea over its western length, was, that the Bay of Bengal tide was considerably retarded in its travel over this length, whereas the Arabian sea tide travelling in the unrestricted sea, entered the western end at the same time as before. Thus the sea tides from the Bay of Bengal and from the Arabian sea now met inside the intermediate sea and the whole of the detritus was now deposited in this sea instead of its being carried away in part into the Arabian sea. The closing up of the western end of the sea must have been rapid at this stage. It is also at this stage that the tongue of land on the Bombay coast was subjected to the tidal water pressure of the sea from both sides over a narrow width and almost simultaneously. This also must have induced the heightening of the Western Ghats over this length, where the low valleys and swamps and backwaters, left behind the coast, were at the same time filling up by denudation of the higher hills that already existed on the islands. After this stage, the whole of the silt brought by rivers from the Vindhyas flowing towards south, and the rivers of Taprobane flowing towards north, was deposited in the intermediate sea, and closed it up entirely at its middle, joining Taprobane and the mainland of India, between Osmanabad and Gulbergha districts. The through flow of sea water having now stopped entirely, it is at this stage that the materials carried by littoral drifts, both in the Bay of Bengal and the Arabian seas, threw up ridges in continuation of their coast lines, or slightly set back inland, thus shutting out the entrances altogether, and it is this stage that we find put down as the stage when Agastya dried the sea up by drinking it.

It is then that further building up of land by the river silt, restricted the area over which their water spread, thus decreasing the area of evaporation to such an extent, that the river discharges were able to keep the limited area left, submerged throughout the year, though previously when the ingress of sea water into the shallow inland sea was suddenly cut off by ridges along the coast, and the area of the inland sea was shallow and so vast that when its water was dried up by evaporation, the combined discharge of all the rivers falling into it was not sufficient to keep it submerged, after replacing the loss by evaporation and absorption. It is thus we find it stated that this sea, after drying up was filled again by yellow water subsequently that is after the surface area was reduced. The subsequent complete reclamation of the area, was a gradual process, left to the rivers to carry out slowly.

Having now shown how the sea was gradually filled up, we are now in a position to consider how the changes in the river courses followed. As the intermediate sea was reclaimed from its western end at the Bombay coast, it would be best to begin with the rivers from the west.

Nanaguna River is the western river and the most important, from its size and catchment basin. It had three principal mouths, separating from Sangamner, the two western mouths Goaris and Benda fell into the western or Arabian sea, and the main outfall Nanaguna had its outlet to the southern intermediate sea. Here I have already shown reclamation of land on the west coast took place earlier, so that Soupara at the mouth of the Goaris, was raised above sea level long before Kâlîdâsa's time, when the southern sea coast was much the same as in Ptolemy's time. The same thing must have occurred near the mouth of the Benda. The gulf here was an indentation, and the travel of silt from the Indus mouth downward was shallowing up this gulf, which was raised again much above sea level by the silt poured in by the Nanaguna river through the Goaris and Benda outlets, these outlets having penetrated the valleys of Western Ghats above Bombay, had their bed fairly high up, and thus they could command a fairly high level at the base of the hills to spread the silt. Soupara is no doubt Shahapur, north west of Bombay, and Igatpuri is Akabarou of Periplus, both near the mouth of the Goaris, and here we find the coast reclaimed to a width of about 40 miles; at the mouth of the Benda also, over 25 miles width was accreted. With these lengths added to the rivers, their bed levels were raised, and as the third and main outlet was still unaffected, the discharges through the Goaris and Benda were diverted into the Nanaguna, and they deteriorated and finally closed up. As they were running through deep valleys, they were keeping the channel alive and open by scouring out from the bed, materials which were brought into them from high hills surrounding them where rainfall was heavy as now, such scouring being from occasional floods, as rainfall in the interior of the basin was occasional and spasmodic. Once the channels deteriorated to a point, which precluded scour from upland discharge, the channels not only closed up as river channels, but must have been brought up to very high levels, precluding their reopening when the main eastern outlet of Nanaguna was closed later on, on the death of the southern sea. This explains why we find the Goaris and Benda, the nearer outlets to the sea, abandoned by the river. The next stage of deterioration of the river mouth came when the intermediate sea coast accreted at the mouth of the Nanaguna main stream, the bed level became higher, with retrogression of bed levels working higher up, which must have led to serious flooding in the Khandesh district for a time, until the flooded levels became sufficiently high so as to spill through the low land immediately to northend of the Western Ghats, and then scour out a fresh channel outlet to the Arabian sea or rather to the Gulf of Cambay, and this channel is the Tapti River, a small nucleus of which was there already for the local drainage. After this, as the southern sea further receded, the upper basins of the rivers to the east of Nanaguna, that is the Pseudostomos and the Baris, could not be drained southwards, and these areas therefore diverted their drainage to the west, and thus we find the central portion of the Purna river channel leave its north and south channels, and turn westwards and join the Tapti. This additional drainage of a high area in the neighbourhood, brought trouble again to the Nanaguna river exit by the Tapti channel, which by becoming higher and higher, threatened the very existence of the channel of the Nanaguna at Khandwa where it pierced the narrow valley between the Satpura range and the Mahadeo hills range. It is at this stage that a serious state of flooding resulted in the area above Khandwa, indication of which is best given in the Skanda Pûrâna, Avantya Khanda, Avantî Mâhâtmya (Ch. 54-55 and 56) as follows "Nîlgangâ (or Sîprâ) flowed by south-east of Pûshkara, and then north of Vîndhyas at the spot sacred to the Son of Marût, then coming to Mahâkâla forest, emptied herself into the Sîprâ-Kûnda at Amarâvatî, and leaving her nîla (blue) clothes put on white clothes. In olden times, the whole country, was flooded by Rêvâ water; goddess Vîndhyavâsînî being propitiated by Agastya, promised that she will prevent the Rêvâ from growing further, but the Vîndhya hills must not at the same time grow further in height, while Agastya will be engaged in Dêvas' work in the Trîkûta gate of the Southern regions. In olden times Rêvâ, Charmanvatî, and Kshâtâ, born from Amarkantaka in the form of rivers as saviours of the three regions, were playing in the Mândhâtrî-Khêtra; when a quarrel arose there, Kshâtâ, left the company of Rêvâ, penetrated the Vîndhya mountain, and arrived at the fair Mahâkâla forest where sacred stream Sîprâ and Amarâvatî city were situated, and that locality is therefore known as the Kshâta confluence holy spot." In the same Pûrâna (Avantya Khanda, Rêvâ, 6) it states that "Narmadâ, girt by the Rîksha island, and penetrating the fierce Vîpûla hills, falls into the sea with great noise (Sanskrit—Rava) for which she is named Rêvâ." This shows the stage when

Narmadâ levels, at Mândhâtrî-Khêtra, which is Mândhâtâ, a few miles to the north of Khandwa, became so high that its spill penetrated the Vindhya hills to its north, and opened out a connection with the Sîprâ river, *via* Kshâtâ river, the alignment of which clearly indicated by the upper Sîprâ Channel, passing near Indore : the closing up the channel at the Khandwa gap must have been to a pretty high level to induce this spill to the Sipra, the consequence of which we are told, was the submersion of the whole country near Mahâkâla-vana and Amarâvatî, that is the Ujjaini Kingdom or the Malwa plateau. The opening of the Kshâtâ connection must have led to further deterioration of the bed at Khandwa which brought about the entire separation of the Narmada and Tapti beds. This diversion I am inclined to believe was also artificially expedited by Haihaya King, Kârtyavîrjya Arjjûna, who closed up the Narmadâ channel in the dry season to create a pool near his capital Mâhîsmatîpûrî which is modern Maheswar, west of Mandhata. Whether he did it to save his capital from the flooding it was suffering from, and whether simultaneously with the obstruction of the channel of Narmadâ, he cut or deepened the connection with the Sipra, for which the connecting channel may have received the appelation of Kshâtâ or a 'cut' river is a matter of speculation. The pent up water in the Malwa plateau was at the same time trying to find an outlet, the small channel of the Namadus River was unable to dispose it off, neither was it able to deepen this channel by scour, as the winding channel through the Aravalli range was too stiff to give way; the obvious line of least resistance lay between the lower reach of the Namadus flowing by Barygaza or modern Broach, and the Mandhata area, and this opening must have at last been made, the point of breach clearly indicated in the relief map, at a point lying between Mathawar hills, and the base of the Satpura range, thus establishing the present channel from Mahesvar, *via* Barwani to Mathawar on to Broach. The change at the outlet at Broach will be mentioned in connection with the

Namadus river. The ridge at Mathawar was pretty high and this is the reason that before it could be opened and furrowed out, the pent up water had to be heaped up to very high levels which flooded the "Vasûndharâ" or the "whole world" in the language of the Skanda Pûrâna.

The area at the western end of the southern sea abutting in the mainland was first to accrete, we therefore find the group of small rivers such as Vênâ, Mula (Mûralâ), Bhîmâ, Ghod, Manjîrâ, Trînâ etc., retaining their names, as they advanced and added on to their channel as the sea receded, and their valleys having no other outlet, was spilled over and raised gradually above flood level. The first river to the east of the west coast, to intercept the drainage of the rivers flowing north to south of the Vindhyas, was the Godavari, and this gave her the precedence as the main river of importance as the sea receded; this river could take up this function best, as its channel fell to the east of the area over which the Taprobane island joined with the mainland in the first instance, and could thus empty herself eastward to the sea connected with the Bay of Bengal, where owing to the gulf widening out the interior level of the gulf was not high. The rivers to the west of Godavari, though sloped eastwards, were struck by the obstruction offerred by the Taprobane island, and their exit to the narrow gulf to the Arabian sea was also cut off at an early stage. It is for this reason that they had to eke out their independent channels as best as they could, overland, and make for the Kistna river as their outlet. The Godavari on the contrary was, in the language of poet Bâna Bhatta, "following the Sea, as a dutiful wife," and was thus receiving in her channel as she proceeded all the rivers of the Vindhyas which she met with on her career of "following the sea on its death."

The changes in the course of the Pseudostomon have already been indicated while dealing with the course of the river (Ch. III). The portion of this river to the north of the Ajanta range was diverted westward into the Tapti; the detached portion, south of Ajanta range became a tributary of the Godavari, while a small portion of the lower basin drained into the Penganga.

The Baris outlet, lying in a gulf was affected earlier than that of the Pseudostomon, and we find that the Ajanta range, which had a low continuation of it eastwards in what are Nirmal and Satmala ranges, cutting off its lower portion, and practically the whole of its waters above the Nirmal range, diverted eastwards by Penganga river which came into being as another intercepting channel which ran eastwards and parallel to the Godavari, running to the north of the Nirmal and Satmala ranges, receiving the waters of the series of rivers, begining with the Pseudostomon, and ending with the Kheberus. The slope of the country had a trend to the east, and gradually we find the Baris waters, diverted into the Penganga system to a series of rivers, running in the south westerly direction, such as the Aran, Waghari, Wardha, Dham etc.

The Solen, is similarly diverted into the northern intercepting river, the Penganga system.

The Kheberus similarly joined the system and we find the big combined river Pranhita, which ultimately joined the Godavari as its tributary.

The Tyna or the Tyndis river had its drainage basin situated in such a place that diversion of part of its water to the rivers running towards the east coast of India was possible; the drainage of this river has accordingly been parcelled out to various directions, a portion to the Kotri river to the west, a portion to the Mahanadi to the east, and a portion of the basin lying lower down, to the Indravati.

The Maisolus river, shut out from the eastern coast effectively by the high Western Ghats, maintains practically its old bed, lengthened over accreted portion of the sea *via* Sileru river, and then the Sabari river, and empties into the Godavari river.

The changes in the river courses in southern India are now completely described. That the Penganga-Wainganga system was for a time running *via* Indravati-

Tel system into the Mahanadi river as the Ganges river of the 17th Cent. maps, is a probability which I have already indicated (vide Ch. V) and need not be repeated.

The changes in the course of rivers in Taprobane offer a simple problem. The Phasis river flowing north, when shut out from that end by the sea closing up, was diverted to the Ganges River of Ptolemy, and it became the Kistna channel itself. The Western Ghats growing higher and shutting out the exit of all rivers of the southern Bombay Presidency towards the Arabian sea, and all the rivers to the south and east of Balaghat range, were therefore forced into the Kistna river, thus we find the Benithora, Sina, Bhima, Nira, Yerla, Malaprabha, Tungabhadra, all joining eventually the Kistna. The reversion of the flow of the Soanus river, or the Varada-Tungabhadra system can only be put down to the land along sea coast at the base of the Western Ghats, and the Ghats themselves rising through the tidal wave pressure from the sea. The same reasons apply to the change in Azanos river, of which, the drainage basin now divided between that of Shimsha and the Cauvery. The Barakes, has been diverted to the sea by the southern Penner river, as the accretion of its delta below Kombakonum, must have raised the river bed high enough to bring about a closure of the gorge near Salem.

The ultimate joining of the small islands lying south of Taprobane to the main island does not require any further explanation; the islands we find are in close neighbourhood in Ptolemy's time, and retarding the free flow of the sea tides near them with sufficient high velocity and, the closing of the narrow channels of the sea between them was therefore to be expected. The group of islands, Goumara, Alaba and Zaba being near each other joined together to form Ceylon, but the sea tide forced through a single narrow opening at Adam's bridge, and so gathering velocity, has arrested the progress of its silting up. Its joining to the mainland is however certain, but a question of a few centuries, though the last closure of the gap will be rapid.

CHAPTER VI

WESTERN BOUNDARY OF PTOLEMY'S INDIA, AND RIVERS FALLING INTO THE WESTERN SEA, THE INDUS IN PARTICULAR

Having established the comparative accuracy of Ptolemy's map of southern India and Taprobane, his map may now be considered fairly accurately delineated for the whole of India and particularly western India, a point nearer to Ptolemy's country. In demonstrating the accuracy of the southern India portion, it was necessary for me to go into details as hitherto it was believed Ptolemy'e map was distorted very much. In describing the western boundary, I shall be very brief, as my work is rendered easier, after having proved that the map is not distorted and may therefore be followed more strictly.

The west coast, is the Mare Indikum, or present Arabian sea, from Simylla northwards to the eastern mouth of the Indus, and then follows the Indus river itself as the boundary, up to the Himalayas.

As far as the boundary abutting on the sea is concerned it has been shown that Simylla is Chaul and Soupara is Shahapur and Barygaza is Broach. This Barygaza or Broach is Vakakachchha of Kathâ-sarît-sâgara (Book I, Ch. VI) which is placed "on the banks of the Narmadâ river, near the Sâtavahana Kingdom", the latter being Satana in Nasik District if not Paithan. North from this corner point of Simylla, we find two indentations or gulfs, one of Barygaza, and the other to north of it, the Kanthi, which stretches right up to the mouth of the Indus. The peninsula of Guzerat is conspicuous by its absence, and this cannot be by accident. Periplus, describing the coast from Indus mouth southwards, mentions first the gulf of Barakê, and south of it gulf of Barygaza, the dividing line between them being a sharp promontory which cannot possibly be Gujerat peninsula as it is now. Periplus has evidently named the Kanthi gulf of Ptolemy as gulf of Barake, after the name of the island Barakê shown by Ptolemy as lying at the mouth of the gulf, and ignores Guzerat, though his description of this portion of the coast is given in very great detail. We must therefore conclude that the Guzerat Peninsula did not exist as it now is, though there might have been some small islands scattered in this place. Having this as our key, the coast-line, may now be drawn after fixing a few of the points. As the Guzerat peninsula did not exist, Ptolemy's map takes us to Malia town in Malia State of Kathewar which must be the Cape Maleo; this is the point where we would expect a sharp protuberance into the sea in continuation of the Mandava hills, and these hills formed the coast in Ptolemy's time, running south-east right up to Bhaunagar, and joined on to the mainland, at the head of what is now the gulf of Cambay. The promontory as described by Periplus, is a sharp tongue of land indeed, as he says that after Papikê in Barake gulf, is the second subdivision of "this gulf running up to north", near up to the mouth of the gulf where he says is Baisnos island, round which he describes are passages into the Mais and Namadus rivers and "after Barygaza the coast immediately adjoining stretches from the north directly to the south". The coast, first running north and then south at this point, shows, the promontory is a narrow strip of land as we would expect in this Mandava hills running into the sea. Kamanê of Ptolemy corresponds to Wankaner. From Kamanê, we find the coast runs clear and straight to Nausaripa, which is Navasari. There is no indentation like the present gulf of Cambay, and we find that the river Namadus, that is the Narmadâ, passing close to the coast near Barygaza or Broach, and then turning northwards falling into the gulf of Kanthi or Barakê. Here we have fortunately tradition to help us to fix the line of the river and the coast. We find in the Râsmâla (Forbes' Ed. p. 3-4) that "Chumardee, traditionally believed to have once been washed by the waters of the ocean. From there could be seen the river towards Wullubhi, and traces of salt water creek called 'Bhownugger' or 'the former' river, which of old bore the argosies of the mysterious race of Kunuksen." From this we find that the Bhaunagar river, was the lower reaches of a big continental river, as it was the passage for argosies from the sea into the country, and the description cannot apply to the present river, if it drained as now a small area of the Guzerat peninsuala, and debouching into the sea in its neighbourhood, the mainland lying to the east of the river, the outlet to the sea must have been towards the west and then north or south; thus we have it that the gulf of Cambay did not exist, and it was firmland through which the Bhaunagar river formerly entered mainland; its outlet to the sea to its west must have been inpeded by the Mandava hills, and thus the river must have been forced northwards, and fell into the Kanthi gulf, which gives us exactly the line of the river Namadus or Narmada as we should expect. That the river near Bhaunagar ran close to the sea coast to the south is also made clear from the statement that Chumardee was one time washed by the ocean. Thus we have the coast running from Malia, by Wankaner, and Chumardee, to Navasari, and the gulf of Cambay firm land, the rivers Mahi and Narmada, turning northwards and falling into the gulf of Kanthi. Poulipoula would appear to be the ancient place Dharampur.

We have now only the coast of gulf of Kanthi left. From Cape Maleo, "the coast turns south and then to east, and on this length the Namiados and Mophis fall, between the mouths of which is Pakidarê village, and opposite the mouths is Baisnes Island." Pakidarê is Bagodra town, some distance inland now, and Baisnes Island of Periplus is Bajana state, of Jhalawad, Kathiwara, formerly an island, now joined to the mainland. The island Barakê is possibly a small part of the Cutch Island lying opposite Malia. After the mouth of the Mophis or Mahi river, which was thus near Dholka, we find the coast turning northwards as shown by Ptolemy and also confirmed by Periplus, who says that after Sinthos is passed, we reach this gulf, over which hangs a promontory "which curving first to east, then to south, and then to west encompasses the gulf called Barakê, in the bosom of which lies seven islands." The coast indicated is along the Sabarmati river to some distance near Ahmedabad, after which the coast made for the mouth of the Luni river which is no doubt the Lonibere mouth of the Indus. The towns in the coast here are, Monoglosson, Syrastra, and Baradaxema. The places I am unable to identify from the names but it is clear from the positions indicated, that Monoglosson is Ahmedabad or in its neighbourhood; Syrastra is Mudhera, and Baradexema is Patan or Anhilwara Patan.

The Mophis river of Ptolemy, or Mais of Periplus is the present Mahi river, which had its outlet in the Rann of Cutch, and Namados river of Ptolemy, or Namnadios of Periplus is the Narmada river, which also like the Mahi, had its outlet to the Rann of Cutch. As already pointed out, these rivers were shut out from their present outlet by the low ridge in continuation of the Mandava hills southwards which touched on the coast at Surat; the silt brought into the Rann of Cutch by the big rivers Narmada, Mahi and Indus, was filling up and raising the Rann, and we find in Periplus it is described that "the gulf surges with vast and mighty billows, and where the sea tossing with violent commotion forms eddies and impetuous whirlpools in every direction; the bottom presents shoals, at others jagged rocks"; the land in the mouths of these rivers was accreting fast, thus raising their beds, till a time came when a breach southwards was effected, the rivers bursting through, opened out their present mouths and formed the gulf of Cambay. The combined discharge of the Indus, Mahi and Namados into the Rann of Cutch, kept the level of the shallow gulf up, at this corner to a high level, which kept the low area of Guzerat peninsula submerged, and the diversion of Indus mouth to the open sea outside the Rann, and also the diversion of Mahi and Namados mouths to the open sea to south, very probably effected the reclamation of the

Guzerat peninsula. The simultaneous pressure of the sea tidal waves on both sides of this peninsula no doubt had and is helping its further rise.

The Namados river course, starting from the outlet to the Rann of Cutch to the east of Bagodra, passed by Broach, and then north towards Kathwara which is Tiatoura of Ptolemy, then penetrating the low hills south of the Malwa plateau, passed by Barnagar an ancient city which is Minagara of Ptolemy, entered the plateau itself and passing by Ujjaini or Ozene of Ptolemy, proceeded northwards to its source by what is now the Chambal river, the flow of which has now been reversed. The bursting of Nanaguna river from its upper reaches, through the Kshâtâ into the Sîprâ, which has been referred to already (Ch. V) raised the Malwa plateau levels, and eventually closed the river exit to south by Barnagar, as the Vindhya was still then "growing". The Namados river was therefore spilt into bits, a portion converted into the upper reaches of Mahi, a portion to the Chambal, a portion to Sipra; the lower portion only retained its name, and when the Nanaguna eventually diverted into it, the whole of the river newly formed as we now see it, was later called Narmadâ. That the Narmadâ course was at one time as indicated by Ptolemy is gleaned from casual reference like that of the Brahma Pûrâna (Ch. 17) which says that "in Bhâratvarsa, lying between Hîmavâna, and Vîndhya mountains, are six, deva-rivers, namely Bhâgîrathî, Narmadâ, Yamûnâ, Sarasvatî, Vîsokâ, and Vîtastâ," clearly indicating that the main portion of the river lay to the north of the Vîndhyas.

The course of the Mais lay from its outlet to the Rann of Cutch southwards to its present channel and the following its present channel up to Dungarpur States, then turning eastwards along its tributary channel towards Mt. Abu, or Orbador of Ptolemy.

The western boundary of India along the sea is now complete and the rest of the western boundary which is the Indus, will now be described briefly.

The point at which the mouth of the eastern effluent Lonibare falls into the Gulf of Barakê, is the north-east corner of the gulf, and it points out to the identity of Lonibare with the Luni or Lavanâvatî river. The most important city on the river in its delta is Barbarei of Ptolemy, Barbarikê of Periplus, up to which the river was navigable freely in Periplus' time, though we find that the river was navigable further up four centuries earlier as Nearkhos' fleet sailed down from the confluence of Akesines. Nearkhos mentions however the point at which there was a bar in the river, and has entered this in his log book as Herma, and this must be at the delta region up to which the river was freely navigable, and would therefore correspond to Barbarei and this exactly fits in with the position of the ancient city Balmer modern Barmer. Susikana would be Sukha, and Bonis is Beon Tar, the former to north and the latter to south of Umarkot. Xoana is Chotan, south of Barmer. These points enable us to mark out the delta of the river. From Barmer, the river, passed by Pasipada which is obviously Pachbhadra, and further up Piska, which appears to Pushkar. Further up is Binagara, which is Minnagar of Periplus, described as a place of importance and metropolis of Skythia, to which cargo is carried from Barbarikê, evidently overland, ships anchoring at the latter port; this Binagara seems to correspond to Nagaur in Jodhpur state, where extensive ruins indicate its former importance as seat of the King. Further up the river is Kanigara, which is Bikaner, or Bikaner-garh corrupted. From this point we can see that the river joined on to the extinct channel, the Hakra or the Ghaggar at Anupgarh, which is undoubtedly the intermediate position of the river between its bed as in Ptolemy's time and the present channel past Dehra Ghazi Khan.

From Anupgarh, the river ran towards Hasilpur which corresponds Aristobathre, and further up by Budh, north of Sutlej, lying about 40 miles east of Tibbi, which is Budoea of Ptolemy. It will be seen that the first big tributary joined the Indus between Budoea and Aristobathre, and that this passed by Malliana. This Malliana, is

Mûlasthâna or Multan, passing by which the channel evidently proceeded by Dehra Gazi Khan and further up received the drainage of the Lorelai river; the lake shown by Ptolemy is the flat valley above the Suleiman Range after this river penetrated into it above Fort Munroe. The alignment thus confirms the identity of Alexandria with Kandahar.

From Budh, the main river, struck north-east to Jiwan-Shah, or Jivan-shah which is Panasa of Ptolemy, and then turned north-west to Harappa. It will be seen that west of this area we have a series of towns with names such as Bhagoana, Paliana, Akaiana, Dogarana, Khandiana, Maghliana, etc., ending in "ana" which is conspicuous not only by their gathering in this area, but also by the absence from other areas in the neighbourhood of place names ending thus. The locality of Ptolemy's Kodrana is therefore clearly indicated in this neighbourhood, and Khandiana, situated 16 miles to the east of Toba Tek Singh, appears to fall in with its identification with Kodrana. The main river channel was therefore to the east of Khandiana, and I have accordingly assumed the channel to run by Harappa. Harappa again has its ancient history, and as such was very likely on the main river itself. This city according to tradition (Cunningham's Ancient India, p. 242) was built by Raja Harappa of an unknown date and its destruction to the same western king in the sixth century who overthrew Shorkot; the remnant of the bed of the river passing by Harappa is still noticeable in what is known as the Gugera bed along which the irrigation canal is now led, and thus Gugera is very likely another form of Ghagar the dry bed of which as already noticed passed by Anupgarh, showing that at one time they were inter-connected. There is good reason therefore to assume that the river passed from Anupgarh by Harappa. Harappa again seems to be only another form of Hydaspis or Hudespes, the tributary of the Indus further up, and the founder was very likely a follower of Darius Hytaspes, and the chief of one of the Satrapies established who named the town after Darius' father, and that this satrapy abutted on the tributary of the Indus which was also named Hytaspis or Hydaspis, discarding the old name of the Vedic period. If Harappa was founded in the 5th century B.C. and destroyed a thousand years later, it must have been at the height of its glory in Ptolemy's time and it is difficult to conceive why it is omitted by him. It is quite possible however that the river may have partially destroyed the city by that time, though the final destruction of the remnants of the city in the sixth century may have come later. It would be reasonable to assume this, as Alexander's movements in this area which lies near the Alexander-Porus battle field indicate that the country was swampy and flooded in the rains in this neighbourhood and the sudden contraction of the channel of the Ravi from a few miles above Harappa to its junction with the Chenab also points out to the conclusion that the river above this point carried a larger volume of flood discharge or that it was part of a bigger river, and that the length from Harappa to its present confluence with the Trim-ab or Chenab is a later avulsion. This Harappa fits in with the position of Asigramma of Ptolemy.

It will be noticed that a tributary of the Indus branches out towards the west, from a point between Panasa and Asigramma, and that it turns southwards towards Modoura of the gods or present Muttra. This tributary, passed by Nigramigramma which corresponds to Hanumangarh, and thus passing by that joined the Sarasvati channel which no doubt joined the Jumna. I will have occasion to touch on this point later on when a short reference on the Sarasvati river will become necessary.

Above Harappa the Indus river followed the present Ravi bed for about 50 miles up to Musa, or Pindi Shekh Musa, which is Iomousa of Ptolemy, at which point the Zaradrius branched out, by what is now the Ravi bed, but the main river struck northwards, over the high level lands which she had raised by her silt, and over which length every vestige of her old channel is now lost. From

Iomousa to Taxila we find the river has no township on or near it, which is a clear indication that, all the tributaries pouring in their waters at this part of the valley which was low then, was flooded in the rains. This also explains why over this length, the want of township and information of the interior, has misled Ptolemy to underestimate the length of the channel from Iomousa to Taxila, considerably. The main river channel passed by Lyallpore, and Sargodh, crossing the present Jhelum course a little below Pind Dadan Khan, and then passing by Taxila to west of Rawalpindi, proceeded north penetrating the hills north of Hazra and joining the Indus river there. The Indus then flowed part Hazra, and had no connection with the Kabul river at Attock, and the latter avulsion from Kalabagh to Isakhel is subsequent to Ptolemy's time, as the Indus and Suastos, *i.e.*, Swat and Kabul rivers combined, are shown as independent at their head.

As the present channel of the Indus along the base the Suleman Range did not exist, the group of tributaries to the west of the Indus, *viz.*, Suastos, Koa, and the westernmost tributary from Paropamisos, joined the Indus further up to the north. The tributary from Paropamisos, is the Gomal and Zhob system or Gomatî of the Vedâs, flowing by Drazinda Kot which is Drastoka of Ptolemy; the Koa river is the Kurrum or Kramû of the Vêdas, flowing by Bannu which is Barborana of Ptolemy, and this joined the westernmost tributary as now at Isakhel, which is the "house of Isa" or as put by Ptolemy, Dionysopolis, its other name being Nagar which is evidently the older Sanskrit name given by Vêdic Aryans, but the name was being transformed by then predominent western hordes. The combined stream, flowing westwards joined the Suastos, the point of confluence was perhaps a little to the north of Khusab on the Jhelum, a mart on the road from Sargodha. The Suastos, passing through Suastene or Swat as already agreed by all authorities, flowing a little north of Peshawar, had no connection with the Indus *viâ* Attock and Hazra, and it thus flowed south from Attock, along the bed now usurped by the Indus, up to near Kalabagh, but as the river had to make for the main river to its east, and as the east and west range of hills from Mianwali to Pind-Dadan Khan offered an obstruction, both the Koa and the Suastos must have turned eastwards to join the Indus at Pind-Dadan Khan, and such an alignment is shown by Ptolemy. Assuming the course of Suastos as indicated, the large city Proklais, or Peukolaites would correspond more to the position of Khushalgarh, than to Peshawar with which the town has been identified by authorities on the subject. As both these cities lie on the channel as chalked out, it does not alter the identity of the channel and I leave the detailed discussion on this point, as unnecessary for my present purposes. This disposes of the tributaries to the west of the Indus near its head, and I proceed now to indicate the alignment of the tributaries to its east.

The eastern tributaries all converge near Bukephela and the combined stream meet the Indus at Iomusa, the position of which has already been fixed near Pindi Shekh Musa, and it remains to fix the position of Bukephela. Cunningham has fixed the position of Bukephela at Jalalpur, whereas others doubtfully at Dilawar. Both these localities appear too far to the north. Pliny has given the distance from Taxila to the Hydaspes near the battlefield as 120 Roman miles (110 English miles) as measured by Alexander's surveyors, and the direction as south, a clear march, up to river Hydaspes without crossing rivers. Jalalpur falls short of this length and the direction is not south but a good deal turned towards east. According to the position indicated by Ptolemy, Bukephela would be Bucheki in Montogomery district, which agrees also in distance and direction from Taxila as given by Pliny. The little village Buchiana Mariala, about 8 miles north of Bucheki, very probably shows the place where Bukephelus was killed or died a natural death. A further confirmation of the identification is forthcoming from the fact that across the river about 40 miles further up we find village Kot Nikka, the suburbs of Pindi Bhatian and I have no doubt that this is the city of Nikh, or 'Nike' meaning 'victory' which Alexander founded to commemorate his victory over Porus. About 20 miles south of Kot Nikka is Sangla Hill which is unmistakably the hill of 'Sang' or 'Zang'' or the great battle. The town Bukephela was very likely established a little to the south of the place where Bukephelus actually died or lies buried, as this site situated at the commanding position at the confluence of the Zaradrius and Hydaspes offered immense advantages for the growth as a city. Alexander's march after crossing the Indus at Taxila, would therefore be on the then advantageous route by the north and south road on the ridge dividing the valleys of the Indus and the Hydaspes over this length. King Porus' country was the fertile region watered by the eastern tributaries of the Indus, and was also protected from inroads from the west by the Hydaspes river which we are told by Strabo was the western boundary of Porus' Kingdom. I am inclined to believe that Porus is Pûrû Kûtsa of the Pûrânas, and that Haryashva is Hydaspes or Raja Harappa, the founder of Harappa. Ferishta (Dow. Vol. I, p. 8) mentions that a chief of the Rajput tribe of Kutswa, became king of India in 586 B.C., and that he was a contemporary of Gustasp or Hydaspes, father of Darius, whose time of accession is fixed at 521 B.C., by Newton, and that this king of the Kutswa tribe, became conqueror after a long spell of unsettled conditions, which fact leads to the view that he may have been helped by Hydaspes in securing the kingdom for him, which fact may also have induced him to name his capital after Hydaspes, or that he may have assumed this name for himself in the first instance. The geneology given in the Harîvamsa, from Haryasva is as follows :—Haryasva—Nîkumbha—Sanhatâsva—Prasênajit—Yuvanâsva—Mândhâta—Pûrûkutsa, which shows 7 generations which would correspond to the difference in time from Darius to Alexander, which is about 200 years. Porus with his old capital at Harappa would therefore select this locality to offer resistance, the best towns and fertile areas of his kingdom being situated in this neighbourhood.

Having now fixed the position of Bukephela, the tracing of the courses of the tributaries becomes easy.

The course of the Zaradrus, proceed from Bukephela, or a little south of Bucheki, eastwards, passing by the ancient town of Raewind, which is Ardons of Ptolemy, joined the present Sutlej channel near Kasur. Above this the old channel of Sutlej, Sanskrit Satadrû, or Zaradrus of Ptolemy remains unchanged. The subtributary of the Zaradrus, namely Bibasis, Sanskrit Vîpâsa, or the present Beas, also remains unchanged.

The course of the Hydaspes, is northwards from Bukephela, and joins the Chenab channel at Pindi Bhatian or Kot Nikka, after which the subtributary Adris or Rouandis separates within a short distance of it.

The Adris or Rouandis, separating here, proceeds eastwards, by north of the ancient town of Shekhupura which is evidently Kaspeira of Ptolemy and then straight on to Lahore which has been identified by many authorities with Labokla of Ptolemy. Amakatis is shown as lying on the river between Kaspiera and Labokla, but from the nature of the print it appears the town is misplaced and that it would be to the west, that is on the Sandabal itself, and that it is Ramnagar, where in the suberbs we find Ramki Chatta and Jamka Chatta, suggesting the name. The Adris after passing Lahore, maintains its old course the Ravi, unaltered.

The Hydaspes, followed up the Chenab course, till at Ramnagar, it bifurcated, the eastern channel being the Sandabals, which is Sanskrit Chandrabhâgâ, which is the Chenab, made up of Chandra and Bhâgâ rivers. From the point of bifurcation at Ramnagar, the Hydaspes joined the Jhelum river perhaps a little way below Jhelum town, and this connecting channel is now entirely gone; the town Jhelum is evidently a continuation of Rohtas, or Rohitapura, a city founded by Rohita of Puru-Kutswa family, separated from Purukutswa by 8 generations or say about 250 years, which would mean that the town was not an old one but evidently had come into prominence as Rohita was an ambitious King, of ideas equally ambitious. Ferishta places Rohita earlier than Porus, and this is not a matter of surprise, when it is remembered that several Kings of this tribe assumed the name of Puru. The eastern tributary of Ptolemy's Indus which is shown as flowing to Modoura or Muttra, takes off from the main river just above Panasa or Jivanshah; from this it is evident it had its bed along the Ghagar-Saraswati bed, thus passing by Hanumangarh, which is Nigramigrama, from which point it must have flowed by Saraswati bed by Thaneswar, and then joined the Jumna. Gagasmira brings us to Garh-Mûktêsvara. Above Jhelum the course is the Jhelum river, unaltered. As regards the name of the river being Hydaspis, I have already mentioned the reasons for this, earlier in this Chapter.

The course of the river Indus and its tributaries as delineated by Ptolemy has now been fully described. The tributaries of the river from the Himalayas were building up the land at the base of the hills and were so confined in their depredations near this Mountain; as the land at the base was built up, their junction points travelled lower down. The conditions of the extent of flooding in the upper reaches of the river will be realised from the statement of Nearkhos reproduced by Strabo, (McCrindle's Strabo, p. 18) that the floods of the Akesines rose 40 cubits high overflowing the plains. In the lower reaches, the river had already shoaled up the corner of the sea at its mouth, throwing up the Cutch Peninsula, and the great shoal, the Rann of Cutch. This had the effect of raising the lever of the river in its lower reaches, where we find the Thar now raised up with the sand spilled over the country by this impetuous river. It was therefore to be expected that the river, having its flood water brought down at a higher level in its upper reaches by the tributaries spreading southwards, and the outlet level also raised in the Thar area, would break through towards the low land to the west, and we find the dry bed of the Hakra or Ghaggar where the river burst through. Once the lower reaches of the channel turned westwards, it has gradually drawn all the tributaries to that direction as we find now. The sequence by which the changes took place, it would be difficult to establish, but the most momentous change is that of the upper Indus, breaking into the Kabul river by the Hazra-Attock channel, which drew the river discharge into the Kabul river at Attock, left the original channel of Indus *viâ* Taxila high and dry, the remnants being the present Sohan river. The Kabul river bed, Attock downwards, became the Indus channel, and in its turn it burst into the unnamed tributary *viâ* Drastoka, that is the Gomal river, and drawn to this channel, this in turn burst into the next southern tributary *viâ* Multan, that is the Rakni and Kaha systems, near where Dera Ghazi Khan is now established. From Dera Ghazi Khan stretching to the sea, it was all low land and the channel of the Indus was thus swerved to the west as we see it now. As the main river shifted westwards, the tributaries from the east naturally had to lengthen their channel to the main river towards the west and also straightened their courses which has given them their present channels focussing towards Dehra Ghazi Khan. The north eastern portion of the basin being now thrown at a very great distance, from the main Indus river, and as this area was on the border line of the basin of the Ganges, the drainage of a good portion of the original Sutlej basin was diverted into the Ganges and its tributary the Jumna. We thus find that Indus had a tributary to the east running towards Muttra, which means that the upper Jumna, basin drained into the Indus even so late as in Ptolemy's time, and the connecting channel by which it is drained was the Sarasvati, the almost extinct bed of which is still to be seen. That this Sarasvati was at an earlier stage an independent river with its outlet to the sea *viâ* the Sarasvati channel into the Rann of Cutch, and that the Indus at an earlier stage in the Vedic Period included in its basins, not only the upper Jumna basin but also the upper Bhagirathi-Ganga basin are not only probabilities but facts. We find an inkling of this given by Apollonius of Tyana who travelled to the sources of the Bhagirathi Ganga, after visiting Alexander-Porus battle-field crossed the Hydraotes, and then after several countries, crossed the Hyphasis (that is the Beas) a river navigable to its source, indicating he made use of it to certain extent, as after this, he crosses the Mt. Kaukasos or the Himalayas at this point, and found on the base of the hill a level plateau, and situated there, Paraka, a large city. From this description we may easily spot Paraka where Plech Dharamsala is situated, about 10 miles to the east of Palampur in Kangra Valley, the antiquity of the place being apparent from the ruined forts of Ratangiri in its neighbourhood. Apollonius next proceeded to the Sophois' stronghold, a four days' journey, which brings us to the neighbourhood of Rampur on the Sutlej. This Sophois' stronghold, seems to be the Sopeithes' place, which Strabo says "some writers place Kathoea and the country of Sopeithes, one of the monarchs in the tract between the rivers Hydaspes and Akesines; some on the other side of the Akesines and of the Hyarotes, on the confines of the territory of the other Porus, the nephew of Porus who was taken prisoner by Alexander, and call the country subject to him Gandaris". This monarch Sopeithes, is no other than Satya-vrata of the Pûrânas, shown variously from 4th to 11th (Harîvamsa 6th, Brahma Pûrâna 4th, Vâyû and Vîshnû Pûrânas 11th, etc.), in descent from Pûrû-Kûtsva or Porus and not as nephew; this prince seems to have been the first in the line to embrace the Vedic Hindu religion, and married a Hindu Princess, daughter of King Satyaratha of Kêkaya, or the Kekian country from which flows Saranges a subtributary of the Akesines (Arrian's Indika I, IV), for which he was banished by his father, and deprived of his kingdom by his people. He was however befriended by the liberal Vîsvâmîtra tribe, the same as the Bisambritae, who are placed by Megasthenes (Frag. LVI.) to the east of Indus near its head, and set up his independent capital and claimed descent from the Solar race of kings inspite of opposition of the orthodox Vasîstha tribe. The Vîsvâmîtra tribe were however too powerful at the time and eventually Satyavrata regained his kingdom and returned to his former capital after 12 years. In these circumstances, tracing his descent from the Solar race, he would naturally name his new capital Ramnagar, and the locality indicated also agrees. That this king Satyavrata, or Sopeithes of Greeks, had two capitals, has led to the confusion mentioned by Strabo. From Sophois' stronghold, Apollonius goes with Ganges to the right and Hyphasis to the left, down to the sea coast, a ten days journey. This indicates that Rampur was the point where the rivers Beas, Sutlej, Jumna, and Bhagirathi were all running close to each other, which even their present channels indicate and that in Apollonius' time Bhâgîrathî-Gangâ penetrated to this area and Beas channel skirted round it turning from Rampur eastwards and bending southwards by the channel known as Baspa river. This would show how the traveller started his return journey with the Ganges to the right and Hyphasis to the left. After this he seems to have journeyed down the Hyphasis, though he does not make it clear how he did it. He "embarked on the river, admired the Hyphasis which at its mouth is narrow and rocky, hurrying through beetling cliffs into sea, with some danger to those who hug the land," and from the sea saw the Indus mouth at a distance, which indicates he must have come down the river, that river is the Sarasvati, which at this time received spill water of the Hyphasis or rather the combined stream Hydaspes, and its upper and lower courses were then joined in one, enabling a navigable passage by it to the sea, independent of the Indus. The upper and lower Sarasvati channels were separated by Ptolemy's time, a century later, the middle section being referred to as "Antahsîlâ" or "subsoil flow" in the Pûrânas. The Sarasvati was thus a river which, situated between the middle basins of the Indus, the Jumna-Ganges, the Narmada-Sipra systems, received the spill waters of all these systems at one time or other. The Padma Pûrâna, (Srîshtî Khanda, Ch. 18 and 32) furnishes the following information regarding "Prâchî" Sarasvatî, which is later called "Prachînâ Sarasvatî", showing that "Prâchî" as used is not "Eastern" but "Prâchînâ" or "Old":— "Sarasvatî, flows at Pûshkara in five streams, Sûprabhâ, Kânchanâ, Prâchî, Nandâ, Vîsâlâ; Sarasvatî emanating from the sacred habitation of Utanka Mûnî and then descending near Plaksha tree, flowed in the direction of the Western sea, but her water was drunk by subsoil fire and Sarasvatî disappearing there reappeared again at Pûshkara. While Sarasvatî was staying in company of Mandâkînî, Brahmâ created Rûpînî as her companion, and Harî gave her Harînî, Vajrapânî gave her Vajrînî, and Nîlkantha gave her Sakûvangarûchî, as companions; then Sarasvatî began to appear as the greatest of them all; the great river Sarasvatî, looked towards the south and then flowing backwards and addressing Gangâ said, 'You go towards the east, do not forget me, proceed to the place you have come from, and by the same path'." Now, the lower reaches of the Sarasvatî flowing from Pûshkara to the Western sea, makes it clear it is the Sarasvatî falling into Rann of Cutch, and at the time indicated, the river was connected with the Pushkar Lake, by a series of five rivers, the bed of the Prâchî the greatest of all, modern Berach river indicating the general direction of the channels. Of the portion of the river in its upper reaches which was already cut up, we find that the channels at the head are Rûpînî, Harînî Vajrînî and Sakûvangarûchî; Rûpînî is river Rupin, Vajrînî is Burang, Sakûvangarûchî is Sharangchu, all tributaries of the Tons, which is therefore the head of the Sarasvatî. All these tributary streams seem to have been connected with the Baspa river, as the passes of Rupinghat, Buranghati, and Sharangchu indicate. This confirms the assumption that Beas or Hyphasis was connected with the Sarasvatî system. Further this Sarasvatî was also connected with the Mandâkînî or Gangâ, which river previous to the time indicated in Padma Pûrâna was showing a tendency to follow the Sarasvatî towards her western course, but that with the deterioration of the Sarasvatî when her "water was drunk by the subsoil heat", Gangâ again flowed eastwards. This establishes the assumptions made before, namely (1) that the Sarasvatî at an early stage was a tributary of the Indus at its head; (2) that a little later her channel swerved southward and joined the Indus, taking with her also waters of the Jumna basin even upto Muttra. (3) that the river at another stage, flowed southward *viâ* Pushkar, Berach river, and Sarasvati independently into the sea at Rann of Cutch. (4) that at a subsequent stage, with the Indus swerved westwards at too great a distance, and upheavel of land at the Malwa Plateau, Sarasvatî was stripped into bits, her southern outlet to sea cut off, a large portion of her drainage diverted by the upper Jumna flowing eastwards into the Ganges, her head-waters also diverted to the Ganges and Sutlej, the connection with the Indus cut off, and the remnant of water she received flowing into the Ghaggar, is now dried up in the deserts of Rajputana. The Brahma Pûrâna shows that the lower Sarasvati had also a connection with the Narmadâ at one stage as it is stated (Ch. 125) that "Vânî river joins with the Gautamî river and this Vânî river again is joined on with the Bhâgîrathî and is named as the Sarasvatî there;" further in the statement of tirthas or sacred spots on the Gautamî gangâ in chapters 91 to 115, Sarasvatî-Sangam tîrtha is placed in the list between Kadravâ-Sangam tirtha and Pravarâ-Sangam tirtha or Nivâsapura, which shows the point of confluence was a little above Sangamner, and that Sarasvati channel was then *viâ* Berach (Prâchî) or Sîprâ (Suprabhâ of Padma Pûrâna).

The conclusions arrived at regarding the alignment of Ptolemy's Indus and its tributaries, enables us to solve the description of Sîndhû river given in the Vêdas and conversely the Vedic description confirms the conclusions arrived at, as regards Ptolemy's Indus. A brief reference to the Sîndhû river as described in the Vêdas will therefore be of interest. The description as contained in the Rîg Vêda X, 75, is given below (Ed. Thomas' translation, p. 3) :—

1. "Waters let the poet declare your transcendental greatness in the abode of the worshipper. Each set of seven (streams) has followed a three-fold course. The Sîndhû surpassed the others in impetuousity.

2. "Varûna hollowed out thy course, O Sîndhû, when thou didst rush to thy contests. Thou flowest from (the heights of) the earth, over a downward slope, when thou leadest the van of these streams.

*

4. "To thee O Sîndhû the (other streams) rush * * * * * Like a warrior King (in the centre of his army) thou leadest the two wings of thy host when thou strugglest forward to the van of these torrents.

5. "Receive favourably this my hymn, O Gangâ, Yamûnâ, Sarasvatî, Satadrû, Parashnî; hear O Marûdvrîddha with the Asîknî and Vîtastâ, and thou Arjîkyâ with the Sûshomâ.

6. "Unite first in thy course with the Trîstâmâ, the Sasartû, the Rasâ and the Svêtî; thou meetest the Gomatî and the Krûmû, with the Kûbha and the Mêhatnû, and with them are borne onward as on the same car.

7. "Flushing, sparkling, gleaming in all her majesty, the unconquerable, the most abundant of streams, beautiful as a handsome spotted mare, the Sîndhû rolls her waters over the levels."

This hymn is to the Sîndhû river, and the rivers, Gangâ, Yamûnâ mentioned are not therefore independent rivers, but tributaries of the Sîndhû. This hymn therefore ignores altogether the Ganges flowing to the eastern sea, mention of which is absent from other portions of the text. It clearly indicates how these tributaries are placed; there are seven sets of rivers, and Sîndhû leading them in the centre, four flowing to the east of the Indus and three to its west, thus

Eastern Tributaries—

1. Gangâ, Yamûnâ, Sarasvatî.
2. Satadrû, Parûshnî.

3. Marûdvrîddha, Asîknî, Vîtastâ.
4. Arjîkyâ, Sûshomâ.

Central Stream—Sîndhû (or Indus).

Western Tributaries—

5. Trîstâmâ, Sasârtû, Rasâ, Svetî.
6. Gomatî, Kûbha.
7. Krûmû, Mehatnû.

We are then told that the river, after receiving these tributaries, rolls her waters over the *levels*, *unconquerable*.

The land built up by the Sîndhû river in Vedic era was thus a comparatively small area, at the base of the Himalayas, roughly confined north of a line drawn from Hardwar, to Dera Ismail Khan; the eastern most set of tributaries being Gangâ or Mandâkînî, Yamûnâ, and Sarasvatî or Tons, and the westernmost set being Gomatî or Gomal and Kûbha or Kophen; and that south of this was level land where the river was *unconquerable*, that is spilling over the land to good depth, and oscillating its channel frequently. The Gangâ, Sarasvatî, Yamunâ rivers of the Vêdas were small tributaries of the Indus, made up of the upper reaches on the fringe of the Himalayas, and that in the Vêdîc period the Gangâ flowing to the eastern sea is ignored. This is in agreement with the view (A. C. Das, Rig Vedic. India p. 21) that in Pleistocene period, sea in Gangetic trough existed, and that it filled up rapidly in post-vedic time.

Kalhan in his Râjtarangînî (1st Taranga) says that from the beginning of Kalpa, up to the time of 6th Manû, the land was under water right up to the base of the Himâlayas Mt., and the great inland area covered with water was therefore known as Satî-sara or Satî Lake. It was during Vaîvasvata Manû's time, that Kasyapa Prajâpatî, propitiating the gods, brought the destruction of the Asura who was creating the floods, and Kâshmîra country was made out of the land reclaimed. From Vaîvasvata Manû the 7th Manû, and father of Ikshvâkû, the first of the Râjpût solar race, to Haryashva is only 12 generations; if Haryasva is Hydaspes, a contemporary of Darius, then the 7th Era, began about 7×40 or 280 years before Darius or 800 B.C. From 800 B.C. to Alexander's time, that is about 500 years, seems rather too short a time to expect reclamation of land in the Punjab and Sindh to the extent as we find it, and Kalhan's account therefore applies very likely to the Jhelum valley only, but even in that case it shows how very rapid changes were going on in the rivers and valleys in the region of the Himalayas near where the Indus and its tributories penetrated them. It shows at any rate that the Kashmir valley was a lake until 800 B.C.

The Indus taken as the Western boundary of India over the land portion in Ptolemy's time was therefore the western borders of Rajputana from north eastern corner of Rann of Cutch northwards, and then striking west towards from Bikaner, then Multan and on to Dehra Ghazi Khan.

CHAPTER VII

EASTERN BOUNDARY OF PTOLEMY'S INTRA-GANGEM INDIA, AND THE RIVERS FALLING INTO THE GANGETIKUS SINUS

India is divided in two portions by Ptolemy, the Intra-Gangem part being the main body of India lying "intra" or "within", that is to the west of Ganges, the portion lying beyond the Ganges up to the hills of Assam from the north, to the Arakan Yomas to the south being Extra-Gangem India. The eastern boundary of Intra Gangem India, is therefore, the Ganges, and the Bay of Bengal, or Sinus Gangetikus from the mouth of the Ganges southwards to Vizagapatam, the point of departure of ships for Burmah. As in the case of the western boundary, the eastern boundary, will be described from the south end at Vizagapatam proceeding northwards.

The first port north of Vizagapatam and close to it is Palura, which from its position fits in with Waltair, or Valter an ancient port, which was of importance as noticed by Marco Polo, who names the port as Betteler (*vide* Ch. V).

Next point, shown to be on the sea set back a little is Nanigaina, which is Vizianagram, ancient Vîjayanagaram.

Katikardama is Chicacole ancient Srîkâkûlam or south Shîkhâpûra, on the Languliya river, mentioned in the Pûrânas as Lângûlînî river. It is the same as Dandagula of Megasthenes. The name Katikardama, is of Jagannâth Katîkârdama, and this town has accordingly been identified by some with Katak and some with Pûrî, though in both these places the Jagannath temple, or the seat of the capital was established at a later date. Chicacole was at one time the seat of the King, and King Sobhana Dev (319-323 A.D.) of Orissa when he had to retreat into the interior at Sambalpore with the sacred images of Jagannâtha, Balarâma, and Sûbhadrâ from the sea coast, during the maritime invasion by Yavanas under Raktavâhû, the neighbourhood of Chicacole must have been the place attacked by the Burmese invadors and all vestiges of the temples destroyed in easily accessible places on the coast by the Burmese Buddhists who were relentless enemies of the Corangees as their former dominators, would explain why Srikakulam or Chicacole was named Katikardama.

Kannagara is Kalînga-patam, or Kalînga-patnam, or Kalînganagara, from which the name Kannagara is corrupted; it was a port on the river Bansadhara, mentioned also in the Pûrânas, and the jutting out portion below the mouth of the river was a cape, the same as Cape Colingon of Megasthenes.

The Manada river falls into the sea, north of Kannagara, and it is the same as the Vansadhârâ river, which near its source passes by Mandagor about 30 miles to the east of Bhowani Patna. The situation of Bhowani Patna agrees with that of Bardamana of Ptolemy, which must have come into prosperity and eminence when the Tel river, which is Pratyalâvatî or Utpalâvatî of Pûrânas, did at one time carry the spill waters of the Ganges from Gangpur district, and thus afforded the locality the best of climate for a thriving population for the time being, and the Vansadhârâ or the Manda river was very likely one of the healthiest effluents of the Tel.

Kottobara is from its position undoubtedly the ancient port of Baruva, a place full of ancient temples, and in maritime trade with Burmah for a long time. The name is very likely from Kota-Baruva.

Sippara is Ichchhapuram, its situation and name agreeing with that given by Ptolemy. The existence of a town named Sripura, the headquarters of Sukara king in Kalînga, in this neighbourhood is mentioned in Padma Pûrâna (Bhûmî 46).

The river Tyndis falls into the sea above Sippara, and its position in the lower reaches fits in with that of the very ancient river Rîshîkulyâ, modern Rushkulya.

The river then proceeds up skirting the northern base of the Nilgiri range of hills in Orissa, which is named by Ptolemy as Orouidian Mts. Yule thinks that Orouidian is from Sanskrit Vaîdurya, the position of which is to the north of the Western Ghats and on this casual assumption says that "Ptolemy has entirely misconceived its position. We conceive that he found in the Indian list, that the great rivers of the eastern or Maisolian coast rose in the Vaîdurya and having no other clue he places the Orouidia (which seems to be a mere metathesis of Oidurya for Vaidurya) near and parallel to the coast." Misconception indeed, but on whose part I leave the readers of the previous pages to judge, but this much is certain that Orouidia Mts., is not Vaîdurya in any case. The alternative name given for the Mt., in Ptolemy's map is Aruarni, evidently after the country or the people occupying the Arouaruoi country to the west of Maisolia which extend north-wards to these hills. The Vâmana Pûrâna, giving details of names of the southern countries in this part puts them in the following order. "Kalînga, Abhîra, Vaîsyaka, Savara, Aranya, Vîndhya, Vaîdarbha etc." In Yoga-Vâsîstha Râmâyana similarly we have "Kalînga, Pûndra, Jathara, Vîdarbha, Mêkala, Savarânana, Savara-varna, Karna, Trîpûra etc." In Vâyû and Markandêya Pûrânas, the order is "Kalînga, Abhîra, Saîvêsika, Atavya, Vâra, Pulînda, Vîndhyamûlîka, Vaîdarbha etc." These three lists will serve to show by comparison that the country of Savara, or Savara-Varna came next to the Aranya or Atavya country and that this latter extended up to the Vîndhyas. This enables us to fix the Aranya or Arournoi country, as extending from the area of Savara country watered by the Sabarî river, to the base of the Vîndhyas, where are the Vîndhya-mûlîka countries, or Badiamai of Ptolemy. The name Arournoi is therefore easily explained. Why the mountains are alternatively termed Oroudian, it is not apparent unless it is corrupted from Mahendra which is the name of these hills now. Whatever it is, there is no doubt as regards the identity of the Mahendra Mt., with Orouidian of Ptolemy. The

Tyndis river passes by the northern base of this hill, where we find the village Kalingia or Ptolemy's Kalliga, 30 miles east of Balliguda. This river must have been an effluent of the Mahanadi or Tel, and thus passing by Kalingia in gorges, connected with the Tel, then followed up along the bed of the Tel, and then the Suktel river, leaving to its west Bolangir, which is Megaris of Ptolemy, and then joined on to the Jonk, and crossing what is now the Mahanadi leaving Seori-Narayan, which is Sibirium of Ptolemy, some distance to its east touched the Vindhyas, by the Arpa, passing on the way the ancient town of Ratanpura which I believe is Opotoura of Ptolemy. One point to notice here is that this river is named Tyndis, and the river flowing to the Southern Sea, east of Aruarni is also named Tyna or the Tyndis. It is easy to conceive that Kalinga area containing Mahendra Giri or Nilgiri Range was at one time an island, and as the land between Vindhyas and Kalinga filled up, it was one river that bifurcated, one branch flowing eastwards and the other southwards, and therefore these two rivers at one time were the effluents of the same river. The very close proximity of the head of the Tyndis with that of the Narmada, which at one time was an effluent of the Ganges, also suggests that at an earlier stage, the Ganges had a branch pouring its water into these rivers. The course of the Tyndis is now described.

The next town on the coast, north of Tyndis mouth is Mapoura, which is Ranpur, northwest of the Chilka Lake.

North of this is the Dosaron river, which is the present Mahanadi, up to its junction with the Hasdo, where it passes between Kakirda which is Karikardama of Ptolemy and Bilaigarh, or Benagurum of Ptolemy; from this point the course was by the Hasdo river passing by Champa or Champâpûram which is Tasopium of Ptolemy, the river having a loop passing by Dharamjaygarh which is perhaps Dosaron, or ancient Dasârna. The Mahanadi was an effluent of the Ganges, and Hasdo or Hesto river was connected with the Son or the Banas (Parnâsâ), which will be shown later on. The Dosaron as an effluent of the Ganges, must have brought into the sea a vast amount of silt which had reclaimed shoaled up sea at its mouth subsequent to Ptolemy's time, and it is for this reason that we find a broad belt of land reclaimed on this portion of the coast.

Next on the coast is Kokala, which is Achala-Basanta on Assia Mts., were extensive ruins of the ancient city exists. In Kathâ Sarît Sâgar (Ch. LVI) we find Nala, after losing his Kingdom in a game of dice, leaves Nîshadha, and proceeds to Kosala and takes service there with King Rîtûparna. In Kathâ-Kosa (p. 211 of Tawney's Translation), it is stated that Dâvadantî, after she is deserted by Nala, eventually goes to Achalapura where King Rituparna ruled. Again in Kathâ-Sarît-Sagar we find (Ch. CIV) a brahmin of Nîshadha, reaches Sankhapûra, not far from Kausâmbî, from there goes to Achalapûra, and then on to the Gangâ for bathing. Now Sankhapûra city is traceable as its name also is preserved intact; it is a suburb of Old Angul, and practically old Angul represents Sankhapûra city. Kosâmbî near Sankhapur, Kosamba of Ptolemy, would therefore be represented by Balarampur or Jenapur. Kosala from this would appear to be the same as Achala-pura, or Achala-Basanta, on Assia Hills.

The Adamas river comes next, and this is unmistakably the Brahmini River, following up its tributary the Sankh, which as pointed out by Yule is the Adamas, or diamond bearing river which he says was the river which supplied diamonds in time of the Moghul splendour. The small village Marakata (meaning 'diamonds') lying near this river in Dhenkanal state, seems to mark the neighbourhood of the mouth of the Adamas river, which at the time of Ptolemy opened out into the estuary of the Kambyson or Kapisa river which was so broad here as to be considered a part of the sea. This Adamas river, following the Brahmini, up to Tikkira river, and then followed the Tikkira bed, passed close to Rairakhol, and then passing by Hira or Hirakhund a little to the east of

Sambalpore had a connection with the Ib river which it followed to its source. It will be seen that the river passes to east of Sambalpore near Hira the old Diamond mines, the area mentioned by Ball as one of the diamond producing tracts of India.

Kaûshâmbi city on the sea, as already mentioned before is Balarampore or Jenapur which was on the sea, and at the mouth of the river, which afforded the city the salubrious climate which induced the Vatsa King Udayana to establish his capital here. Rairakhol seems to be the same as Rorûka, a city which was ranked in importance to Pâtalîpûtra in Buddhist times as mentioned in Divyâvadâna (XXX) where it is stated that "Pâtalîpûtra and Rorûka are two great cities; as long as Pâtalîpûtra thrives, so long will Rorûka exist"; this is an indication that the decline of the two cities was simultaneous, a thing to be expected as the deterioration of Adamas river as a life giving navigable channel to Roruka must have followed immediately on the diversion of the Ganges flow from the Kambyson, the latter affecting Pâtalîpûtra.

After this point on the sea coast, comes the first and perhaps the widest mouth of the Ganges river, that is the Kambyson of Ptolemy, the famous Kapîsâ river of Indian literature. The boundary of Intra-Gangem India now follows the course of the Ganges which will now be described.

CHAPTER VIII

THE GANGES OF PTOLEMY

As in the case of other rivers dealt with already the course of the Ganges will be traced from the sea to its source.

The river before it enters the sea, branches out into five streams. The five mouths, as given in the description, beginning with the west are:—Kambyson, Mega, Kamberikhon, Pseudostomon, and Antibole. In the map, in some prints, another mouth, un-named is shown. As we have described the seacoast from the west, it would be convenient to take up the channels beginning from the west, that is the Kambyson channel.

The Kambyson mouth lies between Kosamba and Polura. Kosamba, as already shown, is near Balarampore or Garh Madhupur. Polura is no doubt the ancient town of Pal Lahara. In Mahâbhârata, Vana Parba 87, in one of the later descriptions introduced, of Asramas and Hills in eastern quarters, it is stated that "The Asrama of Rîshî Matanga is situated in the Mahêndra Mountain, where Bhâgîrathî river enters Manîkarnîkâ, and where Vâhudâ and Nandâ rivers are seen." Mahêndra Mountain is the northern portion of the Western Ghats, including the Nilgiri hills, and the above description therefore refers to where the Bhâgîrathî or Ganges penetrates the northern end of this range, that is the Keonjhar hills. Mankarnacha hill with an elevation of 3,639 ft., lies 60 miles to the north of Pal Lahara, and thus it enables us to fix the position of the channel at the base of this hills, which will be in the valley to the east of the peak. This valley, proceeds northwards in a fairly levelled up area by Chaibassa, which indicates the former huge bed of the river. Chaibassa is the town Srîvâsa, mentioned in Kathâ-Kosa, in story of Lalîtânga, as the seat of King Naravâhana, and as this King's son Lalîtânga is married to the daughter of the King of Champâ, these two places are also near each other, and Champâ is no other than Champua lying midway between Chaibassa and Pal Lahara, and very near to Khiching, the extensive ruins of which place are now being examined. The position of Khiching also agrees to that of Gangê the royal residence of the king of the Gangaridai tribes occupying the delta of the Ganges. This delta region was frequently referred to as the Gângya Kingdom, or the Madhya-Gângya islands in Sanskrit literature. This similarity of name with the neighbouring kingdom of Kalînga, has also led Megasthenes to term the Madhya-Gângya kingdom as Modo-galingae, which he describes (Frag. LVI) as "a large island in the Ganges, inhabited by a single tribe called Modo-galingae." The Mayurbhanja Raj family, who had their capital at Khiching, claims their descent from Asoka, and it is quite possible that Konika or Ajatasatru may have advanced down the river even up to Ganga-Regia or Khiching and that some of his family settled there which may also explain why Champua or Champa is the name of the ruined city to the northwest of Khiching. It is here perhaps that Asoka raised one of his biggest pillars, which the subsequent Hindu writers claimed as the victory pillar erected by the great kings like Raghu etc., and which the neighbouring king Nala of Kosala, when he became lord of southern India, pulled down, a pillar said to be 500 cubits high (Kathâ-Kosa, Tawny's translation p. 203), in fulfilment of a prophesy that the person who does so will be lord of southern half of India.

Thus the western channel the Kambyson, which is the Kapisa, passed by Pal Lahara, and then along the base of Mankarnacha hills on to Chybassa, and then the line of the river will be by R. Sanjai bed to Subarnarekha at Ramgarh, which brings us to the head of the delta. In this reach the channel leaves Kharasawan to the west, which is no doubt Kartasina of Ptolemy. This completes the Kambyson channel.

Having already fixed the position of Gangê regia, as Khiching, the effluent taking off from Kambyson from the neighbourhood of this city is easily fixed, as the Baitarani river, which was the main river or Os Magnum, a branch from this is the Salindi, and it seems that the Baitarani to the west and Salindi to the east, are the remnants of the great channel Magnum Os lying between.

The third channel Kamberikhon lying to the east of Magnum Os starts from Khiching and is the effluent of the Baitarani which takes off from Khiching, of which the flow has been reversed with the silting up of the sea coast. The point where this channel fell into the sea was midway between Bhadrak and Balasore that is to the west of Nilgiri. The name Kamberikhon may possibly have been corrupted from Kairabandhana, the name of the channel at its offtake at Khiching.

The three eastern channels, join into one, and this single channel branches out from the main river at the head of the delta. It is easy to see that the Subarnarekha is the channel which, taking off from the main river at Ramgarh is what is the Pseudostomos channel of Ptolemy, the river already shoaled up at the mouth. The un-named channel to the west of this agrees with that of the Burhabalong, and Tilogrammon is represented by present Balesvar town. The easternmost channel must have formerly been fed by the spill of the main river through the Subarnarekha channel, and the obvious connecting line from Dhalbhum-garh to a little above Midnapore.

This Dhalbhum or the country of the Dhal, which is Dahalâ of Svarodaya (Mont Martin's Eastern India, II, p. 19) which places the south-western divisions in the following order :—Anga, Vanga, Kalînga, Pûrvaja (*i.e.*, the Prasie), Ghosa, Kalasa, Dahalâ, Jayêndra, Yaggnitâ, Uddîyan, Tâla. Dhalbhum garh, the headquarters of the Dahalâs, is Dahalâ-garh or Talarga of Ptolemy which is placed in his map just above the point from where the Antibole channel takes off. This channel, from Dhalbhum-garh, ran in the low-lying land straight towards the Anandapur river, which is now known at its source as the

Kalighye river, running past Narayangarh, Amarshi, and then joining the Haldi River, falling into the sea near Sagaur Island. De-Barros' map in the 16th Century, shows the channel as the "Gangâ" river, confirming this map on this point by the following description given by him (C. R. Wilson in J.H.S.B. Vol. LXI, 1, 2, of 1892) :—"On the west side of Damodar (name not given but no doubt of its identity) enters the Ganges by three mouths forming two islands, and lower down R. Gangâ, just before its junction with the Ganges bifurcates and encloses a small delta; between Gangâ and Damodar are Pisolta and Pisacoly * * * * Gangâ discharges into the Ganges between Angeli and Picholda". Now Anjeli is Hijili, south of Haldi mouth, Pisolta village is north of the Rupnarayan where it meets the Hooghly River, thus the width of the river extended from Pisolta to Hijili or Kedgeri thus including the Haldi and Rupnarayana in one river which shows the former dimensions of the river; the differentiation made by De-Barros between "Gangâ" and "Ganges", the former the Anandapur Channel, the ancient sacred river, and Ganges the river later named Ganges. In Samual Purchas' description of India about 1600 A.D., he refers to this mouth of the Anandpur channel as the Khaberis (Wheeler's Early Travels Vol. I, Ch. II) and as one which "some call Kheberis, Ganges, some Guango the Ganges; some make one river of the two; Barros says both the rivers are sacred" all these clearly indicate this channel as one of the old effluents of Ganges. The name of the Anandapur river, indicates this as being the Antibole channel of Ptolemy. This complets the channels in the delta tract.

In fixing the lines of these former channels, the contour or relief map of India has been the main guide. Now that the position of the channel has been indicated, I would request the reader to have a glance at any relief map of India, and he will be convinced of the apparent and very striking resemblance of the main valleys in this area with the lines of the effluent channels shown by Ptolemy.

Having now fixed the head of the delta at Ramgarh north of Chybassa, the next point is to find out the alignment of the river connection from Chybassa to the Ganges in the valley to the north of the Vindhyas. Ptolemy shows that the channel from Chybassa, flowed a little towards the west and then northwards to the valley, and thus according to him the river penetrated the Vindhya hills at a point, some distance to the west of Chybassa, and thus the channel, past Bhagalpore and Monghyr was not the Ganges course then, and that a connection from Benares southwards penetrating the Vindhyas was existent. If the river did flow to Rajmahal, it would not flow a great way westwards to Chybassa to a higher level again, leaving a shorter outlet to the sea southwards. Fortunately the two rivers North Koel, and South Koel, coalescing at the same point gives us the key, as it clearly indicates that Koel was one river at one time but split up into two sections later on. From Ramgarh, the Subarnarekha channel takes us to very near the channel of the South Koel where the connection must have existed, and then the river entered the Vindhyas, following the course of the South and North Koels, joining on to the Son near Rhotasgarh. The huge bed of the Son northwards from this point carries with it the past history of the river; it has not yet been filled up to a section consistent with the present discharge it carries during floods, though centuries have passed by, since the bed has been deserted by the main river. Now we know from Greek classical sources that the city Palibothra was situated near the junction of the Ganges, and either the Erranaboas which is the Son, or the Yamuna. Palibothra cannot therefore be placed at Patna as has been fixed by previous authorities, as the point of confluence of Son and Ganges, that is Rhotas is too far away from it. The excavations carried out at Patna, have not disclosed ruins which can claim to indicate its importance to an extent consistent with the glorious accounts recorded of that great city. The locality indicated being the neighbourhood of Rhotasgarh, and location on the R. Koel, lying to the north of the Vindhyas, leads to the identity of Palibothra with old Palamau, the extensive ruins of which bear witness to the former greatness of this dead city. That the name of the river near this locality was known as the Ganges even so late as 1665 A.D. will be apparent from what Tavernier in his travels in these parts says :—(Ball's Edition, Vol. II, Ch. XVII) "From Sasseram you turn to south, come first to the seat of the Raja in town 21 coss then Rhotas fort 4 coss; then Soumelpour 30 coss through forests, dangerous from thieves and robbers. Raja lives ½ coss from the town. The Koel passes the fort, and it is in this river diamonds are found. It comes from the high mountains to the south and loses its name in the Ganges." Yule, when unable to explain why the Koel should lose its name in the Ganges, suggests that Tavernier may have been misled from Pliny's accounts that the Ganges yielded precious stones, into mistaking here the Son with the Ganges. It will be realised now that both Pliny and Tavernier are correct, and that Sone-cum-Koel was formerly a section of the Ganges, flowing past Sasseram, Rhotasgarh, and on to Rajahara, the seat of the king, and that Garhi-ghas is his fort nearby, about 4 miles north of Daltonganj. This shows exactly the position where the river entered into the gorges of the Vindhyas, towards Palamau.

Yuan Chwang in his travels indicates that the river previous to his visit passed through gorges at Vaisali, which lies on the bank of the R. Ganges, nearly opposite to that of Palibothra, as he says that (McWatter's Yuan Chwang Vol. II, Chap. XIII, Chuan VII) "from Fei-she-li (Vaisali) 50 to 60 li north-west is the great tope marking the spot where Buddha prevented Lichchhavis' sons to follow him by creating a river with steep banks and swift current." In 673 A.D. when I-Tsing came, he followed the road along the pass of the river Ganges, and even then, we find an indication that the river must have passed a fair amount of spill discharge by its old channel through the Vindhyas; in his journey from Tâmralîptî to Nâlânda, which is a distance of more than 60 yojanas, (Takakusus' Translation, p. xxx) he "proceeded by road straight to the west; at a distance of 10 days' journey from Mahabodhi Vihara passed a great mountain and bogs; the pass is dangerous and difficult to cross; defiles dangerous and attacked by robbers; escaped and reached village at night; from this village northwards for a few days arrived at Nâlânda." The road was through the once important passage of the Ganges, which had already got silted up having lost its importance with the Ganges river deserting this channel, and jungles and robbers were already in evidence. Palibothra must have already been deserted as a city as I-Tsing does not mention it and it is in this neighbourhood that the former population must have degenerated and returned to an uncivilised mode of living. The foregoing remarks make it abundantly clear that the Ganges crossed the Vindhyas here through a gorge, and that course is *viâ* Son and Koel. The Greek accounts confirm this, but as in the Greek accounts Mt. Maleus, which is Malian Mount of the Mallas of Kusinara or Kusinagara, as also Kusinagara itself is mentioned, I propose at this stage to give a conclusive confirmation of the location of Palibothra and Kusinagar, etc., from the Buddhist literature which date to the early Christian era, after which the course of the river from Gange-Regia to Palibothra will be described in detail.

In Jâtakas, and Avadânas, details are given of the last journey of Gautama Buddha from Palibothra to Kusinagara the place of Nîrvâna, and the places on this journey enables us to fix the position of many of the important localities associated with the life of that great Teacher. The last journey as described in some of the texts are given below, the times of the texts are given as far as they are at present known roughly :—

(*a*) Jâtaka (Eshan Ch. Ghose, Vol. I, p. 291), time beginning of 5th Cent. A.D. :—Pâtalîgrâma—crossing the river Gangâ—Kotîgrâma—Nâdika—Vaîsâlî—Châpâla tîrtha —Pâvâ—bath in Kakûthmâ river—crossing River Hîranyavatî—Kûsînagara.

(*b*) Asvaghosas' Mahâyana (Translated from Chinese translation by Suzuki, Ch. II); time 1st Cent. A.D. :—Pâtalîgâma— Kotîgâma— Nâdîkâ— Vêsâlî— Bêlûvâ—

Kûtâgârahall in Mahâvana— Bhandagâma— Hathîgâma —Ambâgâma— Jambûgâma— Bhojanagara (Ananda Chaîtya)— Pâvâ— Kûsînâra near River Kakûthâ— Nîrvâna in the salagrove of Mallas, the upavathana (precincts) of Kûsînâra on the farther side of Hîranyavatî river.

(*c*) Asvaghosha's Buddha-Charîta—(Translated from Chinese translation by Beal, Kiuens, IV & V) time previous to 70 A.D. :—Pâtalîgâma—crosses Gangâ—Kûlî village—Nâdî village—Vaîsâlî—Bhojanagara—Pâvâ in Malla country—crossing rivers Tsae-Kieuh and Hîranyatî to Kûsînagara.

(*d*) Bkah-Hgyur or life of Buddha from Tibetan source by Rockhill (F. 545 to 611), time not certain, :—Pâtalîgâma— crossed Gangâ— Kotîgâma— Nâdîka— Vaîsâlî— Vêlûvâ in Vrîjjî country— Amragâma— Jambûgâma— Bhandagâma— Shur-pai-grong— Hasthîgâma, all villages in Vrîjî and Mallas— Bhoganagara the Malay country—"village of earth"—Jalûkâ Mahâvan—Pâvâ—jungle on other side of Hîranyatî river—Kakûstan river—Hîranyatî river—Kûsînare, the Malla country of Vasîsthas —Nîrvâna and cremation in Makûta-bandhan chaitya after crossing Hîranyatî river.

(*e*) Legend of Goadama (Bigandet, Vol. II, Ch. I & II); time unknown :—Pâtalîpûtra—crosses over to the southern bank of the Gangâ river—Kântîkâmâ—Wâthâlî country—Kântîkâmâ village—Nândîka village—Pêntoogâmâ—Hâtti—Tsâmpou—Apparâ—Baugâ—Pâwâ country —Kakouda river crossed—Kouthenâron, distant from Pâwâ 3 gawots only.

These five lists quoted from independent sources will suffice to show that the names of villages on the route have not been altered ar added to by later interpolations, and that the names given are as they were in the early Christian era, that is, near about the time of Ptolemy's map. We may now follow the route in the present day survey maps.

From Palamau, the place to cross the river was a little to the west, and we find proceeding in this direction to the river Koel, and then across it, is Kutti village, which is Kotigama. A little to the north-east of it, within two miles is Besaria Kalan, which is the famous Vaîsâlî of old. Lying between these, a little to the east is Chando village situated on the land jutting out into the river, and this village is no doubt Nadika, or Nadi which is a distortion of Chandika, this village lying in a jungly country was known as Chandîkâ-Kânana, after Goddess Chandîkâ worshipped here, and from which the place retains its name of Chando to this date. The poet Bâna-Bhatta when invited by King Harsha, proceeded to the King's place, from the banks of the Son river, first to Prîtîkûta village, which is the Kûtâgâra hall in Vêlûvâ near Vaîsâlî, then to Chandîkâ-Kânana—then to Mallakûta village, and then crossing the Bhâgîrathî river to Yasthîgrâhaka village then to King's place. It is clear that Mallakûta village is the Kotîgâma of Mallas, and Chandîkâ-Kânana lay between that village and Vaîsâlî, and Chandîkâ therefore corresponds to Nâdîkâ. We thus see how Chando village represents Nadika, and this distortion is not a matter of surprise as bigot Buddhists had an antipathy to name the Hindu Goddess Chandîkâ at a time when revival of Brahminism was creating a great gulf between these rival religionists.

After Vaîsâlî, Gautama Buddha's route lay towards the south-west, where we find after stopping at the Kûtâgâra hall in Vêlûvâ which is in Vaîsâlî, he next proceeds to Bhandagâma which is Bhunduriya; next we find on the road Amdanda, which represents Ambâgâma or Amragâma; next on the road is Jamua-tikar which represents Jambûgâma; next to this Parhi near Mailan hill, represents Apparâ of Bigandet; near to it on the road is Hatouri, which represents Hatti, or Hatthi-gâma, which is misplaced to an earlier stage in the journey, but correctly placed in Bkah-Hgyur; after this comes the important town Bhojanagara, which retains its old name Bhoja intact, lying near the confluence of the Galphula and Mahan rivers. From here Buddha was taken to Pâvâ after stopping at Jaluka Mahavana, which is the Sal forest of Jaldega, and evidently the intention was to proceed southwards but after crossing the Rehar river which is no doubt the Hîranyavatî river, Buddha fell ill and was hurried back again to Pâvâ, which is represented by Paharbula; his condition not improving his disciple Ananda, did not like the idea of the great Buddha's nîrvâna at this obscure locality and they recrossed the Hîranyavatî river as indicated in Bkah-Hgyur, evidently with the idea to return to Kapîlavastû. The great master grew worse and the nîrvâna took place on the Salgrove of the Mallas which is still known as the Saol-tikra. This place is on the outskirts of Kusinagara as given in Asvaghosha's Buddha Charita and Kûsînagara is 3 gawots or about 7 miles from Pâvâ, and this points out to its identification with Karwa where to this day exists a neglected tope as shown in the maps, the examination of which I hope will throw a good deal of fresh light on the identification of Kusiñagara. Jaluka Mahavana is Jaldega.

Kusinagara has been identified by previous authorities with Kasia near Gorakhpur some disagreeing, some doubtfully, and final argument is the discovery of a copper plate of doubtful date saying that this was the locality of Nirvana. The fact remains that Asoka, only two hundred years after the death of Buddha, was led to doubts about the location of the places connected with Buddha's life, and had to seek the help of Upagûpta, a Pro-Brahmin, to show him these places and it is quite possible that the latter may have misled the king to divert his attention away from quarters where for the time being Brahman influence was predominant. Assuming Patna to represent Palibothra, the details which are given of the route on the final journey, are not traceable. With Palamau representing Pataliputra, it would also be impossible to carry out the journey for a sick person in the few stages given. The identification of Kusinagar is however not the main issue here, but there are three points deduced from the identification of the places which are of importance in connection with the investigation of Ganges course, *viz*:—(1) Pataliputra or Palibothra is Palamau, (2) that the country of Mallas, which lay on the line of this route, extended from Koel on the east to Rehar to the west and that (3) Mailan Hill lies in the centre of this area, the Greek accounts referring to this as Mt. Malleus.

Reference has already been made to poet Bana-Bhatta's account of journey to King Harsha at Pataliputra, to which we return again as it offers some more evidences to confirm location of Pataliputra at Palamau. In his book Harsha-charita he says (Canto I) "Sarasvatî, with Sâvîtrî issued from Brahmaloka, then gradually saw great river Hîranyvahâ which people call Sonâ, and landed at the west bank of that river; * * * * * * * * * * from that across the Sonâ river at a distance of 2 gabyutis (5 miles) is the place of Rîshî Chyavana, a representative of the Bhârgava tribe." (Canto II "Bâna invited by Harsha's brother Krîshna, starts from Prîtîkûta, and crossing Chandîkâ forest stops at Mallakûta village on the first day; next day crossing the Bhâgîrathî reaches Yasthî-grâhaka village and passes the night there; next day reaches the King's camp." The remnant of the small Sarasvatî channel, Sarsootea of the map, still exists near Bhundarya, the Bhandagama of Buddha's route, and the Sutbehee river a little north of it is the Savîtrî of Bana, and Satabahâ of the Buddhists, must have joined and met the Son towards the north and not *viâ* Kanhar as now. This would indicate Chyavana Rîshî's place near the confluence of the Son and the Koel, a point of importance to us, as the locality marking the headquarters of the Bhârgavas, the Vajjians of Buddhists, the Bhargas of Harîvamsa, descended from Dîvodâsa the reconstructor of Vârânasî. We find from the Buddhist accounts that a strip of country intervened in this place from across the river from Palibothra, to the country of the Mallas. We find Bâna, emerging from Prîtîkûta, which is Kûtagara hall in the outskirts of Vaîsalî, crossed Chandîkâ forest or Chando, goes to Mallakuta, or Kotî village of Mallas, Kûttî of maps. Crossing the river here he goes to Yasthîgrâhaka village, which is Latehar, a big village to south-east of Palamau. A look at the map will show that the river Koel flows very near this village now, and that at the time of Bâna (beginning 7th Cent. A.D.) the river channel to the west had already silted up to a tiny channel and Latehar was the village to reach after crossing. This Latehar village, Yasthî-grâhaka in Sanskrit as given by Bâna, is in Pali Lâttâ-gâma. Megasthenes cited by Elian (Francklin on Ancient Palibothra, p. 11) says that near Palibothra was a place Latagê or Lata Gaunh where the king used to feed the monkies, and this place which is no doubt present Latehar, and Yasthîgrâhaka of Bâna, affords yet another proof of Palamau being Palibothra. According to the Bhrigu-Samhita, a MSS, in possession of Major Wilford (Francklin's Palibothra, p. 9) the metropolis of the Baliputra Rajas was built one yojana west of conflux of Ganges and Erran-Bhowah at or near Champanagar; this description is perhaps mis-read and the metropolis is at or near the conflux and one yojana east of Champanagar and this Champanagar is Chanpi Kalan, about 5 miles east of Palamau. In a commentary of 'Dhuruni Kosa' it is stated that (Francklin's Palibothra, p. 9) Jay Singga despatched messengers for investigating to the town of Champaca or Champanagar, the place of Bhagdant or seat of worship of Jains, and the messenger found the city swallowed up by flood of the Ganges and the western extremity of the city was 4 or 5 miles from Bhagdant near Champaca; Bhagdant is without doubt Barwia Kalan, and the seat of Jain worship is clearly indicated in the place Halumani near Sat Barwa, lying between Palamau and Chanpi Kalan; the Dhuruni Kosa has made the situation described very clear by stating (Francklin's Palibothra, p. 10) that "On the retreat of the Ganges from the spot on which Palibothra stood, the place was again filled up with earth on which new villages grew among which is Champanagar"; the position of Chanpi Kalan in relation to Palamau makes this description apply to it correct in every detail; the description cannot apply to Champanagar at Monghyr and Palibothra at Patna; it is also to be clearly understood that this Champanagar, built on the site of Palibothra should not be confused with

Champanagar, capital built some distance away by Konîka.

The name Palamau perhaps requires an explanation. It is evidently Balî-myo, and 'myo' being the Burmese term for a city, it means Balî's city. It will be asked why should this Burmese term be introduced? Major Wilford (Major Wilford in As. Res. Vol. 9, p. 32 and p. 43) shows that Sâmba, son of Krîshna, in order to cure himself of disease introduced a colony of Magas from Sâka country who gave the name of the country of Magadh, and that Behar seems to have risen into great note as the capital of the Magas from the time of Baliputra Rajas in 160 B.C. to A.D. 640. This shows that a section of the Burmese, who are known in India as Magas, migrated to Behar at a very early date, and that their terming themselves as Baliputras, show that they trace their descent from Bali the grandson of Pralhada. The genealogy given in Harivamsa (Ch. III) will be of interest here

Kasyapa (married Dîtî)

- Hîranykasîpu
  - Anûhrâda (Descendants known as Hâlâhala)
  - Hrâda
  - Prahlâda
    - Bîrochana
      - Balî
        - Bâna
          - Indradamana
  - Sanghrâda (Descendnts known as Nîvaâta Kavacha of Manîmatî City)
- Hîranyâksha (Seven sons, Jarjara &c. Descendants known as Bâlêyas who were killed in Târakâmaya war).
- Sîmhîkâ, daughter, married Vîprachîtti (Decendants known as Saînhîkêyas)

Taruk or Taret are terms applied to the Chinese by Burmans (Phayre's Burmah Ch. I, p. 11) and the recent war (13th Century) when the Emperor of China sent a force of 6,000,000 horse and 20,000,000 foot to invade Burmah, and carried out a wholesale slaughter after defeating the main force at Nga-tsaung-gyan near the mouth of the Bhamo river the remnant of the Baleyas were killed, the Burman King driven below Prome to Tarok-man or point of the Tarok or Chinese, and it is quite likely that an earlier war, the great Tarakâmaya Sangrâma of Pûrânas, equally disastrous, took place between these two rival tribes who have been enemies since time immemorial, which caused the emigration of the first batch to India before the Christian era. These Baleyas or Bali-putras are the Magas who migrated to Magadha, and coming from Burmah to Magadha they were termed by the Sanskrit speaking people of Madhya-desha as Prâchya or Eastern People, the Prasii of the Greeks, and not because they occupied the eastern portion of India, as we find this term appearing only at one stage, which is the stage when the migration took place in large numbers and the term not applied to other tribes of eastern India. Megasthenes (Frag. LVI) includes under Prasii the people of sub-Vindhyas, even up to the western coast of India, making Indus their frontier in that direction, showing that the term applied to immigrants from eastern countries and not to occupants of eastern part of India. As these Bali-putras became a powerful race in India, occupying land watered by the Ganges, they made their independent capital and set up their own King, this King being a descendant of Nahûsha. I have already shown that Akrîda, 13th in descent from Nahûsha, is Indian Herakles as referred to by the Greeks, and he became King of the then Southern India, and inaugurated the Pândya Kingdom of Nagpur. While Akrîda is descended from Tûrvasû, second son of Yayâtî, we find Balî descended from Pûrû, the 5th and youngest son of Yayâtî. As given in the Harîvamsa (Ch. 30), Balî, is 23rd in descent from Nahûsha, and I reproduce below the details of the 8 generations above Balî as it will afford an interest in tracing the tribes, which were being formed with rapidly advancing reclamation of land at the time :—

- Janmejaya. (14th in descent from Puru, 16th from Nahusha)
  - Mahâsâla
    - Mahâmanâ
      - Ûsînara
        - Nrîga (progenitor of Yaûdheya tribe)
        - Krîmî (Set up Kingdom in Krîmîlâpûrî)
        - Nava (set up Kingdom in Navarâshtra)
        - Suvrata (with capital at Ambastha)
        - Sîvî (Progenitor of Sîvîs)
          - Vrîsadarbha
          - Sûvîra
          - Kaîkaya (set up Kaîkay Kingdom)
          - Madrapa
      - Tîtîkshû
        - Ûsadratha (became king of Eastern parts)
          - Fêna
            - Sutapâ (named Bhadraka in Matsya Pûrâna and Paîla in Agnî Pûrâna)
              - Balî (was adopted king by Dânavas)
                - Anga
                - Vanga
                - Sûmha
                - Pûndra
                - Kalînga

Each of these sons set up independent kingdoms named after him.

This genealogy is an example of how, the different lines of alien kings, have been merged into the genealogy of Indian kings. Though it is clearly stated that this king Balî of India is descended from Nahûsha with an altogether different genealogy from the king Balî descended from Hîranyakashîpû, yet we find that the Indian Balî has been introduced as son of Vîrochana in another passage, a clear attempt to merge the two into one. The genealogy also indicates the gradual spread of the Central Pândû Kings, eastwards; the Ambasthas appearing in Ptolemy's map, south of the upper Narmadâ valley; Mahâsâla city, referred to in Yuan Chwang's travels, appearing north of Palibothra which is the same as Mussooriya kalan, on the west bank of the Koel lying midway between Palamau and Rohtasgarh; the kingdoms of Anga, Vanga, Sûmha, Pûndra and Kalinga appearing at a later stage, which were therefore kingdoms reconstituted, or perhaps some at least altogether new but named after kingdoms of antiquity mentioned in earlier references, which had been obliterated, and the facts regarding which have been deliberately suppressed. This genealogy also gives a clue as to why Megasthenes ascribed the foundation of Palibothra to Herakles (Frag. I.). For the locality where the Daîtyas Hîranyakashîpû and Hîranâkshya flourished, no tradition or legend exists in India to fix it. I reproduce below the legend of Prince Wilatha as given by Capt. J. G. H. Powell in his book *Mandalay to Bhamo* :—

"At the extreme north of the town Bhamo (from Man-Maw means "pot-village") are the ruins of Sapenago. Long ago, before history began, Setku Min was king of Sapenago; Shan Chronicles state that Setku Min's dynasty reigned in Sapenago till 400 B.E. (1038 A.D.)."

"His wife being childless, after long prayers she conceived. But when she was within two months of her time, the Koktha Min who lived up the Irrawadi where Ayeindama now is, invaded Sapenago territory and the Setku Min and his wife fled to the hills on the east of the first defile north of Bhamo, known as Wilatha (now called Teinpaung)."

"For some time the Prince and his wife remained in hiding but a Mintha discovered their retreat in a cave and informed the pursuers. The Koktha Min then sent a force to seize the fugitives. Setku Min surrendered himself and so succeeded in diverting the attention of the troops from his wife who escaped."

"He was thrown into prison and in the mean time his wife was delivered of a son whom she called Wilatha, after the name of the hill where she was hiding (the hill still exists with a rough cradle cut into the rock inside). When the boy was seven years old, he determined to search for his father, and with the aid of Nats was transported to Sapenago. He arrived the very day that had been fixed for his father's execution and met him on the way to the scaffold. He bowed down and showed his mother's ring and implored the executioners to let his father go and accept him in his stead. The gaoler refused to act without orders and took both father and son before the Koktha Min. Wilatha refused to do homage and so diverted the attention of the Koktha Min's rage upon himself. Koktha Min ordered the father to be set free and the son to be beheaded but when the execution time came the heads-man found that neither Dah nor spear would harm the boy. He was therefore thrown into the river but the crocodiles bore him up and lashed the water in such a foam that the executioners fled. The king then ordered him to be burnt, and Wilatha was thrown into a fiery furnace but in the midst appeared a lotus and seated in this the prince escaped the flames. Elephants were then called out, but they refused to trample on him. As a last resource the Koktha Min ordered Wilatha to be taken to the top of the Nat-faced cliff (Nat-Myet-na-Taungdiek) in the second defile and from thence to be cast into the river and he himself went to see it done. When the party reached the summit, the water raged furiously and a wild storm broke, while the solid earth shook, when Wilatha was cast from the brow of the cliff. Koktha Min was seized with fear and fled back to his palace but as he was about to enter it, the earth gaped and he was swallowed up in the presence of his people and Setku Min reigned in his place. Meanwhile however a

Naga had seized Wilatha as he fell from the cliff and saved him from death. The place where the Naga broke the Prince's fall is now marked by a Pagoda on a rock at the foot of the cliff, called Let-saung-gan, which literally means 'catching hold by the hand'."

The story of Prahlâda as given in the Hindu accounts in the Pûrânas, contains details, exactly the same as in the above account and for the information of the reader unacquainted with it, I repeat below the account taken from the Bhâgavata Pûrâna. (Ch. III, Sec. 17) Twin sons Hîranyâksha and Hîranyakasîpû were born from Dîtî by Kasyapa and they and their progeny were therefore called Daîtyas though they were a section of the Dânavas. They became very powerful under protection of Brahmâ, and Hîranyâksha attacked Bibhâvarî city of Varûna and was in occupation of the kingdom for a long time. Varûna sought the help of Nârâyana Harî, (Ch. III, Sec. 19) who in the form of Varâha killed Hîranyâksha in battle, and then retired to Sukhamayapûrî (Sûkhâ, Bîbhâvarî, Amarâvatî, and Sanyamanî are the four cities near Sûmêru as given in the Lînga Pûrâna.) (Ch. VII, Sec. 3) Determined to avenge the death of his brother, Hîranyakasîpû, propitiated Brahmâ, brought Sîva (Ishâna, which will be shown as Shan states later on) over to his side, and attacked and occupied capital of Mahêndra, that is Amarâpûra. When Hîranyakasîpû was engaged in propitiating Brahmâ to gather strength, and was absent from his capital, Indra the king of Amarâpûra, captured the pregnant queen of Hîranyakashîpû and wanted to kill her so as to get rid of the child, their future enemy, but at the intercession of Nârada rîshî, who assured Indra, that the future child would be one of the staunchest worshippers of Harî, she was released, and stayed at Nârada rîshî's place where Prahlâda was born and bred up. When he was only five years old, he became, the greatest worshipper of Harî, and rebelled with his father's views when he was presented to the king (Ch. VII, Sec. 8). In the meantime (Ch. VII, Sec. 5) Prahlâda, son of Hîranyakasîpû, under the influence of his teachers Sanda, and Amarka, became a worshipper of Nârâyana Harî (the god the Nâgas, later on included in the Hindu list of deities) and refused to discard this worship and return to his own religion and submit to his father, though taught in the Trîvarga-pratîpâdaka Shâstra. Hîranyakashîpû, enraged at this rebellious conduct of Prahlâda, ordered his followers to spear Prahlâda to death, but spears became ineffectual. Frightened at this the king resorted to other methods, *viz.*, trampling by elephants, snake bites, throwing down from hill top, poisoning, and it was found that none of the methods of starvation, exposure to cold and air, throwing into fire or water, dropping down from hill top, was successful (Ch. VII, Sec. 7). When Hîrankayashîpû found all attempts to kill Prahlâda failed, he took recourse to abusing Harî in Prahlâda's presence, and asked the latter, whether he could show that Harî was present in the stone pillar of the palace, if, as he said Harî was omnipresent, and that he was going to slay him and if Harî was in the pillar, let him save you. Saying this he advanced with open swords towards Prahlâda, and repeatedly struck the stone pillar with his fist. The stone pillar gaped wide and out of it came Harî in the form half man and half lion, and catching hold of Hîranyakashîpû, flayed him alive.

In other accounts, the episodes of elephant refusing to trample Prahlâda and putting him on his back instead, of Harî's protecting Prahlâda when thrown into fire, appearing from the midst of fire on a lotus, and of Harî receiving Prahlâda in his arms when he was thrown from the top of the hill, etc., are mentioned exactly as given in the legend of Sapenago.

A comparison of the two accounts will show that so much detail is not a matter of coincidence and they must be the same. The names Wilatha of Burmese and Prahlâda of Sanskrit sound the same. Setku Min and Koktha Min as representing Hîranyâkasha and Hîranya-kashîpû will also be apparent when it is realised that in the legend the kings are terms 'Min' an ordinary term of respect, put properly addressed a king in Burmah is 'Shwe' or golden or Hîranya in Sanskrit, so Hîranya-setku, and Hîranya-koktha do represent Hîranyâksha and Hîranya-kashîpû.

The above goes to show where the Balîpûtras came from, and why these Balêyas from this place, when they were driven out by the Chinese, migrated to India, and were known there as Balîpûtras and Prâchya or eastern people.

Enough has been said for my purposes here, to identify Palibothra with Palamau, and I now turn to the Greek accounts, to trace out the course of the Ganges river from the head of the delta to Palibothra.

Megasthenes says that "(Frag. X) Next (to the Prasii) in the interior are the Monedes and the Suari to whom belong Mt. Maleus. (Frag. XV, B) Crossing the mountains which skirt that portion of India which is most inland, the traveller meets they say, with ravines full of dense jungle in a district called Korouda. (Frag. XX, B) The tribes that dwell by the Ganges are the Kalingae nearest the sea, and higher up the Mandei, also the Malli to whom belong Mt. Maleus, the boundary of all that region being the Ganges. (Frag. XXVI) Palibothra, in Prasian dominion, is situated where Erranaboas and Ganges unite."

Arrian says (I, X) "the greatest city in India is Palibothra in the dominion of Prasians, where rivers Erranaboas and Ganges unite."

Strabo's account seems to be from very meagre information from the nature of the description given by him and he says that (Para 73) : "Artimidoros says river Ganges descends from Emodoi Mt., towards south reaching city Gange, then turns east to Palibothra and sea. Oidanes is one of its affluents; (Para 13) passing by Palibothra Ganges enters sea by a single mouth."

Ptolemy shows Ganges flowing by Palibothra, turning southward and then by a bend towards east and then south leaving Mandalai tribes to the west and Tiladae to the east, and then Kokkonagai to the west, and then separating at the head of the delta into different channels.

It is clear from above accounts that Mandei, Monedes, and Mandalai are identical, and Suari a section of these people in Megasthenes time, though it appears that they may have seperated and migrated further south beyond Kokkonaga, and are the same as Sabarae of Ptolemy, who were occupying the country about Dosaron river in Ptolemy's time. The Mandalai people, have been identified by authorities on the subject with the Mundas, who are mentioned in the Rigveda, and who pressed by the Aryan settlers have been steadily moving southeast towards fresh jungle areas. To this Mandalai tribe, belongs Mt. Malleus, or present Mailan hill, and there can therefore be no dispute about the identity of these with the Mallas of Buddhist literature. Kokkonagar may therefore be the Kusinagar kingdom of Buddhist, which I have shown is south of Mt. Maleus and therefore of the Mandaloi. Suari or Sabarae is therefore Gangpur, the name still preserved in their old capital Suadi. As the localities of these tribes are fixed, there is no difficulty in fixing the course of the Ganges in this section, which must be through the Chotanagpur hills, along the bed of what are now the northern and southern Koel rivers. The Manaiana are the people of Manbhum.

The river course from the head of the delta to Palamau can now be fixed as follows :—From Ramgarh the channel followed the Subarnarekha bed to Patkum, and then turned west following the valley in which runs the Karkori river, thus leaving Manbhum to the east; passing by Khunti or Khuntinagar which is Kartinaga of Ptolemy and leaving the Karkori, it joined the south Koel river at Olmonda which is Oreophanta of Ptolemy; above this point the river very likely had the course bifurcated, one following the Koel and the other the Sankh joining again further up at Gangtar and in Ptolemy's time the Sankh channel was the main channel, and thus leaving the north Koel course, it joined the Sankh at Chainpur, then followed the Sankh to near Checheri where exist the ancient ruins of Tamoli-garh, which is Tamalites of

Ptolemy and which is not to be confused with Tâmralîptî the seaport which must have been a long distance southwards; from Checheri, the channel passed by the ancient town of Netarhat, by the North Koel bed, and following that channel right up to the Son at Rhotasgarh, passing by Palamau or Palibothra; Rhotas was the headquarters of Sagara, king of the Solar race, and the Harîvamsa mentions that this king (Ch. 13) with the aid of the Bhârgavas, reconquered the border countries from which his father Vahu had to retreat, and re-established his kingdom which must be in this area, as the Bhargavas are the Vajjian Lîchchhavîs, and settlers in this neighbourhood; the Rhotas fort was built by his predecessors, but the frontier kingdom was consolidated in Sagara's time and that Rhotasgarh the new capital is Sigalla of Ptolemy. Garî Khas lying north of Amanat river where it joins the Koel agrees with Korygaza of Ptolemy. This completes the course of the river up to Rhotasgarh or Sigalla.

The course of the river was through ravines full of jungle in a district called Korouda, as given by Megasthenes. Korouda is no doubt Karûsha of Sanskrit texts, a country which is classed as Vindhya-mûlîya or situated in the Vîndhyas, in the Pûrânas. In Râmâyana (Adî, Sec. 22, 23), the route given from Anga dêsa where Gangâ branches out in three streams, up the river proceeding by the south bank of the river, is described as dense jungly areas where flourished formerly thriving populated countries of the Malada and Karusha. This is an obvious later addition, but it shows the course of the Ganges in the stage we find in Ptolemy's leaving Gangê regia, proceeding up by the south bank, and then into the jungly ravines between the Malada and Karûsha, that is the Mandalai or Mallas, and Karouda. This description also would show that the course as indicated could not have been through areas, practically plains, *viâ* Patna, Monghyr, Rajmehal as now.

The course of the Ganges from Sigalla (Rohtasgarh) to the sources will now be described. In tracing this, it would be best to remember three important points at the outset. The first is that in Ptolemy's time Jamuna basin up to Muttra is shown as draining into the Indus, the condition of the upper Jamuna and upper Bhagirathi-ganga, was as in the Vedic period already described in connection with the Indus, that is, that the channels draining these basins were affluents of the Indus. The upper Ganges river of Ptolemy is therefore not Bhâgîrathî-Gangâ flowing by Hardwar and the obvious conclusion is that it is Râmgangâ river flowing by Moradabad and Bareilly, joining the present Ganges course near Jalalabad, about 50 miles north of Kanauj. The second point is that the southern affluent Soa river of Ptolemy, which brought the drainage of the lower Jamuna basin, met the Ganges almost at right angles; the point of conflux has therefore shifted down in course of time, and the extent of this shifting down is to be taken roughly the length over which the channels are running parallel, and the confluence was therefore much further up than Allahabad. The third point is, that for the river flowing from the vicinity of Benares to Rohtasgarh, the present channel, *viâ* the Son-Ganges confluence near Patna would be too much of a detour, when a low area from Benares to the Son, near Sasseram was available for the river; the river must therefore have run by a straighter course from Benares to Sasseram, the west bank of the Sone being high up to the latter point. The course of the river from Rohtasgarh (Sigalla) is northwards by the bed of the Son up to Dehri or Baroon on the opposite bank which may be Boraita; from here the river turned westwards *viâ* Sasseram, or Sahasârâma, the headquarters of the Buddhists at an early period, and at a previous period was perhaps a Hindu place the worship of Târâ-chandî, and one of the subordinate frontiers of Mûndâ Daîtya who had his headquarters at Chainpur; passing by Sasseram or Sambalaka of Ptolemy, the channel continued westwards passing by Chainpur and joining the present Ganges channel at Benares; the very ancient town of Chainpur, the headquarters of Mûndâ Daîtya for a time, who had his people the Mandaloi of Ptolemy or Mallas extending from Chainpur, down below to Rehar river, near Bijaigarh or Chan-chu of the Chinese travellers who found the Ganges river channel still passing by that town even in the 7th Century A.D.; passing by Benares with Ramnagar on the opposite bank which is Sâkêta or Sagala of Ptolemy the present channel is followed passing by Mirzapur to near Manda Road, from where, it followed the Tons river, the broad bed of which at this place leads to the conclusion of its being the former channel and this broad bed extends westwards up to Kunda, which is Kindia of Ptolemy lying to the east of Shankargarh an ancient place; the channel then made straight for the Jamuna channel joining it in the neighbourhood of Man south of Kosam or northern Kosâmbî and following this channel up to Asothar, 10 miles south of Fatehpur, this Asothar being Adisdara of Ptolemy; this explains why the channel of the Jamuna is very broad from Asothar downwards to near Allahabad; at Asothar the Soa river of Ptolemy branched out towards south, following the Jamuna bed to Hamirpur and then following the Betwa course past Jhansi which Tamasis of Ptolemy; the main river channel from the confluence of Asothar was across the country by Fatehpur joining the present Ganges channel immediately to the north of that city, and then followed the existing Ganges bed, passing by Cawnpore, Kanauj, right up to Fatehgarh, from where it followed the Râmgangâ river course, thus leaving Unao or rather Thana lying to its suburbs, the Toana of Ptolemy, on the west bank, and then Kanauj or Kânyakûbja which is perhaps distorted to Orza of Ptolemy, where the river may formerly have passed to the west of the city instead of the east as now, or the old city itself when destroyed by the river shifted to the opposite bank and there are indications of the city being rebuilt later on; Sannaba, present Sambhal is left in the interior to the west; the river bifurcates above Orza or Kanauj, the western branch being the main Ganges of Ptolemy or Ramganga river to its source, the eastern branch Diamouna of Ptolemy, must have been a channel taking off from above Kanauj joined with the

Sarda river where it reached the plains from the hills, the channel thus passing by the ancient city of Bisalpore, which is Passalê of Ptolemy; this portion of the channel thus separated from Ramganga in the neighbourhood of Dataganj, then joined the Katra channel which joined the Sardah at Mundiah Ghat, and then followed the Sarda up to its mountain feeder the Dhauli-ganga, which perhaps explains the name Diamouna given in Ptolemy's map; the affluent Sarabos, takes off from the Ganges from Cawnpore, that is past Unao or Thana which is Toana of Ptolemy, then joined with the Sarju, by the low lying area through which the Unao-Lucknow-Barabanke railway line runs, and then following the Sarju bed to its source, thus passing by Hardatnagar or Heorta of Ptolemy lying north of Bahraich, then Satiana which is Storna, and then Phulwa or Sapolus of Ptolemy south of Silgarhi. This completes the course of the Ganges of Ptolemy to its source, and its tributaries excepting the three tributaries in the lower reaches which will now be described.

The lower southern tributary, joins the Ganges at Sigalla. There is no doubt abcut this tributary being the Son, joining the Ganges at Rohtasgarh or Sigalla. Maliaba on the north bank is the ancient place Bijaygarh lying opposite the mouth of the Rehar where it joins the Son, the name is from Umlah river which flows by the Bijaygarh, the ancient place being Umlahghat. The next point shown by Ptolemy is Aspathis, and this I think is the point where the Gopat river meets the Son, the name evidently following that of the river Gopat. The next point is Panassa, and this is a town on the Banas river, which has been identified with Parnâsâ or Pûrânas, where it joins the Son, and Bharatpur on the river represents Panassa. The last point near the source is Balantipirgum and this I have no hesitation in identifying with the old place Bando-garh.

The two other tributaries join the Ganges from the extra-Gangem area. The upper of these, of which no name is given, is the Kosi, the big river on that side above Brahmaputra. The huge bed of the channel of the Kosi from the Himalayas, down to the ancient town of Dhamdoho, stands out prominent in the map, and it indicates that this was one of the rivers which drained out Tibet basin through the Himalayas at some remote date. The channel of this tributary would be, following the Kosi from the source to near Kishenganj, then joining the present Ganges channel at Jahnugira little below Monghyr, then following it up to about Patna and then joining the Son channel, partly along the line of the Punpun river, and then crossing over to the west of Son channel, joined the Ganges near Bhabua. Selimpura near the source of this tributary is Chainpur in Dhankuta; Kassidia, some way down is near the old place Dhamdaha, and I think it is Coondwa, where the road from Purnea meets the river; this Coondwa is another daha, or pool in the river, and may be Krishna-daha, from which the name Kassidia is derived. Kanogiza should be looked for on the present Ganges channel, between Monghyr and Patna. Kanyakubja the capital of Kûmbhîpâla or Kûmârapâla, in Dharmâranya, the details of the names of villages of which are given in Skanda Pûrâna (Brahma Khanda, Sec. 38 and 39), seems to indicate the locality, west of Kosi and north of Ganges, and it is therefore to be expected that the capital Kânyakûbja, that Kûmârapâla wanted to establish in imitation of the great northern capital was in the neighbourhood of Monghyr, its early downfall having been brought about by the river flooding this place shortly after. As examples of the villages, I may mention Rupolâ (mod. Rupailli), Mânajâ (mod. Mansi), Mogodî (mod. Monghyr), Godharî (mod. Gogri), Dûdhîâ (mod. Dudhaila), Baîholâ (Bahera), Hâlalâ (Haya-ghat), Hansâlîâ (mod. Hansa), etc.

The tributary coming from the Extra-Ganjam area to the south, issues from the Bepyrrhos Mts., and is called the Bepyrrhos or the red river. There is no doubt about this tributary being the Brahmapûtra, or rather the Laûhîtya of Pûrânas, the Brahmapûtra channel is still known as the Lûhît or the red river in its course below the Brahmakund. There are two very important points of divergence of the conditions of the river as represented by Ptolemy, from the present condition, *viz.*, (1) that the Brahmapûtra did not continue beyond Bepyrrhos Mts., *i.e.*, it did not continue to Tibet, and (2) that it had no independent exit to the sea, though it joined the Ganges at some distance from the sea, thus running at a fairly high level from the valley between Garo hills and Himalayas to its junction with the Ganges in the Vindhyas, thus indicating that a ridge existed over lower Bengal area between the sea and this tributary. That this tributary did not extend beyond the Himalayas is to be presumed from several facts and traditions; the river Brahmaputra does not appear as a river in earlier lists in Mahâbhârata or the Pûrânas, and that the name of Laûhîtya appears in its place, next to Karatoyâ, thus proving Laûhîtya was the earlier river which has been broken into by Brahmanada; the river is known as Brahmapûtra river below Brahmakund, whereas, above it where the Sanskrit name is used for the Tsang-po, the river is termed Brahmanada, thus indicating that the Brahma-nada did burst into the Laûhîtya, and the latter became therefore "Brahmapûtra", or "son of Brahmâ" river; according to the Kâlîkâ Pûrâna (Ch. 82) Brahmâ's energies were dumped in Amoghâ the wife of Santanû mûnî of Harîvamsa, which created river which was placed in the valley bounded by Kaîlâsa to its north, Gandhamâdana to south, Jârûdhî to west, and Sambarttaka range to east, where the waters pent up formed into a Kûnda or Lake, and increasing in size in the course of immense number of years, appeared like a second sea, after which Parasûrâma for the good of humanity brought her down, first into the Lohîta lake in the base of Kaîlâsa mountain, and then, opening out with his axe the banks of the Lohîta lake again, let the river flow eastward, then again the obstruction put by Hêmasrînga mount was also removed and the river finally was made to flow by Kâmrûpa hills into the south sea; according to the Brahma Pûrâna also, Parasûrâma cleft open a passage from the Brahmakûnda or Lohîta sarovara, and diverted the water into the Laûhîtya river, and according to the Buddhists it is Manjûghosha who diverted the Brahmapûtra river into the plains of India (J. M. Ray, Dhâkâr Itîhâsh, Vol. I, pp. 36-37). Thus there are ample traditions to support the view that Laûhîtya or Bepyrrhos river had no connection with the Tsangpo, and I will show later on, that this Brahma-nada, flowed by the Irrwadi at an earlier stage. As regards the next point, that a ridge existed over the present plains of Bengal, the geological view expressed by Keene (Reclus' Universal Geography Vol. III, p. 22) is as follows :—"A study of the relief of the land leaves no doubt that the border chain of the peninsular plateau was formerly continued eastwards to the Garo hills and the other higher lands skirting the Brahmaputra valley on the east. The now vanished intermediate range was evidently pierced and gradually swept into the Bay of Bengal by the Ganges and the Brahmaputra rivers, the gap so made is no less than 120 miles. The south Assam chain, also, which runs east north-eastwards parallel with the eastern Himalayas, is geologically connected with this system, consisting largely of the same tertiary sandstones and nummulitic limestones resting on older formations;" the Mandara Parvata, used by gods and asuras for churning the ocean was in this neighbourhood, and it evidently points out to the sliding of these hills into the sea which reclaimed at the time a part of the ocean near Kalînga; the mountains in this area were at a stage of floating, which is expressed by the poets by saying that they had wings which Indra clipped and they became stable, but the Maînâka hill escaped and eventually dipped into the ocean. This subsidence brought about with it the changes in the course of the Ganges outfall into the sea. We may now trace the course of the river, which from its source in the Brahmakund must have followed its present course in the valley between the Himalayas at Bhutan, and the Garo hills, up to the neighbourhood of Rangpur; the junction point with the Ganges was above Olmonda (Oreophanta) and below Checheri (Tammalites), and the channel is therefore the Damodar river course which had a connection *viâ* the south Koel, and there is no difficulty from the relief map to pick it out; the junction point was near Rud to the north of Neterhat, from where, the channel passed by Latehar to Chandwa a point at the source of the Damodar and from here, the tributary followed the course of the Damodar within its present valley at least up to Asansol, if not Burdwan; the speculative portion is the connecting channel between Asansol and Rangpur. The difficulty here is that the whole area, shut out from the sea to the south must have been a swamp which explains the dearth of townships as shown by Ptolemy, and then the obliteration of most of what was there, by the extensive changes brought about by the Brahmaputra bursting into Lauhitya, and Ganges diverting its course eastwards, the combined flow inducing the flooding and consequent subsidence of hills by sliding into the sea, till a passage was opened out to the sea for the land locked water. The first thing we find after issuing from the valley enclosed by high hills, is that the river leaves Passalae to the north; Passalae cannot possibly be identified with Baisarh north of Patna, now that I have demonstrated the comparative accuracy of Ptolemy's map; the only suggestion I can offer is that Passalae is Prâgjyotîsa which at the period of Ptolemy's map came into prominence, and Prâgjyotîshpura, the Kâlîkâpûrâna says (sec. 38) is bounded by the Karatoyâ to the east and Laûhîtya flows near it. This shows Passalae to the west of Laûhîtya-Karatoyâ confluence at the time. Karatoyâ was then the biggest river of note next to Laûhîtya, and thus the enormous bed of Teesta shows that Karatoyâ flowed by this channel till it joined the Laûhîtya near Chilmari. Ptolemy's Bepyrrhos, left Passalae to north must therefore have flowed westward from Chilmari, then the next river Jamûnâ must have been joined on, and then leaving Nârad river to its south which is perhaps Nardos of Ptolemy, the next point to pass is Rampore Beualia, from where the Bhâgîrathî channel to Katwa was the bed of Bepyrrhos, which then followed the Ajay course for a time, and then on to the Damodar.

Starting from the lower end of the channel thus indicated, it will be seen that the Bepyrrhos leaves Athenaguram to its north. This town is possibly Bishun-garh or Vîshnûgarh west of Hazaribagh; this city was of importance of old, and possibly the river flowed by a loop along River Kunur which skirts Bishungarh. To the south is Maniena, which is no doubt Manbhum. The balance of the length of the channel has been under-estimated by Ptolemy, as the area was unimportant and sparsely populated. Further eastwards in the area to the south was Rhadamarkotta, which is possibly Hrada-Varttîkâ, or the country in the neighbourhood of the lake or swamp. The towns in Rhadamarkotta, that appear to the south of this river are :—Tosalei, a metropolis; Alosanga; Tougma, a metropolis; and to this has to be added Nardos, a town, which according to some editors have been indicated to be "Nard" instead of Nardos, the name of a town. The people of Teladai who inhabit Besades appear nearest the river intervening between the river and the towns of Rhadamarkotta named above. In Brahma Pûrâna (Ch. 27) the list of countries below Vindhyas, we find the following sequence of names :—'Dasârna, Bhoja, Kîshkîndhya, Toshala, Kosala, Traîpûra, Baîdêsa, Tûmvûra'. In Vâyû Pûrâna (Ch. 43-45) the order is :—'Rasârna, Bhoja, Kîshkîndhya, Toshala, Kosala, Traîpûra, Baîdîka, Tûmûra, Tûmvûra'. In Markandêya Pûrâna (Ch. 5) the order is the same as in Vâyû Pûrâna but Rasârna is Dasârna, Baîdîka is Baîdêsa, Tûmûra is Tûmvula. In Vâmana Pûrâna (Ch. 13, etc.) the order is :—'Utkala, Uttamarna, Dasârna, Gopta, Kîkarava, Toshala Traîpûra, Khellîsa, Tûraga, Tûmvara.' These lists show that between Dosaran or north Orissa and Traîpûra or Tippara, the countries of Toshala, Kosala, existed, and above Tippara Tûraga, Tûmvûra, and Baîdîsa, which confirm the description given by Ptolemy of Tosali which is Toshala, Tugma which is Tûraga or Tûrangama, Besades which is Baîdîsa. Toshala kingdom must therefore have been to the east of Manbhum, that is probably the Bankura-Burdwan area, and the neighbourhood of Vishnupur in Bankura is to be looked for, for Tosali town. Tugma, I have no hesitation in placing on the Turag river, and possibly Dacca indicates the position and neither Toke on the

Brahmaputra not Tagaung in Burmah suits the identity. Nardos is the country about the Narada river and Nator probably was the site of the town itself. Alosanga is probably Tangail, the name preserved in the village Ellenga lying to its north; Ellasin on the Lohajung river suggested by Wilford, though it lies in the locality, has little claim to be Alosanga, being a very recent mart grown up after the jute trade has developed. Besades is Baîdîsa or Baîdîka, and it is the Vaîsya colony mentioned in the Pûrânas as Vaîsya and Sûdra country; the Yogini Tantra mentions that after Naraka and at the commencement of the era of Saka (76 A.D.) there would be Sudra Kings of Kamrûpa (Mont. Martin E. India III, p. 404), which also shows Kâmrupa is Vaîsya-dêsa at that time; Kâlîkâ Pûrana (Ch. 38) says that Nârâyana came with Naraka to Prâgjyotîshpûra and killed the Kîrata king Ghataka of that place and installed Naraka as king, and established the Hindu people over the area from Lalîtakântâra to Karatoyâ river, and the Kiratas, were driven out of the place, and were forced to take shelter in the portion of country from Lalîtakântâra up to the sea. We thus find the Kirradia shown by Ptolemy as occupying country between Besades and the sea. Varâha Mîhîra (Brîhat Samhîtâ, Ch. XIV, pp. 82-86) puts the countries in this neighbourhood in the following order :—"Vîndhya country, Traîpura, Smasrûdhara, Hêmakûta, etc." thus showing that the Smasrûdhara people came between Tippara and Hêmakûta an outcrop of the Himalayas, and thus would appear to refer to this area and Ptolemy says that Tiladai are so called because they are short of stature and shaggy;" "Smasrûdhara" literally means "wearing beards", which would indicate these people to be Tiladai of Ptolemy and Tiladai is obviously corrupt form of Smasrû-dhara. Besades of Tiladai would therefore be the area north of Tippera and south of Brahmaputra, that is of Mymensing and Garo hills and their head-quarters at the ancient town of Tura. On the side of the river opposite to that of Besades is Passalae which as I have already suggested is Prâgjyotîshpûra. Kâlîdâsa (Raghû Vamsa IV, 81) puts it across the river

Lauhîtya, and near to Kamarûpa which is near Gauhati; Kâlîkâ Pûrâna (Ch. 38) says that Prâgjyotîshpûra is in Kâmakhyâ country, and Karotoyâ-Gangâ flows to its east, and it is near Brahmapûtra Laûhîtya river; Brahma Pûrâna (Ch. 219) mentions that "Kokâ river, flowing from the Himalayas was obstructed in its course by stone-boulders which were removed by Vîshnû in his form as Varâha and the river flowed by Kokâ-mûkha, where the place sacred to Vîshnû is situated; Varâha's wife Mahî in the form of Chhâyâ bore a son at that place, which is Bhaûma Naraka asûra to whom Vîshnû made a gift of Prâgjyotîshpûra". These accounts place Prâgjyotîshpûra to the west of Karatoyâ, north of Brahmapûtra, on the bank opposite to and in the neighbourhood of Gauhati, and on the river Koka flowing from the Himalayas; these conditions would indicate the locality opposite Goalpara where the Manas river joins the Brahmaputra and Jogighopa-tirtha is possibly the Vîshnûtîrtha of Brahmapûrâna, or Prâgjyotîshpura. Manasa river has its tributary, the Kokoloong river which may be Koka river, and the town itself would therefore be Bijni; the other localities which may represent the town, is Jogighopa, or perhaps Goalpara itself which may have been on the north bank of the river formerly but now extended to south bank owing to the oscillation of the river channel here. This locality in any case is Passalae of Ptolemy and I am inclined to think that Pachonia to east of Jogighopa and just at the junction of the Manas with the Brahmaputra correctly represents the site, and perpetuates the distorted name also.

Souanagoura lying midway between Passalae (Goalpara) and Kassidia (near Dhamdaha on Kosi), would point out to Koochbehar as the spot and I have no hesitation in identifying Koochbehar as Sounagoura, as it fits the position given by Ptolemy and its claim to antiquity, and lastly that Sonaram Chala village lying 5 miles south-east of the town perpetuates the name of the old town. This village is next to the Hindu-para which shows that the Buddhist advent which started Koochbehar as the Buddhist centre, forced the orthodox Hindu population to seek shelter in this suburbs of the old town, where the old name is still retained. The Bepyrrhos river as described was possibly known in the alternative as the Yamûnâ river; in Kâlîkâ Pûrâna (Ch. 83) it is stated that "the godly Yamûnâ river travels in company with Brahmapûtra, whom she leaves midway, but after travelling 12 yojanas meets the same Laûhîtya-nada again"; this has led Pliny to mention that Palibothra lies near the point where Jomanes meets the Ganges, though he makes a confusion between the two Yamûnâs owing to their identical name; it also suggests itself that the name of the river Amanat is another form of Yamûnâ.

This completes the tracing out of the course of the Ganges and its tributaries as delineated in Ptolemy's map and I will now proceed to discuss the broad changes in the course of this river.

CHAPTER IX

MAJOR CHANGES IN THE COURSE OF THE GANGES

From Ptolemy's map we find that the upper basins of the Ganges and Jumna drained westwards into the Indus, and the river was shut out from the eastern sea through Bengal, its outlet being by gorges and ravines through the Vindhya range at different points from time to time. The Yoga-Vâsîstha-Râmâyana (Nîrvvâna 21-89) states that "at one time Malaya, Darddûrâ, and Sahya mountains were not separate, and they were all one range of Vîndhya mountain". Orouidian Montes from its position is no doubt the Nilgiri range, including in it the Mahêndra Gîrî and Malaya to the east which extended to the Vîndhyas previously joining on to the Kaimur Range, and the whole of this is Darddûra which explains the name Orouidia. Ptolemy shows Meandros Montes, to include Garo and Khasia hills, Arakan and Pegu Yomas, right down to the Dwana range; the presumption is that this Meandros or Mahêndra mountain was joined on to the Darddûra, which was also Mahêndra Gîrî as one, thus forming a barrier on the sea coast over present lower Bengal area, preventing the river Laûhîtya and Ganges from finding an easy outlet to the sea in this length. Thus we find the Gangetic trough shut out from the sea by this continuous range of mountains from the Aravalli range right on to the Assam hills. This is the reason why we find in the Vedas, the Sindhu the main river, the Ganges trough being an inland sweet water sea between the Himalayas and the Vindhyas, but rapidly filling up as the whole of the silt was deposited in the trough, and a larger volume of silt was brought down by the rivers then, than now, as the rainfall on the hill faces was heavier than now owing to the proximity of the inland lake. Only the land near the base of the hills was then habitable. The outlet to begin with was only westwards through the Indus, which river was therefore in the Vedic period, the only river. As the trough filled up the Indus receiving almost all the silt, built up its banks at a rapid rate; at the same time the area of the lake of the Gangetic trough was sufficiently reduced to bring it under the category of a broad river, and the reclaimed land alongside offered an enormous fertile tract available for colonization. This disappearance of the inland lake in the Gangetic trough had a serious effect on the climatic condition of the Tibetan plateau as the proximity of the large water surface previously gave the plateau a more equable temperature to live in, and some amount of rainfall for growing crops. The Aryan population from Central Asia, who previously migrated to the north of the Himalayas, had therefore to force their way southwards and we find one section colonising Indus basin, and the other proceeding to Burmah, the northern Gangetic trough being then too dense a jungle to penetrate into. The spread of civilisation to the Indus basin and Burmah, separating in the north of the Himalayas is the view of Prof. Elliot Smith (*Scientific American*, May, 1926). I will return on this subject later on with more substantial evidence.

The Gangetic trough from Geological evidence is found to extend from the Salt Range to the Assam hills and the depth of alluvium in the trough 13,000 to 15,000 ft. (A. C. Das, *Rigvedic India*, p. 19). In 300 B.C. we find the trough filled up and the Ganges had come into being, but as given by Megasthenes who saw the Ganges and lived in Palibothra, and whose statement is therefore conclusive, the width of the Ganges, at the source even, was 30 stadia or 4 miles, and the mean width above Palibothra 100 stadia or 11 miles and depth 20 orguiae or fathoms, whereas the width of the Indus even at its mouth has been given much less than 20 stadia, as the log of Nearkhos' voyage (Part II, Arrian's Indika) shows his journey along the river at its mouth from Stour to Kammona 30 stadia, in one day, and Kammona to

Koreatis 20 stadia the next day, lengthwise. Then again the width given of the Ganges was presumably in the dry season, as flooding of extensive tracts of the country during rains must have been very frequent which would explain the elaborate laws enacted for safeguarding life and property during the flood season in the Magadha Kingdom, of Chandra Gupta which was along the Ganges above Palibothra and did not extend to the deltaic tract. One of the provisos given in Kaûtîlya's *Arthashâstra* (Book IV, Ch. III, Shamasastry's translation) runs as follows "Villagers living on the banks of rivers, shall, during the rainy season, remove themselves up-countries. They shall provide themselves with wooden planks, bamboos, and boats. They shall, by means of bottle-gourds, canoes, trunks of trees, or boats, rescue persons that are being carried off by floods. Persons neglecting the rescue, with the exception of those who have no boats etc., shall be fined three pans". This shows that in spite of the enormous wide and deep bed of the river available for spread of the flood water, the country along the river banks was flooded in the rains, which necessitated the inhabitants evacuating such areas at the time, and seeking shelter in higher lands up-country or rather the base of hills. In these circumstances, the neighbourhood of the Ganges was still then a veritable inland lake in the rains, of which free drainage to the sea was shut out by the Vindhyas continued on to Assam hills to the east and the Salt Range to the west. The pent up water was not only keeping the soil over the extensive area north of the Vindhyas saturated with water, but held up at a high level above the sea, was exerting lateral pressure on the Vindhya range, inducing its sliding towards the sea and thus bringing about great changes in its levels, particularly that of its several valleys and gorges through which the Ganges drained out from time to time. It is for this reason that the Ganges river outlets both main as also spills, through the Vindhyas, to the sea, underwent frequent changes at this period. We thus find the Ganges outlets at different places referred to in the Pùrânas from time to time, and it is impossible to trace their sequence.

Gaûtamî-Gangâ, which I have already shown to be the Narmadâ, must have been the main outlet for some time. Brahma Pûrâna (Ch. 78) shows that "Gangâ divided into two streams in Mahêsvara's plaits of hair. One stream proceeding at that place through the Vindhyas was known as the Gaûtamî and the other stream continued along north of Vindhyas and was known as the Bhâgîrathî Gangâ". As the dividing point was the Mahadeo hills, the Gaûtamî Gangâ or Narmadâ outlet was southwards from this point, and Bhâgîrathî Gangâ therefore must have flowed eastwards from this point, towards Rohtasgarh; a cursory look at the map will show that the channel must have been along the Hiran taking off from the Narmadâ at Sankot, running past Sihora, then joining the Mahânadî tributary, of the Son, and then the Son itself. The main river bed was thus practically along the Ken, and the place where it divided into Gaûtamî and Bhâgîrathî is Barmhan, which is Brahmatîrtha, about 10 miles northwest of Narsinghpur. This would explain why the Son is Hiranya-vaha, as it did flow from Hiranya or Hiran river, which in its turn is born of Brahmâ from Brahmatîrtha. This also explains why apparently the main river Son in its upper reaches is the 'Mahânadî' or the 'Great river'. The Bhâgîrathî at this stage was carried at a fairly high level, as its outlet past Palamau must have been a narrow gorge as the bed here had never a chance of widening out sufficiently to present to the river a satisfactory outlet in spite of the plentiful discharge of upland water available for a fairly long period to scour out a channel. This is why we find a spill from the Bhâgîrathî from near Rohtasgarh, flowing back into the Gaûtamî when Brahmâ Pûrâna (Ch. 125) says that "Vânî river joins with the Gaûtamî, and this Vânî river is again connected with Bhâgîrathî Gangâ, in which direction she is termed as Sarasvatî." Vânî river is no doubt the Wain-Ganga channel, which presumably flowed eastwards by the present upper Narmadâ channel, on towards Rohtasgarh or rather Palamau where remnant of the channel marked Sursootia Nadi appear on the map near Bhundarya to the west of Palamau. This is the same Sarasvatî river referred to in Bana's Harshacharîta (1st Uchchhâsa) where he says "Sarasvatî, seconded by Sâvîtrî, issued from Brahma-loka, and by and by came to the great river Hîranyavahâ, the son of the great progenitor of mankind (that is Brahmâ), full of clear and cool water, which river people call Sonâ".

The Gaûtamî Gangâ, or Narmadâ, must have been separated from the Gangâ, the locality at which the spill was cut off is clearly indicated by Chhindwara, or Chhînna-dvâra, which literally means the "gate of separation". The Gautamî having been cut off the main river then flowed wholly by the Bhâgîrathî channel or rather the Son, that is southwards from Kanauj to Chhindwara, and then a sharp turn eastwards to Rohtasgarh, a very tortuous channel for the main river. A shorter course must have opened out as a result and thus we find the diverted channel running practically straight from Kanauj to Rohtasgarh, as we see in Ptolemy's time. Until the Kanauj-Rohtasgarh straight channel was opened out and rapid exit of river discharge re-established, the cutting off of the Gautamî outlet must have temporarily resulted in serious rise of flood water level against the Vîndhyas, and it is at this stage that the conditions stated in Padma Pûrâna (Srîshtî, Sec. 19) that "Vîndhya began to grow in height, and Agastya proceeding with the dêvas to the sea coast, drank the sea water drying it up (at the coast). The dêvas finding the sea dry propitiated Vîshnû for relief, and Vîshnû assured them that Gangâ will fill up the sea again. The dêva-river flowing in a reverse direction, issued at Pûshkara near Agastya-rîshî's Asram." The sudden cutting off of the Gaûtamî, due to "the Vîndhya growing in height," deprived the river of a huge discharge of water spilled from the Ganges and the land near its mouth on the sea coast was therefore suddenly reclaimed, that is the sea dried up here and dearth of water made the dêvas approach Vîshnû for relief. The Dêva river, which is no doubt the Bangangâ, then flowed in the reverse direction, that is that the banking up of water behind the Vîndhyas was enough to force a spill discharge westwards through the Bân-gangâ for a time. That this is the Dêva river referred to, is apparent from Skanda Pûrâna (Avantya, Chatûrasîtî-lînga, 13) which says that "Gangâ where it descends from Vîndhya is known as Dêva-nadî, the eastern portion of which falls into the Sûlabhêda Kûnda is the Prâchî Sarasvatî river," and Padma Pûrâna (Srîshtî, 18) which says "Prâchî Sarasvatî river flows at Pûshkara," and (Avantya, Avantîkhêtra, 54) "Nîl-gangâ flowing by the south-east corner of Pûshkara, goes to the Vîndhyas where Marût-sûta is established, and then to Mahâkâla forest, where it falls into the Sîprâ-kûnda at Amarâvatî (Ujjaini), where she changed her blue clothes for white ones". This spill was shortlived, and the establishment of the short and straight channel of the main river from Kanauj to Rhotasgarh and a little deepening of the gorge below Palamau, was enough to divert the whole of the discharge to this channel and Prâchî Sarasvatî became an Antah-sîlâ or "subsoil flow" river in its middle length.

The Vânî-Sarasvatî link between upper Narmadâ and Ganges near Palamau, must have received a fair share of the spill from both from the Narmadâ as also the Ganges at Palamau later on when it rose in level, when Narmadâ connection with the Ganges was shut off, and that connecting river must have been spilling southwards into the intermediate sea and eastern sea at different points; the Skanda Pûrâna gives the names of the spill channels as follows. (Avantya Chatûrasîtî-lînga, 3) "Narmadâ river, born of Rîksha Mountain, asked for a boon from Shankara (Mahâdêva) that as Gangâ was well-famed in the northern country, she may be similarly famed in the southern country under the name Jâhnavîgangâ; of this Gangâ there are fifteen streams, Sona, Mahânada, Narmadâ, Sûrasâ, Kritâ, Mandâkînî, Dasârnâ, Chîtrakûtâ, Tamasâ, Bîdîsâ, Karabhâ, Yamûnâ, Chîtrotpalâ, Vîpâsâ, Balû-vahînî and Ranjanâ." The list shows sixteen rivers and probably Sona-mahânada would read as one river and not two. The important effluents are still traceable, the southern Sona channel running through Balaghat district is now a tributary of Wain-Ganga, Narmadâ is the upper Narmadâ beyond Chindwara which must have then flowed in a reverse direction, Krîtâ is the Krîtamâlâ river of Orissa already discussed, Chîtrotpalâ is the Mahânadî-Tel system already discussed. This shows, which way the spills ran, and it shows that when the Narmadâ connection at Chhindwara was cut off, a large amount of the spill flowed into the Narmadâ above Chhindwara, which found its way to the south sea by channels named above lying to the west, which eventually joined and formed the large river Wainganga or Kaveri or Kheberus of Ptolemy. Harîvamsa (Ch. 27) says "Jahnû married Kâvêrî, the daughter of Yûvanâsva; under a curse from Yûvanâsva, Gangâ, out of half of her own self, created the faultless stream of water Kâvêrî." This Jahnû referred to, is the same Jahnû who dried up the Ganges when the latter flooded the sacrificial platforms. These indicate the genesis of Kheberus or Kâvêrî, born of Ganges. At a later date spills into the Kaveri, from the upper Narmadâ, as also from the Ganges *viâ* the Son or Vânî-Sarasvatî system were gradually cut off, with the deepening of the Ganges bed below Rohtasgarh.

It will thus be seen that when the head of the Gaûtamî Gangâ was closed, the whole of the river discharge was forced into the Bhâgîrathî Gangâ past Palamau, excepting for a small amount of spill water flowing by the Kâvêrî which was the upper-Narmadâ-cum-Kheberus of Ptolemy or Wain-ganga, the bulk of the main river water thus flowing southwards by Palibothra into the sea. After this, the spills by the series of channels towards Orissa developed, considerably, as the opening out of a shorter channel of the main river straight from Kanauj to Rohtasgarh, brought the river water at the latter place with much less fall in surface level, which heaped up the water above Rohtasgarh to higher levels flooding the country and building up land fast as also raising the bed level of the main river along with it, thus inducing further rise of flood level in the locality which had the effect of diverting a considerable portion of the flood discharge into the huge channel of the old bed of the river, *i.e.*, the Son which offered a ready made outlet. The rise of level in this channel opened out spills through the valleys of the Vindhyas, and these valleys were so deepened and scoured out as to reverse the flow of the river at Palibothra for a time. We find that in Buddha's time, or about 500 B.C. Palibothra was the ideal site for building a city; subsequent to his time, the city's downfall was brought about by flooding, as we find it stated in Asvaghosa's Mahâyâna (Suzuki's translation Ch. I, 28) that "Blessed one prophecies, the growth of Pâtalîpûtta, but that three dangers of fire, of water, and of dissention will hang over it," a statement which is repeated by other Buddhist writers of the early Christian era. The temporary reversal of current took place in Asoka's time (273-232 B.C.) or 2½ centuries later as will be evident from the following passage in the Mîlînda-Pânha (Questions of Milinda, Rhys David's translation Book IV, Ch. I, P. 47). "When Asoka, the righteous ruler stood one day at the city of Pâtalîpûtra, amidst his people and ministers of state, beheld the river Ganges as it rolled along filled up by freshets from the hills full to the brim overflowing that mighty stream 500 leagues in length and one league in breadth, he said—Is there any one who is able to make the Ganges flow backwards and upstream? A certain courtesan, Bîndûmatî by name, a harlot woman of Pâtalîpûtra claimed the power and forced the river Ganges to flow backwards." It should be remembered that the reversal of flow at Pâtalîpûtra was also helped by the Laûhîtya or Bepyrrhos river of Ptolemy, pouring in a considerable amount of water at a point below Palibothra but very near to it.

Then filling up of the huge bed of the old river and raising the land along the banks of the Son above Rohtasgarh, was not however a work which the river took much time to accomplish, and we find therefore that before

Ptolemy's time, the Son has ceased to be a spill channel its bed level down to Rohtasgarh filled up to adjust itself as a feeder stream of the Ganges and all connections with the series of rivers in Orissa cut off and the main flow of the river Ganges confined to the channel past Palibothra, but the bed level of the river considerably raised above previous levels which flooded the country on its banks, and covered up under silt large areas on its banks including many of the low lying towns, not excepting Palibothra itself. The vicissitudes of Palibothra led to the removal of the capital to the higher lands across the Auranga river to Champâ-nagar present Chanpi Kalan, as (Ancient Palibothra by William Franklin) "Bhrîgû Samhîtâ manuscript says metropolis of Balîpûtrâ Râjâs was built one yojana west of confluence of Ganges and Erran-Bhowah at or near modern Champâ-nagar. Dhuruni Kosha commentary says that Jaya-Singga's messengers for investigating site of Champaca-nagar found the city of Baliputras swallowed up by the Ganges and the western extremity of the city was four or five miles from Bhagdant near Champaca".

In the upper section of the river, from the source to Kanauj, there was probably no great change from the Vedic period to Ptolemy's time as we find upper Jamuna and Upper Ganges up to Hardwar shown as tributaries of the Indus and draining into the latter. Land at the base of hills and along the main rivers had only come to be thickly populated and prosperous. The Royal road mentioned by Pliny ran parallel to the Himalayas from Thaneswar till it crossed the Ramganga and then turned south at Rudrapura, a town lying about half way between Nainital and Bareilly, which is evidently Rhodopha of Pliny. We see however that confusion has already been started between the two Ganges rivers, *viz.*, the Bhâgîrathî Gangâ past Hardwar and Ramgangâ past Moradabad, as in the distances given along the road, Pliny states that "Rhodopha from Ganges crossing is 119 miles, while according to others 325 miles," though he mentions no such disagreement beyond it. From Rhodopha the road turns south to Kalinipaxa, which is Kalyanpura in the northern suburbs of Cawnpore, a point which was the junction point between the Kalyani river with the Ramganga. Thus we see the river in Ptolemy's time was at the same place as described by Pliny. It must be remembered that Pliny, though he wrote in the first Century A.D., his description is based on much earlier information. There is one point in the channel lower down which requires explanation. Ptolemy shows Yamuna past Mathura, a tributary of the Indus, and the lower section as an independent tributary running from the Vindhyas, which he calls the Soa river, which I have already shown to be the former main river channel and is the present Ken river. How is it that Megasthenes, Pliny and others call it the Jomanes? I think the explanation is simple; before the straight main river channel from Ken-Ganges confluence to Rohtasgarh opened up, it has already been shown that retrogression of bed levels took place, inducing higher levels in the Ken, and water was forced westwards for a time, making a connection with the river past Muttra and the whole system thus had already been known as the Yamuna, which was already joined on to upper Yamuna past Panipat. The opening of the straight Ganges channel from Ken junction to Rohtas however must have subsequently given a great drop in the river levels again, and the Yamuna again was separated into different sections, till the changes in the Indus course westwards, finally restored the Yamuna connections *viâ* Panipat, Delhi, Muttra etc. That the Jumna flowed in the reverse direction for a time at Muttra is amply borne out by traditions which says that during a period of pleasure and plenty in the days of Krishna, Yamuna flowed full to the brim and in the reverse direction.

We have now described the major changes in the Ganges river up to the time of Ptolemy's Geography in the second century A.D., and will now deal changes brought about subsequently. The changes in the upper course of the river, are (1) the diversion of the upper Bhagirathi Ganga from its flow towards the Indus, into the Ramganga, thus forming the present Ganges and (2) similar diversion of upper Jamuna from the Indus, towards the east, thus re-establishing present Jumna river, by joining the upper Jumna, with the end of the Indus tributary towards Muttra, and bringing the combined stream on to Ken which joined the Ganges. The improvement of the straight Kanauj-Rohtas channel early in the Christian era, was probably slowly bringing into the sphere of upper Ganges basin, a part of the eastern Indus basin, but a sudden change of the course of the Indus from its eastern channel in Rajputana to the present western channel in Sindh, brought about also equally rapid changes culminating in the changes (1) and (2) mentioned above. When this exactly took place is difficult to find out.

Kâlîdâsa's time is still an uncertain factor (4th to 6th Cent. A.D.), and in describing Raghû's victorious march in the direction of Sindh, he has mentioned (Canto. IV, 59-69) in detail the westward march along sea coast up to Trîkûta hills (Junnar) after which he says the march was by land to Pârasîka country of Yavanas, and then turned northwards towards Hîmâlaya proceeding by the banks of the Sîndhû-nada (Indus), conquering the Hoon and Kamboja Kings on the way. He does not mention Raghû's crossing the Indus river, and thus it lends to a suspicion that the river had already changed its course westward, throwing a part of the Pârasîka, Hoon, and Kamboja Kingdoms of Indo-Skythia which previously must have extended to the eastern course of the Indus, to the east of the river. The account however is such vague here, that it shows obvious lack of Kalidasa's knowledge of these parts of the country. In Varâha Mîhîra's classification of countries (end of 6th Cent. A.D.) he mentions Panhava, Kâmboja, Sîndhû, Saûvîra, Vadavâmûkha, Araba, Ambashtha with Sîndhû-kâlaka, Raîvataka, Sûrâshtra, and Dravîda sea, all in the same group and this indicates that by then the Indus course must have already shifted westwards separating parts of the old Kamboja and Pahnava kingdom to its east.

Ebn Haukal (902-968 A.D.) describing this area,

starts with Sindh, where he says are cities of Seidan, Meimoun, Moultan and Heidour (page 147, William Ouseley's Translation), showing clearly that the river had been in its westerly course for some time or rather some centuries previously. He mentions however (P. 148) that "Moultan is not reckoned as belonging to Hindusthan" showing that tradition still prevailed pointing out exclusion of Moultan from India having been formerly west of the river Indus which was the former boundary of India. The mouth of the river which he calls the R. Mihran, he says is east of Dambul (P. 155) and to west of Daubul, the former is probably Dambh west of Karachi, and the latter Daben east of Karachi, and the Indus mouth, referred to as R. Mihran was perhaps an effluent, the remnant of which are Malir, Khadeji and Baran. His description shows however that the delta to the west had not been built up to any extent by then, and we may safely conclude that the change in the course of the Indus possibly was within 3 or 4 centuries prior to 900 A.D. that is between 500 A.D. and 600 A.D. The exact date of the flooding of Brahmanabad and its final downfall may possibly help us to bring the date of change of the Indus course to narrower limits.

The upper Jumna seems however to have been forcing the restoration of its connection with its middle section *i.e.*, the former tributary of the Indus from Mathura, *viâ* Muttra, Delhi, Hissar and Ghaggar river, by 400 A.D. as Fa Hien travelling at the time, after crossing Indus river goes south-east to Muttra; then he says (Legge's translation, Ch. XVI) "still following the course of the P'oona river, reached country, south of which is middle Kingdom ** ** ** . From the place where the travellers crossed the Indus to southern India and on to the southern sea a distance of 40 or 50 li, all is level plain. There are no large hills with streams among them; there are simply the waters of the rivers. (Ch. XVII). From this south east for 18 Yojanas to Sang-ka-shi kingdom". This presupposes that the last portion of his journey before he arrives at Muttra was also along the Jumna

(P'oona river), and that the country to south of it towards the southern sea, *i.e.*, towards the Ghaggar river was all one sheet of flooded country, and that Fa Hien found the Himalayan Jumna connected with the river past Muttra, and also that possibly a spill channel of the Jumna from Muttra to Sankissa (Sang-ka-shi) joining on to the Ganges at or above Kanauj, which the traveller followed. From Kanauj, the traveller proceeded "south-east for 7 Yojanas and arrived at Ki-jou-i on the Ganges." Ki-jou-i has been taken to be Kanauj because it is on the Ganges and on the way to Sravasti which latter has been previously identified with Sahet-Mahet on the Rapti river. If Sravasti however is found south of Benares, and if the confluence of Jumna and Ganges was at Asothar we find Kosambi exactly fits in with the site of Ki-jou-i of Fa Hien and I have no hesitation that Ki-jou-i is Kosambi as it was on the Ganges at that time, its direction is south east from Sankissa, and that "crossing the river Ganges and south 3 Yojanas" the pilgrim came to A'le (Ho-li in some texts) village which is without doubt the ancient town Halia, about 45 miles south of Bindhachal station of the East Indian Railway, between Allahabad and Mirzapore. This would go to show that the confluence of Ganges and Jumna had not in 400 A.D., shifted below Kosambi, though it must have shifted some distance below Asothar.

The course of the river from Kosambi to Palibothra as given by the Chinese travellers Fa Hien and Yuan Chwang, depend on the identification of the Buddhist townships in the locality, particularly of Sravasti, Kapilavastu etc., which have been taken to be in the Nepal border by previous authorities but which are all south of the Ganges. A digression here is therefore necessary to help us in tracing the course of the river in this neighbourhood, as described by these travellers. It has been shown conclusively that Pataliputra is Palamau, Vaîsâlî is Besaria Kalan near Palamau across the river Koel, and Kûsînagara is Kerwa and Pâvâ is Paharbula, both lying near the Rehar river on the old road from Besaria towards Bilaspur in the Central Provinces. Both Kapîlavastû and

Srâvastî are places within a fairly short distance of Vaîsâlî and the identification of these places with sites near the Nepal Border cannot therefore be correct, except to the extent I have suggested already that Asoka was led to different quarters for their identifications. It would be convenient to mention at the outset my conclusions as regards the identifications of these different places, and then to verify the sites with their description given in some of the leading Buddhist books. Kapîlavastû, the first capital of the Sâkyas is Rajkheta (23°-45′ N, 83°-13′ E) about 60 miles due west of Palamau; the second capital Dêva-daha is Deorwaha on the Rehar river where the unmistakable remnant of the Daha or Hrada or lake still exists about 30 miles to the west of Rajkheta; Srâvastî is Sarwath, 10 miles north-west of Rajkheta; Achîramatî or Achîravatî river or Sarâvatî river is the Ajher river a tributary of the Rehar, which runs past Sarwath; place where Chhandâka charioteer was left by Bûddha, is Buda-tand on Morne river, 7 miles south-east of Rajkheta; Setâvya is Juba, 14 miles east of Rajkheta on the way to Vaîsâlî. I will now proceed with the verification of these sites as given in Buddhist accounts.

Lalîta Vîstara (Ch. 15. Dr. R. L. Mitra's Ed.) says "Leaving Kapîlâhvya city, proceeding 6 yojans, Siddhârta made Chhandâka return, the Chaîtya on which site still exists." This site is still known Buda-tand or the "mound of Buddha". I have not seen the locality, but the name of the place indicates the remnant of Chaîtya which is called the "tand" or mound and hope a local investigation will disclose the Chaîtya. From this place to Vaîsâlî is not a long distance as from here (Ch. 16) "Bodhîsatva proceeds to Sâkya Brâhman's place, Padma Brâhman's place and then Vaîsâlî city" a distance which can only be reconciled if the distance is within 50 miles as in this case. Then we find (Ch. 17). "Buddha's meditation at Gaya, and King Suddhodana's despatch of daily messengers" a thing which would be unilkely from Nepal borders to Gaya.

In Abhînîshkramana Sûtra (translation of the Chinese

version by Samual Beal Ch. XVII) we find "Sîddhârta leaves Kapîlavastû by the East Gate, arrived at village Mi-ni-ka at sunrise where rishi Po-ka-pi dwelt, which was close to village Loma", and then (Ch. XX) "proceeds forward to village Ho-ni-me-ka and gradually to Pi-ye-li, in the midst of the way was Po-ka-pi rishi's place." Pi-ye-li is Vaîsâlî, and it makes the journey from Kapîlavastû to Vaîsâlî, not a long one like that from Nepal borders to Palamau. Midway between the two places was Poka-pi rîshî's or Bhârgava rîshî's place close to village Loma; Bâna in Harshacharîta (Canto. I) says that west of river Sonâ, is Chyavana rîshî's place and Chyavana rîshî, was of the Bhârgava descent; Chyavana's son Dadhîchî married Sarasvatî, and had two sons, namely Sârasvata the founder of Prîtîkûta and Vatsa the founder of the great family of Vâtsâyana's to which belonged the poet Bâna himself; then (Canto. II) Bâna invited by King Harsha's brother, proceeds from Prîtîkûta to Chandîkâ forest, Malla Kûta village, crossed river Bhâgîrathî and then arrives at Pâtalîpûtra, which makes it clear that Prîtîkûta was west of Vaîsâlî near to which is Chandîka forest, and that it lay between Vaîsâlî and Sonâ river, which fixes the place in the neighbourhood of Bhârgava rîshî's place indicated in the Abhînîshkramana Sûtra. This Bhârgava family are the Kâshî tribe described in Harîvamsa (Ch. 29), where it is given that Divodâsa who refounded Vârânasî, begat Pratarddana, who had two sons Vatsa and Bharga, and 14th in descent from Vatsa is Bharga the progenitor of the Bhârgava section of Kâshî tribe; this indicates that Bhârgava section of Kâshis, the Vajjians in Pâlî literature, had headquarters in Vaîsâlî and its neighbourhood next to the Vatsas of Kosâmbî. The exact place of Chyavana âsrama, or Bhârgava rîshî's place, I am unable to trace but I would not be surprised if Bagra lying midway on the road from Rajkheta to Vaîsâlî is Bharga, or Bhârgava rishi's place, and that Lawa village to its south is Loma village of the Abhînîshkramana Sûtra. Whatever may be the exact identification of Bhârgava's place, it leaves no doubt about the location

Kapîlavastû to east of Vaîsâlî, and in the neighbourhood of Rajkheta as Bhârgava's âsrama the same as Chyavana's âsram lying midway between Kapîlavastû and Vaîsâlî was to the east Vaîsâlî, a distance of one or two days journey and between the Son river crossing and Vaîsâlî. In Ch. IV of this Sûtra, it is stated that five of King Ikshâkû's sons were banished from Mîthîlâ, and "migrating to Hîmâtala Mountains and crossed the Bhâgîrathî, and ascended snowy mountain and founded a kingdom Kapîlavastû named after Kapîla Rîshî whom they found there, and they were called Sâkyas"; the only survivor of these 4 brothers was Kûrû, his son Gokûrû, his son Sînha-hanû, one of his sons Suddhodana married a daughter of Supra Bûddha, "a rich householder of Sâkya family established at Dêvadaha in Kapîlavastû." Rîshî Kapîla's place is clearly noticeable in Khuppurmunda, midway between Rajkheta and Vaîsâlî; Dêvadaha is the lake on the course of the river Rehar forming one of the frontier lines of the Kapîlavastû kingdom, and south of Deorwaha on this river, lying due west of Rajkheta indicates the locality, the lake in the river to its south represented the site Dêva-hrada or Deva-daha itself; the Hîmâtala or snowy mountain referred to must be Malaya gîrî, as this is reached from Mîthîla after crossing the Bhâgîrathî and cannot therefore mean the Hîmâlaya.

In Asvaghosha's Bûddha Charîta (Translation from Chinese by Samuel Beal, Kieuens II & III) the journeys are described without much detail, "Sîddhârta leaves home, morning in Po-kâ rîshî's place; then to Arâda rîshî's place and river Ganges". Po-kâ is evidently Po-kâ-pî of Abhînîshkramana Sûtra, or Bhârgava rîshî's âsrama and Arâda rîshî's place is Vaîsâlî. These localities have already been discussed in the preceding paragraph.

In Dîvyâvadâna (Nepalese Sanskrit edition, Cowell and Neil Ch. I.) Vâsavagrâma is given as a village near Srâvastî, and Bajara village a mile to north east of Sarawath probably indicates the site; the next description is of Sarâvatî river etc., of which the direction from Srâvastî is not indicated, but details given of the neighbourhood are as follows "Pûndravarddhana city, east of which is Pûndakâksha hills, close to which and to its south is Sarâvatî city after which is Sarâvatî river, then to the west is a Brâhmana village named Sthûnapâstha, after which is Ushîra hills". All these localities appear close to Sarwath to its west; Pûndravarddhana city is Padrî; Pûndakâksha hills is Pahar Padri to its east; Sarâvatî city would be given by Sarwath lying close to and south of Pahar Padri; Sarâvatî is the Ajhir river, which is Achîramatî of Buddhists which is the same as Sarâvatî, the river runs by Sarwath; the Brahman village to the west Sarâvatî, is Bomanpahari west of Sarwath, and of Ajhir river; Ushîra-gîrî next is Nowpathar hill. It will thus appear that Sarâvatî here is Srâvastî and that its location is very well defined. It must be noted here that this Pûndravarddhana is not to be confused with Pûndravarddhana city of Bengal.

The Life and Legend of Goadama as given in the Burmese book Mallalinkara Wouttoo translated by Bishop Bigandet, furnishes fairly good details. In Ch. I, the story of Ikshâkû's children establishing the Kapîla-vastû kingdom is given, but Ikshâkû is the king of Benares, the direction to which is perhaps a mistake as later on the king attacked with leprosy retires and settles near Kapilawaot country at a place where he built city Kaulya, separated from Kapilawat by river Rohani; this river Rohani or Hiran is the same as the one which is given as passing by Kusinagar, and is the Rehar, and Kaulya is no doubt Ramkola which though not on the Rehar river, but is on a sub-tributary of it, branching off from the Morne branch of Rehar; the founding of Dewaha is referred to, "the princes of Kapilawat, used to go for sport on the water of a lake, where eventually they built a city named Dewaha which had its king likewise of the Thagiwi race", and Deorwaha on the Rehar, referred to in the preceding paragraph is no doubt this second capital of Kapîlavastû kingdom belonging to the Sagara dynasty. In Ch. IV, we find "Sîddharta leaves Kapilawot travelled 30 Youdzana, arriving at River Anauma" from where

Tsanda was returned, and this exactly agrees with the place Budatand on the river Morne which latter is Anauma river, the distance of the place from Kapilavastu is exaggerated and it is obvious Siddharta did not travel 60 miles during half a night; then "Thidhat stops at Anupya belonging to Malla princes and then 30 Youdzanas to Radzagio, meets king Peimpathara, leaving which place he visits Rithi Alada, and then to Oorouwela"; Anupiya would appear to be Manpura, 2 miles west of Juba, and Rajgrîha of Bîmbîsara here referred to is Rajabas, where the king built his new place near Palibothra when the latter became flooded. In Ch. III, we find "Adzatathat makes a broad road from Koothenaron to Radzgio, 25 Youdzans" which makes Kusinagar on Nepal border and Rajgir in Gya an impossibility, the road is evidently from Kerewa near Paharbula to Gautam ferry at Palibothra.

Enough has now been said to show that Sravasti and Kapilavastu lay to the south of the Ganges, and I will now return to the course of the Ganges from Kosambi downwards.

Fa Hien in 404 A.D., went straight southward from Kosambi to Halia crossing the Ganges river only, and thus the presumption is that the confluence was above Kosambi as already stated in this chapter and also that the present Ganges channel to north of Kosambi had not come into being and that Ganges flowed by the present Jumna channel below Kosambi towards Benares. The pilgrim then goes from A'le or Halia, south east 3 Yojans, to Shache kingdom which latter is evidently the northern frontier of the Sakya kingdom, from where 8 Yojans south-east came to Sravasti, which would exactly fit in with the site as given by me; 4 li north west of Sravasti the pilgrim says is the grove called "the getting of eyes" which is Phulidumar literally meaning the removal of cataract of eyes. The pilgrim then goes to Kapîlavastû, thence (Ch. XXV) 10 yojans east to Vaîsâlî, 3 li north-west of which is the tope of "Bows and weapons laid down" which is Turuk Telya village. Thence (Ch. XXVI)

4 yojans east to confluence of five rivers, the place of Ananda's parînîrvana, where (Ch. XXVII) the river is crossed and descending one yojans reached Pâtalîpûtra. This confluence of 5 rivers is evidently the point to the west of Daltonganj, where the Ganges, *i.e.*, present north Koel, received the Amanat, the Auranga, and the Jinjoi from the east, and the remnant of the Sarasootea from the west. The main river though not named here, is the Ganges, as the pilgrim so names it on a subsequent journey, and thus this course of Ganges was still alive in 404 A.D. The pilgrim then proceeds making a short (Ch. XXVII to XXXI) reference to the distance southward to Nala, then goes evidently from new Rajgriha of Bimbisara to Gya; an explanation is necessary here as to how this route is possible if Palibothra is Palamau, and Rajgriha is Rajgir in Behar, and I would point out that new Rajgriha referred to here by Fa Hien is not Rajgir, but Rajhara, a suburb of Champikalan or the new capital Champa, and about 4 miles north of old Palamau; the details of the neighbourhood are explainable as it will be apparent that the old capital in ruins lying 4 li south, is no other than Palibothra, the Vulture Cavern in Gridhrakuta hill is Harilaong hills, a name from Hargil or Vulture, Parasia or wasteland to north being the Smasâna or cremation ground, Satbarwa is the Sratparni cave, Devadatta's rock is Dewahar east of Palamau in the position given.

Four yojans west of New Rajgriha, the pilgrim mentions he found Gaya city now desolate, to the south of which is Buddha's place of 6 years austerities, ½ yojan northeast is the cave of Buddha's meditation, and ½ yojan southwest, the pâtrâ tree, the place of Buddha's obtaining wisdom. The ruined city Gaya is not traceable in the map, but 8 miles to the west of Champa, there are unmistakable indication of its location as we find the small river now called Buda river or Buddha river which is no doubt the Nairanjana river of Budhists; Bodhi tree is marked on the map, lying to the west of the river; to the west of the Bodhi tree appears Kantaipatra, the site of the pâtrâ tree tope round which Fa Hien found brickwalls built by Asoka; across the Buda river, lying northeast of Bodhi tree is shown Orsa, the Urûvîlva of Buddhists, immediately to the south of which is shown the Orsa Banian Tree, the famous Banian tree of Urûvîlva.

A little digression is necessary here as to the location of Vârânasî as given in the Abhînîshkramana Sûtra (Translation from Chinese by Beal, Ch. XXXIII) where it describes that "after obtaining light at Urûvîlva, Bûddha journeys towards Benares, reaching Chandre (beautiful and bright), then Tchundajira (without horn-strike), then Karnapura (city of ear), then Sarathi (harmonious royal city), then Rohitavastu, then R. Ganges south bank, crossed over to north bank, passes by dragon tank Sankha (serpent) where Nagaraja raised a tower called Medica (earth tower), then reaches Benares deer park." If we follow from the Bodhi tree as above, we come to its southwest to Khando, or Chandre; then further southwest to Siringikona, which is "without horn strike" or Tchundajira; then eastwards to Kanchi, which is taken for Karnapura or "city of ear"; then Saraidi to its east, which is Sarathi; then eastwards to Ratasilli which is Rohitavastu; then river Ganges is reached, which is exactly in the position of Ptolemy's Ganges as indicated by me, and crossing to the north from Ratasilli it brings us to the source of the Sankha river where Sankha-Hrada or dragon tank Sankha is located and then we find Barwenagar on the Ganges at this point which is Vârânasî-nagar of the Abhînîskramana Sûtra. This Varânasî was however missed by the Chinese pilgrims and the Varânasî visited by them was unmistakably the present Vârânasî founded by Dîvodasa which had become so luminous in fame as to dim out of existence other places started with the same name.

The pilgrim then returns from Gya and goes to Benares described as follows (Ch. XXXIV) "Fa Hien returned from here (Gurupada Mt., near Gya) to Patali-putra, keeping along the Ganges descending west ten yojans came to the "wilderness" pursuing the same course west twelve yojans came to Baranasi (Polo-nai in text) city in the kingdom of Kasi; * * * * thirteen yojans northwest is Kausambi". The term descent used evidently has not the meaning of going down the stream, and the description is that the short road ran along the Ganges, from Pataliputra to Benaras, 25 Yojans, and the first length through the "wilderness", which is no doubt the Chandîkâ aranya, and the course is therefore *viâ* 'Chan-chu' of Yuan Chwang, which is modern Bijaygarh, and the course of the river was from Pâtalîpûtra to Rohtasgarh along the Koel, and then turning westward up the Son river to south of Bijaygarh, from where it ran straight towards Benares, through the low lands. Fa Hien then returned to Pâtalîpûtra and (Ch. XXXVII) "following river Ganges, descending eastwards 18 Yojans came to Champâ on the south bank; continuing east 50 Yojans came to Tâmalîptî, a seaport" from where sailed to Sînghala island on his return journey home. He must have followed the Ganges of Ptolemy, southwards, passing by Champa near Mahuadanr, and then to Tamralipti, which is perhaps Tamluk. Thus we see that in 400 A.D., or so, the Gangâ-Yamûnâ confluence was above Kosam, the present Jumna bed the combined Ganges channel below that point, and then from Benares the river ran straight along low lands to Bijaygarh then followed the Son to Rohatasgarh, and then turned south by Koel passing by Palamau, through the Kaimur range to the sea as in Ptolemy's time.

We will now follow the route taken by Yuan Chwang in his travels in 629-645 A.D. Earlier in this chapter, the route taken $2\frac{1}{2}$ centuries earlier by Fa Hien, in the upper course of the river has been given. Yuan Chwang, like Fa Hien, proceeds from the Punjab to Muttra first and then goes up to Thaneswar. This leads to a suspicion that though the Ghaggar had raised the land along near Hissar, affording a negotiable country for a traveller from Punjab to Muttra, the eastern Patiala area was impenetrable, either due to overflowing by the upper Jumna spilling towards Indus, or that though not a swamp it was in the next stage, that is a jungle; this gives as a corollary that the Jumna connection westwards had ceased, even before Fa Hien's time, and it had rejoined its connection with the channel past Muttra. Yuan Chwang then proceeds from Muttra to Thaneswar (On Yuan Chwang's Travels translated by Thos. McWatters, Vol. I, Ch. X, Chuan IV), thus giving a clear indication that upper Jumna connection with Jumna past Muttra had been in existence for at least two or three centuries previous to his visit, as the country along the banks of the river was prosperous and easy for travellers; Fa Hien did not make this detour, but he may have proceeded straight towards Kanauj as his intended stay in India was not as long as Yuan Chwang's, and we are not in a position to draw any conclusions as regards the nature of the country from his omission to visit Thaneswar. Yuan Chwang then takes the Old Royal Road referred to by Megasthenes, going 400 li east from Thanesvar to Su-lu-kin-na on the Yen-mo-na, and then 800 li further east to river Ganges, crossing which is Moti-pu-lo, northwest of which is Gangadvara. Moti-pu-lo or Matipura is Mandwar, and Su-lo-kin-na or Srughna has been taken to be Sugh, north west of Saharunpur; the system of road from Thanesvar to Mandwar however goes southwards, and Singhoa, close to Karnal to its north-east where the road crosses the Jumna, answers to the identification with Srughna. From Matipur the pilgrim goes south east 400 li to Ka-pi-shaung-na, and 400 li further in the same direction to Ngo(or O)-hi-chi-ta-lo, the former identified with Govisana or modern Ufain and the latter Ahîchchhatra ruins of which exist in Ramnagar 20 miles east of Bareilly in Rohilkhund; then south 260 li *crossing the Ganges* to Pilo-shan-na, and then south east 200 li to Ka-pi-tha, the old name of which is Seng-ka-se, the former is identified with Virasana or modern Atrenjikhera on west bank of Kali-nadi and the latter is Sankissa. It will be seen that from Ufain (Govisana) to Ramnagar (Ahîchchhatra) the Ramganga has to be crossed of which there is no mention, though one would expect this as the river in this reach is broad, and the direction of the journey does not agree as Ufain to Ramnagar is south west instead of its being south east. The direct road from Mandwar seems to be indicated in the route, and if we take Ka-pi-Saung-na to be Pipalsana near Moradabad, Bajhera on the Ramganga 20 miles south of Bareilly as Ahichchhatra, Pilkhana lying 9 miles west of Aliganj and about the same distance north of Sankissa as Pilo-shanna we get the obvious route. The conclusion as far as the Ganges course is concerned is that the Pilgrim crossed the united stream of Ganges and Ramganga in his journey from Bajhera (Ahîchchhatra) and Pilkhana (Pilo-shan-na or Virsana). The different localities suggested by me have all claims to antiquity except Pilkhana which identification I offer doubtfully and would not be surprised if Baksena almost opposite Bajhera, is the old town Virasana. Whatever may be the identification, one thing is clear that the Ganges was united with the Ramganga by 630 A.D., at a point near Bajhera; the confluence shifted down rapidly later on to Kanauj, destroying the old city as mentioned by Alberuni in 1030 A.D., who says (Alberuni, translation by Sachau, Vol. I, Ch. XVIII, P. 199). "Kanoj lies to west of Ganges, city being in ruins and capital transferred to Bari, distance from Kanoj three or four days march". The havoc created by the rapid shifting of the confluence downwards may be realised from the precaution taken to shift the new capital to a safe distance of three or four days march from the river and to the east side, as the river having destroyed the city which was to the east of it in Yuan Chwang's time, oscillated back towards west, which was then the vulnerable bank along which the encroachment proceeded. We thus realise here the changes in the course of the Gange up to Kanauj, practically up to the present day, as we see that the confluence point has practically ceased to shift downwards after Alberuni's time.

Yuan Chwang next proceeds from Kanauj which lay to the east of the Ganges (Vol. I, Ch. XI, Chuan V) 700 li southeast, crosses the river Ganges, and reaches A-yu-t'e, and then turns eastwards 300 li crossing the Ganges to north reaches A-ye-mu-ka, thence southeast 700 li crossing the Ganges to its south, and north of Jumna is Prayaga. The directions are quite clear, and A-yu-t'e cannot be Ayudhya, as from Kanauj to west, crossing river goes to A-yu-t'e to east of the river, then the river turns eastwards which is crossed again and to north is A-ye-mukha, after which the river is recrossed at Prayaga. From Prayaga the pilgrim goes 500 li southeast through forest to Kosambi. Thus about 640 A.D., the confluence was still west of Kosam, perhaps confluence of Baruna with Jumna at Kot was the Prayaga of the time, practically the same as in Fa Hien's time no further slow shifting down of the confluence was worked up, the subsequent change must have come by sudden avulsion later on. The Ganges course was therefore, from Kot, *viâ* Baruna channel to Asothar, then joining on to the Ganges north of Fatehpur, thus leaving Chhaunka the Aye-mu-kha of the pilgrim to the north of the channel, and further up the existing Ganges river is followed, and A-yu-t'e is very likely Utri-pura on the main road midway between Cawnpore and Kanauj.

From Kosâmbî, the pilgrim goes to Srâvastî and Kûsînâra and then to Vârânasî. In this circuit of journey we find omission of directions in some, and discrepancies at others which lends to a suspicion that Yuan Chwang did not find the exact places, which were all in ruins and in the jungle, as already found by Fa Hien two Centuries earlier and in a bit of the country of which the author of Mallalinkara Woutto from information wrote that (Bigandet's Goadama, Ch. VII, P. 163) "the inhabitants of Magatha country hate Rahans". Thus Yuan Chwang goes (Vol. I, Ch. XI, Chuan V) from Kosambi 700 li northeast crossing the Ganges to Ka-she-pu-lo, thence 170 li north to Pi-sho-ka, whereas in "the life" Kosambi to Pisoka on way to Sravasti, is 500 li east; then again (Vol. II, Ch. XIII, Chuan VI) from Kapilavastu to Kusinagara is given as northwest through forest country giving no distance, and says that "the salgrove of Buddha's parinirvana 4 li northwest of the capital", whereas Kusinagara was an obscure little village only and Kapilavastu the capital at some distance from the locality of parinirvana. The accounts become clear again from Varanasi onwards, and we can safely conclude that the pilgrim returned to Benares after a vain search for the hallowed places of Buddha's life which lay neglected in ruins in a country overgrown with jungle and where Buddhists were hated. This part of the journey has therefore to be scrapped and we may now follow the course of the river from Benares downwards.

Yuan Chwang proceeds from Varanasi (Vol. II, Ch. XIII, Chuan VII) along River Ganges 300 li to 'Chanchu', which literally means 'War Lord' and I think it must be Bijay-garh, 'Vijay' meaning "winning the War" or "Winner of the War" or War-lord; thus the Ganges channel, left the present channel probably just above Benares, turned southwards, by the present bed of the Chandraprabha river, passing by Bijaygarh joined the Son channel immediately to its south; then 200 li east Yuan Chwang came to A-pi-te-kalana, which is Butto Kalan on south bank of Son; then 100 li on south of Ganges he passed Mo-ha-sho-lo, on the south bank of the Ganges which is Mussorya Kalan on the south-bank of the Koel; then he goes to Vaisali or Besaria Kalan; he refers to Rohtasgarh as "an old city in ruins with few inhabitants, lying 200 li north west of Vaisali, where Buddha in a former life as Mahâdêva gave up his kingdom and became a Bhikshu"; he confirms place of Ananda's parinirvana given by Fa Hien, and places it "on the Ganges and 30 li southwest of Vaisali." We see here that the course of the river was the same as in Fa Hien's time, but described in detail which enables us to trace the exact line. It differs a little from Ptolemy's course, and the change had been brought about by the Ganges river opening out a straight channel from Benares to the Son near Bijaygarh, and abandoning the longer route from Benares *viâ* Sasseram and to east of Rohtasgarh; as a corollary the channel from Monghyr, which joined the Ganges channel to west of Sasseram was now diverted by the channel which is now the lower section of the Son from near Sasseram to its present confluence with the Ganges above Patna. Yuan Chwang evidently did not visit either Gaya of Hindus or Buddha-Gya near it, but refers to them here when he says that "Northeast 500 li from the place of Ananda's Parinirvana to Fu-li-chi (Vriji) country, the chief city called Chan-su-na in a ruinous state; to the northeast of the great river (Mahanadi) is the tope of conversion of fishermen; thence 100 li northwest is 100 ft. high tope on the west of old city; the 1400 to 1500 li to Nipolos (Nepala country)"; it will be seen from the direction given that Chan-su-na corresponds to Parsawan on the Morhar river, about 10 miles to the south of Sherghati on the Grand Trunk Road, a locality full of ancient remains still lying unexplored, and Bich-killa lying about 10 miles south of Parsawan appears to point out the remains of the fort or killa of the Vrijis; the Morhar river is the 'Maha' river referred to by the pilgrim and 100 li to north east of this brings us exactly to Buddha Gaya, the 100 ft. high tope of which is referred to by the pilgrim, near the 'old city' which is no other than the Gaya of Hindus which all the Chinese Buddhist seem to have ignored.

Yuan Chwang now goes to Gaya of the Buddhists and the Bodhi tree in southwest of Dt. Palamau, in the same site as visited by Fa Hien. The pilgrim proceeds (Vol. II, Ch. XIV, Chuan VII) "from Vaisali south across the river Ganges to Magadha, where south of the Ganges was an old city formerly called Kûsûmapûra afterwards Pâtalîpûtra." The description is quite clear and Pâtalîpûtra is now south of the Ganges, and it shows that Palamau being Pâtalîpûtra, the river Ganges is now flowing by its north that is by the Amanat river; then "southwest 200 li is an old monastery, and from there 100 li southwest to Ti-lo-shi-ka", this latter is modern Turer, "90 li south west of which is a lofty mountain," which is the high hill of 3095 ft. altitude near the town; "crossing the river Nairanjana, 40 to 50 in southwest is Gaya Mt. * * * * * * east across the 'Maha' river is Pragbodhi Mt., and 14 or 15 li southwest of it is the Bodhi tree on the Nairanjana river." This brings us exactly to the Bodhi tree of the maps, near the Budh river, the same as visited by Fa Hien.

From here the pilgrim returns towards Palamau as (Vol. II, Ch. XV, Chuan IX), "from the Bodhi tree he goes east across 'Maha' river, 100 li east to Kûkkûta-pâda gîrî" showing that going eastwards, he crossed the abandoned Ganges channel, which took him to Chandwa or Kud-lut which is Kûkkûtapâda-gîrî, the hill extending from Kukud or Kûkkûta hill to north-west of Mahuadanr, and "thence 100 li north east to Buddhavana giri," the latter is Kumandi forest, and "thence 30 li east to Yasti-Vana valley" the latter being modern Latehar, and Yastî-grâhaka of Bâna, Lategaunh of Aelian. Then he gives details, showing that from "Yasthîvana to Kusagrapura is 60 li, connected with a broad road constructed by Bimbisara", and this broad road from Latehar to Chatti Satbarwa exists to this day. Kusagrapura is Rajgaha, present Daltonganj, a city which extended as far east as Chanpi Kalan, that is Champaka of the Jains (Ch. VIII), to the west, the then Ganges river to the east, and Amanat to the south, and towards the north along Ganges to Rajhara and Pandwa the latter being the Pandava mount of the Buddhists; this locality requires a closer examination to trace the details of the old city as given in Buddhist accounts and by the Chinese pilgrims. A superficial examination of the map shows Sat-Barwa, the "Saptaparnî cave in Vebhara hill"; Harilaong as I have already pointed out is Grîdhrakûta; Kalapahar about 15 miles north is the "Black rock on the slope of Mt. Isîgîlî"; Majholi is Maddakuchchhi; all of which are mentioned as situated near Rajgaha in Asvaghosha's Mahâyâna (Ch. III, Susuki's translation from the Chinese). Ambabar lying about 25 miles to west of Daltonganj is no doubt Amba-lathtaka or Ambâ-râstra mentioned in most of the Buddhist books, a place which is very near

Nâlândâ, the site of which must be looked for within a radius of 8 miles of Ambabar.

Yuan Chwang goes from Rajgaha (Chuan IX) or Daltonganj 160 li southeast to Kapota monastery, thence 70 li northeast on south bank of Ganges a Hindu city, thence 100 li east over hills to Lopen-ni-lo, (Chuan X) thence east 200 li through mountains to I-la-na-po-fato country of which the capital towards north was close to the Ganges, thence following the Ganges bank 300 li east to Chanpo country and its capital on the south bank of the Ganges, thence 140 li east to a Hindu town on south bank of Ganges, thence 260 li east to Kie-ch-wen-ki-lo, thence east 600 li crossing the Ganges to Pun-na-fa-tan-na; this shows he travelled from Daltonganj in a general direction north eastwards 1100 li, through mountanious country along the north boundary of which the Ganges flowed, up to Kie-cha-wen-ki-lo, and then 600 li and crossing the river, goes to Pun-na-fa-tana or Pûndravarddhana. From Pûndravarddhana he goes east 900 li crossing large river to Ka-mo-lu-po (Kâmarûpa), thence 1200 li south to San-mo-ta-ta (Samatata) on sea side, then 900 li west to Tan-mo-lip-ti (Tâmralîptî) port, thence 700 li northwest to Kie-lo-no-su-fa-la-na (Karnasûvarna); in the accounts in his life, he does not make this detour but goes from Pûndravarddhana straight 900 li south east to Karnasûvarna, by the side of which is Ki-to-mo-chi ('red mud' or Rângâ-mâtî) monastery, south east of which lay Samatata, thence west 900 li to Tâmraliptî; combining the two, we see that the pilgrim makes Tâmralîptî 1600 li south east of Pûndravarddhana. We thus see that while Yuan Chwang went from Râjgâhâ 1700 li, east to north east, to Pûndravarddhana, midway to which lay Champâ, and from Pûndravarddhana to Tâmralîptî 1600 li south east; while Fa Hien goes from Pâtalîputra near Râjgâhâ, eastwards 18 Yojans to Champâ and continuing the same direction 50 Yojans further to Tâmralîptî; it is apparent therefore that the Champâ of Yuan Chwang is not the Champâ of Fa Hien, though both were on the Ganges and the conclusion is that Fa Hien travelled by the abandoned

Ganges channel, through the Vindhyas, while Yuan Chwang travelled along a new channel of Ganges opened out and established as Ganges bed by 750 A.D. I will now attempt to trace out this new channel, which, it is clear from the pilgrim's account, was in a direction east, and northeast from Daltonganj, and skirting the northern base of a range of hills up to Pûndravarddhana, as he states frequently that in this reach he goes through mountainous tract of country and the chief towns situated at the northern extremity of the hilly kingdoms, and on the south bank of the Ganges; a little before Pûndra-varddhana, the river was crossed when the journey was continued in the same direction, and this shows that the channel turned here towards the sea which was to its south or south east. This shows that the Ganges had found its opening into the sea between the Rajmehal and Garo hills, and was thus flowing from Daltonganj eastwards to Pûndravarddhana and then southwards. The pilgrim says later on (Chuan X) that in going from Pûndra-varddhana to Kâmrûpa he had to cross a large river, which can only be the Karatoyâ-Laûhîtya system, and as the river is mentioned particularly to be large, it indicates that the Tsangpo or Brahmanada had already burst through the barrier below Brahmakund, and has thus been diverted into the Laûhîtya which had thus become the Brahmapûtra. The combined discharge must have raised the level of the swampy country of Bengal, and as its outlet by the Damodar channel to the old Ganges near Tamalites was at a high level and too long a lead, the headed up water in Bengal swamp induced a slip into the sea and subsidence of land on the seaface, through which, the Brahmaputra now found a nearer outlet to the sea over friable soil where it did not take much time to scour out a deep channel for itself. The withdrawal of this discharge of water from the old Ganges channel from below Tamalites must have greatly accelerated the death of that channel, which in its turn affected the reach of the old Ganges channel above Tamalites through the gorges in the hills, that is up to Daltonganj. We thus find the

Ganges flowing straight from Benares towards Rhotasgarh, brought its waters against the Vindhyas at Daltonganj, below which the channel had been closed, and this water thus obstructed, found an outlet eastwards, where the Brahmaputra had already done the spade work by opening out a channel to the sea, lowering the level of the great swamp of Bengal in that direction; the likely sequence of changes we would expect is that the Kosi river which flowed westwards into the Ganges of Ptolemy would, when its waters were headed up first divert its course eastwards into the Brahmaputra or by an independent channel through the subsided land to its west, the line of which was obviously *viâ* Karagola, and that the Ganges, obstructed at Daltonganj, flowed straight from Daltonganj towards this bend of Kosi near Karagola, thus skirting the northern base of Kaimur range and the Rajmehal hills, which gives exactly the direction given by the pilgrim.

Having now fixed the line of the channel roughly I will now follow in detail the track taken by the pilgrim. From Râjgâhâ (Daltonganj), Yuan Chwang goes about "30 li east to Nâlândâ" the exact site of which I am unable to trace from the maps; "20 li southwest of this is Ka-lo-pina-ka town," which is Panki, west of Ambabar; "150 li north-east of this is the Kapota monastery", which is Khapia lying on the road. "North east 70 li of this and on the south of Ganges is a populous town with Deva temples" which appears to the ancient place Kunda which lies almost due north of Khapia, the ruins of which and the remains of nalas and old channels about the old fort shows where the shallow bed of the Ganges was for a time. "From this east 100 li over hills is Lo-pen-ni-lo", which is Lowalang situated about 20 miles southeast of Khapia and right on the hills. (Ch. XVI, Chuan X) "From Lo-pan-ni-lo east 200 li through mountains to I-la-na-po-fa-to country, the seat of Yakkha Bakula, and its capital on its north was close to the Ganges", and this I-la-na-po-fa-to or Hîranyaparvvata, seems to have its peak at Heranhopa, close to and south of Lowalang, but the country at its base lying to its north east in the valley was possibly known by the same name and the town Chatra on the road from Lowalang is evidently the capital of the country referred to by the pilgrim, the situation of which indicates it was on the former river. "From I-la-na-po-fa-to east following south bank of the Ganges 300 li to Chanpu country," and the road from Chatra along the valley eastwards, leads the traveller to Chauparan on the Grand Trunk Road, and this Chauparan is evidently Champâranya, that is Champâ forest which exists to this day as one of the most dense forest, and was the dreaded Danwa-Bhalua jungle of the pilgrims along the Grand Trunk Road during the last few centuries; the capital of the kingdom Chanpu of the Pilgrim, is Chanpi kalan about 3 miles south of Bhalua on the Grand Trunk Road, which was in a commanding position on the point from where flowed the Mohana river, as one of the biggest spill channel of the Ganges when it flowed past Champa. "From Champâ, east 400 li to Kie-chu-wen-ki-lo country, where both Buddhist monasteries and Dêva temples existed pell-mell, and the native dynasty extinguished some centuries before the pilgrim's visit, so capital deserted," and in a note to the text we are told that "the popular name of the country was Ka-ying-kia-lo;" this town is present Kawakol to which we are led by the road from Chauparan *viâ* Kodarma, running in a north easterly direction; the ruins of temples here indicate its importance of old though the ruins have not yet been properly explored but the little that has been done shows that some of these temples are built on, and incorporate parts of very old Jain temples; the pilgrim refers to this city which he found deserted, as "a Belvedere of stone and bricks with inscribed images of Buddhas and Devas", which are probably the unexplored extensive ruins at Satgawan on the Sakri river, south of Kawakol hills, of the later Gupta period. "From Ka-chu-wen-ki-lo east crossing the Ganges, 600 li to Pun-na-fa-tan-na full of deva temples, 20 li east of which is the Buddhist establishment of Po-shih-(kih)-po"; east or a little inclined to north from the east across the Ganges is Purnea or Puronya as its old name is, and the distance from Kawakol is about 120 miles which would answer to 600 li (100 miles) roughly, and the old road passing by Bhagalpore indicates the route of the pilgrim and I have no hesitation in suggesting that Puronya is Pûnravarddhana; the only other place which would obscure the vision in this identification is that offered by Perua or Pandua north east of Malda but the greater distance, and the absence of mention of hills on the journey by the pilgrim precludes this identity, as Yuan Chwang, has all along in this journey from Râjgâhâ mentioned the hills and hilly tracts passed by him and it is unlikely that he would omit to mention the prominent Rajmehal hills which he would have had to cross if he went towards Perua or Malda and his journey in this reach must have been over open area along the base of hills; the Buddhist establishmnet of Poshih-pi, lying to west of Purneah is now untraceable but it is possible that Bishnoopur lying 6 miles to east of Purnea is the locality. From Purnea the pilgrim went "east 900 li crossing large river to Kamo-lu-po", east of which he mentions are hills towards China; the name of the river is not given, but in T'ang-shu it is given as Ka-lo-tu, which may perhaps be Karatoya, which at that time was biggest feeder of the Brahmaputra which had already come into being, but was undergoing so rapid changes, bursting first into the Laûhîtya, and then receiving the Kosi diverted towards it with the Ganges water mixed up, that its name at different reaches offered a problem for the time being. "From Kamrupa 1200 li south on the sea side is San-mo-ta-ta (Samatata) country" and "from Samatata west 900 li to Tan-mo-lip-ti (Tâmralîptî)" and "from Tâmralîptî northwest 700 li to Kie-lo-na-su-fa-la-na (Karnasûvarna) beside the capital is Lo-to-wei-chi (Rakta-mrîttîkâ) monastery"; in the Life, Lo-to-wei-chi is given as 'Ki-to-mo-chi' meaning literally "red earth," and Karnasûvarna is placed 900 li south east of Pûndravarddhana; the distances given are the only guide and though he travelled through a stretch of country where he must have crossed big rivers, he does not mention them, and curiously enough Yuan Chuang after leaving Kamrup, though he proceeded by lower Bengal, Orissa, Southern India, and then along the western countries to Afganisthan, has scarcely mentioned any rivers excepting the Narmada and the Indus in this long detour, not mentioning even recrossing the Ganges which he had to do on his way from Kamrupa to Kalinga or Orissa; these facts lead to a suspicion that the pilgrim returned from Kamrup to Pundravarddhana and then proceeded to Karnasûvarna, and that his information regarding Samatata and Tâmralîptî is given from hearsay accounts. Taking this distance and direction into account, Samatata country must be the flat country of lower Bengal, which was formerly the bed of the swamp which was fed by Laûhîtya spill which could not find an outlet to the sea to its south as a ridge intervened and the level of the river was also banked up to high levels, to the north of the swamps owing to the long distance and high country the river had to go through below to Tamalites to discharge its waters to the Ganges; thus conditions were favourable to induce silt deposit in the bed of the swamp till it was suddenly exposed and reclaimed when the Laûhîtya abruptly opened out for itself a short cut to the sea, in which operation the bursting of the Brahma-nada into the Laûhîtya, and pouring in of a much larger volume of water into the latter than could be passed through the gorges in the Vîndhyas into the Ganges, must have played the major part; Karnasûvarna would take us to near Purulia, and Kesargarh on the Kasai river, 12 miles east of Purulia, from its position and antiquity appears to be the capital of Karnasûvarna country and the Kasai river, is not Kansâvatî as some people have suggested, but Karnasûvarna river, and the site of the "red earth" monastary is in Rangamati on the Kasai, about 10 miles to the west of Purulia.

The identifications of the foregoing places, which are connected with the position of Ganges in relation to them, enables us now to fix the course of the Ganges from Daltonganj downwards in Yuan Chwang's time. The river coming against the Vindhyas obstructed in its course at Daltonganj, spilled its waters eastward passing by the channel of the Amanat up to Ambabar, then through the valley of Chako river, passing to north of Lowalang, then passing close to Chatra to its north, then close to Chauparan to its north, then to north of Kawakol from where passing by Kiul, it joined its present bed at Surajgarh above Monghyr. The question will be raised that if the sacred Ganges flowed by such a channel how is it that substantial remnants do not exist and the reply will be found on the maps; the channel was a short-lived one, through which the waters were spilling; it had no time to deepen its bed for a permanent channel for accommodating the full rainy season discharge and had been thus spilling northwards into the old Ganges-Kosi channel through the large number of rivers intervening which give evidence of it, the chief ones are the Punapuna, Morhar (Buddh), Phalgu made up of Lilajan and Mohana, Panchana, Sakri etc. The biggest volume was disposed of by the nearest channels, that is the first three, mentioned above the Puna-puna deriving its name from its spasmodic existence from a freakful spill, while the enormous beds of the Morhar, the Phalgu and its affluents the Lilajan and the Mohana, from the point of spill to their present confluence with the Ganges as indicated by me, afford positive evidence that such beds could only have been furrowed out by an enormous amount of spill water which must have passed through these channels at one time. The discharge derived from their present catchment cannot possibly account for the dimensions which exist even now, though perhaps 10 centuries have elapsed since the spill was cut off and the bed has partially been contracted by silting; it is this that has given Phalgu river its remarkable sanctity even to this day and an attempt to term it the Sarasvati for a time (Mont. Martin's Eastern India Vol. I, P. 13), and its classification for a time as a "mahâ-nadâ" or a very large river. In a later interpolation in the Mahâbhârata (Vana, 95) also we find the river is termed as "Mahâ-nadî" in connection with sacred Gayâ "where Bhâgîrathî appears like a patâkâ (flag, evidently triangular shape), and descends from hill to hill, and like a mother overflowing the countries to its south as also the country of the Sagara tribe," thus graphically describing the exact condition of the country at this time. To the south of Gayâ the river in spill flooded the whole length of the country to the east of the line from Daltonganj northwards to Sasseram, tapering down eastwards as it disposed of its flood water through the Punpuna, Morhar, and Phalgu, thus appearing like a "patakâ". This condition was short-lived as the river after spilling the country, dropped the silt in the Gaya district spill area, and the clear water flowing eastward into a confined channel deepened it along Monghyr and Rajmehal, while at the same time the bed level above the spill area was raised; the result was a sudden avulsion of the river, making a short circuit from Benares to Patna, and finally abandoning its channel from Benares, *viâ* Bijaygarh and Daltonganj. The narrow tortuous channel of the Ganges from Benares (or rather Chunar) to Patna is ample evidence of this change in fairly recent times, the avulsion being started by spills from below Chunar, which furrowed out the Karamnasa river as one of the outlets and gave it the name as a "destroyer of works" which it then fully deserved; but directly the spill over a broad belt of the country where previously no channel existed, was restricted to a confined and deep bed scoured out by the great velocity with a steeper gradient, the channel adopted a tortuous course to adapt the bed slope to the general slope of the river above and below this reach, giving us the Ganges channel between Chunar and Patna as we find it now.

I'Tsing who visited Bengal, in 673 A.D., that is, shortly after Yuan Chwang left, proceeded (I'Tsing, translation by Takakusu, Para XXXI.) "from Tâmralîptî by road straight to the west; a distance of 10 days' journey from Mahâbodhî Vîhâra passed a great mountain and bogs, the pass dangerous and difficult to cross, defiles dangerous and attacked by robbers; escaped and reached a village at night". Then (Ch. XXXII) "from this village northwards for a few days arrived at Nâlândâ. . . . . Afterwards came to Mahâbodhî Vîhâra". Tamralîptî, he says is 60 Yojans from Mahâbodhî and Srî-Nâlândâ. This description makes it clear that he proceeded west from Tamralîptî by roads in level country, up to the foot of the mountain and then followed the valley of a river with dangerous defiles to the neighbourhood of Mahâbodhî, a description which can only apply to the road to the Bodhî-tree site in Surguja estates; the pass is evidently the valley through which the Ganges flowed in Ptolemy's time but which had at the time of I'Tsings' visit, deserted this outlet and as a result the prosperity of the country on its banks dwindled down, and the old road through the valley had become overgrown with forests, and became a shelter for robbers. His escape from robbers and consequent giving up the idea of visiting Mahâ-Bodhî for the time and proceeding north for a few days of difficult journey to Nâlândâ, shows also that the likely place he encountered the robbers was near Champa, the deserted old capital near Mahuadanr which was now reduced to a village to which he escaped; the direction and possible distance to Nâlândâ near Daltonganj also agrees with his description. This account of I'Tsing shows that the Ganges had already deserted its course through the Vindhyas, sometime previous to his visit.

From poet Kâlîdâsa's work, we can glean that the Ganges near its outlet still followed by Ptolemy's channel as (Raghuvamsa, IV, 34-38) Raghû visits the eastern sea coast, where the Vanga King comes in a fleet of boats to meet him, and he is conquered and Raghû fixes the pillar of victory in the island in the midst of the Ganges, from where he goes to Utkala or Orissa crossing the big unfordable Kapîsâ river by a bridge of elephants; then again winding up his circuit of conquest Raghû (IV, 81, 82) proceeds from Hîmalaya mount. to Prâgjyotîsha and Kâmrûpa after crossing the Laûhîtya river. This shows that east of Ptolemy's lower Ganges was then a country accessible by boats only, that is that lower Bengal was a deep swamp, and that the Brahmapûtra had not then burst into the Laûhîtya. The difficulty is regarding the date of Kâlîdâsa, and I am inclined to accept the earlier date of 4th Century A.D., as by FaHien's time (400 A.D.) the Ganges, as also the Brahmapûtra—Laûhîtya channels must have flowed through lower Bengal as shown already.

In Alberuni's time we find present Ganges course established to the head of Bhagirathi. Going along the Ganges he gives "from Benarasi east 30 farsakhs to Sarwar, Pataliputra 20 farsakhs, Mungiri 15 farsakhs, Junpa 30 farsakhs, Dugumpur 50 farsakhs, Gangasayar 30 farsakhs, where Ganges flows into sea." Sarwar is Garwar north of Buxar, the transcript is possibly due to the double line of g گ being merged into a single line of s ش. Pâtalîpûtra is now Pâtnâ founded by Pâtalî and quite different from Pâtalîpûtra of Buddhists; Mungiri is Monghyr; Jaunpa brings us to Jangipur; thus the river in this portion had adopted the present bed. From Jangipur to Gangasayar which is Gangâsâgara or Sâgar island estuary, the river passes by Dugumpur, which from the distance given would take us to Digambarpur which was in a commanding situation where the Churni river branched off from the Bhyrub. The remnants of the bed of the Bhyrub prove to this day of its being for a time the biggest effluent of the Ganges branching off from Jangipur towards the south-west, and the Ganges channel referred to by Alberuni in this length was along the Bhyrub from Jangipur to Digambarpur and then by the Churni back into the Bhâgîrathî channel at Nadîâ.

We may now sum up the major changes in the Ganges channel, from Ptolemy's time (140 A.D.) onwards as follows :—In the upper section, the Jumna past Muttra was connected with the upper Jumna past Panipat by 400 A.D.; the Ramganga also connected with the Bhagirathi Ganga by that time; the confluence point of Ganges and Jumna, which was at Asothar, was moved down below to Kot by 400 A.D.; the confluence shifted down to Allahabad by 1030 A.D. In the middle reach the river channel from Chunar, *viâ* Saseram and Rohtasgarh towards Daltanganj was abandoned and the route from Chunar (Benares) southwards *viâ* Bijaygarh, joining the previous channel to south of Rohtasgarh, established by 400 A.D., the channel below Daltonganj penetrating the Vindhyas showing signs of closing up; by 750 A.D., the Ganges channel below Daltonganj through Vindhyas had closed up, and the river below Daltonganj, flowing in a reverse direction from Daltonganj to Monghyr by a new straight channel between these two points, but spilling freely over the country to its north, and sending the bulk of its discharge through the Son, Punpun, Morhar, and Phalgu rivers; by 1000 A.D. the Chunar (Benares) to Patna straight connection was firmly established for sometime and the channel *viâ* Bijaygarh, Daltonganj to Monghyr abandoned though this change probably took place a century or two earlier. In the lower reach of river, we find the Ganges course through the Vindhyas below Daltonganj partly closed up by 400 A.D., and by 750 A.D., it is completely closed; the river was thus diverted by Monghyr eastwards and flowed into the swamp of lower Bengal gradually after 400 A.D.; it appears as if for a time the swamp was in its turn draining into the easternmost of the old Ganges delta channel, that is, the Anandapur river or Antibole mouth of Ganges, but with the further closing up of the river channel below Daltonganj, the swamp level was raised high for a time, which made the country of Vanga accessible by boats only, till probably within a century the subsidence of the sea coast of lower Bengal was brought about, and possibly the Bhagirathi route, that is Rajmehal-Saugorisland route opened up; about this time also, *i.e.*, after Kâlîdâsa and before Yuan Chwang, the Brahmanada or Tsangpo burst through the Brahma-kund into the Laûhîtya; the opening out of deep channels of the Ganges and the Brahmapûtra through the subsided land at Bengal coast resulted in the sudden reclamation of the swampy area of Bengal, in about the 7th Century. The 'Swatch of no Ground' at the head of the Bay of Bengal opposite Haringhata estuary, indicates the former existence of a subsoil fissure connecting the Bay with the Bengal swamp when it was kept up at a high level with a barrier at the sea face; this fissure must have been suddenly scoured out to huge dimensions below surface with greater velocity of flow of water through it induced by greater head of water pressure when difference of levels became fairly great, resulting in scouring the bed of the sea at the outlet thus creating the pot hole in the sea now known as the 'Swatch of no Ground'; this in turn induced the subsidence of land arching over the scoured out fissure and the soil caving in closed up the fissure. The position of the "Swatch of no Ground" in relation to the courses of the Ganges and the Brahmaputra, indicates that the Brahmaputra-Laûhîtya river was the first to open out its channel to the sea through the plains of Bengal, and the Ganges changed its course later on, and that they had their independent outlets, the Brahmapûtra and the Bhâgîrathî. In the beginning of the 11th Century the Ganges had sent out a powerful effluent channel towards the east from Jangipur which is the Bhyrub river as gleaned from Alberunis' account. By the 15th Century we find the Padda established firmly as an effluent taking off further eastward than the Bhyrub and supplanting it, as in Vansîdâsa's Padmâ Pûrana written early in the 15th Century, Behûlâ's raft floating up the Bhâgîrathî Gangâ passes by (Padmâ Pûrâna, edited by Ramnath Chakravarti and Dwarkanath Chakravarti, pp. 577-584) "the bend at Godâ was in front, which took a quarter day to pass, leaving which the raft came to the tri-junction of Padmâ, from where the Gûnjarî river also issues" which gives the Padma offtake above Goda-gari Ghat; Abul Fazl writing in 1596 A.D. (Ayeen Akbari, Gladwin's edition, Vol. II, p. 5 and 6) says "Main river in Bengal is Gung; near town Cozyhatta in Sircar Barbuckabad at which it is called Padhawutty, it sends a branch to east which meets sea at Chittagong, the main river going southward forms three streams Sirsutty, Jown, Gung, collectively called Tirpunny. Another river Berhampootter runs from Khatai, to Coach thence through Bazooha to sea," which shows that the Padma course was practically what we see to this day; this course is also shown in De Barros' map of 1510-20 A.D., the Brahmapûtra having an independent outlet, meeting the Padmâ at the lower end of its estuary; the Brahma-Vaîvarta Pûrâna (Ch. 109) mentions that "Gangâ, discovered in company with Srîkrîshna, in fear of Râdhâ, hid herself in Harî's feet, in the shape of Gângînî river, but when pardoned, she came out, when Padmâsana (Brahmâ) took her in his bowl and emptied the bowl pouring Gangâ at the head of Mahêsvara (another name of Bhaîrava), after which Padmâ was ordered to create Brahmânda (new lands evidently)". The time of Brahma-Vaîvarta Pûrâna is uncertain but probably earlier than the 15th Century; this would lead us to conclude that Padma as an effluent probably started in the 14th Century if not earlier. The last of the great change, *viz.*, the Brahmaputra, bursting into the Padma was in the floods of 1787.

The changes previous to Ptolemy's will be more or less speculations based on the changes in the Indus and Narmadâ etc., already given. The starting point is when we see the mountains girt by water, either of the sea or fresh water, that is the Bhârata-dvîpa or the Vîndhyan island, the Vârûna-dvîpa or Aravalli island, the Gândharva-dvîpa or Garo hills island, and Jambûdvîpa or Burmah being the Meru mount island; the Bhârata-dvîpa joined on to the other islands thus enclosing the Gangetic trough; the Sindhû or Indus then came into being building up land of the Punjab and we find the rivers in the Vedic period, which is the Sîndhû only, with Gangâ, Yamûnâ, Sarasvatî in a bunch joined on as one of its tributaries, the existence of the eastern Ganges ignored, it being still an inland sea. The next stage we find the eastern Gangâ formed, but spilling to the sea south of Vîndhyas, by several channels including the Kâvêrî (Kheberus) through these hills; finally the number of these channels were restricted into two, that is the Gautamî Gangâ or the Narmadâ, and Bhâgîrathî Gangâ or Ptolemy's Ganges; next we find Gautami Gangâ cut off, the Bhâgîrathî Ganga (Ptolemy's channel) becoming predominant, but a spill westwards by Prâchî Sarasvatî opened up; upper Jumna formerly a tributary of the Indus, already joined with the Sarasvatî now forms one system and becomes the Yamûnâ and a tributary of the Ganges, as the eastern Bhâgîrathî Gangâ (Ptolemy's Channel) deepens and develops; next stage we find Bhâgîrathî Gangâ (Ptolemy's Channel) deteriorating again, and the western Sarasvatî outlet had become too high, by the Indus raising the land along her course, to be reopened again with the result that the Ganges began to spill through the Vindhyas by several channels, between Bundelkhund and Palamau, (early in this Chapter) the important ones being the Kâvêrî (Kheberus of Ptolemy), the Son (Son and southern Son a tributary of the Wainganga), the Mahanadi (Chîtrotpalâ), and this was in Asoka's time in the middle of 3rd Century B.C. (early in this Chapter), which gave southern India of the time, including Kalînga, the phenomenal prosperity; the Yamuna as a result of Ganges to the east rising in level was again forced to flow westward and again separated into different lengths; the next stage is that the Ganges spills though the Vîndhya were cut off, only Ptolemy's channel through Vindhyas existing, but resulting action was banking up of water in the eastern area in Bengal, and this is the stage we find in Ptolemy's map; the re-assembling of the Yamuna must have followed the shifting of the course of the Indus westwards, subsequent to Ptolemy's time, the exact time of which I am unable to fix.

This completes the major changes in the Ganges from the beginning to date. The minor changes in the delta tract of the Ganges in recent dates are too numerous to be dealt with here.

CHAPTER X

INTRA-GANGEM INDIA OR BHARATVARSHA DESCRIBED IN ANCIENT LITERATURE; SUBSEQUENT BROAD CHANGES

From the examination of Ptolemy's map, we are now in possession of the actual boundaries of India as known to the western world at the time. India as taken by them is divided into two parts, "Intra-Gangem" and "Extra-Gangem", the former is India bounded by Himalayas to north, southern sea running parallel to Vindhyas to south, Ganges flowing by Palibothra to east, and Indus to west; Extra-Gangem India lies to east of Ganges flowing by Palibothra, the sea to its south, the Magnus Sinus or the "Great Gulf" to its east, and to its north the continuation of the Himalayas; this boundary gives an area which practically coincides with Bengal and Burmah of the present time.

Megasthenes confirms the general topography of Intra-Gangem India of Ptolemy, so that we know that India did not undergo much change during four Centuries. Megasthenes (about 300 B.C.) says that the shape of India is rhomboidal, bounded (Fragment II, McCrindle) on the east right onward to south by the great ocean, on the north by Kaukasos mountain to its junction with the Taurus, on the north and north-west up to the ocean by the Indus river and (Frag. IV) on south and east run into the great ocean; the lengths given are, east to west 16,000 stadia and north to south 22,300 stadia. Arrian (2nd Cent. B.C.), amplifies this account, and says that the western boundary is the Indus from source to island Patala 13,000 stadia and then 3,000 stadia beyond jutting out into the sea or a total of 16,000 stadia, which is the breadth of India, and the length west to east up to Palimbothra 10,000 stadia and 10,000 stadia headland projecting into sea or a total of 20,000 stadia. The lengths are exaggerated, as we find from Peshawar to Chaul is about 1,100 miles on a straight line, giving about 10,000 stadia as against 16,000 of Megasthenes and Arrian; from Peshawar to Palamau along the royal road is 1,100 miles or 10,000 stadia is given correctly as it was measured; the length beyond Palamau to the Ganges mouth and then to Vizagapatam is however 600 miles or 5,500 stadia against 10,000 stadia given by Arrian, a very much exaggerated figure, as it is given by guess. The general shape however is exactly as given by Ptolemy. Strabo merely confirms or rather repeats Megasthenes' account. They are all silent about Extra-Gangem India.

The local name of India adopted in Sanskrit literature is "Bhâratvarsha", meaning literally the "country of Bharata". Confusion has arisen from an attempt on the part of authors of the Pûrânas to avoid stating that there are two distinct Bhâratvarshas, one in Jambûdvîpa that is Burmah, and the other to the south of the Himalayas and north of the sea, which is India. The authors of Pûrânas were not prepared to make known the exodus of Aryans from Burmah, at the same time the love for the original home prevented their expurging from the original texts the accounts of the Jambûdvîpa Bhâratvarsha altogether. Thus we find in Brahma Pûrâna that in Ch. 27, Bhâratvarsha, south of Himalayas described in detail and then in Ch. 28 to 60 details of sacred places in India are given, and then in Ch. 70, it says that "The Bhâratvarsha which lies in Jambûdvîpa is a sacred place of paramount importance", indicating clearly a different Bhâratvarsha. In Skanda Pûrâna in Kasî Khanda, Purvarddha, first portion, sacred places in India are described and then in Ch. 22, it jumps to Jambûdvipa Bhâratvarsha, indicating that it is a different one from Indian Bhâratvarsha. In Vâyû Pûrâna in Ch. 43, Bhâratvarsha between Hîmâlaya an dSouth sea is described, as consisting of 9 islands, Indradvîpa, Kasêrû, Tâmraparnî, Gabhastîmân, Nâgadvîpa, Saûmya, Gândharva, Vârûna and Bhâratdvîpa, then details are given of the Bhâratvarsha which is India; subsequently in Ch. 48 Bhâratdvîpa is said to consist of many islands, and to south of it at a distance are Anga, Yama, Malaya, Lankâ, Sankha, Kûmûda and Varâha islands; this description would be quite superfluous unless another Bhâratvarsha is meant, and the islands to its south indicate, this Bhâratvarsha is in Burmah. These two Bhâratvarshas, practically correspond to Intra-Gangem India and Extra-Gangem India of the Greeks. Bearing in mind the distinction of these two Bhâratvarshas, it is not very difficult to distinguish the descriptions of them given in different places in the Pûrânas, though in some cases they overlap each other and in some cases they are merged into each other hopelessly. Indian Bhâratvarsha is evidently named after Bharata, the son of Rîshabha, the first Jaîn Tîrthankara; in Skanda Pûrâna (Kûmârîkâ Khanda 39) it is stated that "In Kalî era, different religions opposed to Hinduism will be introduced in the name of Rîshabha, whose son is Bharata; Bharata's son Satasrînga had eight sons and one daughter named, Indradvîpa, Kasêrû, Tamradvîpa, Gabhastîman, Nâga, Saûmya, Gandharva, Varûna and Kûmârîkâ; Satasringa was king of Sîmhala, and returned to his kingdom; this king divided Bhârata Khanda to his nine children". From the names of the nine islands forming Bhâratvarsha we find that these are named after these nine children. In the same chapter later on we find it mentioned that "Kûmârîkâ subdivided Bhârata Khanda into 72 divisions and allotted each division to 72 of brothers' sons, each of his eight brothers having nine sons". The name of these 72 subdivisions given there show that they must have been at a very much later date, as a single generation cannot account for India passing from the nine island stage to the 72 division stage, the names of which including Bardhamâna, Sîmhala, Lankâ, Gaûd, etc., indicate extensive reclamations since the nine islands stage.

Though in the Pûrânas accounts are given of divisions, rivers, cities, which formed at a recent date, they have in some place or other referred to the Bhâratvarsha composed of nine islands. As there is unanimity in describing this stage it enables us to speculate on the probable form of Bhâratvarsha of that time and I propose to investigate it briefly here.

The nine islands forming Bhâratvarsha as given in the Vâyû, Brahma, Matsya, Vîshnû, Skanda, Sîva, Agnî and Vâmâna Pûrânas are :—

(1) Indra-dvîpa.

(2) Kasêrû, or Kasêrûmâna or Kasêrûna.

(3) Tâmrâparnî or Tâmraparna or Tâmravarna or Tâmradvîpa.

(4) Gabhastîmâna.

(5) Nâga-dvîpa.

(6) Saûmya (Katâha is given in this place in Vâmana Pûrâna).

(7) Gândharva (Sîmhala is given in this place in Vâmana Pûrâna).

(8) Vârûna (Chârana is given in Sîva Pûrâna).

(9) Bhârata, or Bhârata-dvîpa, or Bhâratvarsha (Kûmârîkâ and Kumâra-dvîpa are given in this place in Vâmana and Skanda Pûrânas respectively).

This shows a stage previous to that of Ptolemy's. By Ptolemy's time Tâmraparnî island (Taprobane) had joined with the Naga-dvîpa (Nagadîva), and the seven remaining islands joined on to the mainland. The positions of these islands may now be traced, as each one of them must have included in it, either a range of hills, or high tableland, to maintain themselves as islands, at a time they were surrounded with water.

(1) Indra-dvîpa :—Skanda Pûrâna (Kûmârîkâ Khanda 39) gives the position as follows—"The rear (paschâta) portion of Mahêndra mountain is Indra-dvîpa". Mahêndra mountain is the northern portion of Eastern Ghats, and Indra-dvîpa, its rear portion (or it may mean the western portion which comes to the same) is the area to the north of the Indravati river, consisting of the hills of Bastar district and the tableland to its north.

(2) Kasêrû or Kasêrûmâna—The location is not given, the name indicates, it is Kasêrû or the 'Mêrû', or 'Backbone', island, and I have no hesitation therefore in locating it in Arakan, containing in it the 'Yomas'

which means literally the 'backbone' and which will be shown later on to be part of the Mêrû's of Jambû-dvîpa as referred to on the Pûrânas. This island is therefore the area of Chin and Lushai hills.

(3) Tâmraparnî, or Tâmravarna, or Tâmradvîpa—This is no doubt Tâmbapanni of Buddhist literature and Taprobane of Greeks, with the north eastern portion of Taprobane left out as separate island Nagadiva, which latter was an island previously as indicated by its name given in Ptolemy's map.

(4) Gabhastîmâna—'Gabhastî' means 'Sun' and this island is the island sacred to the Sun; its location is probably the Punjab and western U.P. area, with the Salt Range, and Sewaliks and including the tableland below them, which as an island was probably separated from the Himalayas by a very narrow belt of fresh water sea which closed up as the Indus river started building up land at the base of the mountains. Sun worship was predominant in ancient times in this area; the Mârtanda temple near Srinagar is a noted example; in Skanda Pûrâna (Kâsî Khanda, Pûrvarddha, 49) it is stated that "In ancient times, the god Sun established in Panchanada, the form of Sîva known as Gabhastî-îsvara, which is known as Mayûkhâdîtya; this form of Sîva has been established at Kâshî-pûrî". The eastern tongue of the island probably extended to Kudarkote, 24 miles east of Etawah beyond Agra at a later date, as this has been identified with Gabidhumat which was governed by Haridatta at the time of Siladitya II of Kanauj (*vide* Nando Lal Dey, Geog. Dictionary, p. 59).

(5) Nâga-dvîpa—This is the north-eastern portion of Taprobane, consisting of the tableland of Warangal, comprised in the Nalgonda district, where Nagadiva town of Ptolemy is situated. This is without doubt the first Nâga colony in communication with Burmah, and the innumerable Nâga-kâls spread all over the area marks this out as the Nâga-dvîpa. In Mahâbhârata (Bhisma 6) where although the accounts given of Jambûdvîpa are mixed up, the following statement which refers no doubt to India, is

made :—"Nâga-dvîpa and Kâsyapa-dvîpa are like the two ears of Sasasthâna; in Sasasthâna is placed Tâmraparnî hills and Malaya mountain; Sasasthâna is the second island of Jambûdvîpa". Sasasthâna means the "rabbit area" and it is made clear that it is so called as its reflected outline is seen in the Moon, where the rabbit like outline is noticeable. Kâsyapa-dvîpa is the area referred to in the Mahâbhârata (Vana 114) as "the hilly country presented to Kasyapa by Brahmâ, which falling into the hands of men, subsided in rage to Rasâtala, but through the power of Kasyapa's austerities was again raised above the sea; * * * from Kalînga it appears like a raised ledge on the sea". From this description it is clear that the Kâyaspa island was off Kalînga coast, and ran parallel to the coast so that it appeared like a ledge in the sea; it was therefore an island lying between Indra-dvîpa and Nâga-dvîpa as shown (Fig. 2). Now the island containing Tamraparni hills and Malaya mount is no doubt Tamraparni island, and a look at Fig. 6 will show the remarkable likeness with the "rabbit" outline in the Moon. This Kâsyapa-dvîpa as such is also a 'Sasa-Karna' or "rabit-ear" island, the Sesiura or Sesikrinei—island of Greeks; the description bears out no doubt the location of the Nâga-dvîpa also.

(6) Saûmya—This island is the area which probably formed later on the 'Sûhma' subdivision, one of the five subdivisions of eastern India allotted to each of the sons of Balî, the great Dânava king. This area is placed in Brihat-Samhîtâ (Ch. 16) between Vanga and Kalînga, and the island is therefore to be taken as comprising the table-lands of Mayurbhanj and Keonjhar States, containing eastwards to the Bhâgîrathî mouth. The Vâmana Pûrâna gives Katâha in place of Saûmya, which leads to a suspicion that its author wanted Siam near China to be taken as this island.

(7) Gândharva—the Gândharvas were a race dwelling in the hills and wilds, as given in the Mahâbhârata. The Vîshnû Pûrâna has a legend of these Gândharvas fighting the Nâgas in Pâtâla, which indicates their location in the

proximity of Nâgas. The Sânkhya and Vêdânta schools of philosophy recognise eight lokas or regions of material existence :—(1) Brahma-loka, (2) Pîtrî-loka, (3) Soma-loka, (4) Indra-loka, (5) Gândharva-loka (6) Râkshasa-loka, (7) Yaksha-loka, (8) Pîshâcha-loka; this seems to locate the Gândharvas between Indraloka or Amarapura area of Burmah and the Raksha and Yaksha lokas or Arakan, the home of the Rakaing and Yakaings (*vide* Max and Bertha Ferrars' Burma, P. 3). This island therefore is to be taken as consisting of the Garo and Khasia hills, lying between the valleys of the present Brahmaputra and Surma rivers.

(8) Vârûna—The area must necessarily be near the Punjab, the Vedic India, as Varûna is essentially one of the oldest Vedic deities; he is given as the father of Pûshkara and the place sacred to Pûshkara near Ajmer narrows down the identity. The western Vâsîstha tribes claim Varûna as their ancestor, and the home of this tribe was south of the Bisambritae of Megasthenes or Vîsvamîtra tribes, their opponents. This island is therefore the Kshatrya country with the Aravalli range and tablelands surrounding it.

(9) Bhârata-dvîpa—This is the last island and the most important island, and is described in detail. The Skanda Pûrâna has got Kûmârîkâ island, and the Vâmana Pûrâna Kûmâra island in this place. Kûmârîka or Kûmar-dvîpa forms the western portion of the Bhârata-dvîpa as described in other Pûrânas, so it is not necessary to dwell on these different names given. Matsya Pûrâna (Ch. 114) says "the ninth island of the group forming Bhâratvarsha is the Bhârata-dvîpa which is surrounded on all sides by the sea; this island is 1000 Yojanas wide from south to north, and extends from Kûmârî to the Ganga river Channel". Vâyû Pûrâna (Ch. 43) says "South of the east and west extended tableland on south of Himalaya, and north of south sea, is Bhâratvarsha; the dimension south to north is 1000 Yojanas, and extends from Kûmârîka to the Hîmâlaya 9000 Yojanas along a curve". Brahma Pûrâna (Ch. 19) says "north of the south sea, and south

of Hîmâchala is Bhâratvarsha," (Ch. 37) "south and east of Bhâratvarsha is the great sea and to the north is the Hîmavâna mountain like a bow". Agnî Pûrâna (Ch. 118) says "north of the sea and south of Hîmadrî is Bhâratvarsha, extended 9000 Yojanas in length and 1000 Yojanas north to south". In these descriptions there is no doubt some confusion with Bhâratvarsha, and its component Bhârata-dvîpa but as the Bhârata-dvîpa is clearly described as surrounded on all sides by water, it is certain that this island is separated from the Hîmalayas and that its northern boundary is like an arc of a circle, the southern boundary its chord, thus the whole thing compared to a bow. The width is 1000 Yojanas and length 9000 Yojanas, the length extending from Kûmârîkâ to the Ganges; Skanda Pûrâna, Kûmârîka Khanda, describes in detail Kûmârîkâ, a portion of the country named so (Ch. 37) after princess Kûmârîkâ or Barkarîkâ, the daughter of king Satâsrînga, son of Bharata, the son of the Jain hier-arch Rîshabha; the localities included in Kûmârîkâ are, a part of Saûrâstra (Ch. 4) and country on the sea where river Mahî falls into the south sea (Ch. 3). The length of Bhârat-varsha is therefore from the western tongue of the Satpura Range to the west, to the Paresnath hills to the east, about 900 miles; the width varies from a point to about 250 miles at the broadest part, giving about 100 miles average; the dimensions of length 9000 Yojanas and width 1000 Yojanas are exaggerated, but the proportion of length to width has been given correctly. In the list of Kûlâchalas, or outstanding hills, we find Mahêndra, Malaya, Sahya, Saktîmâna, Rîksha, Vîndhya and Parîyâtra included, which would therefore appear to include the hills in Varûnâ, Indra, Kûmâra islands but here again we must concede Bhârata-dvîpa and Bhârata-varsha mixed up, and necessary allowances have to be made.

Thus we see India formed of a cluster of 9 islands as shown in Fig. 2.

The next change is the joining of the northern group of these islands, *viz.*, Gabhastîmâna, Vârûna, Kûmâra,

Bhârata, Indra, Saûmya, Gândharva and Kaserû, either in a seismic change or by gradual reclamation of land by the movement of the materials from the sea by tidal action, and silt brought by the rivers of these islands. This change would give us Indian continental portion bounded on the south as we see in the 1st Century A.D., but inland seas enclosed which formed the Gangetic, and

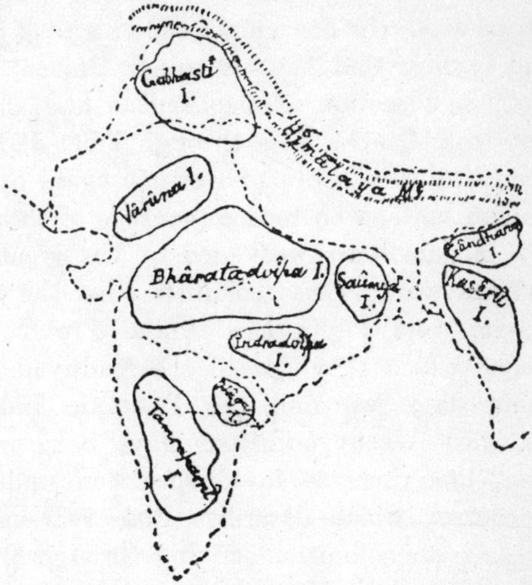

FIG. 2.—India of Nine-Islands Stage.

Indus troughs; the Gangetic trough extending from the Punjab to Assam and enclosed in all sides, and the Indus trough from Punjab to the sea, having an opening to the sea near Rann of Cutch. This in a way gives us the Vedic India, when we see the land formed at the head of the Indus favourable for colonization from the continent; the rest of India rapidly growing up was sparsely populated by the aboriginal inhabitants, who were ignored by the Aryans of the Punjab to the northwest, but they were no doubt getting in touch with the inhabitants of southern Burmah. It is thus in the Vedas we find the rest of India generally ignored, not excepting the Ganges flowing as an independent river to the eastern sea.

The filling up of the Gangetic trough did not take many centuries as the trough was already very shallow, and the whole of the silt brought down by the southern Himalayan and the northern Vindhya rivers were deposited in it, nothing escaping into the deep sea; the Indus trough was deeper and the sea had to do the filling up of the lower area before the river began operations. The valley of the Ganges therefore offered fields for fresh colonization from the continent, and this took place mainly from the eastern end that is upper Burmah or Jambû-dvîpa, where a section of the Aryans had already found their way from Central Asia through Tibet and were about this time being driven out of Burmah again by its original Dasyû inhabitants, who took advantage of the opportunity when the Aryans were weakened by the great internecine Mahâbhârata war. These colonists from the east jumped over Assam, and found the United Provinces the best at the time which they named the Madhyadêsa area. It is at this stage we find the Paûrânîc India. In the Pûrânas, very recent additions have been made during re-writing, but there is so to speak an undercurrent in these accounts, which describes Bhâratvarsha at a time when the Aryan colonists, arriving through Burmah were finally established in Madhyadêsa, and a fusion with the Vêdîc Aryans had taken palce. The eastern colonists' migration, was a most difficult task when the number of male population was reduced by the war, and crossing of the unhealthy Assam swamps, with the Asûras already in possession of the best lands towards the north, reduced them to abject prostration and arriving at Madhyadêsa area, they found the river banks only suitable for occupation, the interiors full of impregnable forests and occupied by the original inhabitants, whom they had to include in their folds as Hindus and thus it led them also to include in their list of minor gods the numerous different deities worshipped by the local inhabitants. Thus we find the Pûrâna accounts very much mixed up. The extent of Paûrânîc Bhâratvarsha can be gleaned from the list of the outstanding mountains called Kûla-achalas and rivers, given in the different Pûrânas, the lists of which is tabulated below :—

KULA-PARVVATAS OR CHIEF MOUNTAINS OF BHARATVARSHA

Pûrâna.	Kûla-parvvata.
Vâyû (Ch. 45) ...	Mahêndra, Malaya, Sahya, Saktîmâna, Rîksha, Vîndhya, Pârîyâtra.
Varâha (Ch. 85)	Mahêndra, Malaya, Sahya, Saktîmâna, Rîksha, Vîndhya, Pârîyâtra.
Brahma (Ch. 27)	Mahêndra, Malaya, Sahya, Sûktîmâna, Rîksha, Vîndhya, Pârîyâtra.
Matsya (Ch. 114)	Mahêndra, Malaya, Sahya, Saktîmâna, Rîkshamâna, Vîndhya, Pârîyâtra.
Vîshnû (Sec. 2)	Mahêndra, Malaya, Sahana, Sûktîmana, Rîksha, Vîndhya, Pârîpâtra.
Padma (Svarga 3).	Mahêndra, Malaya, Sahya, Sûktîmana, Rîkshavâna, Vîndhya, Pârîyâtra.
Mârkandêya (5)	Mahêndra, Malaya, Sahya, Sûktîmâna, Rîksha, Vîndhya, Pârîyâtra.
Kûrma (Ch. 46)	Mahêndra, Malaya, Sahya, Sûktîmana, Rîkshavâna, Vîndhya, Pârîpâtra.
Skanda (Kumârîkâ 39).	Mahêndra, Malaya, Sahya, Sûktîmâna, Rîksha, Vîndhya, Pârîyâtra.
Agnî (118) ...	Mahêndra, Malaya, Sahya, Sûktîmâna, Hêmasaîla, Vîndhya, Pârîpâtra.
Vâmana (13) ...	Mahêndra, Malaya, Sahya, Sûktîmâna, Rîksha, Vîndhya, Pârîpâtra.
Mahâbhârata (Bhîsma 9).	Mahêndra, Malaya, Sahya, Sûktîmâna, Gandhamâdana, Vîndhya, Pârîpâtra.

This table makes it clear that Bhâratvarsha of Pûrânas did not extend southwards below the southern limits of Ptolemy's India. Malaya mountain referred to in the list is the western and Mahêndra the eastern of the Orissa hills group as will be seen from the list of rivers flowing from them which will be given later on;

Sahya is the northern part of Western Ghats; Pârîpâtra or Pârîyâtra or Gandhamâdana is the western part of the Vîndhyas including the Aravalli range, and Rîksha or Rîkshavâna is the eastern portion of the Vîndhyas; and Sûktîmâna or Saktîmâna is the intermediate portion joining Rîksha and Pârîyâtra. Vîndhya is named separately, and from the list of rivers flowing from it, would appear to refer to the southern range, with the Mahadeo hills as its chief component. The omission of Hîmâlaya from the list of Kûla-parvvatas shows that Paûrânîc Bhâratvarsha at first extended northwards to the Gangetic trough only, though we find from the list of rivers given, that the authors of the Pûrânas could not resist inclusion of Himalayan rivers. This shows that in the Paûrânîc period the Himalayan Terai though partially reclaimed, had not yet been peopled to any extent excepting the western or Vedic area of the Punjab. It also shows that the fusion of Vedic Aryans of the Punjab and the Paûrânîc Aryans of Madhyadêsa had not taken place, each section ignoring the other, until the pressure from external invaders from the west brought about a coalition. Paûrânîc Bhâratvarsha is therefore an intermediate stage between the Bhâratvarsha composed of seven islands, and India of Ptolemy, bounded on the north by the Gangetic trough, on the east by partly by the Garo Hills, and Arakan Yomas, and partly by the sea, on the south by the sea in a east and west straight line from Vizagapatam to Bombay, on the west the sea from Bombay northwards in a straight line to Mt. Abu, and then by an arm of the sea which ran into what is now the Thar desert.

In the list of rivers given in the Pûrânas, some additions have been made since they were originally written, but a comparison of the lists given in the different Pûrânas may help us to eliminate the later additions to some extent and thus to give an idea of the rivers of the time. The names of rivers have been arranged in most cases, from the Mountains from which they issue, and this also enables us to fix the identity of the Kûla-parvvatas definitely.

RIVERS FROM THE HIMALAYA.

Purana.	Names of Rivers.	Remarks.
Vâyû (Ch. 45)	Gangâ, Sîndhû, Sarasvatî, Satadrû, Chandrabhâgâ, Yamûnâ, Sarayû, Irâvatî, Vîtastâ, Vîpâsâ, Dêvîkâ, Kûhû, Gomatî, Dhûtapâpâ, Bâhûda, Drîsadvatî Kaûsîkî, Trîtya, Gandakî, Nîschîrâ, Ikshû, Lohîtâ.	
Varâha (Ch. 85)	Ditto Ditto	
Mârkandêya (Ch. 57)	Ditto Ditto	
Brahmânda (50-55)	Ditto Ditto	
Matsya (Ch. 114)	Gangâ, Sîndhû, Sarasvatî, Satadrû, Chandrabhâgâ, Yamûnâ, Sarayû, Irâvatî, Vîtastâ, Vîsâlâ, Dêvîkâ, Kûhû, Gomatî, Dhûtapâpâ, Bâhûda, Drîsadvatî, Kaûsîkî, Trîtyâ, Nîschalâ, Gandakî, Ikshû, Lohîtâ.	
Kûrma (Ch. 46)	Satadrû, Chandrabhâgâ, Yamûnâ, Sarayû, Irâvatî, Vîtastâ, Vîpâsâ, Dêvîkâ, Kûhû, Gomatî, Dhaûtapâpâ, Bahûdâ, Drîsadvatî, Kaûsîkî, Lohînî.	
Vîshnû (2nd part)	Satadrû, Chandrabhâgâ.	
Padma ...	Gangâ, Sîndhû, Sarasvatî, Satadrû, Chandrabhâgâ, Yamûnâ, Sarayû, Irâvatî, Vîtastâ, Vîpâsâ, Dêvîkâ, Gomatî, Dhûtapâpâ, Bahûdâ, Drîsadvatî, Kaûsîkî, Laûhîtya, Lohîtâranî.	Names from mixed up list for Bhâratvarsa rivers.
Skanda ...	Gangâ, Sarasvatî, Kâlîndî, Sona.	Hîmâlaya list not given; these four are from a mixed list.
Brahma (Ch. 27)	Gangâ, Sîndhû, Sarasvatî, Satadrû, Chandrabhâgâ, Yamûnâ, Irâvatî, Vîtastâ, Vîpâsâ, Dêvîkâ, Kûhû, Gomatî, Dhûtapâpâ, Drîsadvatî, Kaûsîkî, Nîsthîvâ, Gandakî, Chakshû.	

Pûrânâs.	Names of Rivers.	Remarks.
Agnî (Ch. 118)	Chandrabhâgâ.	
Vâmana (Ch. 13)	Kalînadî, Pancharûpâ, Sarasvatî, Satadrû Chandrîkâ, Hîranvatî, Nîlâ, Sarayû, Irâvatî, Vîtastâ, Madhûrâ, Hâyarâvî, Kûhû, Gomatî, Dhûtapâpâ, Bahûdâ, Kaûsîkî, Vadhûsarâ, Nîhsarâ, Gandakî, Chîtrâ, Laûhîtya, Ushîrâ, Dhâtakîrasâ.	

In the Mahâbhârata, a combined list for Bhâratvarsha is given. The Vâyû Pûrâna list appears to be the most complete of all and it will appear from this list that land at the base of the Hîmâlayas appears to have been peopled from the Punjab area eastwards to Sarayû and then a portion is practically skipped, till we come to another stretch from the Kaûsîkî or Kosi to Laûhîtya or Brahmapûtra.

RIVERS FROM THE PARIYATRA.

Purânâs.	Names of Rivers.	Remarks.
Vâyû (Ch. 45)	Vêdasrûtî, Vêdavatî, Vrîtraghnî, Sîndhû, Parnâsâ, Vandanâ, Satîrâ, Mahatî, Parâ, Charmanvatî, Vîdîsâ, Vêtravatî, Sîprâ, Avantî.	
Mârkandêya (Ch. 57)	Ditto Ditto	
Varâha (Ch. 85)	Ditto Ditto	Same as in Vâyû except that Sîndhû-Parnâsâ is given instead of Sîndhû, Parnâsâ.
Brahma (Ch. 27)	Dêvasmrîtî, Devavatî, Vâtaghnî, Sîndhû, Venvâ, Chandanâ, Sadânîrâ, Mahî, Charmanvatî, Vrîsî, Vîdîsâ, Vêdavatî, Sîprâ, Avantî.	

Pûrânâs.	Names of Rivers.	Remarks.
Matsya (Ch. 114)	Vêdasmrîtî, Vêtravatî, Vrîtaghnî, Sîndhû, Parnâsâ, Narmadâ, Kâvêrî, Mahatî, Parâ, Dhanvantî, Rûpâ, Vîdûsâ, Vênûmatî, Sîprâ, Avantî, Kûntî.	
Padma (Svarga 3)	Vêdasmrîtî, Vêdasîra, Sîndhûlâ, Parnâsâ, Chandanâ, Kâvêrî, Mahîtâ, Charmanvatî, Vîdîsâ, Sîprâ.	
Kûrma (Ch. 46)	Vêdasmrîtî, Vêdamatî, Vrataghnî, Trîdîvâ, Parnâsâ, Chandanâ, Sadânîra, Manoramâ, Charmanvatî, Dûryâ, Vîdîsâ, Vêtravatî, Sîprû, Sûsîlpâ.	From Parîpâtra.
Vâmana (Ch. 13)	Vêdasmrîtî, Vêdasînî, Vrîtraghnî, Sîndhû, Parnâsâ, Nandînî, Pâvanî, Mahîsarâ, Charvvanvatî, Ulûpî, Vîdîsâ, Vênûmatî, Chîtrâ, Oghavatî, Ramyâ.	

The list given in other places are incomplete or mixed up. It is clear however from this group, that the Pârîyâtra or Pârîpâtra is the western Vîndhyas and Aravalli ranges. The rivers flowing northwards, notably Vêdavatî (Betwa), Sîndhû (Kali-Sindh), Charmanvatî (Chambal) etc., have been indicated more or less as independent rivers, as there is no mention of their being affluents of the Ganges, a fact which would justify to a conclusion that the Gangetic trough was still an inland sea and land at the base of Vîndhyas and Hîmâlayas had not been formed to meet each other in the Ganges valley. In the group flowing southwards from Pârîyâtra, we find Mahî or Mahîtâ (Mahi), Chandanâ or Narmadâ (Narmada), Sîprâ, Sâdânîrâ (? Shedhi or Sabarmati), Vîdîsâ (? Veda), Kûntî (? Kundi) and it appears that some of these rivers had outlets to the sea to the west, but some of them which are now affluents of the Narmada, were then independent rivers flowing into the valley between the Vindhya Range and Satpura range of hills, this valley then being in the nature of an inland sea.

RIVERS FROM RIKSHA.

Pûrânas.	Names of Rivers.	Remarks.
Vâyû (Ch. 45)	Mahânada-Sona, Narmadâ, Mandâkînî, Dasârnâ, Chîtrakûtâ, Tamasâ, Pîppalâ, Sronî, Karatoyâ, Pîshâchîkâ, Nîlotpalâ, Vîpâsâ, Jamvûlâ, Balûvahînî, Sîtêrajâ, Sûktîmatî, Makrûnâ, Trîdîvâ.	
Varâha (Ch. 85)	Ditto Ditto	
Mârkandêya (Ch. 57)	Ditto Ditto	
Brahma (Ch. 19)	Tâpî, Payoshnî, Nîrvvîndhyâ, Kâvêrî.	
Matsya (Ch. 114)	Mandâkînî, Dasârnâ, Chîtrakûtâ, Tamasâ, Pîppalî, Syênî, Chîtrotpalâ, Vîmalâ, Chanchalâ, Dhûtavâhînî, Sûktîmatî, Sûnî, Lajjâ, Mûkûtâ, Hradîkâ.	From Rîshyavanta.
Vîshnû ...	Tâpî, Payoshnî, Nîrvvîndhyâ.	
Kûrma (Ch. 46)	Sonâ, Narmadâ, Sûrasâ, Mandâkînî, Dasârnâ, Mahânadî, Chîtrakûtâ, Tamasâ, Pîshâchîkâ, Chîtrotpalâ, Vîsâlâ, Manjûlâ, Balûvâhînî.	
Skanda (Kûmârîkâ 39)	Satadrû, Chandrabhâgâ.	
Vâmana (Ch. 13)	Mahânadî, Sonâ, Narmadâ, Sûrasâ, Krîyâ, Mandâkînî, Dasârnâ, Chîtrakûtâ, Tamasâ, Ahîvêdîkâ, Pîppalâ-sronî, Chîtrotpalâ, Vîpâsâ, Vanjulâvatî, Falgûvâhînî, Sûktîmatî, Chakrînî, Trîdîvâvasû.	

The names of the rivers Mahânadî (upper Son), Sonâ (Son), Narmadâ (the upper Narmada, the first nucleus of the river which eventually appropriated to herself the bed of the Gautamî-Gangâ when the latter was cut off from the Gangâ), Surasâ (Sombarsa), Dasârnâ (Dosaron of Ptolemy), Ahîvêdîkâ (Ib), shows that the Rîksha mountain is the eastern portion of the Vindhyas, consisting of the Maikal Range, including the Hazaribagh hills to its east. It is to be noted that the list includes names of tributories of the Mahanadi and the presumption therefore is that the Valley of the Mahanadi here was still a shallow arm of the sea in the Paûrânîc times. It will be noticed that the Rîksha mountain of Skanda Purana is a different mountain, north of the Western Ghats.

RIVERS FROM VINDHYA.

Pûrânas.	Names of Rivers.	Remarks.
Vâyû (Ch. 45)	Tâpî, Payoshnî, Nîrvvîndhyâ, Bhadrâ, Nîshadhâ, Vênvâ, Vaîtaranî, Sîtîvâhû, Kûmûdvatî, Toyâ, Mahâ-gaûrî, Dûrgâ, Antahsîlâ.	
Mârkandêya (Ch. 57)	Ditto Ditto	
Varâha (Ch. 85)	Manîjalâ, Tâpî, Payoshnî, Sîghroda, Vêsmapâsâ, Vaîtaranî, Vêdîpâlâ, Kûmûdvatî, Toyâ, Dûrgâ, Antyâ, Gîrâ.	
Brahma (Ch. 27)	Sîprâ, Payoshnî, Nîrvvîndhyâ, Tâpî, Vênâ, Vaîtaranî, Sînîvaha, Kûmûdvatî, Toyâ, Mahâgaûrî, Dûrgâ, Antahsîlâ.	
Matsya (Ch. 114)	Tâpî, Payoshnî, Nîrvvîndhyâ, Kshîprâ, Rîshabhâ, Vênâ, Vaîtaranî, Vîsvamâlâ, Kûmûdvatî, Toyâ, Mahâ-gaûrî, Dûrgamâ, Sîlâ.	
Kûrma (Ch. 46)	Tâpî, Payoshnî, Nîrvvindhyâ, Mahânadî, Sîghrodâ, Vênvâ, Vaîtaranî, Valâkâ, Kûmûdvatî, Toyâ, Mahî, Gaûrî, Dûrgâ, Antahsîlâ.	
Vîshnû ...	Narmadâ.	Tâpî etc., given as from Rîksha, see table above.
Agnî (Ch. 118)	Ditto Ditto	

Pûrânâs.	Names of Rivers.	Remarks.
Vâmana (Ch. 13)	Sîvâ, Payoshnî, Nîrvvindhyâ, Tâpî, Nîshadhâvatî, Vênâ, Vaîtaranî, Sînîvahû, Kûmûdvatî, Toyâ, Rêvâ, Mahâ-gaûrî, Dûrgandhâ.	

The list given includes Payoshnî (Pus a tributory of Penganga formerly the main river), Nîrvvîndhyâ (Narmada lower reaches), Tâpî (Tapti), Vêna (Western Wainganga), Kûmûdvatî (Kunhur), Toyâ (Bara Tawa), Mahâgaûrî (Wagheri), Dûrgandhâ or Dûrgâ (Wardha river passing near old Durga town) and the Vîndhya referred to is therefore the small central portion of the Vindhyas consisting of the Mahadeo Hills with a section of the Satpura range. These independent rivers indicate that to the north of the Mahadeo hills, the Narmada basin was a broad valley with inland lake, and to the south the sea was then not at any great distance to the south of the Mahadeo hills.

RIVERS FROM THE SAHYA.

Pûrânas.	Names of Rivers.	Remarks.
Vâyû (Ch. 45)	Flowing Southwards:— Godâvarî, Bhîmarathî, Krîshnâ, Vênî, Vanjûlâ, Tûngabhadrâ, Sûprayogâ, Kâvêrî.	
Varâha (Ch. 85)	Ditto Ditto	
Mârkandêya (Ch. 5)	Ditto Ditto	
Brahma (Ch. 27)	Godâvarî, Bhîmarathî, Krîshnâ-Vênâ, Tûngabhadrâ, Sûprayogâ, Pâpanâshînî.	
Matsya (Ch. 114)	Flowing Southwards:— Godâvarî, Bhîmarathî, Krîshnâ-Vênî, Vanjûlâ, Tûngabhadrâ, Sûprayogâ, Vâhyâ, Kâvêrî.	
Vîshnû ...	Godâvarî, Bhâgîrathî, Krîshna-Vênî.	

Pûrânâs.	Names of Rivers.	Remarks.
Kûrma (Pûrva Ch. 46)	Godâvarî, Bhîmarathî, Krîshnâ, Vênâ, Vasyatâ, Tûngabhadrâ, Sûprayogâ, Kâvêrî.	
Skanda (Kûmârîkâ Ch. 39)	Tâpî, Payoshnî, Nîrvvîndhyâ, Kâvêrî, Mahî, Krîshnâ, Vênâ, Bhîmarathî.	
Vâmana (Ch. 13)	Godâvarî, Bhîmarathî, Krîshnâ-Vênâ, Sarîdvatî, Vîsamadrî, Sûprayogâ, Vâhyâ, Kâvêrî, Dûgdhodâ, Nalînî, Vârîsênâ, Kalasvanâ.	

The case of the Sahya mountains offers a problem. The authors of some of the Pûrânas have gone out of their way in stating that the rivers from the Sahya are all flowing southwards a remark which would fit in with that of the Godâvarî, Bhîmarathî (Bhima), Krîshnâ or Krîshna-Vênî (Vena a tributary of the Krishna), if it is remembered that the sea was close to the Ajanta Range to its south in the Paûrânîc period, and the rivers named refer only to a small portion near the source of the present courses of these rivers. The inclusion of the names of Tûngabhadrâ and Kâvêrî however seems to be later additions as these rivers could never have been "flowing southwards" near their sources at any time. The names of these river have therefore to be eliminated, and then we see that the Sahya mountains represent Ajanta or Indrayâdhrî group and the northern portion of Western Ghats contiguous to it which are known as Sahyadrî now. Accepting Ptolemy's boundary, it would leave a very small nucleus at the source of the first group of rivers, and it appears greatly probable that in the Paûrânîc period the Tâptî valley was open fully and Narmadâ or Gautamî Gangâ flowed into it; after the Tâptî valley was reclaimed the Narmadâ (Nanaguna of Ptolemy) was diverted southward. When Tâptî valley was open the Ajanta range and north of Western Ghats were joined together, and when Narmadâ (Nanaguna) was diverted southward as we find it Ptolemy's time, the water level at its mouth was raised, thus flooding the part of the country at its mouth and bringing about a temporary separation of Ajanta Range from the head of the Western Ghats as we find in Ptolemy's time. The Skanda Pûrâna includes Tâpî, Payoshnî and Nîrvvîndhyâ in the list, which are included in the Vîndhya list in other Pûrânas, so that according to the Skanda Pûrâna, the Satpura Range is included in the Sahya group.

RIVERS FROM THE MALAYA.

Pûrânas.	Names of Rivers.	Remarks.
Vâyû (Ch. 45)	Krîtamâlâ, Tâmraparnî, Pûspajâtî, Utpalâvatî.	
Varâha (Ch. 85)	Ditto Ditto	
Mârkandêya (Ch. 57)	Ditto Ditto	
Brahma (Ch. 27)	Krîtamâlâ, Tâmraparnî, Pûsyajâ, Pratyalâvatî.	
Matsya (Ch. 114)	Krîtamâlâ, Tâmraparnî, Mûlî, Savarâ, Vîmalâ, Krîtamâlâ, Tâmraparnî.	
Vîshnû ...	Krîtamâlâ, Tâmraparnî.	
Kûrma (Ch. 46)	Krîtamâlâ, Tâmraparnî, Pûspavatî, Utpalâvatî.	
Skanda (Kûmârîkâ, Ch. 46)	Krîtamâlâ, Tâmraparnî.	
Vâmana (Ch. 13)	*Nil.*	(Krîtamâlâ, &c., shown under Sûktîmânâ).

RIVERS FROM THE MAHENDRA.

Pûrânas.	Names of Rivers.	Remarks.
Vâyû (Ch. 45)	Trîsâmâ, Krûtûkûlyâ, Ikshûlâ, Trîdîvâ, Lângûlînî, Vansadhârâ.	
Mârkandêya (Ch. 57)		Same as in Vâyû.

Pûrânâs.	Names of Rivers.	Remarks.
Varâha (Ch. 85)		Same as in Vâyû.
Brahma (Ch. 19)	Trîsandhyâ, Rîshîkûlyâ.	
Brahma (Ch. 27)	Pîtrîkûlyâ, Somakûlyâ, Rîshîkûlyâ, Vanjûlâ, Trîdîvâ, Lângalînî, Vansakarî.	
Matsya (Ch. 114)	Krîtamâlâ, Tâmraparnî, Mûlî, Savarâ, Vîmalâ.	
Vîshnû ...	*Nil.*	(Mahêndra list is not given separately.)
Vâmana (Ch. 13)	*Nil.*	
Skanda (Kûmârîkâ, Ch. 39)	Trîsâmâ, Rîshîkûlyâ.	
Kûrma (Ch. 46)	*Nil.*	(Trîsâmâ, &c., given under Sûktîmâna.)

RIVERS FROM THE SUKTIMANA.

Pûrânas.	Names of Rivers.	Remarks.
Vâyû (Ch. 45)	Rîshîkâ, Sûkûmârî, Mandagâ, Mandavâhînî, Kûpâ, Palâsînî.	
Mârkandêya M. (Ch. 57)	Ditto Ditto	Same as Vâyû.
Varâha (Ch. 85)	Rîshîkâ, Nûsatî, Mandagâ, Palâsînî.	
Brahma (Ch. 19)	Rîshîkûlyâ, Kûmâra.	
Brahma (Ch. 27)	Sûvîkâlâ, Kûmârî, Manûgâ, Mandagâmînî, Kshayâ, Palâsînî.	
Matsya (Ch. 114)	Kâsîkâ, Sûkûmârî, Mandagâ, Mandavâhînî, Krîpâ, Pâsînî.	
Vîshnû ...	Trîsâmâ, Aryakûlâ.	
Kûrma (Ch. 46)	Rîshîkûlyâ, Trîsâmâ, Gandhamâdanagâmînî, Kshîprâ, Palâsînî, Rîshîkâ, Vansadhârînî.	

Pûrânâs.	Names of Rivers.	Remarks.
Skanda (Kûmârîkâ, Ch. 39)	*Nil.*, mentions Trîsâmâ, Rîshîkûlyâ under Mahêndra.	
Agnî (Ch. 118)	Kûmâra.	
Vâmana (Ch. 13)	Krîtamâlâ, Tâmraparnî, Vanjûlâ, Utpalâvatî, Sûnî, Sûdâmâ.	These rivers are shown under Malaya in other Pûrânas.

Independent comments on the three above lists from Malaya, Mahêndra, and Sûktîmâna have not been made as it will be convenient to discuss the three together. It will be seen from the above tables that the different Pûrânas are not agreed as to the nomenclature adopted for these mountains, which form parts of one group of hills in Orissa, which constitute the northern part of Eastern Ghats. These rivers and hills have already been mostly discussed in (Ch. I.A.) in connection with Ptolemy's coast line of India. The rivers from the Malaya are Krîtamâlâ (Kotri), Tâmraparnî (Indravati), Pûspajâtî or Pûsyajâ (tributory of the Godavari passing by Pusgupa), Savarî (Sabiri), Utpalâvatî or Pratyalâvatî (Tel) shows that Malaya mountain is the Bastar district portion of the hills. The Vâmana Pûrâna includes these hills under Sûktîmâna.

The rivers from the Mahêndra mountain end northwards with the important ones Lângalînî (Langulia) and Vamsakarî or Vamsadhârâ (Vansadhara), the Brahma and Skanda Pûrânas adding Rîshîkûlyâ (Rushkulya); the list of rivers from the Suktimana begin with the Rishikulya, thus settling the fact that this river is the dividing line between the Mahêndra to its south and Sûktîmâna to its north. The Rîshîkulya in its upper reaches formerly took a bend southwards, thus, the division line of the two mountains is now represented by the valley of the Vansadhara river, that is a line from Bhowani Patna to Godairi. The Malaya lying to the west of these two is practically detached from them.

Having now described the Kûla-parvvatas or chief mountains and important rivers as given in the common Paûrânîc list, we are able to picture the Bhâratvarsa of the Paûrânîc period; it is an intermediate stage between the seven-island stage and that described by Ptolemy. The southern boundary is much like Ptolemy's, but the land at the southern base of Vindhyas in the central portion still undeveloped, though the eastern or Kalînga area, and western or Sahya area were fully developed; if anything, the western area or Sahya was then connected with the main land and subsequently detached again as the Nanaguna or Gaûtamî Gangâ was diverted from Tapti valley to the south sea; we see also the Narmada, Tapti, and Ganges valleys still broad troughs under water; the same is the case with the Thar desert; at the southern base of the Himalayas, the Punjab area fully developed and joined on to the Madhyadêsa area, north of the Vindhyas, but eastwards the Himalayan Terai was still a mass of forests, not peopled by the civilised Aryan population, until at the extreme east, in the north Bengal area the Terai was peopled by the civilised non-Aryan population. This is Paûrânîc Bhâratvarsa.

Subsequently in the Buddhist period, we find northern India fully reclaimed, the Gangetic trough filled up, but eastern area, that is present Bengal a swamp, possibly an area at the base of the Himalayas formerly populated, was again under water as a result of Gangetic trough filling up, and exit of water southward prevented by a ridge. This is the condition we find more or less the same as in Ptolemy's time.

The subsidence of the ridge in lower Bengal, setting free from flooding the swamp to its north, and joining of the Taprobane Island to main land are changes, brought about during the course of the next 4 or 5 Centuries, giving us India as we see now. The change in the course of the Indus and reclamation of Guzerat and Palanpur areas as a result, must have occurred about the same time but of this I have been unable to fix the date as already mentioned before.

CHAPTER XI

EXTRA-GANGEM INDIA OF PTOLEMY AND JAMBUDVIPA OF PURANAS

Now that we have seen that even so late as the beginning of the Christian Era northern India and southern India separated by an inland sea, Ceylon or Lanka as it is supposed to be, lying further to the south of Taprobane or southern India, Guzerat and Dwaraka non-existent, Ayodhya not yet fully populated by the Aryans, the question will be asked as to what about the Mahâbhârata and Râmâyana episodes and their theatres of action? As I have already referred casually before, Jambûdvîpa is Burmah, and Bhâratvarsha or Râmâyana area is its southern portion, while Mahabharat episode refers to sites mainly in Upper Burmah; Lankâ is Tenassarim district northwards up to about Thaton and including the Mergui Archipelago which were at one time joined with the main land at Tenassarim, and Ayodhyâ is western Siam area. As in the case of the Paûrânîc account of India, the nine-island stage of Intra-Gangem India is given, so in the case of the Extra-Gangem area, the Pûrânîc accounts have given the Jambûdvîpa in a stage of several divisions (6 to 10) and some were islands, and also later on when they joined, and Jambûdvîpa formed one continental area, its sub-islands are given. The confirmation of the accounts given in the Pûrânas, with that we find existing in Burmah and Further-India of to-day, and with the account given in Ptolemy's Georgraphy are all inter-dependent and I propose therefore to take up the discussion of Extra-Gangem India of Ptolemy and Paûrânîc accounts of Jambûdvîpa together. A detailed examination of this large subject can not be included in this short account and I will merely furnish here the outstanding features of the geography of this area.

According to the Pûrânas, the world was composed of seven islands :—Jambû, Plakshâ, Sâlmalî, Kûsa, Kraûncha, Sâka, Pûshkara. Of these, Jambûdvîpa is the largest, and it is divided into several Varshas or divisions, separated by mountain ranges or Kûla-parvvatas, when the divisions have ceased to be islands. In these lists we find some attempt at confusion with the divisions of Indian Bhâratvarsha. The Varshas and Kûla-parvvatas are tabulated below, as it may help the readers to draw their own conclusions as regards the later interpolations.

VARSHAS (DIVISIONS) AND KULA-PARVVATAS (CHIEF MOUNTAINS) OF JAMBUDVIPA.

Pûrânas.	Varshas.	Kula-parvvatas.	Remarks.
Lînga			Same as Vâyû.
Brahmânda Vâyû ...	Bhârata or Haîmavata, Kîmpûrûsha, Harî, Ilâvrîta, Ramyaka or Svêta, or Hîranmaya, Kûrû.	Nîla, Hîranya, Svêta, Hêmakûta, Hîmavâna, Srîngavâna, Nîshadha, Mêrû, Mâlyavâna, Gandhamâdana.	
Vîshnû			Same as Vâyû.
Matsya ...	Bhârata, Kîmpûrûsha, Harî, Ilâvrîta, Ramyaka, Hîranyaka, Kûrû, Bhadrâsva, Kêtûmâla, Ramanaka, Hîranvata.	Nîla, Svêta, Hêmakûta, Hîmavâna, Srîngavâna, Nîshadha, Sûmêrû.	
Brahma ...	Bhârata, Kîmpûrûsha, Harî, Ilavrîta, Ramyaka, Hîranmaya, Uttarkûrû, Bhadrâsva, Ketûmâla.	Nîla, Svêta, Hêmakûta, Hîmavâna, Srîngî, Nîshadha, Mêrû.	
Kûrma ...	Jambû, Uttarkûrû, Bhadrâsva, Kêtûmâla.		
Varâha ...	Hîmavâna, Hêmakûta, Kîmpûrûsha, Naîshadha, Harî, Ilâvrîta, Nîla, Svêta, Ramyaka, Hîranmaya, Srîngavâna, Kûrava, Mâlyavâna, Bha-	Nîla, Hîmâlaya, Svêta, Hêmakûta, Hîmavâna, Srîngavâna, Nîshadha, Sûmêrû.	

Markandêya ...	(As in Vâyû.)	Nîla, Svêta, Hêmakutâ, Hîmavâna, Srîngî, Rîshabha, Mêrû.
Skanda ...	Bhârata or Nâbhîkhanda or Kûrû, Kîmpûrûsha, Harî, Ilâvrîta, Ramayka, Hîranmaya, Kûrû, Bhadrâsva, Kêtûmâla.	Nîla, Svâta, Hêmakûtâ, Hîmavâna, Srîngavâna, Nîshadha, Mêrû, Mâlyavâna, Gandhagîrî.
Sîva ...	Bhârata, Kîmpûrûsha, Ilâvrîta or Kraûncha, Ramya, Hîmavata, Bhava.	Nîla, Hîmâlaya, Svêta, Hêmakûta, Nîshadha, Sûmêrû, Mâlyavâna, Gandhamâdana.
Bhâgavata ...	Bhârata, Kîmpûrûsha, Harî, Ilâvrîta, Ramyaka, Hîranmaya, Kûrû, Bhadrâsva, Kêtûmâla.	Nîla, Hîmâlaya, Svêta, Hêmakûta, Srîngavâna, Nîshadha, Sûmêrû, Mâlyavâna, Gandhamâdana.
Agnî ...	Bhârata, Kîmpûrûsha, Harî, Ilâvrîta, Ramayaka, Hîranmaya, Uttarkûrû.	Nîla, Svêta, Hêmakutâ, Hîmavâna, Srîngî, Nîshadha, Mêrû.
Mahâbhârata ...	Bhârata, Haîmavata, Harî, Ilâvrîta, Svêta, Hîranyaka, Jambû, Uttarkûrû, Aîrâvata, Bhadrâsva, Kêtûmâla.	Nîla, Hîmalaya, Svêta, Hêmakûta, Srîngavâna, Nîshadha, Sûmêrû.
Vâmana ...	Bhârata, Kîmpûrûsha, Harî, Ilâvrîta, Champaka, Kûrû, Hîranmâna, Bhadrâsva, Kêtûmâla.	

It will be observed that the different accounts show a remarkable agreement. In the Varâha Pûrâna, the countries in the hills are also included as Varshas, and Hêmakûta, Naîshadha, Nîla, Svêta, Srîngavâna, Mâlayavâna and Gandhâmadana may thus be eliminated from the list. In the Skanda Pûrâna, alternative names for Bhârata have been given, *viz.*, Nâbhi-khanda or Kûrû; here we find an attempt to assimilate Bhârata of Jambûdvîpa with Bhârata of India, which is named after Bharata son of Rîshabha (*vide* Ch. X), son of Nâbhî (Vâyû Pûrâna, Ch. 33), and with the land colonised by the Kûrûs at a later date. A comparison of the names of Varshas of Jambûdvîpa gives the following common list :—

(1) Bhârata (2) Kîmpûrûsha (3) Harî (4) Ilâvrîta or Kraûncha (5) Ramyaka (6) Hîranmaya or Haîranyaka (7) Kûrû or Uttara-Kûrû or Aîravata (8) Bhadrâsva or Bhava (9) Kêtûmâla.

Similarly the Kûla-parvvatas are :—

(1) Nîla (2) Svêta (3) Hêmakûta (4) Hîmavâna (5) Srîngavâna or Srîngî (6) Nîshadha or Rîshabha (7) Mêrû or Sûmêrû. Mâlayavâna and Gandhamâdana given in some Pûrânas and omitted in others, show that they are only smaller subsidiary hills.

Of the disposition of these Varshas, and their boundary Kûla-parvvatas, details are given in most of the Pûrânas, and a comparison of these accounts cannot be entered into here and I will mention merely one of the accounts, namely that given in the Bhâgavata Pûrâna. Before I do this, I would refer the readers to a map of Jambûdvîpa, given in Gladwin's Ayeen Akbery, which, Beveridge (A Comprehensive History of India, by Henry Beveridge. Vol. I, P. 2) characterises as "a map though sufficiently curious, could scarcely be made more intelligible by any amount of explanation; it is fanciful throughout, and all the attempts which have been made to find fixed localities for its cardinal points have failed", but which map will be found to agree to the description of Jambûdvîpa as given in the Pûrânas; in the map (Fig. 3), the Bhârat-Khanda is divided into seven divisions Indra, Kasêrû,

Tâmraparnî, Gabhastîmat, Nâga, Saûmya and Varhîna all of which except Varhîna are divisions of Bhâratvarsha of India. As this is an attempt to merge the Jambû-dvîpa Bhâratvarsha with Nâbhi-Khanda Bhâratvarsha or a confusion between the two, I reproduce the map omitting the subdivisions of Bhârat-Khanda given in the map. The names given within parantheses appear in the original map, their corresponding Sanskrit names are given in this place.

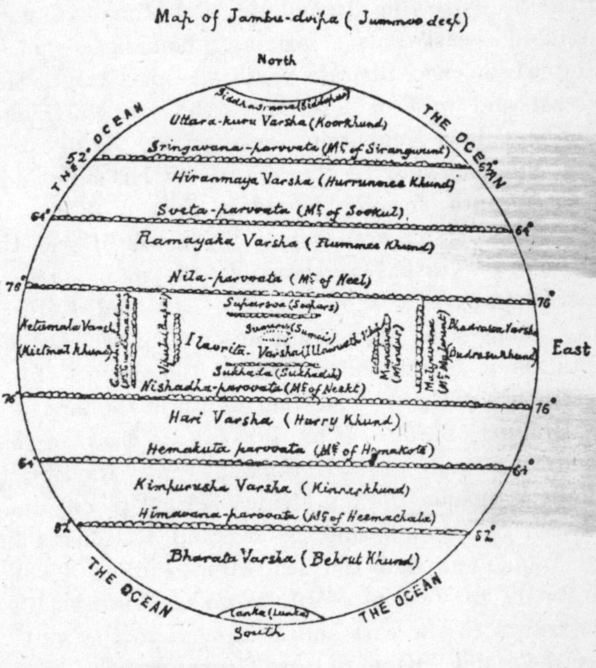

FIG. 3.—Map of Jummoo Deep.

This map as will be seen from the accounts given in the Pûrânas will require some modification, but it is sufficient for a guide to start with, and I will now proceed with the accounts given in the Bhâgavata Pûrâna (V 16). "The world of seven islands is shaped like a lotus, and Jambû-dvîpa is the central island; this Jambû-dvîpa 10,00,000 Yojanas long 100,000 Yojanas broad and shaped round like a lotus-leaf." This indicates the shape is elliptical and not circular. "The nine Varshas (divisions) are separated by eight boundary mountain ranges; the central varsha is Ilâvrîta, in the centre of which is Sûmêrû, the king of the Kûla-parvvatas". *** *** *** *** "North of Ilâvrîta varsha, northwards in stages are Nîla, Svêta, and Srîngavâna mountains forming the boundary lines of Ramyaka, Hîranmaya, and Kûrû varshas respectively; these three mountains are extended eastwards and terminated by the salt ocean at both ends". *** *** *** "Similarly south of Ilâvrîta varsha are Nîshadha, Hêmakûta, and Hîmâlaya mountains extending eastwards, forming boundaries of Harî, Kîmpûrûsha, and Bhârata varshas respectively. Similarly to east and west of Ilâvrîta varsha are Mâlyavâna and Gandhamâdana mountains respectively both stretching from Nîla-parvvata to their north to Nîshadha parvvata to their south, forming boundary lines of Kêtûmâla and Bhadrâsva varshas respectively." It will be seen that the positions of varshas as shown in the map agree, except that Bhadrâsva is shown to the east and Kêtûmâla to west, though the Bhâgavata account of which the interpretation is obscure places them differently; it is quite clear however that the position shown in the map is correct as Brahma Pûrâna (Ch. 18) says "East of Mêrû is Bhadrâsva and west Ketûmâna, and Ilâvrîta in the middle," Skanda Pûrâna (Kûmârîkâ 37) places Bhadrâsva between Mâlyavâna and the sea and Ketûmâna between Gandhamâdana and the sea, Agnî Pûrâna (108) places Ketûmâla to west of Mêrû, Vâmana Pûrâna (13) places Bhadrâsya to the east and Ketûmâla to the west. Kimpûrûsha and Kînnara are synonymous terms and Kîmpûrûsha varsha and Kinner-Khund are therefore identical. Returning to Bhâgavata account (V, 16) we find "on four sides of Sûmêrû mountain are four barrier mountains, Mandara, Mêrû-mandara, Sûpârsva, and Kûmûda." Matsya Pûrâna (113) gives these names as Mandara, Gandhamâdana, Vîpûla, Sûpârsva, Vîshnû Pûrâna and Varaha Pûrâna (77) give Mandara to east, Gandhamâdana to south, Vîpula to west and

Sûpârsva to north. Sukhadâ barrier mountain is therefore Kûmûda of Bhâgavata Pûrâna, and it appears to be an outcrop of the Gandhamâdana-parvvata, running at right angles to it to south of Sûmêru. Thus far we see the map represents Jambûdvîpa correctly.

Now the central point of Jambûdvîpa is the outstanding peak Sûmêrû with reference to which the position of the headquarter cities of the different gods are given and this enables us to fix the site of Sûmêrû. The sites of these cities of the gods have not been sufficiently indicated in anyone of these accounts but taking the different accounts it is possible to come to a fair conclusion as regards them. Instead of proceeding by the analytical method of fixing the site of Sûmêrû, it would be much simpler if I proceed by assuming that Sûmêrû is the small group of peaks in and near Mandalay and then show its relation to the cities in its neighbourhood.

At first we may take up the cities which gives the accepted cardinal directions, North-east, South-east, South-west and North-west. Situated in these directions, or Dîkas, are the dîka-pâlas, or guards of each direction round the central place of Indra in Sûmêrû. North-east angle is the Ishâna-kona, sacred to Sîva or Sankara or Mahâdêva; his city Hsipaw or Thibaw is an ancient one, at present the headquarters of the Hsipaw district; this city lies to the north-east of Mandalay; the name of Sîva's city is given in the Vâyû Pûrâna (Ch. 34) Lînga Pûrâna (48), and Kûrma Pûrâna (45) as Yasovatî, which is evidently another name of Sîva (Hsipaw or Thibaw)-pûrî, though Skanda Pûrâna (Kâsî, Purvvardda, 10) suggests Mahodayâ as the city of Ishâna, at the same time in the name of the cities of the Dîk-pâlas given in the same location is Aîshî, a name which corresponds to Lashio a little to the east of Hsipaw; Mahodayâ is made quite distinct from the city of Ishâna, in the Vâyû Pûrâna (Ch. 34) which says it is Nîshâ-pâtî's (Indra's) city, and lies between the cities of Pavana (Vâyû, that is north-west) and Ishâna (that is, north-east) making it clear that Mahodayâ is to north of Sûmêrû, which is confirmed in

Lînga Pûrâna (Ch. 48) which says Mahodayâ lies directly to north of Sûmêrû; this city is Mya-daung very near to the ancient capital Tagaung lying due north of Mandalay. Ishâna as another name of Sîva, makes it clear he was the chief of the powerful Shan tribes; a curious confirmation of this is given in traditions in Bengal, of Sîva spending his time with women of Kûchnî-pârâ, which refers no doubt to the Kâchins.

South-east, or Agnî-Kona is sacred to Agnî, and the name of his city is given as Tejovatî in Vâyû Pûrâna (Ch. 34), Varâha Pûrâna (Ch. 76) and Kûrma Pûrâna (Ch. 45); this city is the ancient town of Thazi, lying south-east of Mandalay.

South-west, or Naîrrîta-kona, sacred to Nîrrîties or Rakshasas, the name of the city is given as Rakshovatî in Kûrma Pûrâna (Ch. 45), Krîshnavatî in Varâha Pûrâna (Ch. 76), and Mûgdhavatî in Lînga Pûrâna (Ch. 48); this city is present Myohaung, the ancient capital of Arakan, a country named by the local people Rakhaing-pyi or land of Rakshas, who had their abode in Mêrû and were guards round the mansion of Indra (Phayere's Burmah Ch. V. P. 41), as such the Dîk-pâla of the south-west.

North-west, or Vâyû-kona, is sacred to Vâyû, and the name of his city is given as Gandhavatî, in Lînga Pûrâna (Ch. 48), Varâha Pûrâna (Ch. 76), Kûrma Pûrâna (Ch. 45) and Skanda Pûrâna (Kâshî, Purvvaddha, 10), and as Nandavatî in Vâyû Pûrâna (Ch. 34) which latter appears to be slightly altered by mistake. This city is the ancient town of Kindat, lying to north-west of Mandalay.

Thus the centre is the Mandalay area, and we find in Lînga Pûrâna (Ch. 48) that on the south of Sûmêru hill, which is placed like a *Sarâva* or the cover of a cooking pot which is like a frustum of a sphere, is Brahmâ's place; Vîshnû Pûrâna (Div. 2) says that Brahmâ's city is to the north of Sûmêrû; Varâha Pûrâna (Ch. 75) says that Brahmâ's place is Manovatî and it enclosed the Sûmêrû peak all round; Vâyû Pûrâna (Ch. 44) says that

Brahmâ's place Manovatî is on the Mêrû mount; the position indicated is therefore at the centre of Sûmêrû, and Monywa is unmistakably this city, and the Sûmêrû is the bell shaped hill to its east.

East of Sûmêrû is placed Indra's city Amarâvatî, in Lînga Pûrâna (Ch. 48), the same authority (Ch. 54) placing Mâhêndrî city on Mânasa hill to the east of Sûmêrû. This indicates Mandalay or Mahêndra-âlaya as the Mâhêndrî city on the Mandalay hill which is Mânasa-parvvata, and Amarâpûra is the site of old Amarâvatî, on which the new city has been rebuilt. Sûkhâ and Bîbhâvarî are also two Indra's cities near Sûmêrû as mentioned in Lînga Pûrâna (Ch. 54), their position being made clear as lying to the west and north respectively of Sûmêrû in Matsya Pûrâna (Ch. 124); Sûkhâ is evidently Saga about 20 miles west of Monywa and Bîbhâvarî is Ye-u about the same distance north of Monywa.

South of Sûmêrû is placed the city of Yama named Sangyamanî in Lînga and Varâha Pûrânas, and Sanyamana or Susanyama in Vâyû Pûrâna, Sanyamana in Matsya Pûrâna, and Sanyamanî in Kûrma; this city is Yamethin, south of Thazi, as such the direction is not due south of Monywa but it is sufficiently southwards, to put Yama as the Dîk-pâla of the south.

Enough has been given to locate Sûmêrû the central point of Jambûdvîpa, at Monywa. Sûmêrû however formed a part of Mêrû or Mêrû Mandara Range, which as its name signifies is the "backbone" Range; and this backbone is of Jambu-dvipa; the range of hills of which the Sûmêrû is an outcrop is no doubt the Arakan ranges hills which run from north to south through centre of Burmah now divided into two parallel ranges, *viz.*, the Arakan Yomas, and the Pegû Yomas, the former called Anouk-bhat-Yoma-daung and the latter Ashe-bhat-Yoma. Yoma literally means "backbone" or "mêrû," "Anouk-bhat" meaning west point, and "Ashebhat" the east point, thus indicating that the corresponding name to Mêrû is still preserved in the Burmese language for this range.

Gandhamâdana is shown as forming the western as also the southern girdle range round Sûmêrû, and this is therefore Poudaung Range, which towards south curved eastwards, and must have included in it the sacred Popa Mt., which from its position agrees with the sacred Prabhâsa hill of Mahâbhârata. This range is also named Mêrû-Mandara in Bhâgavata Pûrâna (V. 16). Mêrû and Mandara are thus identical, and it explains why we find this range marked as Maiandros Mt., by Ptolemy. We may now picture the Jambû-dvîpa, which though it is compared to a lotus, or a lotus leaf in its outline, is to be taken as elliptical in shape as Bhâgvata Pûrâna (V. 16) puts its length at 10,00,000 Yojanas as against a breadth of 1,00,000 Yojanas, that is the length 10 times its breadth. The Jambû Island is therefore roughly bounded by the Patkoi Range, to the west, the southern end of Pegu Yomas, continuing south to Dwana hill ranges curving eastwards to Bangkok the southern boundary, the the eastern boundary is the ridge to Menam thus passing by Pechabun and then following the upper courses of the Salween river; the northern boundary is a hair-pin-curve formed by the Hkamti-Long range. The south-western boundary thus brings us to Thaton or perhaps Moulmein, which is the north point of Lankâ island, this island extending southwards to the Isthmus of Kra; the eastern boundary is the sea in its southern portion, and in the norther portion separated from Jambûdvîpa by the Me-Klong and Ataran valleys which were at one time broad belts of waters; the western boundary extended beyond to the Mergui Archipelago, a part of land shown in Ptolemy's map as firm land which must have included the Archipelago area in it, the area having been submerged by a subsidence later on. The southern end of the Mandara has undergone subsidence, bringing down with it, completely under the sea the Maînâka Mt., situated to the north of Lankâ island (Râmâyana, Sûndara, 7); it was perhaps formerly in the Sâlmalî island containing the Valâhaka mountain that Maînaka was situated, and later on this island was named Narîkêla island (Kathâsarît Sâgara IX, LI) which contained Maînâka, Vrîshava, Chakra and Valâhaka.

Lankâ-dvîpa of Râmâyana is very often referred to as the Suvarna Lankâ, and the Golden Khersonese island of Ptolemy gives the position of Lankâ as indicated by me. The western portion of the island was low and getting flooded as we find Krîttîvâsa writing in the 16th Century in his Râmâyana (Basumati Ed. Lankâ-Kânda, P. 392) mentions that when Kâlanêmî thought he has killed Râvana's enemies and was entitled to claim half of the Lankâ Island as his own, he dreams of proposing the partitioning of the island by "holding a string dividing line from north to south, and that I will claim the eastern portion of the island and will not go to the western side where the flood embankments on the sea to the west may make inroads into the land, and it is best to concede as much land to Râvana as he desires to get in that direction." Alberuni writing in about 1030 A.D. (Translation by E. A. Sachau, P. 210) describes the condition of the submerged portion as follows :—"The eastern islands of this Ocean (Bay of Bengal) which are nearer to China than to India are :—Zabaz; the western islands are of the Zauj (negroes) and the middle islands are Ramm and Diva islands to which also belong Kumair islands. It is peculiar to the Diva islands that they rise slowly and are reclaimed while another melts away and is submerged in the ocean, the inhabitants migrating in time. Islands of Alwakwak belongs to Kumair Islands. Kumara is not a tree producing screaming human heads as popularly believed but a name of a people whose colour is whitish, stature short and are Hindus." Mahamadan travellers two hundred years earlier (851 to 869 A.D.) describe these islands as follows (Ancient Accounts of India and China by two Mahamadan Travellers by Usebius Renandot, pages 1 to 4 and 61) :—"Between the sea of Harkand and of Delarowi are many islands, as they say 1900, ruled over by a woman queen; beyond these islands in the sea of Harkand is Sarandib or Ceylon, the chief of these islands called Dobijai; up in the country is a Mt., called Rabun on top of which is imprint of Adam's foot. * * * * In the same sea towards Serendib, are also many islands, one of these called Ramni. * * * * The islands of Ramni part the sea of Harkand from the sea of Shelahat. * * * * One months sail from it and opposite China is Zapage province, province 400 leagues circuit plus islands; among these islands one is called Serbera, 400 leagues circuit and also Ramni which is 800 leagues circuit." It will be seen that Ramni or Ramm islands are placed between the Shilahat (Sylhet) sea or Arakan coast, and Harkand sea which must be the Gulf of Martaban thus these islands must be the deltaic islands of the Irwadi, which is the Râmânnya country of the Pali Buddhist literature; Serbeza or Zapage province beyond this towards China is therefore the Sri-Vijaya country its capital at Phrapatoom in ancient Sri Wichaiya Kingdom or rather the Siam Kingdom which dominated all these islands in the sea between the Martaban Gulf and Gulf of Siam at the time of the visit of these travellers (See Siam, in Encyclopaedia Britannica 11th Ed.); the location of these islands with Sarandib or Ceylon as the chief island is between seas of Delarowi (Gulf of Siam) and Harkand (Gulf of Martaban), and it makes it clear therefore that Ceylon or Sînhala or Lankâ of Râmâyana is in this place, the Lankâ island even in the 9th Century claiming memories of Râvana as we find a mount Rabun in it mentioned by the travellers, and that a good portion of Lankâ had already been submerged splitting it into small islands. The sea of Harkand is Hâdhkhâna of Mûkûndaram Chakravartî poet to whose work reference is going to be made now.

Poet Mukundarâm Chakravartî writing in 1577 A.D. in his book on Chandî, when he describes the journey to Sîmhala and Lankâ could only have referred to Lankâ south of Burmah, the journey from the Ganges to Lankâ or Thaton was then possible in small vessels taking advantage of the interminable network of inland channels in the deltas of the Ganges and the Irrawadi that existed at the time, the subsided broad belt of land along the coast lying between the mouths of the Bhâgîrathî and the Irrawadi offering this shelter, till it subsided still further or was deepned by movement of materials by the littoral drift current of the sea sweeping over the low lands and encroaching on it gradually. The journey from the Gangâ river both to and from Sînhala, compared gives the following route from Gangâ (Kavîkankan Chandî, India Publishing House Ed., p. 205, 232-34, 241, 295) :—Magrâ, Mêdînî-malla, Virthânâ, Dhûlîgrâm, Angârapur (to left, Dravîda country with Indrayûmna's temple of Jagannâtha, Fîrîngi's country infested by Hârmâd pirates, Chîngrî-daha, Kânkrâ-daha, Sarpadaha, Kûmbhîra-daha, Karîâ-daha, Sankha-daha, Hâthîâ-daha (or Hâdîa-daha), Bûhîtâla, Setûvandha and Râma's Causeway (to left), Chîtrakûta or Chandrakûta hills in Yaksha Country, Sîtâkhâlî estuary, Harhkhân, Lankâ estuary and Kâlîdaha, entered Ajaya-Vîjaya river—arrive at Sînhala city in Ratnamâlâ landing ghât. It will be seen that on the left of the Gangâ estuary the tongue of land must have extended into the sea in extension of Sâgaur island, almost opposite to Pûrî, which compelled the vessels to pass near Pûrî, which may have been a little down below, but was not missed by Hindu voyagers; passing Magrâ, we find the entrance to Angârapûr Khal to the left, which has since gone into the sea near its mouth, but the creek extended eastwards to the Barisaul district, where the Angeria Khal by Rajapur Police Station still shows the old channel there. The old coast line was roughly about the same as the 250 ft., depth line of the present maps. Leaving Pûrî and its Jagannâtha Temple, the vessels must have turned to the left, as the places met with on the outward voyage are towards the left from here all along; this makes it clear that after Pûrî the journey was not with the coast to right which would be the case if Ceylon was the destination. Immediately after turning to the left after leaving Pûrî, we find the swamps infested by European Pirates or Hârmâdas, the dreaded Portuguese pirates of Sunderbuns whose boats were known as Hârmâdas, a corruption of

Armada. It is to be noted that Valentine's map, 1670 A.D., shows a series of islands along the coast here, and he also indicates the extension of the shoal on the left bank of the Bhâgîrathî estuary. The journey from here is all along in the channels sheltered behind these islands, at the openings of which were the deep pot-holes or 'dahas' in which various living marine animals were met with and the 'dahas' are named after 'Lobster', 'Crab', 'Snake', 'Crocodile' 'Molusca' (Turbinella), and the adventures of the navigators with these pests are mentioned, clearly indicating the journey in inland channels and not in the open sea, a condition which is not to be met with in a journey to Ceylon. After passing the 'dahas' full of marine animals, we come to Hâthîâ-daha or Hâdîâ-daha which is Hanthwadi or Rangoon, after which an inland channel at Bûhîtala is passed probably a point near Pegu on the Pegu river, where islands of weeds, floating over great depth of water, on which cattle graze are mentioned. After this to the left is seen the great Causeway constructed by Râma, and Chandrakûta or Chîtrakûta hills are seen in the Yaksha King's country, and then down the Sîtâkhâlî estuary is entered Hârkhân; it will be clear from the map that from the Pegu river a connecting channel with the Sittang river, which is Sîtâkhâlî of the poet, existed, and that getting into the Sittang, a view to the left will be obtained of the high hills which include the Chîtrakûta hill of Râmâyana as will be seen later on; going down the Sittang estuary, the Gulf of Martabar was entered, which is the sea of Harkand of Mahamadan travellers, referred to in the preceding paragraph and Harkhan of the poet. A short journey along the coast brought the voyager to the estuary of Lankâ river, which must be the Salween river estuary at Moulmein, entering which is the Kâlî-daha, which is no other than the 'daha' or deepwater pool immediately above Moulmein where the Haungtharaw river meets the Salween, and the name Kâlî-daha is perhaps still perpetuated in the village Kado situated at the junction point of the two rivers. Ajay-Vîjay river is therefore the Salween river if not the Donthami river taking off from the Salween above Kado, and the Ratnamâlâ landing stage on the river is the embarking place within 5 miles of Thaton, the Sîmhala city of the poet. Sir Arthur Phayre (Burmah, Ch. III, p. 28) points out that the very extensive ruins of Thaton was once on a creek opening on the Gulf of Martaban, and it is quite possible that this creek may represent the Ajay-Vijay river of Mukundarama. In the return journey from Sîmhala, after leaving Hâdî-daha or Hanth-wadi (Rangoon) river crossing Dhanapatî passed Manohara island to the right and Chîtrabhanga island to the left before reaching the pirate infested creeks of Sunderbuns, which clearly indicates the route lay by Hlang river to Henzada, and Monyo marks the site of Manohara dvipa, which was an island in the Irrawadi, and then by the Okpo channel a connection with the coast existed through the ridge at the head of the channel, and this brought the voyager on to the sheltered side of Cheduba island, the Chitrabhanga island of the poet, which was thus passed to his left, before he entered the Sunderbuns area off Arakan coast. In Rai Dinesh Chandra Sen's Edition, the alternative reading (Vol. II, p. 658) shows that Chataîngâchî or Chittagong was passed in the outward journey after Nîlâchala (Pûrî), then Kaladhauta-pûr or Kaladan River mouth, then Chandraharpûra or Cheduba I. In Manasâr Bhâsân as contained in poet Vansîdas's Padmâpûrâna written in the 15th Century, the route beyond Lankâ island, by the channel of MeKlong which had even at that date a connection with the Gulf of Martaban by the Ataran river is given, where it says (Ramnath and Dwarkanath Chakravarti's Ed. 331 to 338) "After Rama's Causeway the Lankâ capital was in front", which means Thaton in view, then "left Lankâ capital to the right and Malaya hills to the left reached Ahî King's capital Vîjaya City which was passed to the left and then passing a bend Râma's City (Ayodhyâ) was in front" which shows that Thaton was approached from the Gulf of Martaban by the creek mentioned by Sir Arthur Phayre, and that leaving Thaton to the right, the voyage was by the small channel which joins the Salween estuary above Moulmein, then the Ataran river was entered and then the MeKlong which were then connected with each other, thus leaving Vijay city or Sri-Wichaya or Phrapatoom to the left, and then entering the corner of the Gulf of Siam or possibly by an inland connecting creek between MeKlong and Menam bending the course to the north Ayodhyâ or Ayuthia was in front; after passing this bend "the Nîlâskha bend was in front, passing which is the South sea of pearls and corals and Chandrakêtû King's capital", which shows that the voyage was continued to Sîmaharatha the then capital, after turning southward at the mouth of the Bangtapan river. This is another evidence of Lankâ of Râmâyana, to be an island south of Burmah.

The Sîmhala or Lankâ island of Râmâyana, as Golden Kharsonese of Ptolemy we find already joined on to the mainland to its north by Ptolemy's time though a narrow channel for passage of small craft survived, but its south end however extended to C. Maleon Kolon, a point, which from the representation given in the map cannot carry us further south than Kao-Luong peak, and the cape Meleon Kolon is therefore the point Lancon on the Lacon Bight; Kolon in Javanese language means 'west', and this protruding point was at the south-west end of the peninsula as it extended then. That being so, the southern end of the Malay Peninsula was then an island. That this was so, is borne out by travellers of later date, and as a matter of fact Marco Polo passed so late as 1292 A.D., by the open passage between Tenassarim and the Malay Peninsula, the latter being then an island which Polo names as Java the Less. Yule has evidently marked out the route of the traveller by Singapore simply because he assumes that the Malay Peninsula must have been connected with the mainland as now. Let us now follow Marco Polo's journey at this locality. After leaving China, the traveller had arrived in 1292 A.D., at Locac, a station which is identified with Lopaburi, the head-quarters of Siam, by Yule (Marco Polo, by Henry Yule,

Vol. II, Bk. III, Ch. VII) ; (Ch. VIII), "500 miles south of Locac is Pentam I, and 60 miles further Malaur I, the sea in the passage is so shallow (4 paces depth of water) that rudders have to be lifted out for big ships," and (Ch. IX to XI) "from Pentam I, 100 miles is island Java the Less, a compass of 2,000 miles; there are eight kingdoms in this island (1) Ferlec (2) Basma next (3) Samara where owing to adverse winds Marco was detained five months, (4) Dagroian (5) Lambri, inhabited by men having tails, (6) Fansur; only six Kingdoms on this side of the island seen by Messer Marco are mentioned, and two others in the other side are not mentioned." It will be seen that 500 miles south of Lopaburi would bring us to Bandon on the coast, the jutting out land enclosing the district then an island separated from the coast and represented Pentam I, of Marco Polo, and 60 miles further down brings us to Cape Maleon Kolon of Ptolemy, that is present Lacon, where the long tongue of land below Lacon Bight is easily noticeable as an island once separated but recently joined on to the mainland and this island is no doubt the Malaur island of Marco Polo. The shoals in this part of journey are apparent. Then again 100 miles further down is the island, Java the Less, divided into eight provinces, the name of six of which are given; these are (1) Ferlec, which is Perak district (2) Basma is the district round Bernam river, (3) Samara is Selangor district (4) Dagroian is Trengganu district (5) Lambri is Kuala-Lampur, teh reputation of its inhabtiants having tails is perhaps the transformation of Lampur to Lambri or Lomri by Arab travellers in whose language 'lomrî' is a jackal, and (6) Fansur district is the area round Muar river, which claims the old port Maharani Bandar at its mouth, the name of the district derived from its chief town Panchor on the Muar river. A comparison of the identifications of these provinces of Java the Less, as suggested by me, with that made by Yule will probably be convincing to the reader.

Name of District.	As suggested by the Author.	As suggested by Yule (Vol. II, Book III).
1. Ferlec ...	Perak district.	(Ch. IX) Tanjong or Cape Parlak of north-east horn of Sumatra.
2. Basma ...	District round Bernam river.	(Ch. IX) Pasei of Malaya, Passier of modern charts.
3. Samara ...	Selangor district.	(Ch. X) Probably Sumatra, from Sanskrit Samûdra.
4. Dagroian	Trengganu district.	(Ch. X) Unidentified, probably near Pedir.
5. Lambri ...	Kuala-Lampur district.	(Ch. XI) Unidentified, probably north part of west coast.
6. Fansur ...	Area round Muar river with Panchor as chief town.	(Ch. XI) Unidentified, Valentine thinks Pantsur, no longer known by that name but lay in north angle of Sumatra island.

From Lambri, Marco Polo sailed northwards 150 miles to Necuvaram or Nicobars, then to Andamans. This makes it clear that the island Java the Less is the southern part of the Malay Peninsula which was formerly an island, and was not joined on to the mainland by the Isthmus of Kra, even in the 13th Century. The shape of the island was indeed like a 'Java' the Sanskrit name of the island, 'Java' meaning 'Barley'. This explains why we find the Malay Peninsula, northern portion in particular, full of forests and uninhabited until lately (Tytler's ancient Geography referring to the sites of Ophir, Sheba, Taprobane etc., p. 75).

The earlier travellers' accounts confirm this also; thus I-Tsing in 672 A.D. (A record of Buddhist Religion by I-Tsing, translated by J. Takakusu; Introduction, p. XXX to XXI) goes from China to Bhoja, which is either Ayuthia, or Phrapatoom or Sriwichaya; from there "the King sent him to Malayu country which is now called Sribhoja; then going north after more than 10 days' sailed to the country of the naked people, looked at the shores to the east; this country I heard is towards the south-west limit of Shu-Ch'uan; half months sail from here to north-west we reached Tâmralîptî." Now the country of the naked people which lies towards the south-west of Shu-Ch'uan in China is no doubt south of Burmah; in going from Bhoja, to the coast of Burmah, the southern-most point reached by him is Malayu, as he goes from Bhoja to Malayu and then turns north, hugging the coast land to the east, as he says he was looking at the coast to the east in this portion of his journey northwards which took 10 days only, to south of Burmah to the point from where he diverted his journey straight to Tâmralîptî in Bengal. It is impossible to do the journey from Sîngapore to Burmah in 10 days, and it is therefore clear that I-Tsing crossed over from the Gulf of Siam to the Bay of Bengal at a point much nearer to Burmah and Bhoja, and the conclusion is that the southern portion of Malay Peninsula was detached from the mainland as found later on by Marco Polo. I-Tsing found people in southern Burmah uncivilised and naked and it is not a matter of surprise when we remember that in the 2nd Century A.D., the Khersonese area was firm land occupied by semi-civilised Râkshases of Lankâ, and then the east coast became submerged under the sea, bringing about a condition in which people who still stuck to the area suffering from physical vicissitudes, could only have fallen back to wild life.

In the accounts of India and China given by the Mahamadan Travellers, in 851 to 869 A.D., translated by Renandot (Usebius Renandot, First Account, pages 1 and 2) it is stated that "between the sea of Delarowi and that of Harkûnd are many islands, as they say 1900, ruled over by a woman queen". The Sea of Harkund is the Gulf of Martaban and the sea of Delarowi is the Gulf of Siam, intervening which we find the sea dotted over with innumerable islands, under a single queen's control, and this can only mean an inconsiderable area as the Kingdoms of those days were; it therefore can only mean that the parting area dotted with islands was fairly near to Gulf of Martaban, and not so far south as Singapore, and that the opening which was near Isthmus of Kra, was then a point of the sea which was shallow and dotted over with islands much like the Mergui Archipelego area.

The southern boundary of Khersonese of Ptolemy is therefore shown to be fairly correct, and we turn now to its eastern boundary which is a short length from C. Maleon Kolon to the Perimoulic Gulf, at the head of which is Samarade town; the Perimoulic Gulf is therefore the small gulf, where the Menam river falls into the Gulf of Martaban and on the east coast of this gulf the old city Simharatha, which is without doubt Samarade of Ptolemy, exactly at the place where we would expect it.

Having come to this point, and having demonstrated the comparative accuracy of Polemy's map, the next important problem, *viz.*, the location Magnus Sinus, or the Great Gulf, shown as penetrating, a good long way northwards from Perimoulic Gulf is easily solved. It can only mean that the bulk of Siam, forming its central portion, which is barely 300 ft., above sea level now, was under the sea in Ptolemy's time forming the Magnus Sinus; the western boundary was the range of hills to the east of Menam river, up to near old Saketa, or Sokotai of maps, from which point the boundary curved eastwards till it met the range of hills on the right bank of the Mekong river; the boundary then followed the base of the hills on the right bank of the river, forming part of the northern, and whole of the eastern boundary of Magnus Sinus.

The Great Gulf as described, practically forms the eastern boundary of the southern portion of Jambû-dvîpa, that is the Bhâratvarsha of Jambûdvîpa, which is also the Bhâratvarsha of Râmâyana. With the sea so near from the central portion of Jambûdvîpa or Sûmêrû, the main rivers had their outlets towards this Great Gulf not only up to the Râmâyana period, but so late as Ptolemy's time as shown in this map. The great central river, Doanas of Ptolemy, is unmistakably the main southern stream of the Gangâ of Jambûdvîpa and it is shown by Ptolemy as R. Doana and falling into the Great Gulf, a little below Syda city. This Syda city must therefore be taken as old Ayodhyâ, the Thuketa of the Burmese, or Sâkêta of Sanskrit literature, the ancient capital of Siam which is now represented by Sokotai; the name Syda sounds almost the same as 'Judea' to which Ayuthia has been corrupted locally for some centuries. Starting with Syda or Ayodhyâ of Râmâyana, we find that Râma leaving this city for the forest, goes (Râmâyana, Ayodhyâ Ch. 46) to the banks of Tamasâ river the same night; (Ch. 49) next day proceeds to the limits of Kosala country and then Vêdasrûtî river continuing in a southern direction, after a little while reaches Gomatî river crossing which, reaches Syandîkâ river crossing which, (Ch. 50) he meets with the Gangâ river at Srîngavêra-pûra; and then (Ch. 52) crosses the Gangâ river here over to the southern bank the next morning." Thus from Ayodhya to river Gangâ the journey was generally in a south western direction, and the river at no great distance, only two or three days journey from Ayodhyâ. The big central river Doanas is shown as passing at no great distance from Syda, and to its south east, and this therefore must be Gangâ, and its location at this place agrees with present Me-ping river, which is therefore identical with this Doanas of Ptolemy, and Gangâ of Râmâyana; as shown by Ptolemy this river in its upper reaches flows by the valley to the east of the Mandara or the Arakan Yomas, that is, through centre of upper Burmah and must be the Irrawadi near Mandalay or Sûmêrû which means that the Irrawadi formerly flowed eastward into the Me-ping, which was the Doanas or Gangâ, a fact which is borne out by Siam traditions holding the Menam of which Me-ping is the main affluent, as a very sacred river and Gangâ of Jambûdvîpa according to Pûrânas flowed by Brahmâ's city which is Monywa near Mandalay. As the Gomatî had its independent outlet to the sea, we must also assume

Tamasâ river above it must have similarly had its independent outlet to the Sea, and the present town Chumsengsonkgram on the Menam, about 80 miles below Sokotai, is obviously the Sanskrit name 'Tamasâ-Sangama' or the confluence of the Tamasâ with the sea, or the 'Great Gulf,' which enables us to fix another point on this Gulf. Ayodhyâ or Sâkêta itself was on river Sarayû, further north of Tamasâ, also a small river not shown by Ptolemy. Thus we see that the Irrawadi from Mandalay, flowed formerly into the Great Gulf, its channel lower down being the Me-ping; as the sea receded the rivers to the north of Me-ping, having their outlets to the sea interfered with, gradually joined with each other beginning with the northern-most pair, and thus combining finally with the Me-ping, and forming the new combined river Me-nam along the western boundary of the Great Gulf. Similar changes took place on the eastern boundary of the Great Gulf, forming the Me-kong river, which however differs in this, that from beyond the Great Gulf it had already a considerable river to its north as will be seen from the present maps, and the first nucleus of the river was therefore one of some magnitude, which pirated on the others down below it; this upper river at a very early period received some spill of the Gangâ or Irrawadi, and it is for this reason we find in local tradition and history that (Reclus' Universal Geography Vol. III, p. 473) "MeKong was even in the last century, still supposed to be a branch of the Ganges, one of the sacred 'Gangâ' flowing from Mt. Mêrû."

We are now in a position to trace roughly the Gangâ branches of Jambûdvîpa. The accounts of Gangâ given have been very much mixed up in the Pûrânas, as this name has been applied to a very large number of rivers, each fresh batch of colonists in a new area naming their chief river Gangâ, whether it is in Cambodia or Siam, or Burmah, or India in different sections, or Ceylon. It is at first a difficult task to separate the account of Gangâ of Jambûdvîpa and then again, even when this could be done, we find several lengths of different Gangâs of

Jambûdvîpa as the island developed and joined on to the continental area, bringing about with it complete changes in the course of the rivers makes the situation further complicated. In the Bhâgavata Pûrâna we find the initial stage of the main rivers of Jambû-dvîpa when it was an island (V Skanda, Ch. 16) *viz.*, Arûnodâ river and Jambû river, rising from the barrier hills, Mandara and Mêrû-mandara of Ilâvrîta Varsha, the rivers receiving their sources of supply from the juice of huge fruits of Dêva-chyûta, and Jambû trees respectively. The next stage we find, when Jambû-dvîpa has joined with the mainland to its north described in the next chapter (Ch. 17) thus :—"When Vîshnû visiting the sacrificial ceremonies performed by King Balî, assumed his Trîvrîkrama form, and wanted to move his left foot towards the north, a rift was made by his toe accidentally striking against the egg-shell (of the continent compared to an egg), made a rift in the land through which an external stream was diverted into Jambûdvîpa; this stream was draining the saffron-colour water which was accumulated by the washing of the head of Svarga for thousands of Yûgas". The earthly Svarga region is placed to north of Uttarkûrû, that is north of Jambûdvîpa, and this indicates that the Tibetan stream Tsangpo was diverted into the Jambûdvîpa or Burmah area, when this island joined on to Tibet; this Tsangpo would thus appear to be a distorted form of Jambû. The account proceeds "This Gangâ born of Vîshnû's feet, was led by a heavenly channel, and flooding the Chandra-mandala, alighted in Brahmâ's place in Sûmêrû, from where it divided into four streams, Sîtâ, Alakânandâ, Vankhû and Bhadrâ". This portion of the channel is the Irrawadi, the point at which the Tibetan channel burst would be at Brahma-kûnda, and 'Chandra-mandala' is the 'Indaw-gye' or the 'great Indra' lake, Chandra being a term often used in place of Indra, and Brahma-sadana at Sûmêrû is Monywa near Mandalay as already demonstrated. The point where the river divided into four streams is htus to west of Mandalay.

The details of these four effluents have been given, differently in different accounts, and it will not be possible to enter into great details here. I will reproduce here extracts ot some of these accounts, to roughly indicate the channels. The Bhâgavata Pûrâna (V, 17) says Gangâ divided into four streams from Sûmêrû :—(1) Sîtâ, separating from Brahmâ's place, flowing by Gandhamâdana barrier range, and then through Bhadrâsva Varsha, into the salt sea; (2) Vankshû, passing by Mâlyavâna, then through Kêtûmâla Varsha into the western sea; (3) Bhadrâ, flowing northwards, through Nîla, Svêta and Srîgavâna ranges, and Uttara-Kûrû country into the northern salt sea; and (4) Alakânandâ, emanating from Brahmâ's place in Sûmêrû, passing by Hêmakûta and Hîmakûta, and Bhâratvarsha, into the sea towards the south. Vâyû Pûrâna (Ch. 42) says that, Sûra-nadî divides into following four branches on meeting the northern peaks of Mêrû :—Sîtâ, flows by Mandara hill, Sîtânta hill, and through the Bhadrâsva Varsha, and falls into the eastern sea; (2) Alakânandâ, flows by the southerly ridge of Gandhamâdana hills, then through Hêmakûta and Hîmâlaya and then falls into the south sea; (3) Nandâ (replaced by Chakshû in Varâha Pûrâna, and Sarakshû in Markandêya Pûrâna) flowing by Hîmâlaya, Mêrûkûta, and then through the Kêtûmâla Varsha, and falls into the western sea; (4) Bhadra-somâ (replaced by Somâ in Markandêyâ Pûrâna) flowing by Sûpârsva hill, through Nîla-parvvata, Svêta-parvvata, meets the western sea, and Mahânadî (main stream seems to be indicated, and the meeting of western sea is perhaps by a branch of it) after flooding a broad expanse near Sûpârsva hill, and then carrying floating rafts of flowering plants, flows through Uttarkûrû country and falls into the northern sea; later on (Ch. 45) it is stated that Bhadrasîmâ river flows between Chandrakûta and Sûryakûta hills in Uttarkûrû country which is also known as Bhaûmasvarga, or the earthly-heaven. In Vîshnû Pûrâna (II) Gangâ issuing from Svarga, lands in Brahmâ's place and divides into four streams :—(1) Sîtâ, flowing eastwards, crossing many hills, then to Bhadrâsva Varsha; (2) Alakâ flowing towards the south, divides into seven streams in Bhâratvarsha; (3) Chakshû flowing west through hills and Kêtûmâla Varsha; (4) Bhadrâ, through Uttarkûrû country of the north and hills, flows into sea. Brîhad-dharma Pûrâna (Pûrva, Ch. 6) says Gangâ divides at Sûmêrû in Dhârâpâta into four streams, (1) Sîtâ to east, (2) Nandaka to south (3) Vankshû to west and (4) Bhadrottara to north; the four doors of Gangâ (Gangâ-dvâra) are (1) Brahma-dvâra for Kêtûmâla Varsha (2) Sîvadvâra for Kûrû Varsha (3) Têjodvâra for Bhadrâsva Varsha and (4) Harîdvâra for Bhâratvarsha.

The position of the Varshas in Jambûdvîpa has been described in the beginning of the chapter, namely Ilavrîta in centre, with Bhadrâsva to its east, and Kêtumâla to west, and to north Ramayaka, Hîranmaya and Kûrû successively and to south Harî, Kîmpûrûsha and Bhârata successively. The boundary of the Jambûdvîpa can be roughly outlined now as below :—To the north the eastern end of the Hîmalayas; to the west the Patkoi Range and Arakan Yomas and south of Pegu Yomas curving south-east to about Bangkok; the southern boundary practically tapers to a hairpin curve at Bangkok; the eastern boundary beginning from the south is the Menam up to Chumseng-Songkram, then by Pitsanulok, curving eastwards till it meets the MeKong at Kiang-khan, then following the MeKong, and its eastern branch the Ho river from where curving westwards to where the valleys of the MeKong, the Red river and Yangstze-Kiang run close to each other forming the northern boundary at the eastern end of Himalayas or Namku Range. In this area the varshas are therefore distributed as shown in Fig. 4.

A comparison of this figure with the conception of Jambûdvîpa, given in Fig. 3, at the beginning of this chapter, will show the remarkable likeness of the two.

The rivers can now be delineated in it from the description of the Pûrânas quoted above. The main heavenly Gangâ, or Sûrâ-nadî, emanates from Brahma-Kûnd, and flowing by the Irrawadi channel, came to

Sûmêrû head at Monywa; at this point the channel divided into four streams as below :—

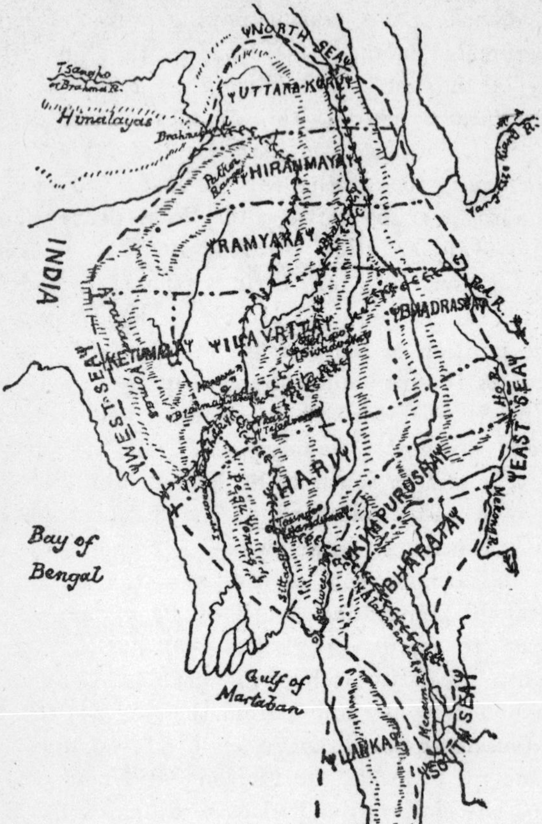

FIG. 4.—Jambû-dvîpa.

(1) Sîtâ, which flowed by Gandhamâdana according to Bhâgavat Pûrâna but by Mandara and Sîtânta according to the Vâyû Pûrâna, and then through Bhadrâsva

Varsa to the Eastern Sea; the Vrîhad-dharma Pûrâna says that the 'gate' of this effluent is Têjodvâra, which must be Tejovatî or Tejasvînî city of Agnî, that is Thazi as given early in this chapter. This channel is therefore from Monywa, by the Irrawadi to Myingyan, and then by the remnant of the channel passing by Meiktila to Thazi, from where it must have flowed eastwards by the Zawgyi, and Nam-lang river valley and then by upper Salween river to the sea to the east, which was near MeKong river.

(2) Vankshû, or Chakshû, or Sarakshû, or Nandâ, flowed by Malyavâna according to Bhâgavat Pûrâna, but Hîmalaya and Mêrûkûta according to Vâyû Pûrâna, and then by Kêtûmâla Varsha to the Western sea; its 'gate' was Brahma-dvâra; the channel thus branched out at Monywa itself, eastwards to Saga, then down the Myttha valley, penetrating the Chin Hills to Myohanng and met the sea below Akyab.

(3) Bhadrâ or Bhadrasomâ, or Somâ, or Bhadrottara flowed by Supârsva barrier hill, and then flowing northwards penetrated into Nîla, Svêta and Srîngavâna Parvvatas and flowing through Uttarkûrû, fell into the North sea; the gate of this river was the Sîva-dvâra, and thus it flowed from Monywa eastwards to Mandalay and then by the Mytinge valley by Hsipaw, which is the Sîva-dvâra, and then turned northwards to the Nam Yao joining the Shweli, made straight for the valley where the upper courses of the Salween, MeKong and Yangtsze-Kiang converge, which was a part of the sea, the northern sea of Jambûdvîpa

(4) Alakânandâ, or Alakâ, or Nandaka, flowing through Hêmakûta and Hîmalaya into Bhâratvarsha; its gate was Harî-dvâra, which must be a place somewhere in Harîvarsha, and Toungoo, suggested to be the place. This channel seems therefore to have bifurcated from the Sîta, at Thazi, then following the Sittang channel, by the valley in which the Burmah Railway line from Thazi to Toungoo runs and then turning eastwards joined the Salween at Bawlake area, and then followed the Salween

channel, to the Thaungyin river flowing at the base of the Dwana Range, and eventually joining the Meping at Raheng, falling into the sea near Nakon Sawan.

The channels of Jambû-dvîpa as indicated, gives us a clue to the channels shown by Ptolemy. The main river is the Doanas, and it flows from the Bepyrrhos Mt., and is therefore to be taken as the Gangâ at this point, and lower down it falls into the Great Gulf, below Syda or Sokotai and it is therefore the Alakânandâ channel as indicated above; its name Doanas is still to be found in the name of the Dwana range of hills along the base of which it flows, and possibly the Sanskrit name Nandaka given to the Alakânanda is corrupted into Doanas.

When the Jambû-dvîpa joined on to China to the north the outlets of the rivers flowing to the north were closed the land in China being high, and their flow reversed; the Bhadrâ river was thus forced to flow into the Gangâ or Irrawadi. This river, when reversed, divided into two distinct branches, one of them the Shweli, and the other the Namyao-cum-Mytinge channel. The Bhadrâ river was one of great sanctity and of early colonisation on its banks, and we find that one section of it now named Nam Yao is termed the Doktowadi in the maps published, even so late as 1907 A.D., by Bartholomew, and also by Harmsworth; this Doktowadi is phonetically the same as Drîshadvatî river of Sanskrit literature; and Shweli must therefore be the revered Saraswatî river. The area enclosed between the Gangâ (Irrawadi), Sarasvatî (Shweli) and Drîshadvatî (Mytinge) is the sacred Madhya-dêsa, and we find the Madaya province here. The affluent of the Doanas shown as branching out towards the east is the Salween which came into being when the sea to north of Jambûdvîpa was closed up; this points to the identification of Adcisaga of Ptolemy with moedrn Saga or Sakoi of maps, and Arisabion of Ptolemy with Yadashe north of Toungoo.

The above enables us now to explain the location of Indraprathai in Ptolemy's map. Indraprathai is shown lying between the main river Gangâ or Irrawadi and its eastern tributary, the Sarasvatî or the Shweli; and it is between these two rivers that the celebrated Indraprastha of Mahâbhârata was located, and there can be no doubt about its identification with the Bhamo area, the "Bhaûma-Svarga" of the Sanskrit classics. McCrindle has suggested that this Indraprathai is perhaps a Brahmin colony from Indian-Indraprastha, but the possibility of its being exactly the reverse does not seem to have struck him.

The foregoing points, fixes roughly the alignment of the Doana river in its upper reaches in Ptolemy's time. In the lower reaches, we have seen, it flows very near Sokotai, or Syda of Ptolemy (early in this chapter). I will now fix the important point Baradaxa or Baradaza, shown near the west bank of the river at the base of the Maiandros Montes. Baradaxa is the famous Bharadvâja-âsrama, a considerable city which is referred to in many places as Bharadvâja-pûra. We have already referred to part of the journey from Ayodhyâ to Bharadvâja-âsrama given in Râmâyana (Ayodhyâ, 49 Et. Seq.); the point at which Râma crosses the river, *viz.*, Srîngavêra-pûra, the nearest point on the Gangâ (Doana of Ptolemy) leads us to Raheng; crossing the Gangâ at this place, the previous evening and (Ayodhyâ, Ch. 54), "leaving early in the morning, reached in the evening Prayâga at the confluence of the Gangâ and Yamûnâ, where Bharadvâja-âsrama was situated" and then (Ch. 55 and 56) "next day following the Kâlîndî river (another name for Yamûnâ) and crossing that river in rafts came in view of Chîtrakûta, and the next day reached Vâlmîkî's âsrama on Chîtrakûta hills on the banks of Mâlyavatî river". It will be seen in Ptolemy's map, that R. Sobanos is shown as issuing from near Bardaxa; and that the Doanas runs quite close to this point, and it is to be expected that the rivers running so close were connected at this point, and Sobanos is therefore the Yamûnâ, and Bardaxa where the river was connected with the Doanas or Gangâ, is the famous Bharadvâja rîshî's place; the Yamûnâ of Râmâyana, or Sobanos of Ptolemy, will thus fit in exactly with the

MeKlawng river connected with the upper portion of the Thaungyin river, and Malyavatî river is the small river taking its rise at Pwemu and passing by Mya-vadi town which preserves the name even now. Bharadvâja âsrama is therefore in the neighbourhood of Ri-Ke, if not Ri-Ke itself, which may be a distorted form of 'Rishi'. Myavadi must be Vâlmîki's âsrama, and an indication to this direction is given when Sîtâ is banished from Ayodhyâ, and (Râmâyana, Uttara, 56) "Lakshman takes Sîtâ to the Gomatî river crossing the first evening, and starting next morning reaches Bhâgîrathî (*i.e.*, Gangâ) the next morning and crossing the river, points out to Sîtâ, the âsrama of Vâlmîki"; it will be seen that Mayavadi will be in view after crossing the river at Raheng or perhaps a little above this point, as in this journey Srîngavêra-pûra is not mentioned, though the crossing was effected by Nîshâda's indicate they were men belonging to the Gûha King of Srîgavêra-pûra. Chîtrakûta hill on which Vâlmîkî and Bharadvâja âsramas are situated is therefore the southern portion of the Dwana Range, and these hills are visible from the Sea as mentioned in Mûkûndarâma poet's work on Chandî discussed in this chapter already. South of this point is the Lesto Regia or Robber's country of Ptolemy; it is in this area that Râma is called upon to extirpate the enemies of the Rîshî; it is also the area to which the original inhabitants of Burmah, the Yakkshas, were forced to take shelter, when pressed by the Aryan colonists from Indraprathai area, as also of the Ayodhya or Syda area; these robbers are the 'Dashyus' whom Arjjûna was incapable to resist at the time of the memorable withdrawal of the Jâdava women, when Dvârâvatî had to be evacuated; the location of the Lesto Regia of Ptolemy between Dwana Range southern portion extending to the Gulf of Martaban and the Gulf of Siam to the south, must therefore be accepted. In Râmâyana (Lankâ, 22), Râma arrived at the east side of Lankâ across to sea, and threatened the sea with his arrow, when "Samudra" (Sea personified) addressing Râma said "Towards the north at this place, there is one of my openings known as Drûmakûlya, which is occupied by fierce and cruel robbers, * * * let your arrow fall there. Râma let go his arrow there, which dried up the sea water and the area was converted into healthy level plains * * * . The Causeway to Lanka was built near that spot later on". This also confirms the location of the Lesto Regia, and incidentally of the reclamation of the sea between Lanka and the mainland in this locality.

We are now in a position to follow the coast line of Extra-Gangem India of Ptolemy, beginning from the western boundary, or the mouth of the Ganges. The first point Petapol or Pentapolis on the coast, must have disappeared altogether by the subsidence and submergence of this coast.

The mouth of Katabeda river, comes next on the coast; this would correspond to the Kutubdia channel, which was possibly a former considerable affluent of the Kaladan river which was the Vankshû branch of Gangâ of Jambûdvîpa; Kutubdia island at the mouth of this river is very likely the small Kataha island of Sanskrit literature, a point which commanded the trade from China; in Kathâ-Sarît Sâgara (I, XIII.) "Gûhasêna, merchant of Tâmralîpta goes in a ship to Katâha for trade", again (IX, LVI.) Chandrasvâmîn, goes in search of his sister "reaching Jalapûra on the sea shore, then in ship to Nârîkêla island, then to Katâha island, then Karpûra island, then Sûvarna island, then Sîmhala island, then crossing the sea to Chîrtakûta city". This trade route from Tâmralîpta to Sîmhala island and Chîtrakûta city, will appear to follow that described by poet Mûkûndarâm Chakravartî as given early in this Chapter, and Karpûra island is Kayukpyo or Ramree island and the position of Katâha island would agree with that of Kutubdia which is evidently corrupt of Katâha-dvîpa, and Katabeda of Ptolemy is yet another corrupt form of the same.

Next point on the coast is Barakoura, a mart which is Baronga island, the mart represented by modern Akyab.

The mouth of the river Tokosanna comes next on the coast, the river is probably the Bemro river, passing by Myohaung, which was formerly a big river and an affluent of the Irrawadi, the Chakshû river of Pûrânas, which perhaps explains the name Tokosanna or Chakshû-nada.

Sambra city near the mouth of the river is Ramree.

Sada city is Cheduba in Cheduba or Chandra-dvipa island, Sada being corrupt of Chandra; Sada river being the An river.

Berabonna mart comes next on the coast, and its situation agrees with Sandway or Dvârâtwatî.

Next we come to the mouth of the Temala. The point to remember here is, that as we find from Ptolemy's map that the Irrawadi (Gangâ) had not opened out its present channel to the west, the whole of the jutting out delta below Bassein district had not been formed; the coast line thus curved eastwards from immediately below Sandway, towards Rangoon. Temala was a river draining the valley between Arakan and Pegu Yomas, that is the lower Irrawady basin extending north up to the Thayetmyo district; Temala is therefore the river which had the present Irrawadi channel from the neighbourhood of Henzada northward to Prome then curving eastwards by the Nawin channel to Thanbulla which latter is the Temala city of Ptolemy. The Temala valley is the Tamâla forest referred to in Râmâyana (Kîshkîndhyâ, 37) which is placed on the sea coast, proceeding west from Kîshkîndhyâ (Kyaikto, see Ch. XII), and on the base of the Mêrû (Arakan Yomas) where it ends near the sea coast, and the area inhabited by Narîkêras, and on this route Râma met the old Savar woman, which agrees with the locality of Sobara of Ptolemy. This river is the same as the Aîrâvatî river, mentioned in Matsya Pûrâna (Ch. 116, 117, 119, 121), where this river is put in the borders of Madra kingdom, its source in Hîmavâna mountain of Jambûdvîpa, the river issuing from near Atrî Rîshî's âsrama, north of which is Trîpûrârî's (Sîva's) country, where Kûvêra was living in Alakâ city, near to which is Mandodaka lake, from which flows Mandâkînî river; the

Hîmavâna mountain is the range dividing Kîmpûrûsha and Bhâratavarsha which curves northwards to this locality, and as the âsrama is south of Sîva's country or Hsipaw district and near to Alakâ which seems to be Laikha, and Mandodaka lake which is Lule lake near Mawnang which brings us to the neighbourhood of Thanbulla, and Ela Ry. station lying between them marks the site of Irâ laks, the source of the Irâvatî-nadî given in Kâlîkâ Pûrâna (Ch. 23), or Aîrâvatî of Matsya Pûrâna. The figure of Bhagavâna Janârddana established in this âsrama is described in detail as "lying on Bhogî's subjects, in reclining posture, one of his knees bent, the other stretched straight, one of his arms resting on the bed of Nâga on which rests his head, second arm stretched downwards little bent with his ankle resting on the thigh, third hand stretched forward and fourth hand holding a flower near the nose." It is one of the figures which shred of two arms, is converted into the reclining Bûddha (see Fig. 5), which is to be seen all over this area, which was the Harî varsha where Narâyana Harî in the form indicated, was worshipped by the Nâgas or rather the Nâts of the Burmese who were guided by their Shin 'Ari (Srî-Harî) lords. Ela town represents the house of Ilâ, and the Doanas or Alakânandâ flowing by it is referred to in Râmâyana (Ayodhyâ, 68) as the river flowing by Aîladhâma or house of Ila and the Aîrâvatî river is the river emanating from Ilâ or Irâ, which are convertible names.

The cape beyond it brings us to the neighbourhood of Rangoon, after which is the Sarabakic Gulf, on the coast of which are the cannibals. It is the head of Lankâ island of Râkshasas who are reputed man-eaters and known to the Burmese as Bilu or ogres, a term which corresponds to Sanskrit Râkshasas, the city Bilin, north of Thaton, and Bilu-gyon or Râkshasa-island at the mouth of the Moulmein river marks out the coast of this gulf. Besynga river must therefore be the Bilin river, and the same as the Godâvarî river of Râmâyana (*vide* Ch. XII). Sobara city lying on the coast between the mouths of the Temala and Besynga rivers, is Thabyegan to the east of Rangoon, and Besynga mart is Bilin city which is now a little inland but on the Bilin river.

Sada city, marked also Saurada on the map, agrees with the position of Thaton, which was Sîmha-râshtra, the capital founded by Thiha Radza in the middle of the 6th Century B.C., and the Sîmhala city of Mûkûndarâm poet; this city was on the sea coast even up to Bûddha Ghosa's time, anterior to 3rd Century B.C., (*vide* Bigandet's Goadama Vol. II, Ch. V, p. 145).

The cape beoynd is now submerged as had been the whole west coast of Khersonese as pointed out previously; the next point, the southern angle of the coast, the Khersone port, is Junk-Seylon or Salang, or the Sûvarna-Lankâ or Golden Lankâ point.

The coast line turns at right angles to the east from Salang, on to Lancon point, the Maleon Kolon Cape of Ptolemy, after which the coast runs northwards, passing by Koh-Lim now an island, formerly joined with the mainland, representing Koli town of Ptolemy; the coast continuing northwards to the little gulf at the head of the Gulf of Siam, where the Menam river falls into the sea, which gulf is the Perimoulik Gulf referred to by Ptolemy, its shape like a small hollow cut into the land, which gives its name. The town Perimoula on the coast is ancient town Phra-mot.

The coast of the Lestii, or Robber's country comes here; this has been located already.

The first city is Samarade, which is modern Simaharatha situated on the east coast of the Perimoulic gulf after which the mouth of the Sobanos river is reached on the coast. This Sobanos river as already shown, is the Yamûnâ river of Râmâyana, the modern MeKlong which formerly curved eastwards a little to the north of the Perimoulic gulf, and fell into the sea to the east of Simaharatha, its new short cut to the gulf *viâ* Ratburi being a later development, though the name of the town at this month, which is Sanun-Savan-Kram, seems to be corrupt 'Yamûnâ-Sangama' or the point of Yamûnâ meeting the sea, indicates that the main outlet probably was here from an early Râmâyana period and the eastern channel shown by Ptolemy is perhaps an affluent. Fontes Fluvii, of which the position is given to west of Samarade, and mentioned by the Latin translator, but the position of which is not given in the map, agrees with the position of the present MeKlong mouth.

At the mouth of this river to east of Simaharatha, we find town Pasê to its west which is Pagrasa of Ptolemy.

Pithonabasti I do not find in the small scale maps.

Akadra must be in the neighbourhood of Chantabun if not Chantabun itself as already suggested by Yule; after this point comes Zabai city jutting out at the corner of the land, which is Mt. Sabab, exactly where we should expect it, situated at the end of the range of hills near Chantabun. This also represents the great cape from which the Magnus Sinus or 'Great Gulf' of Ptolemy begins, the coast here turning abruptly north, and then curves westwards.

The first town on this coast is Thagora, which agrees with the position of Sanem-Chaya-Khet.

Next is Balonga, which must be the ancient city Lopaburi or the city of Lava, one of the twin sons of Râma; the name Balonga is probably from Se Prang, the town to the north-east of Lopaburi.

Throana comes next on the coast; this is Chainat.

After this comes the mouth of the Doanas river or Gangâ of Râmâyana as already demonstrated, the mouth being at Nakawn-Sawan.

Kortatha or Kottadra would be in the neighbourhood of Pechabun, and Doana or Dasana is represented by Dansai.

This completes the outline of the coast of Extra-Gangem India of Ptolemy; the coast line beyond will not be followed further as it is not required for purposes of following up the boundary of either Jambu-dvipa or Extra-Gangem India. Kattigara, the cape, an important maritime port in those days, situated, on the route to China, and the location as shown in the map is almost opposite to the Maleon Kolon cape of Khersonese, and at the eastern end of the Great Gulf, is undoubtedly Cape Camao or Cambodia, the name Kattigara suggests a mutilated form of Kamboja-nagara. The trade route from China up to the 7th Century was mostly by the Great Gulf, which was the inland shallow sea, red with the silt laden water of the river and thus termed by the Chinese "the Red South", touching Kattigara on the way.

We now know of Burmah in three stages.

(1) As Jambû-dvîpa island, time uncertain.

(2) As delineated in Ptolemy's map; in the 2nd Century A.D.

(3) As in present maps.

The first stage of Jambû-dvîpa as a single island is gleaned from the most prevalent accounts given in the Pûrânas and the Mahâbhârata. There are however stray references given of an anterior stage, when this island was also split up into several islands, and as a matter of fact from the descriptions of the seven islands making up the known world, names of which are given in Chapter XI, it is apparent that some of these islands overlap the areas of Varshas of Jambû-dvîpa; then again in some instances as in Padma Pûrâna (Svarga I) it is stated that Bhadrâsva, Kêtûmâla, Jambû-dvîpa and Uttarkûrû are islands round the Sûmêrû. The Jambûdvîpa itself was therefore formerly a group of islands which joined on to each other and formed one island.

This island was separated from the continental area towards China to north, from Indian islands to the east, from French Indo-China which was then the island of Mahâ-Champâ, to the east, and from Lankâ island consisting of Tenassarin district, and Yama-dvîpa, or Java the Less forming now the Malay Peninsula towards the south.

The silt poured into the intervening seas by the Tsang-Po or Brahmapûtra river gradually filled up these shallow intervening seas, and joined the Jambû-dvîpa to the mainland, at first towards its north-eastern corner, and in time the Tsangpo river, began to flow through the centre of this island, and from the description of the rivers of Jambû-dvîpa as given in this Chapter already, it will be seen, that this river had then advanced to Mandalay, and was then divided into four broad streams, which were perhaps remnants of the shallow seas formerly intervening the component islands of Jambû-dvîpa. In this stage of Jambû-dvîpa, it has been compared to the delineation of the rabbit outline in the moon, a comparison which has been applied to the Jambû-dvîpa of Burmah, as also in later interpolations, to the peninsular part of India. It is not difficult to separate the original and the later interpolations in the accounts given in the Mahâbhârata where (Bhîsma Ch. 5) Sanjaya tells Dhrîtarâshtra that "Jambû-dvîpa is round like a wheel. As a man sees the reflection of his face in a mirror, so is the reflection of Jambû-dvîpa seen in the Moon. Two parts of the Jambû-dvîpa are Pîppala-sthâna (Peepul-tree area) and two parts the great Sasasthâna (Rabbit area)". Then (Ch. 6) Dhrîtarâshtra asks Sanjay to "describe the area of Sasasthâna first, and then of the Pîppala-sthâna" and Sanjaya in reply, gives at first the details of the Jambû-dvîpa divisions, with Sûmêrû in the centre and Bhadrâsva, Kêtûmâla, Jambû, Utterkûrû and Bhâratvarsha as its divisions, making it clear that it is Jambû-dvîpa of Burmah; after he has given these details which must be of Sasathâna, Sanjaya goes on to add (at the end of the chapter) as follows :—

"The Sasathâna of which you (Dhrîtarâshtra) have asked, I am describing now, which please listen; north and south of Sasathâna (Rabbit area) are two Varshas (divisions of the Country), Nâga-dvîpa and Kâsyapa-dvîpa are like the two ears of the Rabbit-area, and Tâmraparnî hill and Malaya Mt., are placed in the Rabbit-area which is counted as the second island of Jambû-dvîpa."

Then in Chapter 7, the details of Sûmêrû Mt., and Uttarkûrû are resumed. It is clear from this that the concluding portion of Ch. 6, is later interpolation and it refers to the Taprobane island containing Malaya Mt., as the Rabbit-area, with the Nâga islands and Kâsyapa island as its ears, whereas the rest of the description is of Jambû-dvipa which is also compared to the rabbit outline of the moon. Though Sanjaya says that two parts are Pîppala-area and two parts are Rabbit-area, and Dhrîtarâshtra asks him to describe the Rabbit-area first and then the Pîppala-area, it is curious that Sanjaya does not mention the details of the Pîppala area at all; this fact would lead us to conclude that as he was dealing with the Jambû-dvîpa the Rabbit outline referred to the Jambû-dvîpa of Burmah, and that the Pîppala-area and Rabbit-area of India, which are not described in detail, refer to India and are later interpolations, and a clumsy attempt to merge the Rabbit-area of one into that of the other. The Rabbit outline of the Jambû-dvîpa of Burmah, and the Peepul and Rabbit outline of India would be recognised from Figure 6.

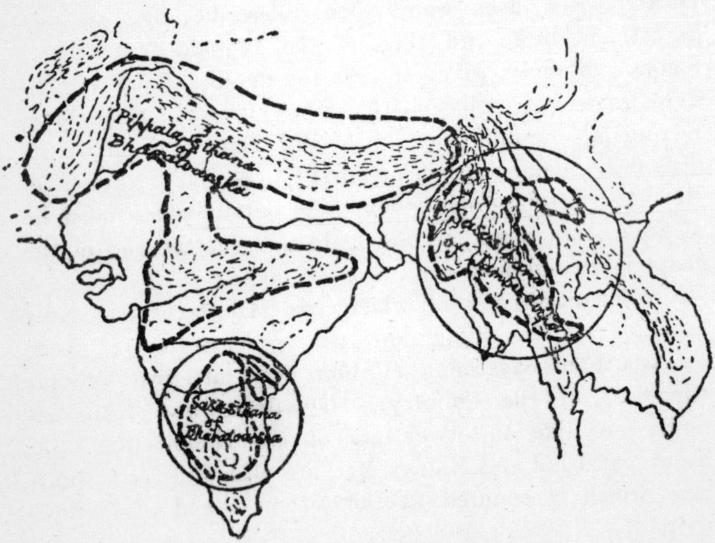

FIG. 6.—Sasa-sthâna and Pîppala-sthâna of Jambû-dvîpa and Bhâratvarsha.

It will be noticed that the figure of Pîppala-sthâna or Peepul tree area of India is made up by the Vîndhyas or Indradvîpa portion representing the roots, the Aravalli Range forming the stem, and the Himalayas with the

Hindukush Mt., west, and Garo hills to the east forming the branches; the Sasa-sthâna or Rabbit area of India is made up of Taprobane island of Greeks or Tâmra-dvîpa of Pûrânas, as the body of the Rabbit, and Nâga-dvîpa and Kâsyapa-dvîpa referred to in Chap. X, as its ears. The Jambû-dvîpa as the Sasa-sthâna or Rabbit-area is made up of the Pegu and Arakan Yomas with Patkoi Range forming the body, and the tableland of Yunnan or Gândhâra of Pûrânas forming the ear.

The next stage we find the northern (Bhadrâ), eastern (Sîtâ) branches closed as effluents; the eastern branch flowing into the Great Gulf of Ptolemy to its north, having already reclaimed the sea between China and northern French Indo-China, the main stream was the Alakânandâ or Nandâ to south, flowing into the Great Gulf to its west. The next stage with a little further change in the river, *viz.*, that the western stream (Vankshû or Chakshû) separated from the main river, and flowing as an independent stream, and the Lankâ island joined to the mainland from the silt from water spilled by Yamûna effluent of the Alakânandâ or Nandâ or Gangâ, Sobanos of Ptolemy, filling up the narrow belt of sea between Jambû-dvîpa and Lankâ island thus joining the latter to the former; this is the state we find in Ptolemy's time.

The important changes since then are :—

(1) The diversion of the Alakânandâ-Gangâ into the Aîrâvatî river, or Têmala river of Ptolemy, making a passage through the tablelands between the Arakan and Pegu Yomas.

(2) Filling up of the Great Gulf by the silt brought down by the Alakânandâ or Doanas of Ptolemy, and the MeKlong.

(3) The subsidence of western portion of Lankâ island.

(4) The joining of the island Java the Less, with the mainland of Burmah by the Isthmus of Kra, thus forming the Malay Peninsula.

The whole coast of India and Further India having been traced, I will conclude this Chapter with a suggestion for correct reading of Ptolemy's map pertaining to this area. The reader is requested to refer to H. Kiepert's representation, reproduced with McCrindle's Ancient India as described by Ptolemy (Edited by Surendranath Majumder Sastri), the outline of which is given in dotted lines in Fig. 7. Up to Long. 95, Ptolemy's outline follows

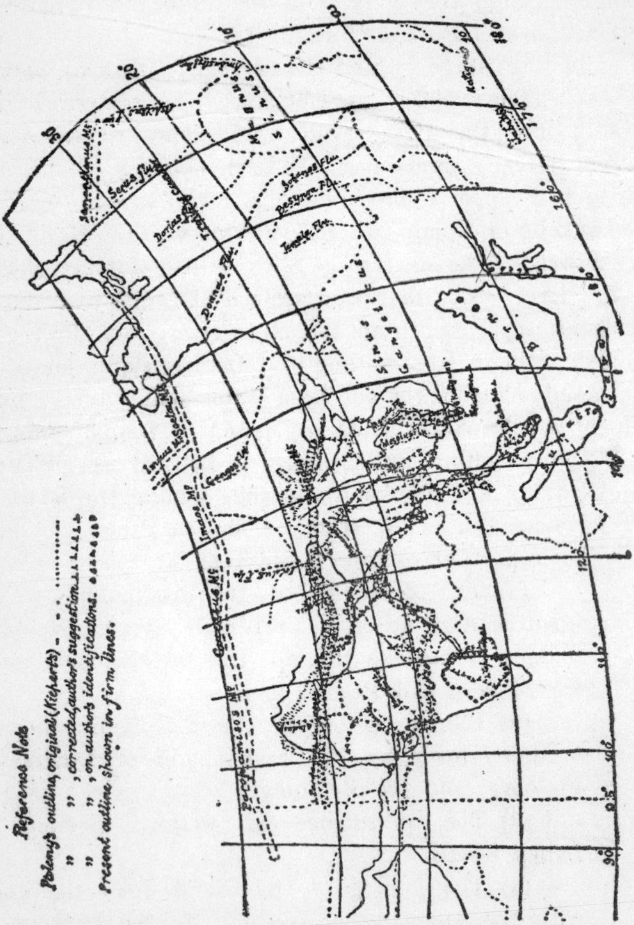

FIG. 7.—Ptolemy's Map corrected and compared.

actuals fairly well and it is to east of this, that Ptolemy has exaggerated the distances both along latitudes and longitudes, and that, by 100 per cent. If the distances from 95° long., is reduced to half, measured eastward of this 95° long., and distances from the Tropic of Cancer, both north and south are similarly reduced to half, the outline will be as shown in ⊥⊥⊥⊥ ; this outline compared with the actual outline from identification now made by me which is also shown in the Figure, shows the remarkable accuracy of Ptolemy's information, subject of course to the correction suggested. The plan brings out unmistakably into prominence, the identity of

(1) Taprobane island with peninsular India.

(2) Sabadias I, or Java-dvîpa with Malay Peninsula

(3) Magnus Sinus or Great Gulf with Central Siam

(4) Doanas river with Alakânandâ Gangâ of Jambû-dvîpa

(5) Dorias, Ambasthas, Sainos and Cottiaris rivers, which were independent rivers formerly, as parts of the present MeKong river.

(6) Kattigara as Cambodia.

CHAPTER XII

GENERAL OBSERVATIONS REGARDING THE CHANGES IN INDIA AND BURMAH, TOUCHING BRIEFLY ON MAHA-BHARATA AND RAMAYANA AREAS, AND FLOW OF ARYAN COLONISATION

I have shown in the foregoing pages that in the Paûrânic accounts of Jambû-dvîpa and Bhâratvarsha, the places in India and Burmah are so much mixed up that, there is practically not a single chapter in them, where the old and new have not been blended and where sites in Burmah and India of the same name are not treated as the same. To read them, we must consider India and Burmah together. From some brief references already made, it has been shown that the Râmâyana area lies in southern Burmah and western Siam. I would now touch on the Mahâbhârata area briefly.

The Mahâbhârata Kings are Chandra-Vamsa or of Lunar Race, claiming their origin from Chandra or the Moon. In the Mahâbhârata we do not find the geneology of the Kings, a discreet silence being maintained. The geneologies are however given in the Pûrânas, each one differing from the other in some details; even in the same Pûrâna we find discrepancies, and I will just mention those in the Harîvamsa where more comprehensive lists than in any other Pûrânas have been given, to show how it has been rendered almost impossible to trace, which part of geneology refers to any particular line of Kings. In Ch. 25-28, we find Prajâpatî— Atrî— *Soma*— Bûdha— Pûrûravâ— Ayu— Nahûsha— Yayâtî— Tûrvasû— Vahnî— Gorbhânû— Traîsânû— Karandhama— Marûtva— Sammata— Dûsmanta— Karûtthâma— Akrîda; Akrîda had four sons, Pândya, Kêrala, Kola, and Chola, the inaugurators of four famous provinces after their names; here we find that the western colonists

Dionysos and Heracles, after setting up kingdoms in the southern India, laying claim to their descent from the Chandra Vamsa, though it is clear from the omission of Pandu in the geology, that the Pândyas of Nagpur had no blood relation with the Pândyas of Mahâbhârata. Yayâtî of this list has four other sons besides Tûrvasû, *Viz.*, Yadû, Drûhyû, Anû, and Pûrû, of whom Yadû is the first of the Yâdavas, and Pûrû of Paûravas to whom belong the Pândyas of Mahâbhârata. The Paûrava line is given as follows :—Yayâtî— Pûrû— Mahâvîrya— Prâchînvana— Pravîra— Manashya— Abhayada— Sudhanvâ— Sûvâhû— Raûdrâsva— Rîchêyû— Matînâra— Tatsû— Sûrodha— Dûsmanta— Bharata— Vîtatha or Bharadvâja— Sûhotra— Kâsîka— Dîrghatapâ— Dhanvantarî— Kêtûmâna— Bhîmaratha— Dîvodâsa (of Vârânasî) etc. This branch clearly indicates an offshoot of the western colonists, as Vârânasî does not seem to have ever been a name for the Kâsî Kingdom of Mahâbhârata, and Dhanvantarî and Dîvodâsa have local traditions in India. In Ch. 20 of Harîvamsa we find the geneology of Brahmadatta, a contemporary of the grandfather of Bhîsma of Mâhâbhârata is given thus :—Vrihatkshetra— Suhotra— Hastî (the founder of Hastînâpûra city)— *Ajamîdha*— Vrîhadîsû— Vrîhatdhanû— Vrîhatdharma— Satyajît— Vîsvajît— Sênajît— Sûchîra— Prîthûsêna— Pâra— Neepa— Neeparâja— Samara— Para— Prîthû— Sûkrîta— Vîbhrâja— Anûha— Bramhadatta— Vîsvakasena— Dandasêna— Bhallâta last of the line killed by Karna of Mahâbhârata. The powerful Visvâmîtra family of western India lay claim to the Lunar race, and accordingly we find the following geneology in Ch. 32, spring from Ajamîdha, son of Hastî in the above list as follows :—Ajamîdha by wife Kêshînî— Jahnû— Ajaka— Valâkâsva— Kûsîka— Gâdhî— Vîsvâmîtra etc.; though in Ch. 25, the claim is laid through Pûrûravâ, grand-father of Nahûsha as below :—Pûrûravâ— Amâvâsû (brother of Ayû, the father of Nahûsha)— Bhîma— Kânchanaprabhâ— Suhotra— Jahnû— Sûsaha— Ajaka— Valâkâsva— Kûsîka— Gâdhî— Vîsvâmîtra etc., which shows clearly mixing up Sûhotra with Ajamîdha, as the Vîsvâmîtra clan had to be accommodated in the Lunar race. Again in Ch. 32, we find the geneology of the Pândavas of Mahâbhârata, from Ajamîdha as follows :—Ajamîdha, by wife Dhûmînî— Rîksha (I)— Samvarana— Kûrû (left Prayaga and founded Kûrûkshêtra)— Parîkshît— Janmêjaya—Vidûratha— Rîksha (II)— Bhîmsêna— Pratîpa— Sântanû— Vîchitraviryya— Pandû— Dhananjaya— Abhîmanyû— Parîkshîta— Janmêjaya; it is curious that Dhananjaya is shown here as the only son of Pându in this list, though Dhrîtarâshtra and Vîdura are shown as brothers of Pândû, and that the prevalent name of Arjjûna is not given in its place. Later on in Ch. 34, two other brothers of Dhananjaya are mentioned, *viz.*, Yûdhîsthîra and Bhîmasêna, as sons of Prîthâ who married Pândû, but Nakûla and Sahadêva omitted, which may possibly be due to the fact that they were born of Mâdrî, the second wife of Pându. The Harîvamsa has not followed the geneology further down, though we find in Vâyû Pûrâna, the following :—Arjjûna— Abhîmanyû— Parîkshît— Satânîka— Asvamêdhadatta— Adhîsamakrîshna— Nîrvvaktra (who removed the capital to Kausambi when Hastînâpûra was destroyed by the erosion of the Ganges)— 6th in descent, Sûtîrtha— 9th in descent Kshêmaka (the last of the line). In Matsya Pûrâna Sûtîrtha is replaced by Sûnîtha from whom 9th in descent is Vrîhadratha— 2nd in descent Satânîka— Udayana— Vahînara— Dandapânî— Nîrâmîtra— Kshêmaka. In Kathâ Sarît Sâgara (Book VI, Ch. XXX), we find Arjjûna— Abhîmanyu— Parîkshît (head of Bharata race)— Janamêjaya— Satânîka— Sahasrânîka— Udayana. Here we find that Udayana, King of Kosambi on the Kalînga coast of India had to be included in the list, when he became one of the most powerful Hindu Kings of India. In Puri temple records, Madala Pânjî, geneology of the Orissa Kings are given (Sewell's Madras, Vol. II, p. 204-5) as follows :—Yûdhîsthîra— Parîkshît— Janmejâya— Sankara— Gaûtama— Mahêndra— Ishta— Sêvaka— Vajra—

Narasîngha— Mânkrîshna— Bhojendra— Vikramadîtya— Karmârjît— Hatkêsvára— Vîr Bhûvana— Nirmal— Bhîmdêva— Sobhandêva— Chandradêva— Yayâtî Kêsarî; credit for long reigns of even 731 years for individual kings had to be given, to reconcile the dates between Yûdhîsthîra in B.C. 3101 to Yayâtî Kêsarî in 474 A.D.

The geneoligies have been given just to show that the powerful Vîsvamîtra Kings had to be included in the Lunar line, so additions have been made; the same is the case when the later Vatsa King, Udayana near Kalînga and Kêsarî Kings of Orissa area had also to be included in the list as belonging to the same race; it also shows that Arjjûna and Dhananjaya may not have been the same person.

Similar additions have been made in the Yadû Vamsa, to which Krîshna of Mahâbhârata belonged, the notable inclusions in the list being the Haîhay kings of western India, including Mahîsmâna, the founder of Mâhîsmatî, and Arjjûna (Kartya-Vîrjjya) and his son, Sûrasêna. As a matter of fact not only were the writers of Pûrânas forced to include these powerful kings in the geneological list, but they went even so far as to identify powerful rebels who attempted to re-establish Brahmanism, with Krishna of Mahâbhârata. A single glaring instance will perhaps suffice to give an idea of such attempts.

Thus in Burmese history (Sir Arthur Phayre's Burmah, Ch. II) we find that in the 10th Century one such attempt made by Soa Rahan who reintroduced Nâga worship in Burmah, as against the prevalent Buddhist religion there; this Nâga worship, or the worship of Harî or Nârâyana, resting on Ananta-nâga, it must be remembered was already included in the later Hindu books. This episode is given in greater detail by G. E. Harvey in his history of Burmah which I reproduce here (p. 19).

"Farmer King Nyangu Sawrahan (931-64 A.D.) became King of Thamahti and worshipped Naga dragon. * * * The Ari lords kept false manuscripts and let a Champaka tree grow over it on which the Pugan Kings fell into this misbelief. * * * Moreover he consulted heretical Shin Ari regarding building of Zigon Pagoda in the Kingdom of Yadapye (Prome) and Thaton.

"Nyangu Sawrahan was overthrown by a pretender Kunshaw Kyaungh Pyu who in his turn was overthrown by Nyangu Sawrahan's two sons, they enticed him into a monastery of theirs in the pretext of invoking his blessing and then forced him to take the robe. He lived in the monastery with his wife and their son, Anawratha. Of the usurping brothers, Kyiso was accidentally killed with an arrow while hunting thamin (?) stag in his favourite haunt in Bangyi in Monyua district; Anwaratha raised a following at Popa hill, challenged the surviving brother Sokkate to single combat, slew him at Myinkaba near Pagan and seized the throne in 1044 A.D. (Hmannam I, 225).

"The Ari priesthood centred at Thamahti village a few miles south-east of Pagan".

For the elucidation of the reader unacquainted with the life of Krîshna as given in the Pûrânas, I would mention here, the episodes in his life which bear on the points given in the Burmese historical accounts quoted above. Krîshna was born when his mother was confined in prison by Kangsa, King of Mathûrâ, a city on the Yamûnâ river. Krîshna's mother Dêvakî was a cousin sister of Kangsa, and as the Sage Nârada foretold that the son of Dêvakî by her husband Vasûdêva would be the future King of Mathûrâ after slaying Kangsa, the latter wanted to destroy the child as soon as he was born. The child when born, was however exchanged for a female child which was destroyed by Kangsa, while the male child was transferred to the care of the farmer King Nanda of Vrîndâvana, a city lying across the river Yamûnâ, where Krîshna was reared. Vasûdêva by another wife Rohînî had a son named Valadêva, who was also named Sankarsana. These two brothers became powerful leaders in their youth, and their first action was to make a sudden entry to the palace of Kangsa and to kill him there in a hand to hand fight, after which they released Kangsa's father Ugrasêna, from imprisonment imposed by his son, and placed him on the throne of Mathûrâ. Later on Krîshna became King of Mathûrâ. Krîshna was accidentally struck by an arrow in his leg when he was sitting on the branch of a tree, by a Vyadh, who mistook his legs for a bird on the tree.

The two accounts make it clear that Kyiso was hailed as an 'Avatara' for his partly successful attempts to revive Brahmanism, and even so late as in the tenth Century A.D., the events of his life, has been incorporated in the Pûrânas, as episodes in the life of Krîshna of Mahâbhârata, thus introducing the love episodes of Vrîndâvana with Kyiso as Kêsava (another name of Krîshna), his brother Sokkate or Sanskritised Sankarsana (another name of Valarama), farmer King Nyangu Sawrahan who introduced Nâga worship in A.D., 924 (Phayre's Burmah, Ch. II, p. 21) as the pastoral (gopa) King Nanda of Vrîndâvana, Kangshaw Kyaungh pyo as Kangsa the King of Mathûrâ and Anawratha was introduced as Anîrûddha, the son of Krîshna. There is some difference however in the two accounts, which is to be expected as Anawratha, to the great disappointment of the Pounhas (Brahmans), turned later on, a staunch Buddhist, and an inveterate enemy of Brahmanism (Phayre's Burmah, Ch. IV, p. 33). The reforms inaugurated by this king and his introduction of the written Burmese language completely shattered the influence which the Brahmans held in the Burmese court for centuries after the exit of the main body Brahmans from Burmah. That these are later interpolations is also indicated in the Pûrânas; thus we see in Vîshnû Pûrâna (Sec. IV), the death of Krîshna after Kûrûkshêtra war, and then (Sec. V), Krîshna born again in Yadû line (Thado) with Kangsa's sister Dêvakî as his mother; in Brahma Pûrâna (Ch. 213) that "in a future kalpa (after Kûrûkshêtra war) Vîshnû, reborn in Mathûrâ, for the good of mankind was known as Kêsava."

Another example is that of identifying the great general Dâmodara of Srûtasarman's army, with Krîshna. Dâmodara had led the Srûtasarman's forces, which arrayed themselves in favour of the Dêvas, against the forces of

Sûryaprabhâ in the great battle of Kalâpagrâma, a battle which was almost as great as the Kûrûkshetra war as described in detail in Kathâ-Sarît-Sâgara, (Bk. VIII, Ch. XLVI to XL).

My object in discussing the geneology given in the Pûrânas, and also in quoting the instances of interpolation in the Paûrânîc accounts of episodes in recent Burmese history, is to show (1) that the powerful tribes which sprang up in India in post-vedic time from the intermingling of the Vedic Aryans of the Punjab, with the successive western invaders including the Macedonean Greeks who settled down in India, as also of the original inhabitants and colonists from the Burmah side, who had no connection with the Mahâbhârata and Râmâyana Kings, claimed lineage from the Solar, and Lunar lines of Kings, and forced their names in the Paûrânic geneologies in recent times; (2) that recent episodes of Burmah are included in the Pûrânas by colonists from Burmah to eastern India, into the life of the greatest heroes of Pûrânas, which indicate that in the revision of Pûrânas the Pandits from Burmah area had a great hand and that Burmah was therefore an area where the Pûrânas were preserved by these Pandîts. From the Paûrânîc accounts I have shown that Jambû-dvîpa is Burmah; it has also been shown that Râmâyana area is in western Siam; the Irrawadi near Mandalay has been shown to be the Gangâ of Jambû-dvîpa; the celebrated Drîshadvatî river of the Pûrânas appears in the Hsipaw district retaining its name intact even in recently printed maps and the absence of any river of that name in India is noticeable; Indraprastha or Indraprathai appears in Ptolemy's map at the confluence of this Gangâ and Drîshadvatî, that is in the centre of Upper Burmah whereas Indraprastha is not shown by Ptolemy in India proper, and Indabera as shown by Ptolemy cannot possibly to taken to mean Indraprastha when the more correct name Indraprathai has been given by him elsewhere. These considerations are sufficient to locate the Mahâbhârata area of Indraprastha etc., in upper Burmah. This area is in Ilâvrîta Varsha, that is the central plain of Upper Burmah. Mandalay though a recent town, is one that was built to keep the remembrance of an ancient town, as is the case with Ayuthia; Mandalay represented Mahêndra-âlaya, or the place of the 'Great Indra'; Amarâpûra or Amarâvatî is yet another name of his city, is represented by Ava near Mandalay; this must therefore have been the ancient site of the town, as has been found already from the Paûrânîc accounts discussed in the previous chapter. The plan of old Ava by John Crawford, Envoy in 1929, as reprinted in V. C. Scott O'Connor's Book "Mandalay and other cities of Burmah" shows 19 gateways of the city, prominent amongst which are Sanda-puri, Ong-baung, Myinta, Hansawadi, Yo-da-ya, and Ta-nen-tha-ri, showing the close connection which the central city had with Chandra-pûrî (Mandalay), Anga-Vanga (Ong-baung or Paung section of the original Burmans to east of Mandalay), Mathura (Myin-ta represented by modern Myothit), Hansâwadî (modern Pegu, or Hansavati rebuilt in 6th Cent. A.D.) Ayodhyâ (Yo-da-ya represented by old Thûkete or Sokotai), and Kûrûkshêtra or Thânesvara (Ta-nen-tha-ri, represented by modern Kyaukse), all places of note in the Mahâbhârata.

The location of Kûrûkshêtra is defined in many places, and Kyaukse answers to all these descriptions. Thus Brahmânda Pûrâna (Ch. I) says that "The Sages performed their sacrifices in Kûrûkshêtra, on the banks of the sacred Drîshadvatî river"; the Doktwadi river now a branch of Mytinge was then the main river which must have curved southward by Kyaukse to meet the Gangâ (Doanas of Ptolemy) flowing by Thazi. In Mahâbhârata (Vana, 83) Kûrûkshêtra is placed on the north of Drîshadvatî and south of Sarasvatî, and (Adi, 109) the Kûrûjângala, Kûrava, and Kûrûkshêtra country lying between Gangâ and Yamûnâ; Manû says, "Kûrûkshêtra is (II, 19) in Bramharsî region, distinguished from the Brahmâvaratta region which lies (II, 17) between the Drîshadvatî and Sarasvatî rivers"; these two statements are at variance with each other, but I think this gives us an indication that the Drîshadvatî (Mytinge) which in the Mahâbhârata period flowed southward by Kyaukse towards Thazi had by Manû's time (? 320 A.D., revised in present form) diverted her course straight towards Ava, which explains this divergence; Agnî Pûrâna says (Ch. 109) "Kûrûkshêtra is close to the Sarasvatî river", a statement which shows that the site is at a place where the Sarasvatî and Drîshadvatî were running close to each other as we see they must have done near Kyaukse; Vâmana Pûrâna (Ch. 22) confirms that "Kûrûjângala is between Sarasvatî and Drîsadvatî, and that it is Brahmâ's north Vêdî which includes Hastînâpûra and lies near the Brahma-Sarovara", which indicates in a way that Brahmarshî region is the south Vêdî and thus the portion cut off by the Drîshadvatî to its south, and it is therefore a stage as described by Manû; Brahmâ's Lake which was near Monywa, described as near to Hastînâpûra and Brahmâ's north Vêdî, which is Brahmêvartta, lying north of Brahmarshî region in which Kûrûkshêtra is situated, also points out to its location at Kyaukse; Manû (VII, 193) says "Kûrûkshêtra is near Indraprastha", which is also another confirmation of the site, Indraprastha being Mandalay-Ava area. The Brahmâvartta region was the home of Manû as he says it is the most holy area, and it is thus we find his codified laws accepted as the basis of laws in Sîam and Cambodia later on.

Another important area is Gândhâra, the princess of which region was the wife of Dhrîtârâstra, and the mother of Dûryodhana. It is in alliance with this country that Dûryodhana was instigated to fight against the combined forces of the Pândavas and the Jâdavas. The old Gandalarit province of Yunnan (Phayre's Burmah I, p. 8), is without doubt this Gândhâra, as lying fairly close to, and towards the north-east of Hastînâpûra, this would be the country to take sides with Dûryodhana, in his fight against the Pândavas who were allies of the Harî worshipper Telaings occupying the south of Hastînapura area. The Chinese of Yunnan, known to the Burmese as Taruks or Tarets (Phayre's Burmah I, p. 11), the old enemies of the Aryan settlers, series of wars with whom are recorded in the Pûrânas as Tarakâmaya wars, were all along trying to make a split amongst the Aryans, and the character of Sakûnî of Gândhâra represented in the Mahâbhârata bears out this; Sakûnî, phonetically will be seen to be a Chinese name. From the statement made by Father Lacouperie, the leading family at Tali Fu in Yunnan was the Mong whose emergence into Chinese annals occurred some 2800 years ago. The Mong Mao legends assert that king U. Ding had a gardener who secretly married a dragon (Nâga) woman and lived three years in the dragon's country. Their offspring founded the town of Tinglong and became so powerful that king U. Ding gave his kingdom to him and his daughter to wed. They had two sons of whom Hkun-yi-Hpang-Hkam became the king. During his reign a big battle was fought against the Chinese and the Dragon's son was defeated and escaped to Chengmai in Siam where he founded another kingdom. This Hkun-yi or sho Hkun-yi, sounds very much like Sakûnî of Mahâbhârata.

The location of this Gândhâra with reference to the Kûrû's country fits in with possibilities as closely, as the present idea of its identity with Kandahar, with Kûrû country near Delhi, diverge from such possibilities.

Prabhâsa hill of Mahâbhârata is the Popa hill, which retains its sanctity even now amongst the Burmese, though the country has turned a Buddhist country for centuries. This is the place celebrated for many episodes in Krîshna's life, of merriment with pastoral gopa people, and of his death, which from what has been said early in this chapter, will appear to refer to the life of Kyiso in the 10th Century; Krîshna's death is also placed in Paûranic accounts in the neighbourhood of Prabhâsa, which agrees with the Burmese account of Kyiso's death in Bangyi forest in Monywa or Lower Chindwin district. This sacred hill seems to have been associated with episodes both in the Mahâbhârata period, as also the later pastoral life of Kyiso, perhaps mostly the latter. Popa hill is near Pagan, the Upper Prayâga of Pûrânas.

Chhatrâvatî city is of importance as the capital

of Drona, and it is placed (Mahâbhârata, Adî, 166) to the north of the Bhâgîrathî (Gangâ) while across the river to its south is Pânchâla Kingdom and the Pândava brothers proceeded to this place from Bharadvâja âsrama on the Jâhnavî (Gangâ); Bharadvâja âsrama has been shown to be Ri-Ke, and travelling along the Gangâ (Doanas) channel as chalked out in Ch. XI, from Ri-Ke following the river up its course, it goes north to near Baw-lake when it turns westward, and it is therefore north of this reach that Drona's Kingdom Chhatrâvatî was situated, and we find the ancient Gantarawadi State here representing the same. South of this east and west stretch of the river was Pânchâla, and Pazaung, situated on the west bank of the Salween, answers to the locality. Next to Pânchâla was Kânyakûvja to its west, and Kanyulkwin town, now a Railway station on the Rangoon-Mandalay line, shows unmistakably the old city; this city was the capital of Vîsvàmîtra who usurped the kingdom of Harîschandra, and it is curious that even to this day, the principal representation in the annual procession of Pagan (Bhâratvarsha, Srâvan 1335 B.S. article by Pares Chandra Sen) is of King Harich-changa (Harîschandra) being deprived of his wife and child by Tejja-min (Vîsvamîtra). This also fixes the Syamanta-Panchaka area which according to the Vâmana Pûrâna (Ch. 22) extends from Kanyakuvja to Hastînâpûra, and is thus the Pegu Yomas.

The Kingdoms of Magadha and Mathûrâ are intimately connected with Krishna's movements during the Mahâbhârata period, as also during the later episodes introduced in his life and thus presents great difficulties in sorting out the references which refer to the different episodes. Generally speaking, Mathûrâ of Madhû Dânava (Harîvamsa, Ch. 93) given as situated near the sea, which was accepted by the Yâdavas of Saûrâshtra descended from Haryasva, as their new colony is without doubt Mathûra of Nagpur, Madhûrâ of Buddhists and southern Madhûrâ of Kathâ-sarît-sâgara, and (p. II, 7-9) Modoura regio Pandionis of Ptolemy; Mathûrâ, the Modoura of Gods of Ptolemy, modern Muttra, is the headquarter of the first colonists of Yâdavas from Burmah; Mathûrâ of Kamsa episode of 10th Century, must be taken in the neighbourhood of Thamhati, southeast of Pagan (early in this chapter) where Kunshaw Kyangh pyu was forced to take the robes by Kyiso, and where subsequently the Ari priesthood centred; Mathûrâ of Mahâbhârata was also in this neighbourhood, and Myothit on the Yinzum river points out to be the locality, and it lies about 40 miles to the east of the old city Magwe on the Irrawady which answers to Magadha of Mahâbhârata, and Kyauk-ye, about 30 miles up the river is the Kêkaya capital referred to as Kêkayapûra or Gîrîvraja or Râjgrîha. Possibly the Mathûrâ of Kyiso episodes, was in the neighbourhood of the old Mathûrâ of Mahâbhârata, and it was the Brahman element still lingering in that city in the 10th Century, that was responsible for hailing the new deliverer of Brahmanism, Kyiso as Krîshna, thus making Kêsava of 10th Century as Krîshna of Mahâbhârata; Vrîndâvana of this recent episode is Wundwin, a little to the north of Thazi; it is a place to which direction the pastoral colony of Myttha would be expected to retreat when threatened from Magwe, by Jarâsandha of Magadha; from Magwe, Wundwin, lies towards Kehsi-Mansam, the headquarters of the powerful Kêshî Daïtya, and we find (Harîvamsa Ch. 60) Vasûdêva warning King Nanda not to retreat towards Vrîndâvana as they will be open to attacks by the cruel oppressor Kêshî in that direction, who had already advanced towards Vrîndâvana and was staying near the place at that time. Magadha must have been a place close to Mathûrâ; we know that the Magas, who later, were driven towards India and colonised in Behar, had traditions, claiming descent from Jarâsandha of Mahâbhârata, then again these self-styled Rajvamsi tribes of Magadha of Behar (Phayre, Ch. V) claimed that "they were descended from the immigrants into Arakan from Magadha, and that the name Maga, given to them by the people of Bengal correctly designated their race or the country from where they came". Further "Arakan called by the natives Rakhaing-pyi (Rakshângapûrî) or land of

Rakhaings, is applied to beings who had their abode in Mêrû and are guards around the mansion of Indra"; it has already been shown that Nîrrîtis or Rakshasas were the Dîk-pâlas or guards of Indra's mansion to the southwest and that the locality was Arakan (Ch. XI) which clears up this point. The original migration of the Arakanese is therefore not from Behar in India, but from 'Maga' in Mêrû, and thus Magwe is clearly indicated as the country of their origin. In Arakan (Phayre, Ch. V, 43) we find a remnant of the Mru tribe still exists a chief of which is the founder of Dhinyavati at a period (? extravagantly) put at 2666 B.C., and he appears to agree with the Mûrû Daîtya of Pûrânas, who was killed by Krîshna. The migration of the Magas is therefore from Magwe area in Burmah to Arakan in the Mahâbhârata period or thereabout, and when the wholesale migration took place later on, on a larger scale to Behar of the Magas of Magadha, and Sûtas of Anga or Drona's Kingdom of southern Shan States and Bâlêyas or Balîpûtras of Northern Shan States, under pressure of the Târakas or the Chinese, we find the whole body moving to Behar in India. Connected with the fights with the Daîtyas and Dânavas, we find Shat-pûra mentioned, as the city of Dânavas, which was attacked by Krîshna of Mahâbhârata after Magadha was conquered. This was the city where a section of the Arakanese were driven already as we find hinted in Harivamsa (Ch. 139) which says that "after Trîpûra was killed by Rûdra, the remnant of the Asûras, went to Shat-pûra and lived there"; the location of this Shat-pûra is given in (Ch. 131) saying it was in Parîyatra hill which is named as Shâna-pâda and the "Gangâ, born of Vîshnû's feet came there when, she was remembered by Nârâyana" and that by this "Gangâ, known as Avîndhyâ Gangâ, the powerful Daîtyas of Shat-pûra, will be shut in there and their egress cut off, so that even though they are powerful they will not be able to harm others"; it is stated later on (Ch. 144) that Andhaka, the great Asûra wanted to secure the Pârîjâta flower and inquired of the Mandara hill as to the location of the Pârîjâta gardens situated at the base of that hill, and the hill disappeared. Now Shat-pûra is the city to which the Asûras retired, and we find it is the area where Gangâ burst in and flooded all round the city, the diversion being effected by the Mandara, one of the hills near Sûmêrû, subsiding; all these clearly point out to the identity of Shat-pûra with Thayet-myo; Myo is city or "pûra" and Thayet represents 'Shat' of Shat-pûra. Thayetmyo has an ancient history to confirm this assumption in mythical times (Statistical and Historical accounts of Thayetmyo, by Col. Horace Browne, p. 40) it was part of the country occupied by Pyus. The name of the city in its present form, taken as Burmese means "Mango city" but, this meaning is not even by local tradition applied to be the correct import; it must either mean the Daîtya-myo or Daîtya's city, or Shat-pûra, both of which practically becomes of the same import when it is remembered that Shat-pûra is a city of Daîtyas.

This identification, and the two facts mentioned in connection with this city, *viz.*, (1) that Gangâ was made to flow by it and (2) Mandara hill subsiding gives us a clue to the diversion of the Gangâ (Doanas of Ptolemy) into the Aîrâvatî (Temala of Ptolemy) as indicated in Ch. XI. The Mandara is the eastern girdle hill of the Sûmêrû, and the subsidence of its southern end would let the Gangâ (Doanas of Ptolemy) flow to the valley between the Arakan and Pegu Yomas to the south east, and a glance at the relief map will show that Thayetmyo is situated just above the place where these Yomas were connected with a ridge; the city was situated on an eminence but all round it must therefore have been flooded with the spill of the Gangâ (Doanas) till a breach was made subsequently in this ridge by the pressure of the impounded water behind it, and gradually the Gangâ (Doanas) diverted into the Aîrâvatî (Temala) channel giving the present lower Irrawadi river course. The local name of the Pegu Yomas in Thayetmyo district is Galladzat Mt., and (Browne's Thayetmyo, p. 8) "the derivation of which does not correspond in the slightest with any native local name is a puzzle"; the name sounds very much like Pârîjâta, which is ascribed to it in the Harîvamsa as quoted above.

We are now in a position to hazard an attempt to chalk out roughly the line of the Yamûnâ river channel which presents a good deal of difficulty. The lower course of this river during the Râmâyana period passed near Bharadvâja âsrama, and it has been shown (*vide* Chapter XI) that the channel was identical with Sobanos of Ptolemy, and present MeKlawng river with the upper portion of Thaungyin river. We find that the Gangâ (Doana) and Yamûnâ (Sobanos) were connected with each other near Bharadvâjapûra (Bardaxa) as stated in Râmâyana (Ayodhyâ, 54) which states clearly that "Bharadvâja âsrama is in Prayâga at the confluence of Gangâ and Yamûnâ"; it states in the next chapter (Ayodhyâ 55) that "the river Kalîndî, (another name of Yamûnâ) which was flowing in a reverse direction, was crossed by rafts, and then after 10 Krosas by road reached Valmîkî's âsrama Mâlyavatî (modern Mayavati) on Chîtrakûta hills"; later on (Ayodhyâ, 105) it says that "Yamûnâ, in full flow meets the sea and does not return, and that this can be seen from the Chîtrakûta hill". This shows Yamûnâ to be an effluent stream of Gangâ, taking off from Bharadvâja âsrama (mod. Ri-Ke, Ch. XI); there is however the statement that the current of the stream was reversed at Bharadvâja âsrama, and that means the Yamûnâ was an affluent stream previously and if that is so, it is clear that the independent outlet to the sea was established later, but the river must have flowed previously further inland and upland. This is made clear in a passage where Râvana complains of the refractory attitude of Sîtâ towards him, and Kûmbhakarna consoles him thus (Râmâyana, Lankâ, 12) "Like Yamûnâ, when she first descended and flooded the swamps in your Kingdom, but after a connection with the sea was established her impetuosity was no longer felt, so will Sîtâ be reconciled to you." This makes it clear that the Yamûnâ was an affluent of the Gangâ, coming from upland and meeting the main river at Bharadvâja âsrama, and that subsequently an independent connection with the sea was established by an avulsion, and thus the direction of flow of the river near the âsrama was reversed; that the flow of the stream was a sluggish one after the independent outlet was established is apparent from Kûmbhkarna's remarks as also the fact that the river was crossed by rafts. We know now that from Bharadvâja âsrama the Yamûnâ as an affluent formerly flowed upland, and the obvious conclusion is that this affluent is the same Yamûnâ on which Mathûrâ (Myothit) is situated, and which passes through the Magadha country (with Magwe as capital); further up from Mathûrâ the river passed near Vrîndâvana (Wundwin), though in doing so, the river flowed in a tortuous course as indicated in Harîvamsa (Ch. 102) which states that "Valarâma by his plough furrowed out a course from the banks of the Yamûnâ; the river though flowing down in a straight course generally, flowed upward to pass by Vrîndâvana". The Yamûnâ-aranya or forest of Yamûnâ extended to the area east of Magadha, thus in Râmâyana (Ayodhyâ, 71) when Bharata marches from Kekayapûra to Ayodhyâ on receipt of news of death of his royal father he goes "from Rajgrîha eastwards, reaches Sarasvatî(Shewli)-Gangâ (Irrawadi) confluence, then the Matsyadêsa and then crossing the Hlâdînî (Doana) reaches Yamûnâranya (Yamûnâ forest), after which he crosses the Gangâ (Doana), and then by a long round journey further east, reaches Ayodhyâ (Sokotai). Thus the Yamûnâ forest extended between Magwe and Sokotai, and it lay to the west of the Doana river of Ptolemy, which clearly indicates that the river must have run parallel to the Doanas and to its west. We can therefore conclude that the Yamûnâ flowed from the neighbourhood of Wundwin southwards passing by Myothit, and then piercing through the Pegu Yomas, to Lewe, a little to the east of Ela, now a railway station. Here the river ran possibly very close to the Gangâ (Doanas) but parallel to and to the west of it, then joining the Sittang course near Pegu and curving eastwards towards Bharadvâja âsrama, and joining the Gangâ (Doanas) there. It appears however that much of the information regarding the Yamûnâ, is later interpolation, and the course I indicate doubtfully.

Mîthîlâ is without doubt the ancient and important city Meiktila, the headquarters of the Meiktila district. As the place retains its original name, and its position in relation to the neighbouring places agree, it is not necessary to enlarge upon the obvious. This is the locality from which "Mîthîlâ, female celebates who observe a rule parallel to that of the Pothudaw" (Max and Bertha Ferrar's Burmah, p. 40) emanated, and the birth of Sîtâ is therefore from the earth. The queen of Mahasambwa, King of Burmah ruling at Tharekhettara, is named Bedayi, who according to tradition (Powell's Mandalay to Bhamo, p. 65) was also born of a deer, and brought up by prince Labaduha, the adopted heir of King Thado-nagain or Thado Maharaja. The legend says that "one day a huge boar 18 feet high was devastating the land and under the King's orders, prince Labaduha marched out and the boar fled south and sought refuge in the Shan country, and the place is known to this day as Wet-wun (boar-entry), near Thonze, north-east of Mandalay; the chase continuing, the boar crossed the Irrawadi at Wet-ma-sut (boar not wet), and was not overtaken till it reached island Wettogyun (boar-strike-island) where it met its death; the prince decided not to return to Tagaung, but lived in Pegu country as an ascetic hermit, and here he found born of deer the female child Bedayi whom he brought up; later on Bedayi was married to Maha-sambwa the elder of the two sons of Thado-nagain, who was born after Labaduha retired as a hermit; the two sons were floated down the river Irrawadi in rafts as they were blind, but they recovered their eyesight through the treatment of a Bilu-ma (Râkshasî or female Ogre) and the place they recovered their eye sight was Salin (got-sight) in Minbu district; it was after this that the two princes met Bedayi on the river bank and was brought to Labaduha, who arranged the marriage of Bedayi with Maha-Sambwa". It is clear that

Bedayi's birth was therefore near the old Magadha area, if not Mîthîlâ, and Bedayi is another form of Vaîdêhî, a girl of Vîdêha country which is another name for Mîthîlâ. The episode is given in a slightly different form in Padma-Pûrâna, Bhumîkhanda, (Ch. 28 to 46) where it stated that "Prîthû gave the Taîlanga and Haîhaya countries to Sûta, Magadha, Vandî and Chârana tribes; Ikshâkû, king of Ayodhyâ with his queen Sûdêvâ, went to the Gangâranya (Gangâ forest), where he met the Sûkara Râjâ (Boar King) and fought a great war with him; he chased the Boar King to the Jâhnavî-Gangâ near Mêrû, and fought with him again and the Lûbdhakas also fought for him, and the Boar King was killed by Ikshâkû". It will be seen that Lûbdhakas, which means men living on chase, is prince Labaduha; King Thado-nagain is the Ikshâkû King from Ayodhyâ, which representation is not incorrect as this King is the sixteenth of a line from Daza Raja, who headed the second band of Kshatrya immigrants from the east of Irrawady at a period when Gautama Buddha was alive (Phayre's Burmah, Ch. I, p. 9), and so they claimed descent from the Solar Race of Ikshâkû. An important change to be noticed is that the Magadha and Mîthîlâ area is given as Gangâranya or Gangâ forest and is not the Yamûnâranya or Yamûnâ-forest (*vide* earlier, this Chap.) of Râmâyana, which goes to show that at the time the Padma Pûrâna was written, the upper Yamûnâ channel had already been cut off or diverted into the Gangâ, parallel to which it ran. Another point of importance to notice here is the gift of the country in the neighbourhood to Sûtas and Magadhas. The Sûtas are the tribe claiming descent from Karna of Mahâbhârata, to whom devolved the area given to Drona which has been shown to be Gantaravadi states of the Karenni country (*vide*, earlier this Chap.); they are the Karens (Max and Bertha Ferrar's Burmah, p. 147) "whom Burmans, Telaings and Shans have kept out of the plains; the 'White Karens', Sghaw (Sghrraw), and Pwo occupy the mountains between Burmah and Siam; they have colonies in the mountains far to the east and west and have spread themselves to the plains adjoining; they call themselves Baganyaw (Bghrraganyaw) and call Burmans Bayaw." In Markandêya Pûrâna (Ch. 58) in the Kûrma-Sangsthâna (Tortoise representation of Bhâratvarsha) we find in the eastern-most area next to Magadha and Mîthîlâ, the Sûrpa-Karna and Vyâghra-mûkha countries are placed; the Sûrpa-Karnas seem to agree with the Sghaw Karens, and Bghrraganaw or Vyâghra-Karna, with the Vyâghramûkha, a section of the Karnas or Karens. The Burmans as Byaw is no doubt the "Vâyû" people of Jambûdvîpa (*vide*, Ch. XI) whose original place was at Kindat but who were forced southwards with the gradual spread of the Aryans in the upper Irrawady valley; these sections represented as Pavananandanas or sons of Vâyû, and occupying the Dwana range became an ally with the Siamese Aryans of Ayodhyâ, in the Râmâyana period to fight with the Rakhasas or the powerful Telaings of Lanka island or Thaton country.

Dvârâvatî is a city which figures very prominently in the Mahâbhârata, as the city of Krîshna, a new capital built and fortified by him, with a view to resist the attacks from Jarâsandha, the King of Magadha. The Vrîndâvana episode must be left out as a later interpolation as explained already. Dvârâvatî is mentioned as a city near the sea coast, and that its destruction was due to flooding from the sea; the sea, even in Ptolemy's time, passed by Thârâwaddy which would appear to represent Dvârâvatî, though at first sight the city of Thârêkhettara in the kingdom of Yadapyi or Yâdû-pûrî or city of Yâdûs, near Prome, built in the 5th Century B.C. by Dwattabaung would suggest to be the city; Tharawaddy by its name and situation fits in more with Krishna's city and we must remember that the whole city is perhaps several feet under the soil now. Krîshna was the leader of the Yâdavas, or Yados, or Thado Kings of the Burmese, the worshippers of Nârâyana Harî; in Burmese history, the Shin Ari sects represented them. Originally they occupied the upper Irrawadi Valley, as I have already shown (*vide*, Ch. VIII) that in Sapenago country, near Bhamo the then headquarters of the powerful Daîtyas, the Harî worshipping

Nats in the neighbourhood played an important part in restoring Walatha (Prahlâda) to his kingdom, and it also appears from the Paûrânîc accounts that Prahlâda became a convert to the Harî worship; in the Pûrânas we find that though Harî-varsha, south of Ilâvrîta or the central area of Burmah, is the country of the Harî worshippers, they are also in evidence partly in Ilâvrîta-varsha itself as (Vâyû, 46) Sêshanâga, Vâsûkînâga, and Takshakanâga as also the Rakshas lived there along with the Pîtrîs; as the Aryans advanced, the Harî worshipping Nâgas and Nats as also the Daîtya of Sapenago were forced towards the south; we find in the time of the Mahâbhârata, the Daîtyas had moved southward to the Magadha (Magwe) area in Irrawadi Valley the Harî worshipping Nâgas to their east, in the Sittang valley. The two tribes had not forgotten their old feudal enmity and the great leader Krîshna, of the Harî worshippers, effected a split in the Aryan household between the Kûrûs and Pândavas in the Kûrû country, thus to check the power of the Aryans to the north as also the Daîtyas or Asûras of Magadha to his west, and of the Karna country of Karens to his east, and that of their general enemy the Chinese or Târakas, who were sending out hordes after hordes at intervals from Gândhâra or Gandalarit country of Yunnan, by involving the whole lot of them in a general war. The result of this was the great Mahâbhârata war. Evidently this war anticipated in time by the great mastermind of Krishna, and this led him to retire from Mathûrâ and make the headquarters of the Yâdavas lower down near the seacoast at Dvârâvatî, where the treasures and women were to be kept in a fortified place during the war, and then to return after the war was over, and the joint power of the Yâdavas and Pândavas established in the country. Little did he foresee that Karnas and Gândhâra would prove such powerful allies of the Kûrûs, and that even a section of his own warlike people living in the north, who were known as the Nârâyânî Sênâ, will join the opposite camp; little did he foresee that the result would be an annihilation of the whole Aryan and Nârâyanî army; little did he foresee that his own people in Dvârâvatî will become emasculated, leading merry lives in security in an isolated and fortified place during the war and engaging in petty quarrels amongst themselves; little could he anticipate that even the forces of nature would turn against him and just at the critical moment, the sea would encroach on the coast near Dvârâvatî and thus bringing about the flooding and destruction of the city itself, and the isolated position of the city instead of its being a source of security turned out to be the greatest danger as his retreat was cut off at the time of the direst need. The result is too sad a story to relate and thus we find the 'silent conspiracy' to keep something out of view amongst Paûrânic authors as complained of by modern writers, but we may well conclude from what has been hinted out by them the dire calamity brought about. When the town was threatened with destruction, Krîshna, disappointed, dejected, decided not to leave his favorite city but to perish with it; he found the Yâdava male population too small and incompetent for the orderly evacuation of the city and for transporting the Yâdava women to safety to Indraprastha and he had to requisition the services of Arjjûna to do this. (Mahâbhârata, Maûshala, 7) "Arjjûna left Dvârakâ, taking with him the innumerable destitute women of the Bhoja, Andhaka, and Vrîshnî, and great numbers of Yâdavas, when Dvarakâ was swallowed up by sea water, and for a time stayed in the Panchanada (Pyinmana) country; attacked there by Dasyûs (Robbers, the Lestos of Ptolemy were still occupying the area to south) and unable to prevent the forcible elopement of women, he retreated with the remnant of women to Kûrûkshêtra (Kyukse), and settled the Hârddîka boys and Bhoja women in Mârttîkavata (? Myttha) city, the balance of aged and young males with women in Indraprastha (Ava), and Sâtyakî boys in Sarasvatî nagara; then he proceeded to Hastînâpûra (Thehaw-daw) and reported facts to Yûdhîsthîra". Thus we see Arjjûna, the once greatest hero of the Mahâbhârata war, unable to resist the attacks of a small number of the original Burmans who were driven to seek shelter in the hills of Dwana Range, when previously pressed by the Yadavas from the west, and the Aryans of Ayodhyâ from the east. In Brahma Pûrâna (Ch. 212) the helpless situation is described thus :—"Arjjûna with the inhabitants of Dvârakâ, and there leader-elect Vajra, and thousands of Yâdava women, left Dvârâvatî, and proceeding to Panchanada fixed their residence there; seeing the large number of widowed women, escorted by single-handed Pârtha (Arjjûna), the Dasyûs felt tempted, and these cruel Abhîras (Pastoral people) followed them armed with sticks and stone-chips and forcibly took away the women in the very presence of Arjjûna; some women even voluntarily went over to them; Arjjûna, worsted by those low Mlêchchhas, deploring his abject condition, proceeded to Indraprastha and installed the Yâdava prince Vajra as King". It will be seen that the site of Tharawaddy as Dvârâvatî is well indicated if the whole history of fortifying the city near the sea for purposes of strategic retreat during the Mahâbhârata war, and the route of the subsequent retreat as given above are considered together. From the same considerations, it will be realised, that Dvârakâ in Gujarat, Mathûrâ as Muttra, Indraprastha and Hastînâpura near Delhi in India, are impossible sites to reconcile; retreat from Muttra to Vrîndâvana lying on the opposite bank, for purposes of safety against dangers from Kangsa of Mathûrâ aided by Jarâsandha at Patna, would obviously be useless; retreat over the long distance through alien countries to Guzarat from Muttra in days of transport by road journey on foot is not seriously to be thought of; in their last evacuation, the journey from Dvârakâ in Guzarat, to the Punjab, and then to Kûrûkshêtra, and then to Indraprastha near Delhi, and then reporting events to Hastînapûra near Meerut, is also not the natural route to take.

The Panchanada country in this final retreat, I have suggested to be Pyinmyna; references to Panchanada are meagre in Mahâbhârata, or in Jambû-dvîpa and it is therefore to be concluded that as the Aryans consolidated lower down in the Gangâ (Doanas) valley, they must have tried to instal the Panchanada or 'five river' country, and the five rivers are Satadrû, Vîpâsa, Irâvatî, Chandrabhâgâ, and Vîtastâ; the Manipur river from Log-tak lake was known as the Vîtastâ river and at one time was an affluent of the Chindwin; the Chindwin is Chandrabhâgâ; Irâvatî retains its name intact; Vîpâsâ and Satadru are replaced by the Sarasvatî and Drîshadvatî, the courses of which are given before (*vide*, Ch. XI).

Naîmîshâranya, the sacred place for rîshîs, the hub of the Brahmarshî-region, is Namme-Kon lying about 50 miles due east of Pyinmana; the town lies on the river issuing from the great Lu-le-lake, and this river is therefore to be taken as the Gomatî.

Indraprastha has already been shown to have been situated in the Ava-Mandalay area (early in this Chapter); this is the site of Mahêndra's city or Mahêndrâlaya (Mandalay) and Amarâpura (Ava) another name for Indra's city. The old city Indraprastha must have been in this neighbourhood.

Hastînâpûra lay further north and on the Gangâ, and at first sight Tagaung would suggest to be the site of this city. Hastînâpûra was however entirely destroyed during the Mahâbhârata period, by the erosion of the Gangâ, and this fact would lead to the conclusion that Tagaung built by Kshatrya King Abhiraja in 1000 B.C. (Max and Bertha Ferrar's Burma, p. 201), was to replace Hastînâpûra and if that is so, then Thi-ha-daw, the small island in the Irrawadi, 20 miles below Thabeitkyin, is the remnant of the old city; this island contains very ancient ruins and a look at the map will show that the river has widened out and oscillated here a good deal. The island answers to the description of it as given in Harîvamsa (Ch. 119) which says:—"Sâmva (Krîshna's son by Jâmvâvatî) forcibly taking away Dûryodhana's daughter Lakshanâ, for which he was captured by the princes and brought to Hastînânagara and imprisoned there; Valadêva wedged in his plough here against the masonry rampart walls, and so to dislodge the city and force it into the Gangâ; from that time this partly revolved (dislodged) city, appears as a barrier across the stream of the Gangâ." Thi-ha-daw would therefore appear to be the remnant of old Hastinapura, its appearance fits in with the description in every detail.

The sites of cities of outstanding importance in the Mahâbhârata have been described and it is not necessary to follow up the identifications further. In describing the journeys for conquests, or the sacred places or tîrthas, much that is later and recent have been introduced and the identification of those places will not help us in connection with sites connected with the main Mahâbhârata story, and I have not touched on them.

I will turn once more to the venue of the Râmâyana. The site of Lankâ island has already (Ch. XI) been shown to be south of Burmah, with Thaton as the capital city of Râvana. The site of Ayodhyâ has been shown to agree with that of Sokotai (Ch. XI) and that of Bharadvâja âsrama or Bardexa of Ptolemy in the neighbourhood of Ri-Ke (Ch. XI). I will now refer in brief to some of the other important sites of Râmâyana.

Chîtrakûta hills play an important part. The âsrama of Sage Vâlmîkî is situated on it, and on the banks of the Mâlyavatî river; Mâlyavatî is the same as Maya-wadi, and Chîtrakûta the lower Dwana Range. Poet Mûkûndarâma states that from the Sîtâkhâlî Mohânâ, or estuary of the Sittang river (see Ch. XI) the Chîtrakûta hills could be seen at a distance from the sea, and that the causeway built by Râma is also passed close to the coast there. This description narrows down the locality of Chîtrakûta to Dwana range. On the road from Ayodhyâ to Vâlmîkî Asrama on the Chîtrakûta, we find the first important point in crossing the Gangâ (Doanas) at Srîngavêra-pûra which must be Raheng (see Ch. XI); from this point the road bifurcated, one after crossing the Gangâ and then going direct towards Bharadvâja âsrama, and the other by the Ayodhyâ bank of the Gangâ to Sarayû-Gangâ confluence, where the âsrama of Kâma is situated (Râmâyana, Adî, 22) and where the river is crossed to join the other route. This asrama of Kâma is clearly Kamau-kala-Hat.

Crossing the Gangâ at Srîngavêrapûra, and following the road along the right bank of the river, (Râmâyana, Ayodhyâ, 54) going up the river a good days march, was the Bharadvâja âsrama, from where the effluent Yamûnâ (Sobanos) takes off, and from where 10 Krosas is Chîtrakûta and Vâlmîkî âsrama on the Mâlyavatî (Ayodhyâ, 56); this brings us to Maya-wadi.

Near Chîtrakûta is Dandaka forest, and Janasthâna (Adî, 1, Ayodhyâ, 117); on the high peak of Chîtrakûta (Aranya, 7) is Sûtîkshna âsrama, four Yojanas south of which is Agastya âsrama (Aranya, 11); a short distance from Agastya âsrama, is Panchavatî forest near Godâvarî river (Aranya, 13) and lying on the way from Agastya âsrama to Panchavatî is Jatâyu's recess (Aranya, 14), southwest of which is Kaûncha forest (Aranya, 69) at a distance of three Krosas from Janasthâna; three Krosas east from Kaûncha forest is Matanga âsrama situated on the west bank of Pampâ lake, and a road towards the west leads to Rîshyamûkha hills (Aryana, 73) with very steep slopes. As all these sites are situated close to each other, it is convenient to deal with them together, and fixing the sites of some of them would indicate others of which sites cannot be traced from the small scale maps. The name of the Janasthâna valley is perpetuated in the river Donthami, which now flows by Thaton, but which river must have been a creek from the narrow belt of sea between Lanka island and the mainland; to north of Janasthâna, we find Pawutta obviously representing Panchavatî; this being so, the river which flows by Pawutta, which is the present Bilin river represents Godâvarî river; north of Pawatta is Potsuwah, which represents Rîshyamûkha, the name it will be seen does not differ much as 'wah' in Burmese means mouth which is "mukha" of Sanskrit and its description as a hill with very steep ascent is a very apt one; Kaûncha forest is Kunzeik, situated about 20 miles north of Sittang and about the same distance to the west of Pawutta ; from the relative position of Kaûncha forest, given as 3 Kroses east of the west bank of Pampâ lake, we can conclude that this lake was in the valley of the Bilin river, and the broad expanse of the valley immediately to the north of Yin-On is the site of the Pampâ lake, now completely reclaimed, and Godâvarî and Pampâ river are the same, represented now by the upper section of the course of the Bilin river.

Kîshkîndhyâ lies near Matanga âsrama (Kîshkîndhyâ, 13), southwest of Vîndhya in which Agastya âsrama is situated, from where the great sea is visible (Kîshkîndhya, 58) and Kyauk-taung lying northeast of Bilin points to its site; 'taung' means 'hill'' and Kyauk-taung is corrupt Kîshkîndhyâ hill. The southern portion of the Dwana range was the area to which the original Burmans, known as Vâyû (see early this chapter) or Pavana, were forced to take shelter when driven from the plains by the Aryans advancing by the Gangâ (Doanas) valley and during the Râmâyana period we find them here in Kîshkîndhyâ region, and the powerful, yellow race headed by Hanûmâna as "Pavana-nandana" or "son of Vâyû" joining the forces of Râma to fight their common enemy Râvana, the Râkshasa king of Lankâ. That the powerful "Vânara-sênâ", or "Monkey-army" under the great Hanûmâna, belonged to a yellow race like the original Burmans, as distinguished from the Aryans on the one side, and the Harî worshippers Nâgas on the other, is made clear in the Râmâyana (Lankâ, 4) where this Vânara-sênâ marching in Sahya Mt., is described thus :—"Like the earth adorned with ripe paddy crops standing on it, so the yellow Vânara-sênâ appeared to cover the whole country." Further south, the headquarters of 'Sûparna' or Garuda, represented by modern Sapannye; Sûparna at one time the ally of the powerful Vîshnû or Aryans of northern Burmah, evidently later on found their enemies, the Nâgas of southern Burmah too powerful and had to retire south; a section of these people, under Jatâyû in Rîshyamûkha hills were involved in the war against Râvana and after the war they probably moved to Sûpanbûrî or Sûparna-pûrî, on the west bank of Menan-Chao-Phrya. In Râmâyana (Sûndara, 1 and 56) we find Hanûmâna's subjects, and Nâgas to their north occupying this southern tongue of the Mahêndra Mountain (Pegu Yomas continued to Dwana Range), which place could be seen from Lankâ island lying opposite to it, and that the hills abutting on the sea "slipped and became level" after the time that Lankâ was burnt by Hanûmâna. The position of Râma's causeway it is difficult to locate exactly, but Theinzeik would appear to be Trîkûta hill, and between Theinzeik and Bilin appears to be the site. Thus the Râmâyana area lies in southern Burmah and western Siam.

Having now proved conclusively from the identifications of the places referred to in Mahâbhârata and Râmâyana, that the venue lay in Burmah, a short reference to the history of Burmah will be necessary to explain that references to Mahâbhârata and Râmâyana statements are not incompatible with the traditions of Burmans. The references made to the history and traditions of Burmah will mostly be from Sir Arthur Phayre's History of Burmah, and the references quoted will be from that book unless otherwise mentioned.

"The Burmans formed into a nation by the union of Mongoloid tribes * * * worshipping Nats; the union of the tribes was accomplished, gradually, under the influence of Aryan immigrants, the Kshatryas from Gangetic delta. * * * The Indian settlers, adopted themselves the name of Brahma, now written Mramma and pronounced Bama." The Ganges referred to is Jambû-nadî or Tsang-po, and the obvious route of the Aryan immigrants was by this valley. Coming from Central Asia, to the north of Himalayas north of Punjab, one section colonised the small Punjab area, then recently formed at the base of the hills, the area south of the Himalayas and east of the Punjab being a narrow belt of forest on the fringe of the Gangetic trough, a vast inland sea of fresh water; this section were the Vedic Aryans. A second section followed the northern slope of the Himalayas, that is the south of Tibet plateau, which had then a more equable climate owing to the proximity of the inland sea to the south of the Himalayas, as also inland lake in the Tibetan Plateau, as this area must have then had greater rainfall carried from clouds of the Gangetic trough area, and there was thus some reservoir of water resting against the Himalayan embankment to its north; the pressure of this accumulated water, from time to time, made breaches in the Himalayas letting out the water into the Gangetic trough, which would explain the tremendous width of bed of some of these rivers such as Kosi, Gandak, and also the chasms of Hamsa-dvara etc. This draining out of the Tibetan plateau reservoir, must have forced that band to proceed eastwards to Burmah, carrying with them, some amount of Vedic civilization. The draining out of the Tibetan plateau also effected a junction of Burmah island of Jambûdvîpa with the mainland of Tibet and thus we find this band of Aryans, pouring in through the Kubo valley and settling down in the plains at centre of upper Burmah.

The disposition of the different tribes given in the Jambûdvîpa, marks a stage previous to that given in the history of Kings of Burmah which start with King Abhi Raja (1000 B.C.). The Jambûdvîpa position gives the central area occupied by the Aryans, or Brahmas; to the northeast is Ishâna, that is the Shan tribes who have still maintained their area intact as Ishâna is acknowledged as one of the most powerful gods, to whom Indra had to go to very frequently for help; to the northwest were the Vâyu, or the Burmans who were gradually forced to seek shelter in the hills of Pegu Yomas as given earlier in this chapter; to the southwest in the Arakan coast were the Nîrrîties or Râkshasas or cannibals, who were in evidence even up to 10th or 11th Centuries as borne out by the description given by travellers; to the south east was Yamas who seem to have merged themselves to other tribes and lost their identity; south we have Harîvarsha, a great area occupied by worshippers of Harî in the forms of Nârâyana, and they are themselves the original Nâgas, who partly separated towards Manipur, but the bulk occupied the lower Irrawady valley, and had active maritime relations with Taprobane island, as we find Nârâyana in his Anantâsayyâ or resting on the bed of Sêsha-nâga or Ananta-nâga is in strong evidence in Madras Presidency area; we also find stupendous figures of Nârâyana in his Anantasayyâ pose, converted into reclaiming Buddha all over the lower Irrawadi valley, the notable examples in easily accessible places being those at Winkaba near Rangoon, and Shwethalyaung at Pegu. These people the Yâdos—under Srî Krîshna were powerful allies of the Aryans in the Mahâbhârata period, and were included in the fold of Hinduism, Krîshna being acknowledged as Vîshnû incarnate. A section of the Aryans proceeded along the Gangâ (Doanas) to western Siam in the Râmâyana area; they were cut off from the main body at the centre as we do not find help rendered by the latter in the wars with the forces of Râvana of Lankâ, and eventually they merged with the local tribes some going over to Cambodia and a few chosing to migrate to India, on the downfall of Aryans in Burmah and Siam.

We have seen, how, weakened in the Mahâbhârata war of extirpation, the Yados made their final exit from lower Burmah, almost the whole tribe perishing, and Arjjûna of the Pândavas escorting the women, aged people, and children, from Dvârâvatî to Indraprastha, and unable to resist the attacks of Burman robbers on the way. That was the sad story of the Yâdavas. The fate of the Aryan survivors of upper Burmah was equally sad, if not worse. The aboriginal tribes, who were forced under pressure from Aryans to seek shelter in the hills and jungles, discovering the sad plight of the Aryans weakened by internecine war, did not lose any time to re-assert themselves in their native land, and in their turn drove out the irreconcilable section of the Aryans who refused to submit to them and crossed over to India; a large body of Aryans must however have submitted to the new order of things, and thus we see a fusion taking place of Aryans and the original Burman tribes. Even after this fusion the Aryans in Burmah continued to exercise a dominating influence in the courts for a good length of time, as they kept to themselves the written language and literature, in the country, and modified the Hindu religious books to include in the folds of that religion the local deties, Sîva, Nârâyana, Harî, etc. In Max and Bertha Ferrar's History (Burmah, p. 158) it is stated that "the Pohnas (Brahmans) were patronised by Kings of Burmah as astrologers and calendar makers; those settled in Burmah came at different time from different parts of India but principally from Manipur. They strictly guarded their castes. * * * They study and teach Sanskrit after the Burman mode". This shows the power exercised by the Brahmins; the way they came as stated is an assumption, as all historians hitherto assumed the migration of Brahmans from India to Burmah, taking the reverse course as an improbability. This also explains why the Burmans claim their ancestry from the Jambûdvîpa king, and why in the traditional list of ancient kings the Jambûdvîpa Raja, Dewata Raja, Munika Raja, Naga Raja, Indra Raja, find places, and later on Kamsa (Kantha), Kalînga, Sîmhala (Hihaĺa) Rajas are also included. This also explains why the ancient kings of Tagaung are Yâdavas (Thado), evidently descendants of the Yâdava nominee Vajra installed at Indraprastha by the Pândavas. The power of the Brahmins was gradually lost by the introduction of Buddhism in Burmah, of the Pali language and literature, and finally by the radical reforms and the introduction of written Burman language by Anoaratha Soa in 1010 A.D., when the last batch of Sâkadvîpa Brahmans of the Brahmarshi region in Burmah, left for Bengal. The evacuation of the band of Kshatryas after the Mahâbhârata war after Arjjûna arrived at Indraprastha with the Yâdava women and installed Vajra the Yâdava representative on the throne at Indraprastha, is thus described in Brahma Pûrâna (Ch. 212). "Vyasa told the Pândavas that by Harî, the terminator of all things, their end is drawing nigh; and it is fit that these (Pândava) brothers should leave this kingdom and proceed to the forest; realising this the Pândavas installed Parîkshîta on the throne, and left the kingdom." The migration and its tribulations can be realised from what is given elsewhere as also in Harîvamsa (Ch. 186 and 187). "Mlechchhas will occupy the Kûrû-Pânchâla country, and Kûrû-Pânchâla people will go to the Mlêchchha country; * * * the people with their friends will rove about aimlessly in their land in a demented state awaiting their end; it is then, that driven by fear and pangs of starvation, they will migrate, carrying the children on their shoulders, and crossing the Kaûsîkî river, take refuge in Anga, Vanga, Kalînga, Kâshmîra, Mêkala, and Rîshîkantara hilly countries; they will live along with the Mlêchchhas in the base of the Hîmâlaya, or on the salt sea coast, or in the forests; they will be forced to live on meat, fish, reptiles, snakes, fruits and to wear animal skins and barks of trees like Mûnîs; they will live near rivers for their water supply." The time given for this final migration is at the advent of Buddhism in Burmah though the first band of Kshatryas left after the Kûrû-kshêtra war. Kâshmîra referred to in the statement above is not to be mixed up with Kashmira in Punjab; this Kashmir was a province to the north-east of India. The migration is indicated by Kosi valley, as northern Bengal country at the base of the Hîmâlayas was already populated by powerful alien tribes, and the refugees had to cross over to the west of Kosi before they found unoccupied forest land where they could settle down, and thus they spread largely to the area west of Kosi R. spreading south towards the sea coast.

Sir A. Phayre then proceeds, (Burmah, Ch. I, p. 5) :—"That the Indians should have arrived by a northern or north-western route, and not to have ascended from the delta of the Irrawadi is rendered certain from the history of Pegu. Only three names have been handed down as borne by the original tribes, *i.e.*, Kanran, Pyu or Pru, and Sak." Later on we find (Ch. II, p. 18) "Burmese chronicles relate the story of Tharekhettara monarchs :—the tribes under the monarchy were Pyu, Kanran and Mramma; the two former tribes fought for pre-eminence, Thupynia died during the struggle after a reign of 11 years, Pyu were victorious and Kanran retired westward. Pyu fought amongst themselves and divided into two parties, one division occupied hilly district south-west of Prome, was attacked by Telaings, and then crossed the great river into country west of Padaung, when they were attacked by Kanrans in possession, and were driven north to Mendon. They retired farther north and crossing Irrawadi under their leader Thamuddarit, nephew of Thupinya and arrived at Yunhlwutguen on the river, near to which the city of Pugan called New Pugan was founded. Thirteen years had been occupied in wandering of the tribe. After this separate tribes are not mentioned and Mramma was the general national designation." This history it will be seen has a remarkable likeness to the Mahâbhârata episode, if Pyu are taken to be Pândûs, Kanran as Kûrûs, and Sak or Thek or Theit as the Daîtyas who were the original inhabitants of Burmah towards the north-east, but who were already fused with the local Burmans of the south under pressure of the Aryans. The thirteen years period of fight is repeated in Mahâbhârata, during 12 years of which their whereabouts were known, and for one year was absolutely unknown, or 'Agnâta-vâsa'. The division of the Pyu into two section, appears to be into Pândavas, and Yâdavas, as the retreat of the latter to south-west of Prome, probably Dvârâvatî as headquarters, and their retreat when attacked by Telaings to the country west of Padaung (Panchanada) in the first instance and then to Mindum (Indraprastha). There is no doubt the blending of new with the old traditions and the name of King Thupinya of 7th Cent. A.D., has been brought into this old tradition, and substituted for Sûyodhana, another name of the Kûrû leader Dûryodhana whose reign must also have been about 11 years.

The gradual migration of the first batch is hinted in the Arakan chronicles. We find the Kshatrya (Phayre's Burmah, p. 8) "King Kan Rajagyi went with his followers (from Tagaung) down the Irrawadi, reached Khyendweng river, and established himself at or near a hill called Kaïe (? Kalâpa village of Pûrânas) in Kubo valley, occupied by Pyu, Kanran and Sak tribe, and made his son

Mudusitha king over them. He then proceeded to north Arakan and established his capital at Mt. Kayukpaudaung. Arakan chronicles fix the date which answers to B.C. 825".

While the Kshatryas were moving towards India by northern Arakan, the Daityas claiming descent from the great Prahlada had already been forced westwards and were occupying Magadha area (Magwe and Thayet-myo) during the Mahâbhârata period and we find the Kanran tribe migrated also to south Arakan (Phayre, p. 42) and that (p. 43) Mru (Mûrû Daîtya) tribes established there in 2666 B.C., a date, extravagantly put, as Sir Arthur Phayre remarks. These people then bore the general name of Magas, having migrated from Magadha of Burmah. Further pressure must have made them move on further west where we find them established as Balîpûtras or Magas in south Behar in the Buddhist period, and the Kanran section as Sûtas settled in Anga country south of the Ganges in Monghyr and Bhagalpur. That the relation between the Arakanese and Magas of Magadha continued to be maintained for a long time is evident from the fact that King Maha Taing Chandra of Arakan named his new capital as Vaisali after Vaisali of Magadha.

This migration need not be followed further, as my object is merely to indicate the direction of flow. The sum total of the observations is that the Aryans from Central Asia, spreading to north of Kashmir, divided into two sections, one occupying the Punjab or Vedic Area, the other proceeding along northern base of Himalayas to Burmah and established along the main river valley which then flowed towards western Siam; this section, weakened by quarrels amongst themselves were driven out by the original inhabitants in turn, and they retreated to India, along the southern base of Himalayas this time, and then a meeting and fusion of the two batches of Aryans took place. Before this fusion took place the Vedic Aryans had been mixed up already with Persian and Macedonian hordes a good number of whom also settled down in the Punjab; the Aryans of Mahâbhârata and Râmâyana were also similarly mixed up with the original inhabitants of Burmah and eastern India; the great allies of the Mahâbhârata Kshatryas were the Telaings, and Harî worshipping Nâgas, and these tribes had to move on to southern India to what was then the Taprobane island. The inhabitants of Lankâ island, had also to leave their country in large numbers, as they were already pressed by the Burmans from the east, and the western portion of the island was submerged by the sea; their final migration was to Ceylon, as is amply borne out by the story of the migration given in Mahavanso, (Vol. I, Ch. VII) that "Vijay, son of Sinhabahu, King of the land of Lata, with 700 followers landed at Lanka and colonised the island and named it Sihala"; the date of Vijay given in the list of Kings in Mahavanso (Part I, I, Page IV) is 543 B.C., which coincides exactly with the date of death of Thiha-Radza of Thatun (*Vide* list of Kings in Ch. XX, of Phayre's Burmah), and there is no doubt that Sinhavahu, father of Vijay, is Thiha-Radza of Thatun. The reference to the country of Lata may either be due to a confusion with Thatun, or that Vijay's boat at first drifted towards Surat or the Lata country where he landed at first but owing to his impetuous behaviour he was driven out from Lâta-dêsa and then he proceeded to Ceylon.

The ignominious retreat of the Aryans from Burmah is a subject which the Brahmins and Kshatryas could not possibly have stated in the Pûrânas, Mahâbhârata or Râmâyana not only because it was a sore point which it was as well for them to cast to oblivion but it would have meant the loss of their prestige with the aboriginal tribes in India in the new field of colonization. The details of their previous history was therefore clouded by omission of the points of their weakness and under imagination adding where necessary to fill up such gaps. They could not forget the memories of the favorite play ground of their ancestors, and each band as it spread in a new locality, named their new villages and township after those old places, and later on blended their Paûrânîc history with the new places, when they found out by the 10th Century that the dream of re-occupation of their old play ground will never be realised. The Punjab section of the colonists, or the Vedic Hindus had already been mixed up with powerful Macedonian tribes and their superiority had to be acknowledged, and the result was the Rajput element, and these kings had to be admitted as descended from the Solar or Lunar races. The Vîsvâmîtra and Parasûrâma lines also were forced in. The first band of Aryans from Burmah were from the Mahâbhârata area, and we therefore see the tribes claiming the Pândya lineage established near Delhi; the later batch was from Siam or Râmâyana area, and they are therefore in evidence to the east of the Pândyas, that is in Ayodhyâ area, from where they spread towards south-east as new land formed, and the powerful Sagara Râjâ made his Yagna or sacrifice in the land south of Ganges and north of Vindhyas. The Dânava and Daîtya colonists from Burmah through southern Arakan, occupied the Magadha or south Behar area, while the Karna descendants of Anga country of Burmah, occupied Monghyr Bhagalpore area; these people were looked down upon, by the Aryan settlers to the west, and were thus classified as Châranas (Bards) and Sûtas (Charioteers), but we find that they had become a powerful nation at the time of the advent of the Greeks, and Balî, 21st generation from Pûrû, son of Yayâtî, son of Nahûsha, became Danavêndra or King of Dânavas as given in Harîvamsa; the Balîpûtra kingdom with headquarters at Palamau under the Maurya Gupta Kings was the greatest power in India in the 3rd Century B.C. The development of Kalînga went on about the same time, and south-west of Magadha towards the sea we find Vatsa Kings of Kosambi when they became powerful at a later date, claimed their descent from the Pândyas and Satânîka, Sahasrânîka and Udayana included in the geneology (Matsya Pûrâna, Ch. 50, see also Ch. VIII), as descended from Arjûna. Somadêva, in Kathâ-Sarît-Sâgara, refers to the trend of colonisation by the Pândava descendants (Book II, Ch. XVIII), when he makes Yogandharayana tell the Vatsa King:—"The north though rich, is defiled by intercourse with barbarians, west is not honored being the side of the setting sun, south is in the neighbourhood of Rakshas and gods of death, in east presides Indra, Sun rises, and Ganges flows, so east is preferred; among countries between Hîmâlaya and Vîndhya mountains, country watered by the Ganges is the best: *your ancestors conquered the regions by beginning with the east* and made their dwellings in Hastînâpûra on Ganges, but Satânîka went to Kaûsambi on account of its delightful situation." This indicates the first advance of the Pândyas from the east (Burmah) to west jumping over the rich country to the north of Bengal as it was defiled by intercourse with barbarians, and Satânîka came back again towards the sea coast to east of India on account of its delightful situation.

The Harî worshipping Nâgas, we find made their way to southern India in Taprobane island, their first colony must have been Nâgadvîpa (see Ch. I, C), from where they gradually spread to the whole of the east coast of Taprobane island; their influence spread along the coast northwards, and thus we have Nârâyana Harî as the prevalent form of god, from Bengal southwards to southern Madras coast; the Anantasayyâ form of Nârâyana, the once prevalent form in Burmah being very prominent in the southern coast, and we find Manîâkkhî nâga in power in southern Madras (as island) during Buddhas' time as given in Mahavansa (Wijesinha Mudaliyar's translation, Part I, Ch. XV), where it is stated "the fourth divine teacher in the Kappa (Kalpa or era) was Gotama (Buddha); in his first advent he reduced Yakshas to subjection, in his second he established power over Nâgas; again on the third occasion at the entreaty of the Nâga King Manîâkkhî, repairing to Kalyani, pertook of refreshments." The Dipavamsa confirms this (Translation by Oldenberg, Part II, p. 42). We thus find the Nâga Kings established firmly before the Christian era, and the nucleus of the present Mînâkshî temple is evidently due to him, though later advent of Saivism advancing from the west coast worked changes; the Vaigai river is the ancient Kalyani river.

On the west coast of Taprobane, the aboriginal population had their Priapus form of worship, and this was the area to which, the followers of Sîva of Burmah found their way, and we find a blending of different forms of Sîva; the Saivites seemed to have gathered strength with the Aryan colony migrating during Parasûrâma's time and so their influence we find also in the southern Madras coast.

The Rajput or rather the mixed Vedic-Aryans advanced by the then east bank of the Indus, that is the present Rajputana area, southwards, and then a small band proceeded along the then southern coast to Nagpur area and founded the southern Pandya Kingdom (Ch. I) and another band proceeded along the western coast colonised by Parasûrâma.

The observations in this chapter, indicate the general lines of spread of the Aryan influence in India. From my point of view I consider they have a greater significance, as this gradual spread will, when considered with the gradual changes the geography of India and Burmah indicated in the different chapters which preceded, will help to solve many of the problems hitherto unexplained.

GLOSSARY OF LOCAL TERMS, USED IN PLACE-NAMES &c., IN INDIA AND BURMAH.

Varsha, Khanda, Kshêtra, Râshtra, Prastha, Pat—*Division of Country.*

Dêsa, Dês, Sthâna, Thân, Bhûmî, Bhûm—*Country.*

Samûdram, Samûdra, Abdhî, Sâgara, Sâgar, Sagaur—*Sea.*

Nada, Nadi, Kiang—*A river; Nadî is the feminine form of Nada, the latter accordingly used to denote a big river.*

Hrada, Sarovara, Sara, Sar, Sâgaram, Sâgara, Sâgar, Sagaur—*Lake or Inland sea.*

Kûnda, Kund, Daha, Doho—*A pool; a pool in a river.*

Mohânâ, Mohân—*Estuary.*

Vêlâ, Kûlam, Kûla, Kachchha—*Coast.*

Sangama, Sangam—*Confluence of two or more rivers, or the debouchure of a river into the sea.*

Achalam, Achala, Adrî, Gîrî, Saîla, Parvvata, Pahar, Taung, Daung—*A mountain or hill.*

Konda, Kota, Kotai, Mundi, Mund, Betta—*A hill.*

Tanr, Danr—*A mound, or hill, or plateau, or high ground.*

Atavî, Kânana, Aranya, Aran, Vana, Van, Bun—*A forest.*

Nagaram, Nagara, Nagar, Pûram, Pûra, Pur, Pore, Poor, Pûrî, Buri—*A city.*

Kalan—*An important place.*

Grâma, Gram, Gam, Gaon, Gong, Gaunh—*A village.*

Myo—*A town.*

Nadî-grâma, Naîgame—*A village on a river, or on the coast.*

Ganja, Ganj, Gunj, Petia, Pet, Peta—*A market-place or mart.*

Bandar, Pattanam, Pattan, Patan, Patam—*A port.*

Ghât—*A landing stage or port, or a river-crossing or ferry.*

Ghât—*A pass in a hill, or hill.*

Garh, Gur, Gar, Killa—*A fort, or a fortified town.*

Serai, Chatta, Chatti, Chati—*A halting stage on a route.*

Asrama—*A habitation, usually of a saint; hence the headquarters of a religious sect.*

Tîrtha—*A sacred place; a place of pilgrimage.*

Dvâra, Dwara, Dwar—*Door; gateway.*

Dvîpa, Dwip, Dip, Diva, Div, Gyun, Kyon—*An island.*

Mêrû, Yoma—*Backbone.*

Râjâ, Rajah, Raj, Radza—*King.*

Hîranya, Hêma, Sûvarna, Subarna, Shwe—*Gold; golden.*

Asva, Ghoda, Ghod, Kudre—*A horse.*

Bilu, Biloo, Bilin—*A Rakshasa, or ogre, or cannibal.*

Hîma—*Snow.*

Pûtra—*Sons, children, descendants.*
Mûkha, Mukham, Wuh—*Mouth.*
Kûlya—*Cut, or excavated* (by).
Kâtâ, Chhînna—*Cut, or separated.*
Mahâ, Gyi—*Great.*
Nge—*Small.*
Yasthî, Latta—*A stick.*
Rakta—*Blood; red.*
Lal, Nal—*Red.*
Neela, Nîla, Nil—*Blue.*
Uttara, Ooter, Ottara—*North; northern.*
Pûrva, Prâchya, Prâk—*East; eastern.*
Dakshîn, Dakhin, Deccan—*South; southern.*
Paschîma, Paschim, Pratîchya, Aparânta—*West; western.*
Ishana, Aîshî—*North-east; north-eastern.*
Agnî, Agneya—*South-east; south-eastern.*
Naîrrîta—*South-west.*
Vayû—*North-west.*
Madhya, Modo, Madaya—*Middle, central.*
Vâna, Vân, Vanta, Mân, Manta—*Possessing of* (used as a suffix).
Vatî, Matî—(Feminine form)— Do. do. do.

LIST OF BOOKS CONSULTED

The Rivers of the Vedas and how the Aryans entered India—*By Edward Thomas.*

Vedic India—*By Zenaide A. Ragozin.*

Rg-Vedic India—*By Abinash Chandra Das.*

Vayû Pûrâna.

Matsya Pûrâna.

Vîshnû Pûrâna.

Padma Pûrâna.

Skanda Pûrâna.

Varâha Pûrâna.

Kûrma Pûrâna.

Mârkandêya Pûrâna.

Agnî Pûrâna.

Vâmana Pûrâna.

Lînga Pûrâna.

Brahmânda Pûrâna.

Sîva Pûrâna.

Dêvî Pûrâna.

Brîhannâradîya Pûrâna.

Kâlîkâ Pûrâna.

Brahma Pûrâna.

Brîhaddharma Pûrâna.

Kalkî Pûrâna.

Mahâbhârata.

Harîvamsa.

Râmâyana (Vâlmîkî).

Yoga-Vâsîstha Râmâyana.

Manu, with Kulluca's Glossary—*Translated by Sir W. Jones.*

The Ashtâdhyâyî of Pânînî—*Translated by Sris Chandra Basu.*

Avesta—*Translated by Arthur Henry Bleeck.*

Kaûtîlya's Arthasâstra—*Translated by R. Shamasastry.*

Geography of Herodotus—*By J. Talboys Wheeler.*

Geography of Herodotus—*Translated by Wm. Carey.*

Ktesias—*By J. W. McCrindle.*

Megasthenes' India—*By J. W. McCrindle.*

Arrian's Indika—*By J. W. McCrindle.*

Periplus of the Erythrian Sea and Arrian's Account of the Voyage of Nearkhos—*By J. W. McCrindle.*

The Indian Travels of Apollonius of Tyana—*By Osmond-deBevoir* Prillaux.

The Geography of Strabo—*By H. C. Hamilton* and *W. Falconer.*

The Christian Topography of Cosmas (Cosmas Indicopleustes)—*By J. W. McCrindle.*

Ancient India as described by Ptolemy—*By J. W. McCrindle.*

Lalîta-Vîstara—*Edited by Dr. Rajendralala Mitra.*

The Questions of King Milinda (Mîlînda—Panha)—*Translated by T. W. Rhys Davids.*

Buddha-ghosa's Parables—*Translated by Capt. Rogers.*

Asvaghosa's Discourses on the Awakening of Faith in the Mahayana—*Translation from the Chinese version by Teitario Suzuki.*

Legend of Buddha, being a translation of the Chinese version of the Abhiniskramana Sutra—*By Samuel Beal.*

The Fo-sho-Hing-Tsan-King or Asvaghosha's Buddha Charita—*Translated from the Chinese translation by Samuel Beal.*

Dipavamsa—*Translated by Hermann Oldenberg.*

Sumangala-Vilasini, Buddha-ghosha's commentary on Digha Nikaya—*Edited by T. W. Rhys Davids* and *J. E. Carpenter.*

The Buddha-vamsa and the Cariya-pitaka—*Translated by Rev. R. Morris.*

The Life of Buddha, derived from Tibetan Works in the Bkah Hgyur and Bstan-Hgyur—*By W. W. Rockhill.*

Divyavadana, a Collection of Early Buddhist Legends from the Nepalese Sanscrit—*By E. B. Cowell* and *R. A. Neil.*

The Life and Legend of Gaudama (from Burmese translation of Pali text of Mallalinkar Wouttoo)—*By Rev. P. Bigandet.*

The Mahavamsa—*Translated by L. C. Wijesinha Mudaliyar.*

Buddha Bharata—*By Sarat Kumara Ray.*

Buddhist India—*By Rhys Davids.*

Chips from a German Workshop—*By Rhys Davids.*

Ancient Geography and History referring to the Sites of Ophir, Sheba, Taprobane, &c.—*By Robert Tytler.*

Asoka—*By Vincent A. Smith.*

Buddistic Remains of Bihar—*By A. M. Broadly.*

Inquiry concerning the Site of Ancient Palibothra—*By William* Francklin.

Raghû Vamsa, of Kâlîdâsa.

Kûmâra-Sambhava, of Kâlîdâsa.

Mêgha-dûta, of Kâlîdâsa.

Kalhan's Râj-Tarangînî, translation into Bengali—*By Prof. Haralal Chattopadhaya.*

Brîhat-Samhîtâ of Varâha Mîhîra—*Translated by N. Chidambaram Iyer.*

Jâtaka—*By Ishan Chandra Ghosh.*

Uttara-Râma Charîta of Bhavabhûtî—*Translated by C. H: Tawney.*

Kâdamvarî of Ban-Bhatta—*Translated by C. M. Ridding.*

Kathâ-Kosa—*Translated by C. H. Tawney.*

Kathâ-Sarît-Sâgara of Somadêva—*Translated by C. H. Tawney.*

Harsa-Charîta of Bân-Bhatta—*Edited by Kashinath Panduranga.*

Nâgânanda of Sri-Harsha-Dêva—*Translated by Palmer Boyd.*

Mahâvîra-Charîta of Bhavabhûtî—*Translated by John Pickford.*

Prâkrîta-Prakâsa of Vararûchî—*Translated by E. B. Cowell.*

Dasakûmara Charîta of Srî Dandî—*Edited by H. H. Wilson.*

The Travels of Fa Hien—*Translated by James Legge.*

On Yuan Chwang's Travels in India—*Translated by Thomas McWatters.*

A Record of Buddhist Religion—*By I'Tsing, translated by J. Takakusu.*

Ancient Accounts of India and China by Two Mahomedan Travellers of 851 to 869 A.D.—*By Usebius Renaudot.*

Oriental Geography of Ebn Haukal—*Translated by Sir William Ousley.*

Alberuni's India—*Translated by Prof. Edward C. Sachau.*

Marco Polo—*Edited by Henry Yule, revised by Henry Cordier.*

The Travels of Ibn Batuta—*Translated by Samuel Lee.*

Tabakat-i-Nasiri of Minhaj-ud-din Abu-umar-i-usman—*Translated by Major H. G. Raverty.*

The History of Hindostan (Ferishta)—*Translated by Alexander Dow.*

Ayeen Akbery of Abul Fazel—*Translated by Francis Gladwin.*

Krîttîvâsa's Râmâyana—*Basumati Edition.*

Kashîdâsa's Mahâbhârata—*Dey Bros'. Edition.*

Chaîtanya Bhâgavata of Srî Vrîndâvana-dâsa Thâkûr—*Basumati Edition.*

Chaîtanya Charîtâmrîta of Krîshna-dâsa Kavîraja Gosvâmî—*Edited by Harish Chandra Mazumdar.*

Narottama-Vîlâsa of Naraharî Gosvâmî—*Basumati Edition.*

Bhakti-Ratnakara of Narahari Gosvâmî—*Edited by Ramnarayana Vidyaratna.*

Padmâ-pûrâna of Vamsîdâsa Râya—*Edited by Ramnath Chakravarti* and *Dvarakanath Chakravarti.*

Kavî-Kankana Chandî of Mûkûndarâma Chakravarti—*India Publishing House Edition.*

Early Travels in India, of Samuel Purchas and Van Linschoten—*Edited by J. Talboys Wheeler.*

A Collection of Voyages and Travels from the Library of the Earl of Oxford, of F. Bernier, Capt. Robert Coverty and William Bruton—*Edited by Thomas Osborne.*

Travels in India by Jean Baptiste Tavernier—*Edited by V. Ball.*

Travels in the Mogol Empire by Francois Bernier—*Edited by Archibald Constable.*

Storia du Mogor by Nicolas Manucci—*Edited by William Irvine.*

Riyazu-S-Salatin of Ghulam Husain Salim—*Translated by Abdus Salam.*

The Seir-Mutaqharin of Syed Ghulam Hossein Khan—*By Nota-Manus.*

A Voyage to the East Indies—*By Fra Paolino da San Bartolomeo.*

A History of the Military Transactions of the British Nation in Indostan from 1745 A.D.—*By Robert Orme.*

Memoirs of a Map of Hindoostan—*By James Renell.*

History, Antiquities, Topography and Statistics of Eastern India —*By Montogomery Martin.*

The British Colonies—*By R. Montogomery Martin.*

The Analytical History of India—*By Robert Sewell.*

Ancient India—*By R. C. Dutt.*

India in the Fifteenth Century—*By R. H. Major.*

A Comprehensive History of India—*By Henry Beveridge.*

The Indian Empire; its History, People and Products—*By W. W. Hunter.*

The Early History of India—*By Vincent A. Smith.*

Lists of the Antiquarian Remains in the Presidency of Madras—*By Robert Sewell.*

Archeological Survey of Western India—*By James Burgess.*

Antiquities of Orissa—*By Rajendralala Mitra.*

Archeological Survey of India—*By Alex. Cunningham.*

Reports of the Archeological Survey of India.

List of Ancient Monuments in Bengal—*Published by the Archeological Department of India.*

Ancient Geography of India—*By Sir Alexander Cunningham, edited by Surendranath Mazumdar Sastri.*

Portuguese in India—*By Frederick Charles Danvers.*

History of Portuguese in Bengal—*By J. J. A. Campos.*

Land of Five Rivers and Sindh—*By David Ross.*

Universal Geography—*By E. Reclus, edited by E. H. Keene.*

History of the Parsis—*By Dosabhai Framji Karaka.*

Good Old Days of Hon'ble John Company—*By W. H. Carey.*

A Manual of the District of Vizagapatam—*By D. F. Carmichael.*

Râs-Mâlâ or Hindu Annals of Goozerat—*By Alexander Kinloch Forbes.*

Notes on the Topography of R. Hughli in the 16th Century as represented in the DaAsia of De Barros—*By C. R. Wilson.*

Early History of Bengal—*By F. J. Monahan.*

Dhâkâr Itîhâsha (History of Dacca)—*By Jitendramohan Ray.*

Pâbnâ Jêlâr Itîhâsa (History of Dt. Pabna)—*By Radharaman* Saha.

Mêdînîpûrêr Itîhâsâ (History of Midnapur)—*By Jogesh Chandra Basu.*

Jasohar-Khûlnar Itîhâsa (History of Jessore-Khulna)—*By Satish Chandra Mitra.*

Bîrbhûm-Vîvarana (Birbhum Description)—*By Kumar Mahimaniranjan Chakravarti.*

Bângâlâr Itîhâsa (History of Bengal)—*By Rakhaldas Bandopadhaya.*

Prâchîna Râjmâla (Ancient Kings)—*By Ramprana Gupta.*

A Letter to Lord Dalhousie, on the Storm Waves of Bengal and their effect on Sunderbans—*By Henry Paddington.*

Tide-Tables for the Indian Ports—*By O. C. Ollenbach, F. J. Selby* and *W. H. H. Brookes.*

Report on the Mahanuddy River—*By Col. A. Cotton.*

Journey to Lhasa and Central Tibet—*By Sarat Chandra Das.*

History of Burmah—*By General Sir Arthur P. Phayre.*

Burma—*By Max* and *Bertha Ferrars.*

History of Burmah—*By G. E. Harvey.*

Note on an Archeological Tour through Ramanadesa, the Telaing Country of Burmah—*By Taw Sein-Ko.*

A Preliminary Study of the Kalyani Inscriptions of Dhamacheti 1476 A.D.—*By Taw Sein-Ko.*

A Preliminary Study of the Po-u-daung Inscription of Sin Byinyin, 1774 A.D.—*By Taw Sein-Ko.*

Inscriptions of Pagan, Pinya and Ava, 1442 to 1774 A.D.

Statistical and Historical Accounts of Thayetmyo—*By Lieut.-Col. Horace Browne.*

The River of Golden Sand—*By Capt. Gill.*

From Tonkin to India, by the Source of the Irwadi—*By Prince Henri d'Orleans.*

Mandalay and Other Cities of Burmah—*By V. C. Scott O'Connor.*

Mandalay to Bhamo—*By Capt. J. H. G. Powell.*

China—*By Prof. R. K. Douglas.*

Earthquakes and other Movements—*By John Milne.*

A Treatese on Rivers and Torrents by Paul Frisi—*Translated by Maj-Gnl. John Garstin.*

Note—Books on Rivers and River Engineering, and Geology, are not included in this list.

INDEX.

A

B

D

E

F

H

I

J

K

L

M

N

O

R

S

T

W